DAWN BEHIND THE DAWN

DAWN BEHIND THE DAWN

A Search for the Earthly Paradise

GEOFFREY ASHE

A JOHN MACRAE BOOK / HENRY HOLT AND COMPANY / NEW YORK

Published by Henry Holt and Company, Inc.,
115 West 18th Street, New York, New York 10011.
Published in Canada by Fitzhenry & Whiteside Limited,
195 Allstate Parkway, Markham, Ontario L3R 4T8.

Library of Congress Cataloging-in-Publication Data
Ashe, Geoffrey.
Dawn behind the dawn : a search for the earthly paradise.—1st ed.
p. cm.
"A John Macrae book."
Includes bibliographical references and index.
1. Mythology—History. 2. Gods—History. 3. Ritual—History.
I. Title.
BL311.A74 1991
291.2'11—dc20
91-21838
CIP
ISBN 0-8050-1070-X (alk. paper)

Henry Holt books are available at special discounts
for bulk purchases for sales promotions, premiums,
fund-raising, or educational use. Special editions
or book excerpts can also be created to specification.

For details contact:
Special Sales Director, Henry Holt and Company, Inc.,
115 West 18th Street, New York, New York 10011.

First Edition—1992

Designed by Katy Riegel
Map designed by Claudia Carlson

Printed in the United States of America
Recognizing the importance of preserving
the written word, Henry Holt and Company, Inc.,
by policy, prints all of its first editions
on acid-free paper.∞

1 3 5 7 9 10 8 6 4 2

Contents

Preface   vii

1.   Departed Glories   1

2.   The Return of the Goddess   9

3.   Beasts, Mountains, Stars   24

4.   The Indo-Aryans   40

5.   The Paradisal Heights   52

6.   Numerology and Psychology   67

7.   The Prototype   77

8.   Sumerians and Babylonians   89

9.   The Bonded World   107

10.   The Israelites   117

11.   The Two Dwellings of the Lord   131

12.   A Greek God   146

13.   A Greek Goddess   157

14. Beyond the North Wind   169

15. Expansion   184

16. Starting Points of Science   195

17. Enigmas and Eccentrics   202

18. Vindication?   213

     Notes   227

     Bibliography   255

     Index   263

Preface

Some time ago I wrote a book called *The Ancient Wisdom*. It explored a notion aired by persons of speculative bent in quite a number of ways—the notion that in some sort of paradisal past, humanity was taught arts and sciences and spiritual truths by superior beings: sages from lost Atlantis, or "Hidden Masters," or visitors from distant worlds. While not greatly tempted by such fantasies, I found that my exploration turned up clues hinting at *something* unprovided for in official prehistory. There was, however, no way of getting these clues into a logical shape, or reaching conclusions seriously better than guesswork.

Then, a decade later, things began to happen. Mr. Harry Hicks of Menlo Park, California, introduced me to a strange art object he had acquired in India. If this was as old as it appeared to be, it suggested a radical new insight into a certain ancient society, an insight that could bring some order into the mass of facts I had previously found so confused. Soon afterward, major studies by the archaeologists Colin Renfrew and J. P. Mallory publicized results of radiocarbon dating and other research that could carry matters farther along the same line. Meanwhile a third eminent archaeologist, Marija Gimbutas, was proposing a fresh approach to prehistory that seemed to converge strangely with some of my own conjectures, and, if I could accept it, would enable me to put them on a much firmer basis and to make more challenging sense of them.

This book is the result. Or, let us say, an interim result. Remarkable vistas are only just beginning to open up, with implications for our thinking about the present as well as the past.

One or two details. In the transliteration of Sanskrit, academic precision requires a specialized kind of spelling, which I decided not to employ. It has to be explained for uninitiated readers, and I have preferred spellings that they need not stumble over and are not seriously misleading. Biblical quotations are from the Revised Standard Version unless otherwise stated. When writing of Greece and the Middle East I have kept to the long-accepted chronology, while realizing that this is now questioned in places by Peter James and other scholars. Thus far, there is probably not sufficient reason to modify what is said, and if the new datings were to be proved, I still doubt if that would make much difference to the main discussion.

Besides acknowledging Harry Hicks's role in making the first step possible, I would like to record my gratitude to Persia Woolley for her interest and encouragement; to Timothy Taylor, for his elucidation of a geographical term that surprised me; and of course to Eric Ashworth, my agent.

DAWN BEHIND THE DAWN

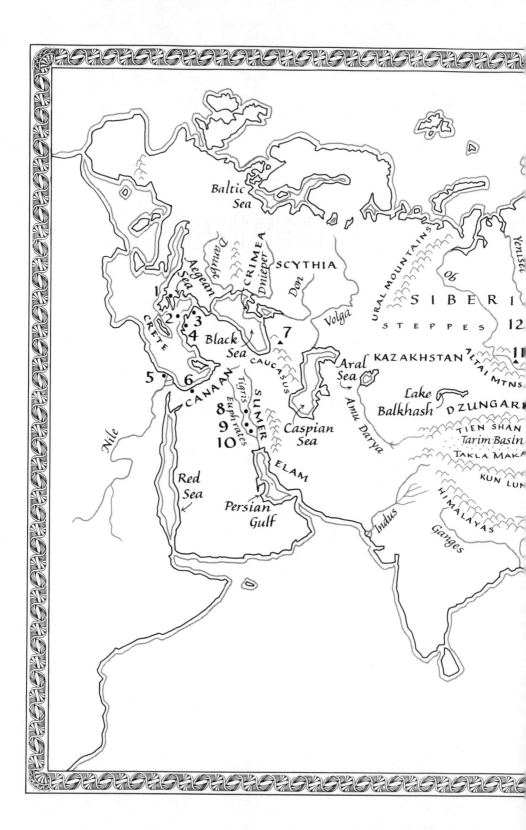

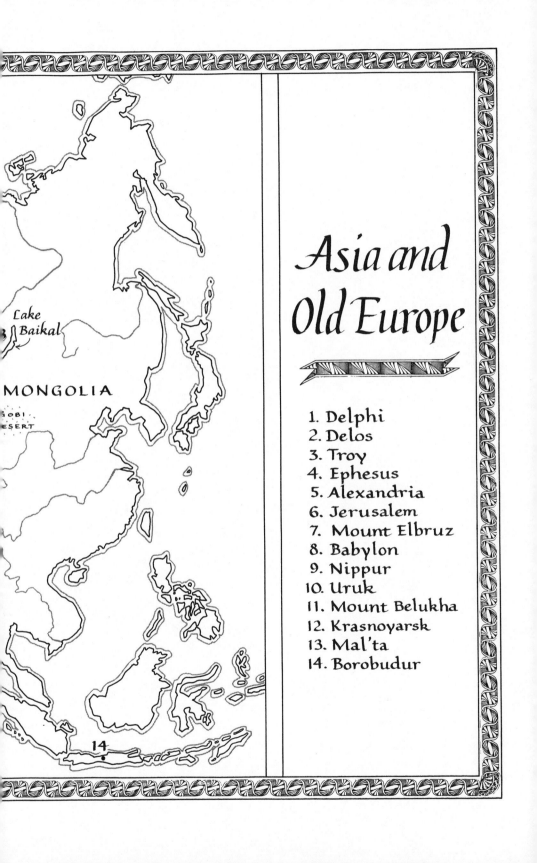

Asia and Old Europe

1. Delphi
2. Delos
3. Troy
4. Ephesus
5. Alexandria
6. Jerusalem
7. Mount Elbruz
8. Babylon
9. Nippur
10. Uruk
11. Mount Belukha
12. Krasnoyarsk
13. Mal'ta
14. Borobudur

Lake Baikal

MONGOLIA

GOBI DESERT

14

CHAPTER ONE

Departed Glories

1

How did early societies take shape, and what happened before their emergence into historical daylight? Prehistorians have their answers. They describe various forward steps: the invention of farming, the clustering of settled communities, technological advances, the concentration of power, urban beginnings. All of this is sound. Nothing can be a substitute for the facts revealed, or for the scholarship that reveals them. Yet when we turn to myth and legend, we find assertions about the context of these developments that have a paradoxical air. They imply an attitude and an overall picture that are in sharp contrast with the imagery of progress.

Myths and legends do not ignore the developments. They tell of the beginnings of useful arts, the establishment of kingship, the foundation of cities. Often, though, and quite often enough to call for scrutiny, a jarring element slips through the net—a belief that the movement is not forward, or not consistently forward; a belief in loss rather than gain; a belief that far back in time, life was better and more enlightened, and that whatever made it so has ceased to be an effective part of experience.

Something is lacking in our patterns, something that should be fitted into ideas of prehistory (or psychology, or both) to resolve the discord. To put it picturesquely, there is a need to identify a lost paradise, whether illusion or, in some sense, reality. What was it? The question is no mere antiquarian puzzle. We confront a sort of syndrome here. Humanity never has escaped from it, and it remains a contemporary issue. Two closely related themes, over the centuries, have given the belief expression. One is the golden age. The other is Ancient Wisdom.

The theme of the golden age is widespread. Of course the term is applied loosely to any phase of prosperity, to golden ages of art or literature. But that usage echoes a profounder and older one. Supposedly, humanity or some part of it once enjoyed harmony, well-being, companionship with deities. People were innocent of misconduct that flourishes now. Life was free from want, without backbreaking toil. The golden age ended for reasons given variously—through sin, or evil magic, or an usurpation of power, or a built-in principle of decay. Decline may have been swift or it may have been gradual. Progress on specifics, when this is admitted, is seen in a setting that is retrograde overall.

In traditional versions, much of this is daydreaming on obvious lines. Two less obvious aspects should be noticed. The first is a correlation with freedom from the curse of mortality. Humans in the golden age were long-lived or even immortal—perhaps potentially, perhaps actually. Death, or at any rate the fear of death, came in with the sadder epoch that followed. The second noteworthy aspect is an association of what is missed in the here and now, happiness or wisdom or divine companionship, with a good place—an earthly paradise, an Elysium. This may exist even yet. But human beings are separated from it, except maybe for a favored few. Perhaps the golden age was a time when all were in contact with its beatitude.

Ancient Wisdom is a variant with a shift of emphasis. Benign deities or sages, knowing much that ordinary humans did not, once illuminated and aided them. The illumination faded with the departure of Ancient Wisdom's teachers. Humanity retains arts and crafts, science and religion, but a basic impulsion lies buried in the past. When progress occurs, it is apt to be joined with forgetfulness or error, a loss of coherence, and principles that should inspire it. Ancient Wisdom survives, to the extent that it does, only in fragments or in the minds of an elite.

Ideas like these have persisted for thousands of years, and they persist still, adapted to present ways of thinking. They are not to be dismissed as archaic illusions.

To look first at ancient examples, the golden age of Greek and Roman mythology resembled some others in being a previous dispensation, an era of "gods before the gods." The Greek poet Hesiod, in the eighth century B.C., sketched five epochs.[1] Each had its own human species, with the golden coming first. The golden race flourished when the world's ruler was Cronus, or, as the Romans called him afterward, Saturn. He was the chief of the elder deities known as Titans. The golden people lived carefree lives, feeding on nature's gifts, such as fruit and honey, without disease or decrepitude. According to some versions—not Hesiod's—Astraea, goddess of Justice, dwelt among them. They could die, and they did, but death held no terrors for them, and their kindly ghosts wandered unseen befriending mortals.

Their end resulted from a divine coup d'état. Zeus, Cronus's son, banished him with most of the other Titans and took over supremacy with a clique of colleagues on Mount Olympus. The golden race disappeared and was followed by a second, the "silver," when men were dominated by their mothers (foolish, says Hesiod). Astraea was still there, but she was distancing herself, and she presently departed skyward and turned into the constellation Virgo. Then came two "bronze" races, eating meat, using bronze weapons, and delighting in violence. Hesiod's second bronze race is superior to the first, rallying against the trend. Its men included the heroes who fought at Troy. Some were translated, exempt from death, to a blissful Elysium over the western ocean, where Cronus was still sovereign. This respite from decline was brief. It was followed by the time of the "iron" race, our own, the basest and most benighted.

Hesiod's account of a bronze age succeeded by an iron age agrees with archaeology. He was not entirely ignorant of the real past, whatever his golden age was, if anything. Greeks of a later day, who inclined to romanticism, liked to think that something resembling the golden age was still going on somewhere, not only in the fabulous Elysium but in a vague northern place, the home of a people called Hyperboreans, who lived happily and virtuously for a thousand years.

Hinduism is more cosmic.[2] It has its golden age in what is known as the Krita Yuga, a very long time ago. Then, all beings were righteous, wise, prosperous, and healthy, and fulfilled the laws of their nature and status. The Krita yielded to a shorter and inferior Yuga, the Treta, and that to another, the Dvapara, and that to the Kali Yuga in which we live. The Kali Yuga is the worst and the shortest. This running down of the world is preordained. Even in our Kali Yuga the world still contains an abode of divine beings, an inviolate paradisal fastness, but this is far beyond mortal accessibility.

Instances could be multiplied from other mythologies. What is not often realized, however, is that even with antique myth-making left behind, the basic notion continues to surface in fresh guises.

Christian reformers in the sixteenth century, both Catholic and Protestant, agreed that the church was in a bad way. Yet neither party envisaged what normally would be urged now, and *is* urged by liberal theologians: reform through development and progress, through pushing forward to new ground, discarding a superseded past. Both appealed instead to the past itself. They evoked the golden age of the apostles and early saints, when Christianity was pure. Reform meant sweeping away abuses so that the young church, as the reformers conceived it, could return.

In the eighteenth century, Jean-Jacques Rousseau became the arch-prophet of the French Revolution partly by reinventing the golden age as an era of unspoiled natural humanity. Human beings, he maintained, once were free and equal and good. They had been corrupted by civilization and by such upholders of it as kings and priests, who subverted natural law by enforcing their oppressive wills. The political moral was palpable. In an intriguing throwaway line, Rousseau admits that his golden age might be a myth and not a fact. The natural condition, he says, is one that "exists no longer, perhaps never existed, probably never will exist, and of which none the less it is necessary to have just ideas, in order to judge well of our present state." The compulsion to impose such a myth, not merely as a theory but as a necessity, is a thing to be reckoned with. So is the readiness of Rousseau's many disciples to accept the myth and act on it, believing in the lost natural felicity and trying to wipe out obstacles to its restoration. It was hardly Rousseau's fault that the most powerful of them, and the most dedicated wiper-out, was Robespierre.

At sundry times the compulsion has imposed further mythic conceptions. One is a classless idyll of "primitive communism" which Karl Marx's followers tacked on at the beginning of their version of history, before the rise of oppressors and the beginning of class war. It was no part of the original theory, but Marxists decided that without a golden age of their own—rather like Rousseau's, as a matter of fact—their system was incomplete. At some indefinite time after the revolution the classless idyll would be reborn. A few decades later, Mahatma Gandhi created a mystique for Indian nationalism out of his vision of an ancient India of saints and sages and village communes and cottage industry, which alien conquerors had blotted out. He launched a mass patriotic program of hand spinning and weaving as a movement of practical revival. Like Rousseau, he acknowledged that his golden age might never have existed, but, also like Rousseau, and in much the same way, he justified talking about it.

A more recent expression of the same syndrome is the Black Muslim myth, which commended itself to some black activists in the 1960s.[3] According to this, the whole human species was formerly black, civilized, and moral, and the majority were happy. But sixty-six hundred years ago a scientist, less moral and happy than his colleagues, carried out a eugenic, or rather antieugenic, project that generated monsters, namely white people. All of the evils of white power and black subjection go back to this disaster. It should be added that Malcolm X, the creed's ablest convert, soon abandoned it.

As for Ancient Wisdom, the companion concept, that too has a long pedigree and an enduring vitality. On a naive level mythology offers its culture heroes, who taught the arts of life to primeval humanity. Here the Greeks kept a link with their golden age, the reign of the Titans, by allotting the chief culture-hero role to Prometheus, a Titan himself. We find primordial sages in Babylonia and India; we find other sages, divine ones, presiding over a golden age in China, their wisdom invoked by Confucius; we find the god Krishna communicating the teachings of the *Bhagavad Gita*, supposedly four or five thousand years ago.

As with the golden age, what is seldom realized is the stubbornness with which such ideas persist. During the European Renaissance, Ancient Wisdom was almost a norm of advanced thinking. Many of the finest minds of that age worshiped at the shrine of rediscovered antiquity and sought solutions to the profoundest problems in long-lost "Hermetic" treatises, which had been concocted by mystical Greeks early in the Christian era. Isaac Newton himself thought he was not a discoverer but a rediscoverer and said his findings were symbolically foreshadowed in classical myth.[4]

Western society has gone on displaying the same compulsion and producing new editions of Ancient Wisdom. Eighteenth-century England saw the launch of a notion, still by no means defunct, that the Celtic priest-magicians called druids were primordial world teachers. Later, theorists of a quasi-academic type ascribed all earthly enlightenment to super-Egyptians or super-Babylonians. From 1875 onward Ancient Wisdom was bursting out with a fresh luxuriance in the doctrines of theosophy, proclaimed by Helena Petrovna Blavatsky. She declared, in effect, that everything was known long ago and was taught selectively to initiates by Masters of Wisdom in remote Asian retreats. The Masters are still there and have exerted a hidden influence over world events, although their teachings have been obscured and perverted. More recently Ancient Wisdom donned science-fiction garb in the writings of Erich von Däniken, for whom the gods of mythology were sky people, astronauts from distant planets, who visited our own planet thousands of years back and uplifted its brutish inhabitants, but then went away.

These manifestations seldom have been Christian in any clear sense, and some have been anti-Christian. During the 1980s, however, Ancient Wisdom took yet another form in a Christian reaction. Fundamentalists sponsored Creation Science. This was grounded on a claim that the Bible gives literal truths about the world's beginnings, taught by the divinely inspired Moses for ancient Israel's edification. Regular science has lost sight of these truths and will not admit them, propagating such fictions as evolution to keep them suppressed. The elect, however, can recapture them and enlarge on them, and Creation Science has a right to a place in schools, as an alternative to evolution.

2

Such modes of thinking can be explained in part by psychology. Nostalgic pseudo-memories of a trouble-free childhood are projected onto the world at large, onto its past beyond coherent record, childhood's equivalent. A sense, in the individual life, of things closing in, of frustration and decay, of an inexorable slide toward death, is projected likewise. The golden age was real, but it didn't last. A further aspect of these phenomena can be explained in the same way. This is the recurrent conviction that the lost glory is not truly lost and can be won back and reinstated: a conviction that has inspired Christian reformers, French revolutionaries, and others, and long since created a mythic expression of its own in the prophesied return of King Arthur. We might detect a need to defy the tragedy of the mortal condition, and a need to do this by affirming not only that the golden age existed but that although it went into eclipse, death has no lasting dominion over it and it remains capable of resurrection.

Yet perhaps this is not enough. Perhaps psychological myth-making is not a full explanation, or rather, a full explaining-away. Could there be a factual substratum, as the myth makers, with all their disagreements, unite in implying; a substratum able to inspire variations on the two themes, though below the conscious threshold itself; a substratum that the psychological factors somehow latch on to? Can the themes be integrated into a real past, without minimizing the data that have a different message?

To suggest that such backward-looking yearnings may have a factual basis, beyond history's reach, is no novelty. One of Europe's mightiest creative spirits, with far less information to work on, made this very suggestion. In his *Purgatorio* Dante airs the conjecture that the golden age is a dim reminiscence of life in the real lost Eden, the earthly paradise of unfallen, undegenerate, and innocent humankind (28:139–41). Speaking to him as a visitor, its resident lady says,

> *Those men of yore who sang the golden time*
> *And all its happy state—maybe indeed*
> *They on Parnassus dreamed of this fair clime.*

Dante provides for something like Ancient Wisdom too, although he does not say so. The notion that the first humans' innocence was thought of in the Middle Ages as ignorance is a mistake. Theologians whom Dante read maintained that Adam and Eve before their fall were wiser and more profound in insight than we are. The ban on the tree of knowledge was not a ban on knowledge as such. One of their intended duties was the education of their descendants.[5]

As a Christian, Dante believed in the lost paradise, if perhaps not literally in his poetic vision of it. With or without belief, Christian conditioning certainly has strengthened the double syndrome in Western society and encouraged some of the dreams that Dante refers to. Further, the dreams proliferate. After the waning of Christian faith, the sense of loss has gone on without the dogmatic anchor, and the golden age and Ancient Wisdom have branched out in a medley of directions.

One result has been a suspicion, and often more than a suspicion, that standard accounts of history are inadequate and may have been falsified. Somehow, somewhere, there has to be a huge missing piece . . . or to adapt Voltaire's remark about God, if there isn't, it has to be invented. In a society that bears the stamp of Christian conditioning but is no longer in tune with the old orthodoxy, something has to take the place of the paradise story. Broadening horizons demand a larger something, of which the paradise story may be a reflection, but only a partial one. The idea of the missing piece has been fostered in the last century or so by an assortment of mysteries and alleged mysteries—Stonehenge, Easter Island, the pyramids, et cetera.

Its most flamboyant product has been the modern myth of Atlantis. From the way this has developed and the form it takes, we may extract a hint for deeper inquiry. The phrase *modern myth of Atlantis* is important. There is no credible trace of a sunken land where Atlantis is alleged to have been, out in the Atlantic Ocean, and the only account of it, Plato's, is a myth of his own contrived out of several ingredients for a didactic purpose. Few Greeks took his Atlantis literally; nor did more than a handful of other readers till 1882. Then Ignatius Donnelly, an American politician who also found Baconian code messages in Shakespeare, published *Atlantis: The Antediluvian World.*

Donnelly's book launched a school of Atlantologists, who reconstructed the lost land in amazing detail. Atlantology was taken up by Madame Blavatsky and her theosophists, who improved it in their own style. Many believers continue to this day. They have made out that Atlantis was the true site of the Garden of Eden and all other earthly paradises. It was the home of a blessed and brilliant race, one whose leaders became the gods and goddesses of mythology. It was the seat of a high, even supernatural civilization that created those of Egypt, Mexico, and Peru as offshoots.

Here we have the golden age and Ancient Wisdom combined, together with a stupendous downfall when Atlantis plunges beneath the waves. We also have an attempt to integrate them with history, through the notion that the lost civilization was ancestral to other, known ones. Atlantis is the most spectacular missing piece ever thought of. But however the missing piece is conceived, it tends to have this ancestral quality: it is not only missing, it is an exciting Something Else that is senior to what official history admits and, if brought into the open, would put it in a different light.

The questions can be stated more specifically. Could there indeed be a missing piece? Did an ancient culture exist, unacknowledged or overlaid by successors, that was a seedbed of motifs in recorded ones? We can dismiss the common origin of Egypt, Mexico, and Peru. That is fantasy. We can wonder more seriously about a shared source of inspiration behind those ancient cultures where we recognize our own in the making—behind, for instance, the Greek and the Israelite. These were certainly not products of diffusion from Atlantis. Might there, however, have been a prior fountainhead of influence that passed into them and into others—a true something else that lingered in various disguises, molding beliefs in a golden age or paradise and contributing to traditions of Ancient Wisdom, below the historical horizon? If it could be defined it may disclose a more-than-psychological background for the themes, where they have been most powerful, versatile, and significant.

This is more than rootless guesswork, more than idle fancy about folk memory. The whole issue has been raised quite suddenly by a new version of the golden age, which has made it, with its affiliated topics, a living issue in a different class from such constructions as Atlantology.

CHAPTER TWO

The Return of the Goddess

1

Since the late 1970s, a golden age has been part of the ideology of the women's movement. That is not to say that all feminists have adopted it, that it has become an orthodoxy for more than a school of thought within feminism, or even that the school of thought is unanimous. But effective voices have been raised, and unlike some other golden ages, this has support among academic prehistorians.

The central idea is that although men have been the ruling sex for thousands of years, it has not always been so. A balanced society once existed. For a while the term *matriarchy* was popular, but it fell into disuse as suggesting a mere mirror image of present society, with women predominant instead of men. Two new adjectives have come into use—"matristic" and "gylanic." The latter was coined by Riane Eisler as a derivative from Greek words for "woman" and "man" and comes nearer to conveying the intended equality. A matristic, or gylanic, society is obviously an aim for the future. But it is now affirmed also as a reality in the past, which an informed women's movement must seek to reinstate on a new level.

When did it exist? In relevant scholarship the outstanding figure is Marija Gimbutas, an archaeologist of the highest repute.[1] Her main field of study is what she calls Old Europe, the central and eastern part of that continent, and especially the Balkans. As defined it extends a little way into Russia, but only a little, although Russia's archaeology has an important supplementary role. In Old Europe, agricultural societies flourished from about

6500 B.C. onward, and according to Gimbutas they were peaceable, creative, and free from sexual chauvinism. Inheritance was traced through the mother. Old Europe's climactic achievement was Minoan Crete. Crete's beautiful art is said to reflect not only a society that was nonviolent but one in which women were respected, influential, and equal with men. And this was so, more or less, throughout Old Europe, before a slow process of change that began in roughly 4000 B.C. and was completed in Crete and other islands by about 1500. The outcome everywhere was a male-dominated society, tracing inheritance through the father, warlike, culturally inferior. This is labeled "patriarchal" or "androcratic" or "androcentric." Much the same happened in other parts of the world, notably Anatolia (Asia Minor) and the rest of the Middle East. Humanity never has recovered.

All of this sounds like a partisan myth, yet it does not lack a degree of respectability. J. P. Mallory, Lecturer in Archaeology at the Queen's University, Belfast, while dissenting from the more interpretive part, has acknowledged that some of it is plausible. The Gimbutan view of Old Europe may look like a wild generalization from Crete, as the only exhibit we really know about. That, however, is not the case, largely because of a further factor—the widespread evidence, or asserted evidence, for Old Europe's religion and a religious change. The matristic society worshiped the Goddess; its male deities were secondary. The patriarchal society that supplanted it worshiped gods, and eventually God, the almighty and exclusive Sky Father. Artifacts everywhere are said to reveal the same story. The upsetting of intersexual balance and the triumph of the male went with a transformation of ritual, theology, and myth, which likewise happened in other places.

One present consequence is the growth of what is sometimes called women's spirituality, involving an attempt to re-create the Goddess religion as a rival to the Christian and Jewish religions, which are condemned as products of the change and as oppressive of women. In part this is a development from a revival of witchcraft, or Wicca, professedly the Old Religion, which began in about the mid-twentieth century under the influence of the anthropologist Margaret Murray. The terrible witchhunts of the past have been annexed to feminist history by being construed as Christian persecution of women, not only because of their sex but because witchcraft preserved a residual paganism with a female deity in it. A conference held in 1978 in Santa Cruz, California, under the title "The Great Goddess Re-Emerging," may be said to have launched the Neo-Goddess religion. It has been expounded by Merlin Stone, Monica Sjöö, Elinor Gadon, and others, who draw on Gimbutas's work and generally have her approval.

The ancient Goddess, it is stressed, was not God with a mere difference of gender. An old joke about a feminist who advised, "Pray to God and She will help you," now might be thought misleading. God the universal sovereign, "out there," apart from the world he made, is regarded as an invention of men and as having come on the scene later. The Goddess was and is the Great Mother, Earth rather than Sky, the life bestower, the creative energy, the giver of birth and rebirth, within nature. Goethe's phrase at the end of *Faust* about the cosmic *Ewig-Weibliche*, the Eternal-Womanly, has a certain aptitude. The question "Does the Goddess exist?" cannot be asked as it can of God, or argued about metaphysically, or answered yes or no. The noted Californian witch Starhawk says that asking "Do you believe in the Goddess?" is like asking "Do you believe in rocks?"[2] The Goddess is *there* in experience, and she transcends, and takes endless forms, as the goddess figures of myth and religion and as living women.

Her era of supremacy was the golden age so far as there ever was one. However simple or backward in modern terms, it had a basic rightness. When the matristic culture was overthrown, its patriarchal successors took over some of its achievements, but they debased and distorted them. The Goddess was not totally banished, except (officially, at least) by the Israelites, but she was fragmented into a medley of goddesses and nymphs, made out to be daughters or wives or subordinate partners of ruling gods. Such is the picture we get in Greek mythology, because the original myths were rewritten, in the interests of Zeus and his Olympian gang. Zeus ends up with a wife and fifty-three mistresses.[3] Similar rearrangements took place in the Middle East.

One result was a change in attitudes to death.[4] In the time of the Great Mother, death led to rebirth and was not feared. The horror of mortality came into the world with the male takeover, because the male is not the life giver. Although there was still an afterlife, it was, for all but a few favorites of the gods, a dreary near-nullity in a realm of shades.

The mythic part of all of this was worked out in essentials before the modern Goddess movement, in the poetic imagination of Robert Graves, who followed up his extraordinary 1952 book *The White Goddess* with a massive study of the Greek myths. Some of the reconstructions were foreshadowed by others. Lewis Richard Farnell, author of the monumental work *The Cults of the Greek States*, remarked as far back as 1896,

> The female deities of the Greek religion have so much of common character as to suggest the belief that they are all different forms under different names of the same divine personage.[5]

In 1959, E. O. James published a sweeping survey, *The Cult of the Mother-Goddess*. In 1961, Sibylle von Cles-Reden's *The Realm of the Great Goddess* interpreted Europe's megalithic structures in Malta, Brittany, the British Isles, and elsewhere as Goddess temples.

However, anyone who listens to the neowitches among the Goddess revivalists will find that they have a longer perspective. They claim not only that their religion is the oldest, but that it descends to them from the Stone Age. "According to our legends," says Starhawk, "witchcraft began more than 35,000 years ago."[6] Gimbutas opens up a similar vista, shorter but not all that much shorter, archaeologically. She argues that the Goddess worship of Old Europe and Anatolia was continuous, with a substratum of Paleolithic cult traceable well before 20,000 B.C., and that the substratum can be detected or inferred over a vast expanse of the Eurasian landmass.

She does this by building up a network of "Goddess" artifacts and imagery.[7] The key items, recognized for some time, are female figurines. Hundreds have been unearthed, in several styles. Some are apparently pregnant, some have exaggerated sexual features, others are more austere. Archaeologists, accepting them as images of female divinity (although not all do), have applied the restrictive label *Venuses*, which Gimbutas rejects. Using the figurines and a medley of carvings and ceramic designs covering many millennia, she effects a kind of decipherment. She exhibits linear motifs and gives them Goddess interpretations. The most elementary is a

Paleolithic figurine: the so-called Willendorf Venus. *American Museum of Natural History*

V, which is explained as the female pubic triangle. The argument proceeds step-by-step to inverted V's and then to wavy lines and spirals. These are associated with water and with stylized animals—birds, sheep, deer, bears, swine, and, conspicuously, snakes—all of them thereby being related to the Goddess. Artistically minded followers have added more—butterflies, spiders, scorpions, fish. Support is invoked from later, documented myths and from identifiable icons that bring in some of the same creatures, making the Goddess (or rather, the goddess figures derived from her) a Mistress of Animals and giving her a special companionship with serpents—in Crete, for instance.

The Gimbutan cryptogram is not formless. Its geography is given a certain shape by chronology. Most of the older objects are in the Soviet Union,[8] and some of the very oldest, dating from 24,000 B.C. or thereabouts, are also the farthest from Europe. Where the USSR meets Mongolia and China is the great curve of the Altai mountain chain, its peaks numinous to this day in Mongol eyes. Farther east is Lake Baikal, one of the world's largest bodies of fresh water, called a sea by aboriginal tribes, and with a fauna of its own. The Altai-Baikal stretch of Siberia has yielded some of the richest and earliest Goddess hauls.[9] At Mal'ta, fifty-five miles northwest of Irkutsk, the figurines are among the best artistically. Those nearer Europe are apt to be cruder and less inventive, hinting at imitation. Some of the Mal'ta objects have been assigned to a later date, but if the later dating is right it simply may reflect a long period of cultic activity. There is no doubt that Mal'ta does have Goddess material going back to about 24,000 B.C. No sites west of Russia have produced any that is proved to be quite so old, though in some cases the margin may be narrow.[10] Logically pressed, the arguments imply something more specific than a Paleolithic Goddess culture spread over a wide area. They imply a point of origin for it, a center of diffusion, artistic and religious. In the Altaic region, something began. There may have been other sources, but that, at any rate, was one source.

Goddess logic would suggest that the Stone Age Altaic tribes lived in a state of primitive wisdom and intersexual balance under the Great Lady's aegis. It would not be seriously disputed that life was hard, sometimes violent, and, on average, short. But it had an imponderable spiritual rightness.

Pursuing the prehistory, we might infer that Altaic influence drifted across the Soviet Union and into Europe, becoming part of the substratum. With the growth of farming economies from the seventh millennium B.C. and social, technological, and artistic progress, the Goddess culture blossomed and culminated in Crete. Its religion gloriously outgrew the Siberian heritage, but that heritage had prepared the ground and played a formative part.

Goddess image with serpents, Minoan Crete. *Mansell Collection*

2

A Goddess-devoted writer, the Swedish-born artist Monica Sjöö, draws a conclusion that is like Dante's transposed into non-Christian terms. Golden age and paradisal mythology springs from a long-range nostalgia for the Goddess era. That presumably is why the divine Astraea is on earth in the classical golden age but is there no longer.[11] Such a view implies that traditions, however hazy, have descended all the way from the Goddess era and perhaps even, specifically, from the north Asian region in which it may have begun—a prototype paradise. Witches like Starhawk, with their claimed continuity of legend, would find no difficulty here. Others might.

Can anything really be identified in that region as having gone into the making of other cultures, whether in the way Goddess prehistory indicates, or in any other way? Can it be cast in the seedbed role, as a place from which motifs and conceptions spread to ancient societies? If we can trace an outward transmission of anything significant, we can consider its harmony or otherwise with the Gimbutan model. We can ask whether anything emerges about an unknown Altaic factor in human development, a missing piece, such as romantic fancy has supposed Atlantis to be, doubtless humbler than Atlantis, yet bestowing a sort of vindication on the mode of thinking that conjures it up.

In the Paleolithic Altai country, or anywhere near it, we cannot hope for inscriptions or kindred items. These people were hunters and gatherers, using stone implements, dressing in skins and furs, living in caves or the crudest shelters. They had art of a simple kind, but no metals and not even a beginning of literacy. Nothing follows, of course, about mental inferiority. Genius and creative talents can take forms that leave no tangible traces. Even in classical Greece, as Mortimer Wheeler once remarked, an archaeologist may find the tub in which the philosopher Diogenes lived while completely missing Diogenes. The European cave paintings at Altamira and Lascaux are later, and megalithic monuments like Carnac and Avebury are later again, yet those gifted artists and builders were still as backward in some respects as Paleolithic Siberians.

With the figurine makers, we do not know what the relation between the sexes was. Yet a gylanic balance is possible. While hunting would have given importance to men, women might have had equal importance, through magic and healing, for instance. We cannot tell from the figurines alone whether the Goddess really was the chief deity and whether the art objects are rightly interpreted in that sense. Again, however, it may be so, and at least one counterargument does not work. Whatever hunting's social role, it need not have promoted a divine masculinity. Anthropologists have spoken of goddesses, mistresses of wild nature, who "link the mystic identity of the hunter with the hunted."[12] Even the myths of Greece include a huntress goddess, Artemis, afterward Diana.

In the upshot, Gimbutas's code-breaking exercises, sketching a network of Goddess symbolism, do amount to a case for a primitive ideology, and the recurrence of imagery over a vast area may favor a dissemination from the Altai-Baikal region. Still, it is hard to see anything so distant in time and space playing a major part in later history, or leaving a powerful enough impression on folk memory to influence more advanced societies, mythwise or otherwise. It would be more plausible if the Altaic part of the network harbored something truly distinctive, a unique "strong magic," a special paradise-generating factor. It also would be more plausible, *much* more, if that area had not simply produced figurines and then closed down— if there had been cultic continuity, if it had gone on being "live," so to speak, for thousands of years. The idea is not absurd. The Australian aborigines, with their imaginative mythology, seem to have remained very much as they are now for forty millennia.

At Mal'ta, the cult center where some of the oldest and best figurines were found, there is evidence from other objects that the place's importance might have gone on. But among the earliest of all, retrieved from a cave burial, is an oblong panel of mammoth ivory dated about 24,000 B.C.[13] On one side of it, three snakes establish its place in the Goddess network. On the other side is a design composed of lines of dots. They curve around to form seven spirals, six little ones framing a seventh that is much larger. In the large spiral the line goes around seven times, circling inward to a hole in the center. This design, being linear and serpentine, also is in accord with Gimbutan ideas. It is more, however. It is the first instance anywhere in the world of something destined to emerge far and wide as very strong magic indeed—the peculiar mystique of the number seven.

The large spiral, or others like it, could be at the root of a known phenomenon, one of the most intriguing forms that the seven mystique takes. A mathematician, Robert P. Thomas, has pointed out that if you complicate a seven-circuited spiral like this by making the line double back, running alternately clockwise and counterclockwise instead of going continuously around, there is only one way of doing it that is aesthetically satisfying. And that precise design occurs as a maze pattern or labyrinth in a far-flung variety of contexts. It is sometimes round, sometimes square; some instances are mirror images of others; but the pattern is always, basically, the same.[14]

It is on a tile from Pylos in Greece dated about 1200 B.C. Cretan coins are stamped with it as a symbol of the labyrinth. The coins are much later, but the original labyrinth, in the Minoan age, was probably not a building housing the Minotaur (whatever he was) but a dance following the double spiral. Such a dance was performed ritually on the Aegean island of Delos well into classical times. The same backtracking septenary figure is on an Etruscan vase from Tagliatella in Italy, dating perhaps from the seventh century B.C.; it is part of a picture of an equestrian maneuver called the Game of Troy and mentioned in Virgil's *Aeneid*. A graffito in the same form is on a pillar in Pompeii with the words LABYRINTHUS HIC HABITAT MINO-TAURUS ("The Labyrinth, here lives the Minotaur"), doubtless a rude reference to the owner of the house.

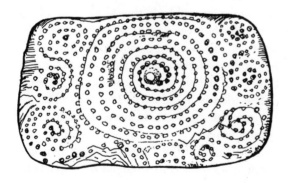

Design on ivory panel from Mal'ta, Siberia. *Thames and Hudson*

The backtracking spiral is inscribed on a stone from Wicklow in Ireland and on another in the Rocky Valley near Tintagel in Cornwall. In Wales it used to be a recognized pattern for turf cutting as a pastime of shepherds, and boys challenged other boys to draw it correctly.[15] For the Welsh it was *Caerdroia*, the Walls of Troy. A large-scale instance, disputed but defensible, is a hillside earthwork system on Glastonbury Tor in Somerset, England, judged, if the reconstruction of the pattern is right, to be Neolithic.[16] Glastonbury's long history has been heavily overlaid with legend and speculation, but it has a fair claim to have been a Goddess sanctuary before its better-known career as a Christian one. Present-day devotees of the Goddess climb the Tor and follow the track. Thousands of miles away, in a manuscript illustration to the Indian epic *Ramayana*, the same pattern represents a fortress where the hero's wife is imprisoned. It is also on the floor of a Jain temple in Karnataka.[17]

Since the spiral on the Mal'ta panel is a simple one, its role as prototype is very much a conjecture and may seem farfetched. But archaeology does not in fact offer a prototype anywhere else, and an argument in favor arises from the developed spiral's most surprising appearance—among the Hopi of Arizona, who call it the Mother Earth symbol.[18] In their eyes it represents a road of life that, if followed, leads to rebirth through the eternal Mother. The rebirth is a reenactment in the individual of a myth of history, the Emergence. Three human races were destroyed before this one, but in each case a remnant lived underground and "emerged" to repopulate the world. Other native American myths tell related tales, to the effect that the survivors reached the surface by a tunnel following the same course and that the double spiral depicts the umbilical cord and fetal membranes of the Earth Mother when she gave birth to her children.

Now, if the scattered instances are products of diffusion at all, the starting point could hardly have been anywhere but in northern Asia. There is nowhere else from which people or motifs could have spread both across the Eurasian landmass and to a North America that received its settlers from Siberia, when the continents still were connected. Finally, if the septenary spiral did spread abroad as a magical or sacred image, the dates of the developed versions show the development apparently happening much later than the Mal'ta panel, with the implication that the source did continue to be "live," and veneration of the spiral continued there till a time came when it was elaborated and propagated.

Whatever weight should be given to the spiral itself (and one of its aspects will presently make these guesses look more solid), cultural diffusion from a broadly Altaic center is a hypothesis worth discussing. Gimbutan prehistory supplies a hint here for an exploration that not only may support it but may range beyond it . . . or, alternatively, may call it in question. Diffusion could have carried Goddess motifs and imagery, or maybe non-

Goddess motifs and imagery, and it could have built up paradisal traditions looking backward to a mythified source. If, however, we are to try confirming this source and defining its character, we shall need to be more specific. It also will be important to ask whether we can ever see the diffusion actually happening. And in assessing possibilities, we shall face a complication due to Gimbutas herself.

Her golden age has the same Paradise Lost quality as others. It is brought to a close. We are told that the Goddess-worshiping gylanic order was tragically replaced by male-ruled, god-oriented societies, ancestral to the present world. Some anthropologists, who more or less accept the gylanic age, see its eclipse as due to technological progress, giving men wider scope and advantages. Not so Marija Gimbutas and her followers. The end came through active destruction—gradual, piecemeal, but deadly. The story has villains. They are the Indo-Europeans.

3

Who were the Indo-Europeans? Why, when, and how are they supposed to have extinguished the golden age?

They were a mysterious people—it may be franker to say a hypothetical people—whose language is thought to have been ancestral to many others and whose descendants are thought to have spread these derived languages over a huge area, its extent shown by the fact that the Gaelic of Ireland and the Hindi of India both belong to the Indo-European family.[19]

Well over a century ago philologists realized that many languages, widely different on the face of it, have overlaps and parallels implying a common origin. This is easy to see in such cases as Italian and Spanish, both of which are derived from Latin. But the argument can be pressed much further. Besides Latin and the Latin-derived group, the Celtic, Germanic, and Slavic languages and Greek are all classed as Indo-European. English counts as Germanic, although its main Anglo-Saxon element has been augmented by many words from other sources. The reason for the "Indo" is that the same logic brings in Sanskrit and its Indian descendants. It also brings in Persian and several dead languages, such as Hittite. This linguistic family is distinct from the Semitic family, of which Hebrew is a well-known member, and from the languages of Africa and the Orient.

All Indo-European languages seem to have been derived, through a long process of separation and evolution, from a Proto-Indo-European original. This parent tongue may have been a single language or a cluster of closely related dialects. Proto-Indo-European is completely undocumented. There are no inscriptions, no texts, no secondhand reports. However, a little of its vocabulary can be inferred from words that are shared, with only limited divergence, by all of its derivatives—such words as those for "father" and "mother."[20]

The speakers of this original tongue, the Proto-Indo-Europeans, presumably had a homeland in one geographic region. Some of their descendants spread over Europe, carrying dialects that evolved and grew, till they resulted in Greek, Latin, and the rest. Others spread over parts of Asia, with a branch reaching Iran and creating Old Persian, and a branch reaching India and creating Sanskrit.[21] The latter are known as Indo-Aryans. The term *Aryan* is of Indian origin. It used to be applied more widely, even to Indo-Europeans in general, but racist exploitation brought it into discredit and it is confined now to the Indo-Europeans who reached India, plus one other grouping to the west of them that was closely akin.

Strictly, it is inexact to speak of Indo-Europeans as if they were a race or nation. A more accurate term is "Indo-European speakers."[22] But in view of manifest kinships and continuities, it is hard to discuss them without at least some ethnic meaning. Many attempts have been made to locate the homeland, the starting point of the great dispersal, and to identify the first Indo-Europeans with a known ethnic or cultural stock. Speculation has roamed over a good deal of Europe, a good deal of Asia, and parts of Africa, and extended to the North Pole.[23] However, some of the territory can be ruled out by study of the inferred "Proto" vocabulary. Shared words for certain trees and animals imply that these were known to the Proto-Indo-Europeans. Therefore their milieu was one that contained these trees and animals, as, to take the extreme case, the polar regions do not. Still, theories have ranged from central Europe to central Asia.

This is where Marija Gimbutas comes in.[24] She equates the first Indo-Europeans with Neolithic dwellers on the steppes of the Soviet Union, who disposed of their more important dead in chambered mounds known as kurgans, so that burials of this type can be used to plot their movements. Kurgan society began to take shape in the Volga basin as far back as the seventh millennium B.C. The Kurgan people were pastoral, practicing small-scale agriculture and animal husbandry. After a while they domesticated the horse and had wheeled vehicles. They were patriarchal, male-dominated, with a male pantheon, and they were combative and fond of weapons, making these from copper and bronze as metallurgy developed.

Gimbutas has Kurgan people expanding into Old Europe in several waves over a long period, from about 4300 B.C. to about 2800 B.C. Old Europe's gylanic or matristic society was *pre*-Indo-European and had been in possession for a long time, worshiping the Goddess in various forms and living peaceably by farming. The change for the worse was due to Kurgan mobs entering as conquerors, imposing not only Indo-European speech but the ascendancy of male warriors and a male religion. The process was not complete everywhere till centuries after the last actual invasion, but there was no reversing it.

Some female prehistorians have adopted all of this, treating the Goddess culture and its Indo-European destruction as a single package. However, the part involving the Indo-Europeans presents difficulties, even if, as is far from proved, their equation with the Kurgan people is right. It may be relevant to events at the other termini of expansion, in Iran and India. It fails to account for the triumph of patriarchy, or whatever we call it, in countries the Indo-Europeans never overran—Israel, for instance. There, the same kind of thinking has to evoke a different set of macho villains. (Merlin Stone, author of *When God Was a Woman*, tries valiantly to hold everything together by making out that the priestly Levites *were* Indo-European.[25]) But even in Europe it is doubtful how far the combined package is acceptable. In *In Search of the Indo-Europeans*, J. P. Mallory gives a respectful summary of the Gimbutan position but concludes:[26]

> Almost all of the arguments for invasion and cultural transformations are far better explained without reference to Kurgan expansions, and most of the evidence so far represented is either totally contradicted by other evidence or is the result of gross misinterpretation of the cultural history of Eastern, Central and Northern Europe. (P. 185)

Robert Claiborne, who gives the Indo-Europeans a Danubian homeland, offers a further argument.[27] It hinges on geography. Conquerors can impose their languages, but the language of the conquered survives in the landscape, and especially in the names of rivers. Until the fifth century A.D. the inhabitants of Britain were Celtic. Then Anglo-Saxons from across the North Sea gradually took possession of much of the country, and wherever they were supreme the Celtic British language yielded to Anglo-Saxon, the ancestor of English. Yet many river names in England are British to this day—Thames, for instance. In North America, by the late nineteenth century, English speakers of European stock outnumbered the indigenous tribes from coast to coast and were absolutely dominant. Yet dozens of native river names survived, and survive still, witnessing to a previous population.

Now throughout central and eastern Europe, most names of rivers are derived from Indo-European languages. Very few are clearly non-Indo-European. All of the continent had inhabitants before Indo-Europeans spread over it, and local traces of them remain even linguistically, as in the Basque country of northern Spain. But it is difficult to believe that this pre-Indo-European population was large when the map fails to testify to that effect, except in patches near the Atlantic. If that judgment is correct, while

Gimbutas's gylanic society may have existed, it could not have been pre-Indo-European, because there never were enough pre-Indo-Europeans in the region where she says it flourished. It must have been Indo-European itself or predominantly so, and the nature of the change that subverted it is more problematic.

Colin Renfrew, famous for a revision of carbon dating that revolutionized ideas about Stonehenge, has put forward a rival theory with support from a Soviet philologist, Tomas Gamkrelidze.[28] For him, Proto-Indo-European was the language of early farming communities in Asia Minor in the seventh millennium B.C. The beginning of Indo-European-speaking society may well be as far back as the beginning of agricultural society, may in fact be a phase of it, in which case the Gimbutan thesis of something radically unlike in bias is mistaken. These people multiplied, and a slow, unspectacular wave of advance, without major migrations or conquests, carried agricultural groups into Europe and farther and farther across it. They absorbed an earlier population that, as the river names suggest, was extremely sparse. Renfrew accepts Indo-Europeans on the steppes, in the fifth and fourth millennia, but considers that they branched off from the ones who settled Europe and adopted a life-style of their own. Another wave of advance might have rolled eastward from Anatolia toward India. Renfrew's account is controversial. It has been given qualified support by Marek Zvelebil, professor of archaeology at the University of Sheffield, in Sheffield, England.[29]

Mallory, following critically on Renfrew's heels, proposes a model that is more like Gimbutas's, in spite of his skepticism about her Kurgan invasions.[30] His Indo-European homeland is the Pontic-Caspian region, meaning, mainly, southern Russia and the lower Volga basin. Cautious in handling scanty evidence, he is more venturesome than most in tracing the dispersal through Asia, which he believes might have been rapid, as folk movements go.

No consensus has emerged, beyond agreement about early Indo-Europeans roaming the steppes. Still, recent discussion has had a decided tendency to push the whole process back in time. It used to be supposed that the first Indo-European stirrings did not begin until the late third millennium B.C.[31] Today they are put in the fourth, the fifth, even the seventh. Indo-European influence on, say, Sumer, the pioneer civilization of the Middle East, once would have been ruled out on the ground that Sumer was earlier than any possible Indo-European propinquity. It still may be ruled out, but not for that reason. Indo-Europeans of some sort could have been there, as far as chronology goes.

So a distinction is called for. The golden age of the Goddess may be real, the casting of Indo-Europeans in the role of destroyers is gratuitous and an obstacle to impartial inquiry. They may have been, they may not.

We don't know enough about them. The archaeology of the Kurgan people is inconclusive, since they may not have been the first Indo-Europeans anyhow. Whoever those Indo-Europeans were, some of them, especially the steppe dwellers, were probably patriarchal. Honorable interments of men but not women tell their tale. But there is no evidence that even the steppe dwellers were exclusively god-oriented. Attempts have been made to infer their religion from a few divine names shared by different branches of the linguistic family. Results have been meager.[32] Thus, the Greeks had their sky god, Father Zeus, and the Indo-Aryans too had a sky god, Father Dyaus. It is easy to infer an Indo-European god with a name like "Dyeus," ancestral to both. Comparison, however, reveals almost nothing about him. Zeus and Dyaus, in their respective mythologies, are not at all the same. Divine names for the sun also are cognate. We have Sol, Sulis, and so on in Europe, and Surya in India. They do not tell us how Proto-Indo-Europeans thought of the sun, and their solar deity may quite well have been female.[33]

Gimbutas and her followers have made the golden age, Ancient Wisdom, and paradisal myth into serious issues—not as embodying literal realities but as reflecting and echoing realities. The rise of a reborn Goddess religion has made these issues not only serious but vital and current, bound up, in the eyes of Goddess devotees, with the spirituality and status of women. The aim of this inquiry is to ask how far Goddess prehistory works, and to approach that question by way of another that it raises but that may have unsuspected bearings: whether an immemorial seedbed—a more or less Altai-Baikal seedbed—is credible. And to keep all possibilities open, the destructive part of the package must be set aside, for the moment at least. The Indo-European role may not be as supposed. Study of Indo-European cultures could turn up evidence, even supportive of the Gimbutan prehistory, that has been obscured by their dismissal as merely barbaric. Whoever they were, Indo-Europeans were scattered across the steppes very early, not only in Russia but far into Asia. On Gimbutas's own showing they occupied what was, or had been, Goddess territory. Cults and mythology from the hypothetical seedbed could have lingered on; there could have been a fertilization of Indo-European groups from Siberian cultures in which they did linger on. There may be traces of such an influence in Indo-European societies farther afield, carried there with the great dispersal. It is not a question of finding them throughout the Indo-European complex, borne along everywhere with the linguistic baggage, but simply of finding them somewhere in it. If apparent traces exist—and if they can be detected farther afield, among peoples with whom Indo-Europeans came into contact—then it may be proper to draw inferences about the seedbed area.

Any such influences transmitted through Indo-Europeans would be much later than the early Siberian Goddess artifacts or, indeed, the assumed rise of Goddess worship in Old Europe. Evidence for them cannot be direct evidence for the Goddess prehistory. Yet this line of inquiry can be valid and relevant. The first step is to ask what really can be said or inferred about ancient religion and mythology in Siberia, and in the Altai-Baikal region in particular. Then we can ask whether any of the motifs that come to light do seem to have had a dynamic quality; whether they do suggest a seedbed and an influence going out from it. The case of the septenary spiral could be a foretaste. If such influence is apparent in Indo-European or other cultures, we can say something about those background motifs— that they always could have had the outgoing quality. Such results, if achieved, will have their own interest quite apart from the feminist issue. But they will lead into it, raising the question how far the seedbed motifs harmonize with Gimbutan conceptions and whether a continuity spanning the millennia was indeed a Goddess continuity. Researches not hitherto brought to bear may turn out to offer a key, or several keys.

This discussion is an exploration of myths, beliefs, and practices. It begins with some neglected clues. I make no apology for an inquiry that may look fanciful. The proof of the pudding is in the eating. Fanciful or not, I think the inquiry does go somewhere. When the data are assembled we may glimpse a common origin for things widely separated; a beginning behind recognized beginnings; a dawn behind the dawn and an Eden, if you will, behind Eden.

CHAPTER THREE

Beasts, Mountains, Stars

1

To assess the old north Asian culture and its influence (if any) on others, the most hopeful approach is by way of myths and religion. The exploration cannot be confined to one region, because the same myths and religion, with variants, extend widely over Siberia and adjacent areas. But it may become feasible to narrow it down and focus on Altaic country.

The aboriginal Siberians have lived from time immemorial by hunting, fishing, and a limited kind of stockbreeding.[1] Historically most have been nomadic to some degree. They are scattered sparsely but widely and their kindred are to be found outside Siberia. None are Indo-European. There are Finno-Ugric speakers, related to Uralic tribes, north of European Russia. Across the territory from there to the Pacific are Tatars and Samoyed and Chukchi and Buryat and Yakut. In the east are Tungus. The Altai range runs through Mongolia, and Altaians and Mongols are akin. The more comprehensive terms *Turkic* and *Turko-Tatar* also are in use. Some prehistorians have distinguished Paleo-Siberians from Neo-Siberians; the latter, who include the present Altaians, are supposed to have wandered from a homeland in central Asia, but this was an extremely long time ago.

The key word for this inquiry is "shamanism." That does not cover everything, not by a long shot, but in all of this region shamans are the religious elite. To study their activities is to learn a great deal; to study the mythology that surrounds them—some of it taught and perhaps invented by them, some of it coexisting—is to learn more. The shaman, to sum it up briefly, is a person who has learned techniques of ecstasy, who attains superhuman knowledge and power, who communes with gods and spirits in trance, and who does it by controlled methods. Such accomplishments are found among many peoples, but Siberia, with parts of central Asia, is the shamanic territory par excellence.

The standard work on this topic is by Mircea Eliade, who draws together a mass of older research and subjects it to illuminating scrutiny. Another author not to be neglected is Maria Czaplicka, an Oxford scholar who, in 1914, published *Aboriginal Siberia*, a book that gives information not found in Eliade's work and is still valuable as an adjunct to his. A third is Nicholas Roerich, a Russian who was not a specialist in this field but touched on it in the course of a distinguished career as an artist and archaeologist.[2] He supplied Stravinsky with material on pagan Russia for the *Rite of Spring* ballet and designed scenery for Diaghilev. After the revolution the Bolsheviks offered him a post in their Ministry of Culture, but he chose to emigrate. From 1925 to 1928 he led a leisurely expedition through central Asia, impelled by a mixture of motives, anthropological, religious, and mystical. His travel diary, published in English as *Altai-Himalaya*, is full of curious lore. Some of it can be supplemented from the work of his son, a more academic scholar who went on the expedition.

Nicholas Roerich, Russian artist, archaeologist, and anthropologist: portrait by his son Svetoslav. *Nicholas Roerich Museum—used by permission*

Anyone who tries to survey shamanism in depth faces two problems. The first is that much of the research was done by investigators in the nineteenth century and the early twentieth. Owing to the dwindling of shamanism under Soviet rule, it may not be easy to check their reliability or confirm the beliefs and practices they describe. The second problem is more daunting. Data amassed in modern times, however trustworthy, may not be evidence for what shamanism was long ago, or even for the existence of shamanism.

As to the first problem, the rational course is to follow Eliade and speak in the present tense, assuming that the investigators correctly reported what happened and, if sketchily, happens still. Soviet anthropologists have published encouraging studies of remote tribes, and some cross-checking can be done from other societies in which something like shamanism flourishes.

The second problem is the serious one for the present purpose. The usual opinion is that shamanism has indeed existed for thousands of years, in communities that may have shifted location but have remained fairly static in character. If that is so, we have a method of deciding the likelihood or otherwise that this northland did contain a cultural seedbed. Where other societies underwent an ancient contact with it, direct or indirect, do they exhibit parallels to the motifs of the shamanic world, as we retrospectively judge these to have been? Evidence of this type will be especially forceful if it converges; if independent facts, far apart, agree in pointing back to the same part of the world as a source of inspiration.

Against shamanism's great age, some have argued, on the basis of likenesses and word borrowings, that it was created or at least deeply affected by Buddhism, which reached Mongolia in the thirteenth century A.D.[3] If it was a spurious offshoot of Buddhism, obviously it tells us nothing about antiquity. But there is no real reason to think that shamanism as observed is a Buddhist creation or that Buddhism radically altered it from what it was anciently. Over most of Siberia, no evidence exists. Even in the part where it does, the eastern Tungusic part, the Buddhism that left its mark was the Tibetan, Lamaistic variety. This owes much that is characteristic to a pre-Buddhist religion called Bön . . . and Bön itself was shamanistic. So the discussion goes in a circle.[4]

Eliade denies that shamanism was a Buddhist creation. He shows good reason, some of it archaeological, to detect Paleolithic roots.[5] Cave paintings are supportive, and Soviet archaeologists are prepared to concur. The British prehistorian Stuart Piggott, seeking antecedents for druidism, finds some among the shamans—perhaps even Altaic ones—and argues that this subject opens up a vista of fully twenty thousand years. He also raises a more specific issue. America, as remarked, was first populated from Siberia by tribes that wandered along a land bridge, spanning what is now the Bering

Strait and joining Asia to Alaska. Forms of shamanism are attested in America too, and Piggott suggests that migrants from Asia took it with them. Toward 6000 B.C., however, the Bering isthmus vanished when the melting of ice raised the water level. After that the migration was over, or virtually so. Therefore, any propagation of shamanism to the New World happened before 6000 B.C., and any motifs attributed to the migrants must have existed in Siberia before they left—in other words, before 6000 B.C. Quite apart from anything known to be shamanic, we have the septenary maze pattern or double spiral among the Hopi and its possible ancestor on the ivory panel at Mal'ta; and in this case the inference would be valid, since the Mal'ta object is a long way prior to 6000 B.C.

For Starhawk, as a witchcraft authority, continuity with the Paleolithic is no problem. She takes ancient shamanism for granted on the basis of "our legends."[6]

Across the rich tundra, teeming with animal life, small groups of hunters followed the free-running reindeer and the thundering bison. They were armed with only the most primitive of weapons, but some among the clans were gifted, could "call" the herds to a cliffside or a pit, where a few beasts, in willing sacrifice, would let themselves be trapped. These gifted shamans could attune themselves to the spirits of the herds, and in so doing they became aware of the pulsating rhythm that infuses all life, the dance of the double spiral, of whirling into being, and whirling out again. . . .

Male shamans dressed in skins and horns in identification with the God and the herds, but female priestesses presided naked, embodying the fertility of the Goddess.

Let us at least allow that shamanism as observed *may* be evidence for the distant past, and let us see how things look if we accept its great age, provisionally, as a working hypothesis.

2

To begin with, it needs to be clear that we are not talking about savages, either now or in the past. Some anthropologists fancy that the ancient milieu may have been more impressive than the present. To quote Nora Chadwick, author of an acute study,

It is, indeed, to be suspected that the most primitive peoples living today are not originators, but the heirs of millennia of culture, imperfectly transmitted and now deteriorated often beyond recognition.

The loftier conceptions of former civilizations are reduced to degenerate magical formulae.[7]

But even if shamanism has deteriorated, it is far from being a mere affair of "degenerate magical formulae." The shaman is a person deserving respect and qualified to exert influence. He is not a witch doctor in the worse sense, exploiting superstition, nor is he a holy lunatic, despite his often bizarre outfit, his dancing and drumming (the masculine pronoun is for convenience; it does not imply that all shamans are male—far from it). On receiving his vocation he undergoes a rigorous training, with grueling initiatory ordeals. He comes through, if he does, as a person superior to his fellow tribesmen in wisdom, self-control, and strength of character, a guide, healer, and diviner for his community. Important in the shamanic scheme is the idea of a soul distinct from the body, capable of taking different forms, living and adventuring on its own and surviving death. The shaman's repertoire includes not only the mediumistic ecstasy in which he consults gods and spirits, but out-of-the-body traveling, sometimes (at least in his own belief and others') physical traveling by no normal method, and bilocation and flight.

Despite the shamans' gifts, the conception of a lost golden age occurs here as elsewhere.[8] They speak of a past when all human beings could make contact with the gods and spirits, and could do it easily. Now only shamans can do it, and even they cannot do it easily. Their powers are less than those of their predecessors. It may well be significant that male shamans sometimes show a penchant for transvestism and sex change, as if their nostalgia looked backward to an older feminine magic, with a notion that the true source of inspiration is female and that assumed femininity can set up a rapport with it.[9] Occasionally a shaman may dress like a woman, arrange his hair like a woman, talk like a woman, sew like a woman. Although this conduct is not homosexual (as the term usually is understood), cases are on record of a feminized shaman taking a male lover and even marrying him.

Women can be shamans themselves, sometimes with an effectiveness that may help to explain the actions of sex-changed men.[10] Shamanesses' performances have deeply impressed outside observers. A Tatar poem tells of a knowledge contest between two sages in which both were defeated by a woman who knew more words than either.[11] Women's status might have been higher once because of this very command of magical arts. A more radical view, favored by some Soviet anthropologists, is that female shamans were formerly the only ones, so that the nostalgia reflects historical fact.[12]

A reason for thinking so is that a medley of tribes all have different terms for male shamans, whereas the term for a female shaman is always a variant of the same word.[13] A male Tungus shaman is simply that, but an Altaic one is a *kam*, a Buryat is a *bo*, a Yakut is an *oyun*. A female shaman is a *utygan* or a *udagan* or a *udaghan*, but never anything etymologically different. The inference is that these tribes are descended from groups that were closer together, or in closer touch, and then all shamans were women, known by a single term—*utygan* or something like it—that stayed in use after the connections were broken. Male shamans appeared only after the separation, so the words for them were invented independently. (This view, though a product of mainstream anthropology, is more feminist than Starhawk's.)

The priority of women has been invoked to explain an undoubted fact: the association of shamans and smiths.[14] A Yakut proverb declares, "Smiths and shamans are from the same nest." And according to another saying, "The smith is the elder brother of the shaman." They can overlap; a smith virtually can *be* a shaman. The extraction of metal from ore and the metallurgical use of fire are post–Stone Age arts taught by a smith god. The smith's status as the elder implies some kind of seniority, and Troshchanski, who proposed the theory that shamanesses were first, suggested that male shamans originated as smiths who made metal gear and ornaments for the female ones and gradually usurped their functions. If so, the rise of the male shaman is comparatively recent, as prehistoric time scales go. We would have to suppose that in the American shamanism derived earlier from Asia, the process happened independently and perhaps otherwise.

Eliade acknowledges guardedly what he calls echoes of matriarchy.[15] He notes that Siberian folklore includes female fairies who possess and confer magical powers. They are pictured as auxiliary to male shamans but with a superiority of their own. Thus, they can help men to make journeys in the spirit when the men cannot manage it, journeys they themselves make unaided.

Shamanic deities vary, but with a certain consensus.[16] Some tribes recognize a Supreme God, Tengere Kaira Khan, Merciful Emperor Heaven. However, if believed in at all, he is far off and little sought after. The effective high god is Bai Ülgän, who dwells in celestial regions and is concerned with the atmosphere, fertility, and human needs. Down below us is an underworld god, Erlik Khan, lord of the dead. In Altaic tradition Ülgän created Erlik as a helper, but he turned hostile, and Ülgän made further beings, including the first humans. Creators are always male. But alongside them is often a female presence taking different forms. The Ugrians on the Ob River have a creation myth set in "the house of the Master of the Upper World and the Great Mother." A goddess figure appears in other contexts as Mistress of the Universe, mother of animals and people, and among the Altaians, with a gender fusion, "Mother and Father of the Man." Earth itself is personified as a woman, notably among the Tungus. Storytellers attach the word *mother* to names of rivers and mountains, as the more masculine English dubbed their best-known river Father Thames.

There seems reason to accept that this variable divine female is residually the Goddess of the Gimbutan network, carrying on after her fashion and witnessing to millennial continuity. The shift from female to male deity might be linked with the shift from female to male shamanism, if that really happened, for metallic or other reasons. The female-shaman word *utygan* may have derived from the Mongol "Etugen," or Earth Goddess, suggesting that shamanesses, in their exalted state, embodied her.[17] The religious change in Siberia might therefore have been due to internal causes, without alien conquest.

Animals have a major shamanic role. One feature of the golden age is a lost harmony with nature that only shamans can recapture, and then only temporarily. Shamans have animal helpers and dress in outfits imitating the animals, whose power they draw on.[18] They turn themselves into birds, for instance, learn their language—which is a key to secrets of the Unseen— and imitate them in spiritual flight. There is a high regard for the horse. Horse-headed sticks and wooden images are talismans carried in ecstatic dancing. Among Altaic shamans the sacrifice of a real horse is, or has been, an elaborate ritual in which the shaman accompanies the victim's soul to the highest heavens.[19]

In the taiga, the coniferous forest between the steppes and the tundra, the most powerful wild creatures are elks and bears. Tungus tribes recognize a cosmic Elk with a place among the stars, and also a cosmic Bear.[20] At the earthly level, bears have an eloquent importance across this whole northern world.[21]

The bear, in its larger varieties, inspires not only dread but a peculiar awe. It eerily combines terrible strength with a half-human look when on its hind legs, and it resembles humans in the wide range of its diet, so that it conveys an impression of being both overpowering and not quite animal. Legends tell of "bear-son" heroes who are the offspring of a bear and a human parent.

Psychologists have claimed that the she bear is an ancient maternal symbol.[22] Archaeologists have claimed that the bear is the oldest identifiable deity.[23] They base this opinion on Neanderthal sites in Europe where cave dwellers made niches to hold the skulls of bears and arranged the thigh bones with evident care. The object, by inference, was to return the bear's spirit to its home in an amicable atmosphere. However that may be, the bear has always had ready-made mythic qualities. A former popular belief that its cubs were mere lumps of flesh and fur, to be licked into shape by the mother, carried a hint of primeval chaos and its transformation into a world. The animal's winter sleep paralleled the seasonal cycle. Some native American tribes still perform a spring ritual called the Grizzly Bear Dance, which imitates the grizzly waking from hibernation.

Bear cults are on record among peoples linked by the Finno-Ugric languages, in Lapland, Finland, Estonia, and around the Ural mountains. These languages form a branch of a Uralic family of which the other branch is a Samoyedic group in northern Siberia. Such cults have existed among the aboriginal tribes all the way to the Pacific. Beyond, native Americans too have bear cults and myths. Many of the Siberians say they are descended from bears, and a word, *mangi*, means "bear" in one dialect but means "spirit of ancestors" in another. A Slavic belief used in the *Rite of Spring*, thanks no doubt to Roerich's researches, makes bears the ancestors of the whole human race.[24]

Lapp shamans in historical times attached parts of a bear's carcass to their magical drums to strengthen the magic and "became" bears in their prophetic ecstasy.[25] Lapps gave the bear nicknames—Grandfather, Woolly One, Old Forest Apples, Honey Paws—and performed a ritual when they went out to hunt it on its emergence from its winter den. After killing one, they begged its pardon, and the subsequent feast was ritualized. The Finnish national epic *Kalevala* treats bears with reverence.

Over the expanse between Lapland and the Pacific, bear cults and shamanism interpenetrate.[26] Among the Yakut, each shaman has a tutelary spirit in animal form, and with some of the greatest this is a brown bear. Many put on a bear costume, imitate the animal, and undergo ecstatic changes. By "becoming" bears, they do not sink to subhuman level, they grow to be more than human.

A number of Siberian tribes hold bear festivals.[27] Those in the eastern region, among the oldest strata of population, are the most impressive. The Kuryak of Kamchatka have a festival in which people in general, not shamans alone, dress up as bears, and a sacrificial one is ceremonially "sent home" (that is, sent to the spirit realm) in the belief that respectful treatment will smooth the path for bear hunters. The Kuryak say that when a bear kills someone, that person's soul goes to the forest and is reborn as another bear. The Gilyak, on the mainland opposite the island of Sakhalin, nurture a tame bear, venerate it, and sacrifice it. The festival is a unifying public occasion, like the Olympic Games in ancient Greece. In Gilyak eyes, bears are superior to people, in mind as well as in body. The sacrificial victim becomes an intermediary between mortals and gods.

Across in Japan, the Ainu, a pre-Japanese minority, still practice a reduced bear worship. In past times its chief ceremony was like that of the Gilyak. They used to capture a young black bear, raise it with kindness till it was fully grown, and then "send it away" to its spirit home with a swift, merciful killing. Afterward everyone feasted in the victim's honor, eating its flesh, with its head and hide mounted so that it still was present.

As for kindred beliefs and customs in America, they may not have been an independent growth. They are, in fact, part of the case for a spread of shamanism from Siberia before the Bering connection was severed, and hence for the great age of such beliefs and customs in the ancestral land. American shamans are more than medicine men.[28] Assumption of the ursine nature is one feature of their experience that they have in common with Siberians. Special reverence for bears has been noted in the New World as well as the Old. Some native Americans used to be reluctant to kill bears at all, or to lay a hand on a dead one. Others would kill them for food but apologize, like the Lapps, and arrange the remains carefully so that the creature would be intact in the spirit world. An Eskimo deity appears in polar bear guise. Among the Sioux, the Chippewa, the Pueblo, and the Iroquois, bear gods are benign healers. The Apache politely call the male of the species "the Old Man."

3

In the beginning, says an Altaic myth, the Creator sat on a golden mountain in the middle of the sky. No other solid ground existed as yet. When he had made the earth, he lowered the mountain onto it.[29]

Altaic shamans tell of the mountain at the heart of the world. This is one form of a shamanic conception that is not solely Altaic and appears in other regions in other versions. The essential idea is that the world has a kind of axle, a pillar that connects the earth and the heavens, holding them in position. Where the sky pillar is not pictured as a mountain, it may be a cosmic tree.[30] That image is familiar in Siberia and elsewhere. While the mountain too has parallels, it is more shamanic. Above is the upper world.[31] One name for this is *Tymanitki*, which means "Toward Morning" and, to judge from other mythologies, has an implication about the place where the sun reappears at dawn. A river flows down the mountain from the upper world, across our own, and into the depths below. Beside it are the dwellings of female shamans surviving in spirit from the past.

The central mountain is one of the alleged evidences for a modification of shamanism by Buddhism. Buddhist mythology does include a central mountain, called "Sumeru," and Mongols apply similar names, such as "Sumer" and "Sumbur," to their own version. However, they are well aware that Sumeru as such came in with Buddhism. They have a native network of sacred mountains, in the Altai and Tien Shan ranges, that are vastly senior.[32] These are the abodes of spirits and deities, and some are so numinous that people avoid using their proper names, preferring epithets like "the high," "the holy," "the beautiful." Mongols have been burying important persons on the high places since the Stone Age, as archaeology proves, and they practice an ancestor worship inspired partly by a belief that the dead draw power from mountain spirits. Marco Polo found the funerary custom flourishing in the thirteenth century:[33]

All the great lords who are of the lineage of Chinghiz Khan are conveyed for burial to a great mountain called Altai. When one of them dies, even if it be at a distance of a hundred days' journey from the mountain, he must be brought here for burial. (P. 97)

Khan Tengri ("Lord God" or "Heaven-Lord") in the Tien Shan is one of the Mongols' sacred mountains, and "all the thirteen Altai" are prayed to. An invocation to the gods of Dzungaria includes Altai Khan, Lord Altai.[34] These cults are shamanic and embody the oldest conceptions in folk religion. The lamas persecuted shamanism—an ironic thing to do, since their version of Buddhism was so largely derived from Bön, itself shamanic.[35] Shamanism survived in Mongolia by adaptation without changing its essential nature and continued into modern times, preserving the reverence for mountains. Kindred cults are widespread in the neighboring part of Siberia. The northerners, in fact, were quite equal to imagining their cosmic mountain unaided. Positive reasons will appear for believing that they did.

Shamans in their self-induced ecstasy make trance journeys on the celestial river.[36] It has many rapids, and the journey is risky and can be fatal. Perhaps because of the dangers, one name for it is *Engdekit*, which carries a notion of exclusion. Another and more frequent out-of-the-body feat is an ascent of the mountain itself, and up and onward through a series of "clouds" or levels to consult the god Bai Ülgän.[37]

As above, so below. The entrance to Erlik Khan's underworld corresponds to the center of the sky.[38] It is a hole, approached by passing another mountain, which is made of iron (a detail that might be thought to preclude great age, or at least imply a reworking of the original, but meteoric iron goes indefinitely far back). Shamans may undertake the descent to escort a deceased person's soul to Erlik's kingdom or to plead with him for the soul of someone who is sick and near death. This is another hazardous feat. The shaman goes down in spirit through a series of levels called *pudak*, or "obstacles," and sees weird and alarming sights. Erlik lives in a stone palace with his sons and daughters. At the séance's climax the shaman is dealing with him face to face. If the purpose is to ask for a sick person's reprieve, he offers gifts and drink, and if all goes well, Erlik agrees not to take the patient yet.

A recurrent feature of shamanism is representation.[39] Among the Evenks, a Tungus people, the shaman of a clan has a clan tree that is mystically identified with the cosmic tree. His own life and the clan's are bound up with it. Spirit ancestors sit on its branches watching over the clan and choosing shamanic candidates. Artifacts can deputize for the cosmic center, the tree or mountain. Tatars and Buryat revere a pole, even a tent pole, as standing for the prop of the sky. Altaic shamans keep a symbolic tree or post, notched to correspond to the celestial levels. The shaman's spiritual ascent may be accompanied by a physical one. While rising in his trance through the heavens, he is also literally climbing the tree . . . or post.

4

This theme of centrality draws attention to the polestar, the unmoving center of the sky, its "nail" in some dialects.[40] It is often supposed to mark the top of the sky pillar, whatever form this takes, and it is even called a pillar itself. It may be the point of entry to the upper world. Its prominence partly explains that of the constellation that circles it and is often linked with it, and circled the celestial pole even when that star did not quite mark it—Ursa Major, the many-named Great Bear, Big Dipper, Plough, or Wain. A few other constellations have a place in these northern mythologies—Orion, for example—but only a few. Ursa Major is outstanding. Nicholas Roerich refers to this in his *Altai-Himalaya*:

> The cults which surround some constellations such as the Bear and Orion amaze you by their widespread popularity. The wisdom of the Shamans designates them for worship.[41]

There is nothing special about an interest in Ursa Major as such.[42] Throughout most of the northern hemisphere it is in the sky at all seasons and at all hours of the night, circling the pole and never setting. For many peoples it is the only recognized constellation, or nearly so, and the only one that has stories told about it. Egyptians used to say it was the astral form of the god Set, or maybe of his thigh only. Mexicans said it was the foot of the god Tezcatlipoca, nipped off by an alligator, so that he limps. For Lapps, Eskimos, North American Indians, and some Africans it is the sole constellation agreed on. The early Lapps made it the bow of a hunter. The Sioux saw it as a bier or coffin, and so did the Arabs. In Kirghiz mythology its seven stars are watchmen who guard the two brightest stars of Ursa Minor, called the horses, from a menacing wolf; one day the wolf will kill the horses and the world will end. Kindred myths identify the stars themselves with wolves, which pursue the horses and, just before doomsday, will catch them. In Latin the constellation is the *Septentriones*, the "Seven Oxen," imagined turning a heavenly mill.

Ursa Major is the only constellation that popular folklore, free from literary influence, picks out and names. It is the Dipper or the Plough, and the image of a vehicle is very ancient indeed. A Roman astronomical writer, Hyginus, calls this constellation the Wain or Waggon, and the much earlier Homer concurs, though he knows the name *Bear* also, as Hyginus does; he uses both in the *Iliad* (18:487). Often the constellation is a conveyance for someone in legend or the Bible. Its rider may be the Emperor Charlemagne or King Arthur, so that it becomes Charles's Wain and, in Cornwall, Arthur's Wain. He may be Odin or Thor. He may be David, Elijah, Christ himself.

The constellation, therefore, is prominent everywhere. But shamanism, especially in eastern Siberia and Mongolia, gives it prominence of a special kind—partly because of a primitive cosmic myth, partly because its stars are individualized and enumerated with a quite peculiar emphasis.

With the Evenk, and very likely other groupings that have not been similarly studied, folklore about this constellation is rooted in a hunting society of unknown antiquity.[43] Hunters need orientation, and the Evenk manage it chiefly by knowledge of surface features, but their attitude to Ursa Major is exceptional. They are so familiar with its movements that they can tell the time by it, even within minutes. They have a word, *kheglun*, that, in reference to the sky, normally means this constellation. On earth it means an elk. Ursa Major, in the Evenk scheme of things, is the cosmic Elk.

A folktale introduces three men who went elk hunting. One boasted that he would reach the animal first; the second carried the cooking pot and was slow; the third, the smallest, confessed to being weak and said he would trail behind. When they sighted the elk, the boaster was scared and fell to the rear, and the little one advanced to the front. This version of the constellation brings in the men as well as the animal. They are the stars of the "handle," the other four constitute the elk. The star nearest to it is the faintest of the three, while the one in the middle has a tiny companion— the cooking pot.

Whether the cosmic Elk is the whole constellation or only the rectangular part, it is a "she."[44] Ursa Minor is the Elk's calf. In the first age of the world, the Elk ran out of the thickets of the heavenly taiga and carried off the sun on one of her antlers. Darkness fell till a human hero chased her and got the sun back. That sequence is repeated daily forever. She lives in the thickets but makes an evening sortie and captures the sun, and the hero retrieves it. In the west, of course, the same constellation is a bear. The cosmic Bear of the shamans is sometimes the associated group Boötes, the Ploughman or Waggoner. Both Elk and Bear roam the banks of the cosmic river.[45]

This elk myth resembles many in viewing the constellation as a whole. What is very rare is for the stars to be individualized as persons. In shamanic country, however, it happens. The story of the three hunters is a partial instance. Mongols pray to all seven stars for increase and fertility and identify them as the Seven Old Men, sages or magicians living on the cosmic mountain, with the polestar and the sky's navel or center above.[46]

In the Altai-Baikal region, Roerich took down a story of Gesar Khan (or

Gessar-Khan, as he spelled it), a hero of Mongolian epic, credited with shamanic feats himself.

> To Gessar-Bogdo-Khan were sent seven heads, cut off from seven black blacksmiths. And he boiled the seven heads in seven copper kettles. He fashioned out of them chalices, and inlaid these chalices with silver. And so out of seven heads came seven chalices; and Gessar-Khan filled these with a strong wine. Thereupon he ascended to the wise Manzalgormo and bestowed upon her the chalices. But she took the seven chalices fashioned from the seven heads of the blacksmiths and scattered them into the heavens and the seven chalices formed the constellation Dolan-Obogod (the Great Bear).[47]

Crucial here is the near interchangeability of smiths and shamans. "Black" smiths have a special magical status. With some Siberian peoples—the Yukagir, for instance—a shaman's wisdom lingers on in his skull after death and the skull can be preserved and consulted.[48] So the stars are formed from seven seers, an idea not far out of line with the Seven Old Men, and their arrangement as the constellation is the act of a goddess, herself a wisdom figure.

The pounding iteration of sevens forges a link with the Mal'ta panel and is one of many proofs that the number has a mystique in the shamanic world. Seven and nine both carry weight, but seven carries more. In the Ugrian poem of creation, which brackets a Master of the Upper World with a Great Mother, their house has a birch tree behind it.[49]

> *On the golden-leaved, golden-boughed birch*
> *Seven golden-winged, golden-tailed*
> *Cuckoos sit.*
> *Seven nights they sing,*
> *Seven days they sing . . .*
> *On the whole earth living*
> *Men thanks to their power*
> *To this day endure.*

The goddess's brother summons creatures from the waters to reinforce this humanity-sustaining magic.

> *From the depths of seven rivers, of seven seas,*
> *Seven golden-backed beetles*
> *Are raised . . .*
> *Men thanks to this* [the beetles' power]
> *To this day endure.*

In out-of-the-body journeys to Bai Ülgän, when the shaman has to ascend through celestial levels, the number varies; but in Altaic shamanism it is normally seven. Bai Ülgän has seven sons, though he also has nine daughters.[50] The Altaic descent to Erlik Khan is through seven subterranean levels. Erlik has seven sons and seven daughters. The number of rapids to be negotiated on Engdekit, the cosmic river, may be seven or nine. In the Yenisei basin it is unambiguously seven.[51]

Bai Ülgän's sons and colleagues make other mythic appearances, and while, again, there are groups of nine, seven predominates.[52] The Vogul recognize seven Sons of God; the Vasyuga-Ostyak have seven gods, one for each of the heavens; the Yakut even have seven Supreme Gods. Sevens occur with other deities. The Yurak-Samoyed pay homage to an Earth spirit with seven sons, and their sacred images have seven faces, or a single face with seven gashes or cuts in it. The Ostyak, on the middle Yenisei, speak of a goddess on a seven-story mountain who writes the fate of each human being at birth on a seven-branched tree. Tatars have seven gods who likewise record the destiny of newborn children. Stories like these last ones, however, presuppose writing and must be late, whether or not they adapt older tradition.

Shamanic procedures show the same bias. To quote Eliade, "The mystical number 7 apparently plays an important part in the shaman's technique."[53] Among the Ostyak, a man about to become a shaman cooks a squirrel, divides it into eight portions, discards one, and eats the other seven. After seven days, revisiting the spot, he receives the sign of his vocation. Among the Yurak-Samoyed, a man on the verge of the same step lies unconscious for seven days and nights passive to assailing spirits. An account of such a shaman's initiation tells of a trance experience in which he was taught the healing virtues of seven plants, found seven talking stones on a beach, and remained with them for seven days listening to secrets they taught him. A fully fledged shaman of the same tribal grouping wears a glove with seven fingers. Ostyak and Lapp shamans put themselves in a trance by eating a mushroom with seven spots. An Ugrian shaman has seven helping spirits.

An Ugrian mythic or visionary woman wears her hair in two braids, with seven seagulls at the end of one of them and seven goldeneye ducks at the end of the other.[54] In the poem described earlier about the woman who knew more words than the sages, the margin by which she won was seven.[55]

Most of these instances are scattered and could be mere oddments due to wandering tribes or individuals. Only two groupings show a heptadic concentration suggesting a real, rooted significance. Either the Samoyed or the Altaians might qualify. They live a fair distance apart, the Samoyed being north of the Ostyak between the Ob and the Yenisei. On the whole, Altaic shamanism emerges ahead.

One pioneer collector of shamanic lore was Gregory Potanin, a Russian born in Siberia in 1835, who spent a large part of his life as a political exile and studied Mongols and other distant peoples with the aid of his wife.[56] He left a description of an Altaic shaman's outfit. It included seven small images or dolls sewn to his collar, and seven bells. The dolls stood for the "seven celestial virgins" and the bells, tinkling, were the virgins' voices summoning spirits. Images on the drum of another Altaic shaman symbolized spirits associated with seven "nests" and "feathers," and seven maidens inflicting seven diseases.[57]

What we have here, outstandingly in the Altaic clusterings, is the idea of seven as a key to matters of deep import. It is impossible to derive it from Buddhism, and there is no sign of septenary influence from any other quarter. In view of the veneration of Ursa Major and its worship as the Seven Old Men, the implication of Roerich's story may be correct and the seven-star constellation may be the prototype.

In any case, we can now close in, as desired, on the Altai-Baikal region. Some of its mythology may be simply Siberian in a general way, but its seven mystique, coupled with myths of Ursa Major and deities, is distinctive. So are the myth of the golden mountain and the cults looking to the real range.

Mal'ta's septenary spiral is worth recalling again, for other reasons, connected with the fact that one of its possible descendants is the Mother Earth symbol of the Hopi.[58] They have a strong folk memory of ancient migrations and they have traces of a seven mystique apart from the symbol, being unique in this respect among native Americans. Their creation myth tells of nine universes, two of which belong to creator gods exclusively, leaving, for practical purposes, seven. They concur with the Greeks in a rather unusual count of the Pleiades as seven, and they have seven hymns that are sung ceremonially before the Pleiades sink below the horizon. The argument already stated applies again. In view of the spiral and the seven-nine duality, these Hopi heptads may be remnants of a shamanic package conserved by Proto-Hopi migrants from Siberia. If so, its ingredients must have existed in a Siberian home before they left, before about 6000 B.C. That would be evidence for an early Siberian seven mystique apart from the evidence of the Mal'ta panel, but linked with it. And since Mal'ta is in the Altai-Baikal region, things perhaps come together a little, and a cultural fountainhead somewhere in that region grows more definable, whether or not the maternal Hopi view of their spiral favors its Goddess character.

Chronologically, however, such arguments are not to be pressed. It should now be clear that the motifs and myths opened up by shamanism *may* be very old; and it seems easier, on balance, to believe that at least some of them are. But to search for ancient influence means searching for ancient echoes and parallels outside, and if we find them, we cannot determine who influenced whom (if anyone did) on the basis of dates alone, because at the Siberian end, the date cannot be certain. For instance, there are myths in other countries that are very like the shamanic descent to Erlik Khan. One may have taken shape between 2500 and 2000 B.C. If the shamanic theme is much older that that, influence from Siberia is credible. But while it may be older, there is no way of proving directly that it is. Influence can be urged seriously only if apparent cases come to light that work in one direction but not in the other, that cannot be turned around logically. There are such, and because they exist, other cases associated with them can be admitted.

CHAPTER FOUR

The Indo-Aryans

1

Five thousand years ago people of Indo-European stock lived in the western part of the Altai Mountains and in the Minusinsk river basin just to the north, as far as Krasnoyarsk on the Yenisei. Through contact with shamanism they created a fertile ideological hybrid. The remoter consequences are still with us, and most profoundly so. That, I believe, is the conclusion to which inquiry leads, ranging over a large part of the earth and many centuries.

It is at least certain that these Indo-Europeans existed. No one knows what they called themselves. Archaeologists speak of the Afanasievo culture, taking the name from a place where it was identified.[1] It was the extreme outpost of the medley of Indo-European groupings that stretched from the Ukraine across the steppe lands. To judge from its remains, the Afanasievo culture resembled others by the Don and the Volga, and while the gaps in knowledge still are wide, similar communities, pastoral and, in a limited way, agricultural, undoubtedly were scattered over the space in-between. At such a distance of time, radiocarbon readings are far from precise, but they have pushed the origins back from dates formerly favored by Soviet archaeologists. The Afanasievo folk were in place by 3000 B.C., very likely earlier, and they continued for a full thousand years.

While they may have had nomadic forebears, they themselves were sedentary, living in settlements of up to ten families. These may have been seasonal camps, not occupied all the time. They fished in the rivers and practiced subsistence farming on a small scale, with a little livestock—cattle, sheep, and (a significant species) horses. Bones of bison, roe deer, foxes, and chipmunks show that they hunted. They used stone axes and arrowheads, but they also used copper knives, needles, and fishhooks, and made arsenical bronze, an alloy of copper with arsenic.

There is no proof that they had wheeled vehicles, but the probability is that they did. They cooked in big jars and made pots with linear designs on them. Ornaments were of silver and gold. Gold (another significant item) was highly valued, and earrings were made from it. Bracelets were decorated with small white stones and had clips of meteoric iron. The dead were buried in pits, with rough stone structures on top.

From these people, and others akin to them on the steppes, Indo-European expansion proceeded south and southwest. J. P. Mallory suggests that some of the descendants of the Afanasievo grouping may have penetrated Chinese Turkestan, where a maverick Indo-European language, dubbed Tocharian by Western philologists, has long been a puzzle.[2] Tocharian speakers were to embrace Buddhism and play a part in its spread to China. More important for present purposes is the course of events nearer the Aral Sea and Lake Balkhash, where Mallory sees Indo-European pastoralists mingling with agriculturalists during the late fourth and early third millennia. Over a large area there arose the Andronovo culture.[3] On its southern fringes, through contact with embryonic urban society, Indo-Europeans made strides in metalworking, ceramics, and architecture.

Meanwhile, they were differentiating.[4] A large body continued south as Iranians. Others, known as Indo-Aryans, were the first members anywhere of their vast linguistic family to speak to us in literature that survives. On them, attention must be focused.

Some of the Indo-Aryans may be identified with a group called the Tazabagyab, along the Amu Darya River.[5] Some of those may have left the area and moved on along a tributary, the Vaksh, to Gandhara in the Swat Valley, where graves hint at their presence about 1800 B.C. In due course they could have made their way onward into the Indus Valley from the north. That remains a "could have," but whatever exactly these Indo-Aryans did, we do presently find them in the Indus Valley, superseding an older civilization. They have a language that evolves into Sanskrit; they produce a sacred book, the *Rig Veda*; and their own descendants expand farther into the subcontinent, creating the India of Hindu history and tradition.

The *Rig Veda*, compiled in its present form over several centuries around about 1200 B.C., consists of 1,028 metrical "hymns" (they are hymns in a very broad sense).[6] While many address the gods, others are concerned with myths, rituals, and a variety of life situations. With the aid of archaeology, a certain amount can be inferred about the Indo-Aryans of the Indus Valley.

This was a male-ruled and male-centered society, though not devoid of respect for women; several hymns, for instance, allow that a woman may take the sexual initiative.[7] While no part of the *Rig Veda* approximates to epic, male values have inspired a glorification of battle. Some of the hymns extol the Indo-Aryans' victories over a darker people, whose forts they stormed.[8] It used to be thought that they conquered the previous civilization, known to us from its cities Harappa and Mohenjo-daro, but this was far gone in decay before Indo-Aryan settlement was established, and the ruins show few signs of violent destruction. The dark enemies probably were aboriginal tribes.

These Indo-Aryans lived in simple buildings. They had no cities themselves, and little state organization; their kings had few functions beyond performance of rituals and leadership in war. The hymns refer to iron and ships, although they were not seafarers in any enterprising sense. Their most valued animals were horses and cows, both of which were held in religious veneration.[9] Warriors rode in horse-drawn chariots with spoked wheels and shot arrows at their opponents. Intoxicants and gambling are mentioned. There was no writing—the hymns were transmitted orally for a long time—but there was music, with the same scale as in Europe. Overall this Vedic society has distinct resemblances to the one portrayed in the sagas of ancient Ireland, at the other end of the Indo-European world.

Later Hindu commentators, for whom the *Rig Veda* is holy writ, find a coherence and even an implied monotheism that are not really there. Their approach is selective, singling out, for instance, a verse doubtfully translated "Truth is one: the sages call it by various names."[10] Actually the hymns saluting deities give discrepant views of their origins, character, and status.

The god who stands out most is Indra, a flamboyant warrior chief expressing the Indo-Aryans' macho ideals.[11] He is a doer of heroic and beneficial deeds, wielding a thunderbolt, slaying monsters, and bringing rain to the earth. Another prominent figure is the fire god Agni, who has a vital role in sacrifice.[12] Another is Varuna, a sky god, representing cosmic order. Vishnu is present, but he is far from the supreme godhead he attains in later Hinduism. There are dozens more. Several hymns speak of a "One" beyond and above everything else, but they have no theological precision. A hymn of creation poses a series of unanswered questions and ends with what is best described as a punch line:

> Whence this creation has arisen—perhaps it formed itself, or perhaps it did not—the one who looks down on it, in the highest heaven, only he knows—or perhaps he does not know.[13]

Goddesses are mentioned, though seldom with evidence of worship. They are apt to be personifications, of dawn, for example, and night, and the forest. However, a being with a touch of the Goddess makes mythic appearances, as a primal Mother of Gods called Aditi.[14] She is a female creative power in logic-defying symbiosis with a male one, Daksha: "From Aditi Daksha was born, and from Daksha Aditi was born." Her name is explained as meaning "the Infinite."

The atmosphere of the *Rig Veda* is, on the whole, optimistic and positive. Ethical aspects of religion are not absent, but neither are they central. There is more interest in securing good fortune and averting ill through one's relationship with the higher powers, and hence in ritual, especially sacrificial. This has a bearing on any probing of the Indo-Aryans' past. The *Rig Veda* says nothing about their ancestral migrations, but it may preserve authentic themes from that period, because of a paramount stress on the exact, sacrosanct wording of all texts involved in worship.[15] The priests' oral tradition was meticulous, and it is unlikely that the texts have been altered radically. That fact may place a query over conjectures about "patriarchal" rewriting, but it encourages a belief that the *Rig Veda* sheds light a long way back. The literature of mature Hinduism, even centuries later, gives surprising hints at how far back the traditions may reach.

Take, for instance, the *Mahabharata*, better known in the West than it used to be because of a famous and brilliant dramatized version. A huge composite work developed in stages from a much shorter epic, it amounts now to an encyclopedia of Hindu mythology. The event at its nucleus is a war in north-central India between two branches of its chief royal house, one led by a usurper, the other by his cousin, the deposed king, claiming his rights. The epic's geography, its portrayal of Indo-Aryans so far into India, and related archaeological data put the narrative in the eighth or ninth century B.C.[16]

Yet Hindus have always taken it for granted that the war was fought much earlier. Some, who ignore archaeology or are unimpressed by it, continue to do so. Astronomical statements in the text are said to indicate 2449 B.C. or even 3102.[17] It is fair to cite what has been called "the most remarkable trait of Indian psychology, a complete, instinctive indifference to history and the preservation of historical records." All the same, the gap seems enormous and gratuitous. What does the early dating really refer to?

Europe may offer a clue in Arthurian romance. Sir Thomas Malory's fifteenth-century work, long the standard English version, makes Arthur king of England in a feudal, chivalric setting, with many details implying the Middle Ages. The map is medieval, and one of Arthur's major campaigns, an invasion of France, is conceived in terms of the real wars of Edward III and Henry V. What Sir Thomas actually is doing, in the steps of other romancers, is updating a story that is in fact very old. The Arthur saga is rooted in traditions and legends about events in the so-called Dark Ages, the fifth century A.D. and thereabouts, when the original Arthur (if there was one) lived. Sir Thomas even gives a plausible fifth-century date, despite the impossibility of the story, as he tells it, having happened in that century.

Such a process may underlie the *Mahabharata*. The real dynastic quarrel may have belonged to "another time, another place." Perhaps the author of the primary epic, say, in the eighth century B.C., took up an old tale of rival cousins, a tale carried orally from far back in the migrations, and turned it into a story of a time and a place he knew. The scene of the fighting is Kurukshetra, a real battle site not far from Delhi. But the sites of real battles in Scotland and Cornwall, long after Arthur's time, have been associated with Arthur.

Whatever the value of these reflections, a tradition claiming to tell of events in 2449 B.C. or 3102 makes much better sense if it is like the one that gave Sir Thomas his distant date—if Hindus actually had traditions going back validly to a distant past, and to an ancestral culture already existing then, somewhere. It could have existed in an area, say, in Kazakhstan, peopled by recognizable Indo-Aryans who were forebears of those who reached the Indus Valley and created the *Rig Veda*, and passed farther into India and created the *Mahabharata*.

Logically, some such area, in Kazakhstan or wherever, is needed for an entirely separate reason. There were other Indo-Aryans who did not go to the Indus Valley at all, having branched off from a point farther back in the migrations—from a point, therefore, where some sort of Indo-Aryan culture was already in being. They have been neglected for lack of data. It will become steadily clearer that they should not be neglected.

What can we say about them? First, they were in contact with Iranians, who, of course, settled in Iran but had attained some degree of identity well before. Terms in the languages prove ancestral kinship but also a divergence amounting to conflict. Indo-Aryans had a word, *asura*, that meant a divine being, and Iranians had an equivalent, *ahura*.[18] But whereas in Iranian *ahura* kept its "good" sense, the Indo-Aryan *asura* was inverted to mean a demon. Indo-Aryans had another word for a god, *deva*, and Iranians likewise had an equivalent, *daeva*. But they made *daeva* mean an evil spirit. In the outcome, for Indo-Aryans, *deva* was good and *asura* bad; for Iranians, *daeva* was bad and *ahura* good.

Scholars have tried to connect this with Zoroastrian religious reforms in Iran itself.[19] However, the split seems likely to be rooted in an earlier enmity. These Indo-Aryans of western Asia, as Mallory calls them, did suffer at Zoroastrian hands in Iran, more or less fading out in that country. But some went beyond and survived.

Egyptian records testify to a prince in Palestine named Indaruta, and this is the same as Indrota or Indrauta, which occurs in the *Rig Veda*.[20] In northern Syria the empire of the Mitanni flourished in and around the sixteenth and fifteenth centuries B.C. Its records reveal an Indo-Aryan presence, perhaps for a while an influential presence. A treaty in about 1380 between a Mitanni king and a Hittite king in Asia Minor calls a list of gods to witness.[21] Among them are Mitra, Varuna, Indra, and the Nasatyas, all of them deities of the *Rig Veda*. A Mitanni named Kikkuli in the Hittite kingdom wrote a manual for horse trainers using Indo-Aryan terms. A text in another language, Hurrian, also on horses, uses Indo-Aryan words for their colors (brown, gray, and reddish). Plainly, these western Indo-Aryans, descendants of horse owners on the steppes, were acknowledged experts.[22]

Their importance will emerge. So far as anyone knows, they left no records of their own. For the moment we must return to the Indo-Aryans who did, the ones in the Indus Valley, and their *Rig Veda*—not only for what it says about their beliefs and ideas around 1200 B.C. but for what it implies about the beliefs and ideas of their forebears, continuity with an ancestral north where the Afanasievo had flourished, and yes, influences from it.

2

First, and further, to matters equine and a connection noted by Stuart Piggott and Mircea Eliade.

It will be remembered that over much of Siberia a shamanic ritual from time immemorial has been the horse sacrifice.[23] The Indo-Aryans also sacrificed horses, not with any implication of contempt or indifference but precisely because of the unique value they put on them. They looked upon their wonderful animal with pride, delight, and awe. Hymns in the *Rig Veda* salute the horse as divine and a companion of gods. Sometimes literary convention is turned around and gods are complimented by being compared to horses. The chief Indo-Aryan deities of the Mitanni treaty, Mitra, Varuna, and Indra, are spoken of in the *Rig Veda* as riding them and blessing them and giving them power.

A hymn that describes the ritual slaying of a fine racehorse opens with an invocation that includes the same three. To judge from this echo, and from their known activities, the western Indo-Aryans were at one with their distant cousins in the Indus Valley. The hymn of sacrifice makes it clear that the horse's spirit goes to heaven, as it does in the Altaic rite, where the shaman escorts the spirit to higher regions.

The horse with his smooth back went forth into the fields of the gods,
just when I made my prayer. The inspired sages exult in him. We

have made him a welcome companion at the banquet of the gods. . . . You do not die through this nor are you really harmed. You go to the gods on paths pleasant to go on.[24]

In the *Mahabharata* a horse sacrifice called the *Asvamedha* is one of the most splendid royal ceremonies.

None of this would suggest shamanic influence, if the sacrificing of horses were a major rite of Indo-European peoples in Europe and Asia. Not so, however. They had a variety of horse myths and horse rituals, reflecting the animal's high status. Single periodic killings are mentioned in one or two places, and a horse was put to death at royal inaugurations in Ireland.[25] But nothing is on record anywhere else like the important and complex rituals of the Indo-Aryans or the mythology surrounding these; nothing, except in Siberia; and the migrations spanned the space in-between.

The horse leads to other animals. In the shamanic scheme of things it is an aid or catalyst for ecstatic flight but has no cosmic character.[26] That is confined to the two most powerful wild creatures, the elk and the bear, the latter being the greatest of cultic beasts.[27] Both have their places in the sky as the neighboring constellations Ursa Major and Boötes. In our own stellar imagery, the first of these, the Big Dipper, is the Bear; in parts of Siberia, Boötes is the Bear and the seven-star Dipper is the Elk. These equations are not universal. What does appear deeply rooted is that it is Ursa Major that is held in special reverence and that shamans, while having myths of it as a whole, have other myths that personalize the stars as seven beings—the Seven Old Men on the central mountain or the smith shamans in the Manzalgormo story recorded by Roerich. From that celestial counting, perhaps, came the mystique and shamanic role of the number seven, with unmistakable significance in the Altaic region.

While the constellation is recognized by many peoples, this individualization of its stars is rare at myth-making levels. Elsewhere, if it is not the Dipper or the Plough or the Wain, it is a bow or some other object seen as a whole. When the stars are counted at all, they are animals—wolves or oxen. Outside the shamanic northland itself they appear as persons in only two settings. One is the Kirghiz country of central Asia, where they are guardian spirits who, by watching over Ursa Minor, keep the world in being.[28] This myth belongs to an area traversed by Indo-Europeans in their expansion from the north. The other and far more important setting is the Indo-Aryan complex itself. In the *Rig Veda*, the *Mahabharata*, and elsewhere the stars of Ursa Major are the Seven Rishis, translated "Sages" or "Seers." The seven stars, in effect, are the northern Seven Old Men or shamans in a more august guise. The principal name for the constellation is *Saptarshi*, the "Seven Rishis."

Rishi means primarily a poet who composes hymns to the gods, but the

Seers forming the sky heptad are much more.[29] They have been described as "mysterious beings connected with the origin of man and knowledge" and as representatives of a sacred past. They are responsible for Hinduism's basic scriptures. Their status is unique, between humanity and divinity. Hymns in the *Rig Veda* speak of them as acting in concert with a creator figure, helping to "carve" the sky and earth and "harmonizing" the cosmic patterns.[30]

While as stars they circle majestically around the pole of heaven, they have earthly lives. In a Hindu version of the Flood they are the only companions whom the ark builder Manu takes aboard with him. When the earth is submerged they moor the ark to the highest peak of the Himalayas. Divine power presently enables Manu to fill the world with new creatures, and the Rishis play a part in the renewal. The heptad's composition varies from cosmic cycle to cycle. The names of the set for our present cycle are Gotama, Bharadvaja, Visvamitra, Jamadagni, Vasishtha, Kasyapa, and Atri.

Some commentators think their astral aspect is a later development and cannot be proved in the oldest literature.[31] However, at least one verse of the *Rig Veda* can hardly be taken in any other sense. It occurs in a hymn extolling the Creator, the One, dwelling in heaven:

> Mortal men rejoice that their votive offerings are heeded there where they say the One is, beyond the Seven Seers.[32]

Here the Seven Seers are a fixed group, with the Creator "beyond." This has to be the group in the starry sky. In any case, the astral identification, whenever precisely it was made, implies a long-standing reverence for the constellation and its septenary nature.

So we have Ursa Major as a source of Ancient Wisdom, with its seven stars, *as* seven, personified, numinous and powerful, as nowhere else . . . except in the Indo-Aryans' ancestral north. And as we saw, the north harbors another myth of the constellation, maybe not in a place close to the ancestors, yet still intriguing in the light of the Hindu myth.

Beside Ursa Major's second star is Alcor, not always visible and too faint to count as one of the seven. In the Evenk tale that interprets the constellation as three hunters and an elk, that star is given recognition—only as a humble cooking pot, but still, recognition. It surely would be hard to find another allusion to it in any myth throughout the world. There is one, however, and it is in a myth of the Seven Rishis.

Here the bright star with the faint one beside it is Vasishtha, and its little companion is his wife, Arundhati.[33] In a discourse on celestial bodies the *Mahabharata* tells of "the Seven Seers and the divine Arundhati." Most of the time she was nobler and more loyal than the wives of the other Rishis. In a crisis they divorced theirs, but Vasishtha did not, and that is why, in the heavens, he has a companion and the rest are alone. Yet since Arundhati is so faint, there must be a reason, and the epic provides it in male-oriented terms:

> Even the faithful and good Arundhati, famous in all the worlds, distrusted Vasishtha, the eminent seer. He was always completely pure-hearted and devoted to her happiness and well-being, yet she despised that hermit among the Seven Seers. Because of this contempt she is now a tiny star like a red ember overlaid with smoke, not very lovely, sometimes visible sometimes not, which appears like a bad omen.

Recognition of Alcor in the northland, recognition of Alcor in Indo-Aryan myth. Influence? There is a further point. This constellation has another Indian name, seldom used but strangely related.

A verse in the *Rig Veda* praising the god Varuna runs, in a modern version:

> *The stars fixed on high appear at night.*
> *By day they depart, we know not whither.*
> *Varuna's laws are faithful.*[34]

In the first line the translator sidesteps an issue he may have wished to avoid. Almost certainly the reference is not to stars in general but to seven special ones, a group, Ursa Major. The word, in the singular, is *riksha*. Very rare in the *Rig Veda*, it can mean a star but also can mean a bear, that being its primary sense.[35] In other contexts the plural of *riksha* is certainly employed to mean the preeminent stars, the seven. A Vedic scholar even suggested that they acquired their dignity as *Rishis* only because of the verbal echo. But ambivalence of *riksha* is a fact. For Indo-Aryans (as also, eventually, for Greeks and Romans) the septenary constellation could be ursine. It could be picked out as a special group of bear stars.

This is very odd. In the Indus Valley the bear would not have been a natural creature to think of. It was known, but it was far from familiar. The word *riksha* in its basic zoological sense occurs only once in the 1,028 hymns of the *Rig Veda*. Why apply it to stars at all, and especially such outstanding ones? A thought presents itself. The Rishis are seers. Who is the seer, humbler than those august beings but a seer still, who also can be a bear? It sounds like a riddle, but it does have an answer: a shaman. Shamans dress in the skins of animals and profess to take on their nature. Powerful shamans favor the powerful bear. In one Tatar dialect the word for a woman-shaman, *utygan*, actually does duty for a bear also.[36] Such a background supplies a better logic for the two names of the constellation than a hypothetical wordplay putting *riksha* first with *Rishi* as a chance result. And, of course, the tribes of the ancestral north knew bears very well, as the Indo-Aryans did not.

We now have a case of apparent influence that is firmly evidential, because it is one-way. It has to go from the north to the south; it cannot be turned around. Since shamans assume the nature of animals—sometimes, though not by any means always, bears—the great shamanic stars might have become bear seers. That idea could have traveled south with the migrations, to emerge at last in the Indo-Aryan ambiguity, with the stars regarded as seers *or* bears. The process would have been most unlikely to start at the other end, in a country where bears scarcely were known and without mythic or folkloric significance, and where seers' ursification was not known at all. Even if it happened, it could not have affected the established phenomena of the north.

Other cases of apparent influence can be looked at fairly with the same bias in mind.

3

The seven-star constellation, however styled, opens up a wider issue. Shamanism, whether or not directly because of it, has its marked mystique of the number seven, most persistent in the Altaic region. A god with seven sons dwells above seven celestial levels; another god with seven sons dwells below seven subterranean levels; shamanic initiations abound in sets of seven objects; and so on. Does it appear that the seven mystique reached the Indo-Aryans in the company of mythic ideas about the constellation? It does.

To begin with, the *Rig Veda* has another great septenary group, the Adityas, who include Indra and Varuna themselves. Aditi, Mother of Gods, bore eight sons, but one, Martanda, was unformed. His brothers shaped him and made him into the Sun. Then, as the Adityas, the mighty seven "went forth among the gods." Seven bay mares were provided to draw the Sun's chariot.[37]

The philologist Max Müller, who, in the 1880s, published portions of the *Rig Veda* in English translation, claimed that while seven was sacred to its authors, three, five, and ten were equally so.[38] At least on the basis of a frequency count, this is quite wrong. A complete rendering of the 1,028 hymns by Ralph Griffith came out a few years later. It shows that seven is the most common number, with three as the runner-up and all others far behind. Many of the heptads occur more than once. Griffith's index, supplemented from Müller, indicates about forty different ones. Doubts over translation and interpretation mean that the list must be treated with reserve, and not all of them can be resolved by consulting the original, because, for example, two different terms may or may not be synonymous. Griffith, at any rate, has the following:

> Seven Adityas, castles, celestial streams, communities, cows, fiends, flames of Agni, forts, germs, glories, guards, heroes, horses, hotars [a kind of priest who invoked the gods in rituals], lights of sacrifice, metres, mothers, mouths [of a river], oblations, priests, regions of the earth, reins, ridges, Rishis, rivers, sages, singers, sisters, spears, splendours, stations of sacrifice, sunbeams, threads of sacrifice, tones, treasures, troops. Seven-headed beings, a seven-wheeled vehicle, a sevenfold human race, occur also.[39]

Wendy Doniger O'Flaherty, a modern translator of 108 of the hymns, stigmatizes both Müller and Griffith as unsound but agrees with them on some of the heptads in her selection.[40] Her disagreements produce, in English, several more. However, it is doubtless a matter of translation.

Vedic sevens occasionally cluster together. Müller quotes a verse bracketing the seven Adityas with seven regions and seven hotar priests.[41] In a long and obscure "Riddle of the Sacrifice," which makes considerable play with numbers, seven occurs more often than any other. Its fifty-two verses begin, according to O'Flaherty:

> 1 *This beloved grey priest has a middle brother who is hun-*
> *gry and a third brother with butter on his back. In*
> *him I saw the Lord of All Tribes with his seven sons.*
> 2 *Seven yoke the one-wheeled chariot drawn by one horse*
> *with seven names. All these creatures rest on the age-*
> *less and unstoppable wheel with three naves.*
> 3 *Seven horses draw the seven who ride on this seven-*
> *wheeled chariot. Seven sisters call out to the place*
> *where the seven names of the cows are hidden.*[42]

The translator assures her readers that this can be decoded.

In mature Hinduism—this is a qualification to the foregoing—the mystique of seven does not persist. The Indo-Aryans who pressed on to dominate the subcontinent created a vast literature and an elaborate religion. They continued to revere the *Rig Veda* as a sacred book, but they gave it new meanings and enlarged and varied its myths. In that gigantic growth the seven mystique faded out or was swamped. The Rishis remained seven; the Adityas became twelve.[43]

There are two major exceptions. One is the doctrine of seven chakras, the supposed foci of the human organism, much in favor with modern enthusiasts for things oriental. However, these belong to specialized cults, known as Tantric, that may have their roots in the same Indus Valley as the *Rig Veda*.[44] The other exception is more important and will appear shortly.

Meanwhile, if we look west, the topic plunges abruptly into deeper waters. Antiquity discloses another group like the Seven Rishis, and to all appearances the Rishis inspired it, it was not a separate growth. If they did, the chain of influence would extend further—mysteriously further. One of the world's first literary masterpieces came from Mesopotamia, the country watered by the Tigris and Euphrates rivers, to which Iraq roughly corresponds. That masterpiece was the *Epic of Gilgamesh*, relating the exploits of a legendary hero. In its opening and closing passages it mentions a tradition about the way civilization began. Seven of Mesopotamia's senior cities owed their foundation to the Seven Sages. They were known as the Sebettu, and there are grounds for thinking that they were derived from the Seven Rishis.

One clue lies in an unexplained detail, a loose end. The Seven Sages have a female companion, only one, Narundi.[45] The Rishi Vasishtha has a wife—none of his colleagues have—and his wife Arundhati and Narundi are surely the same. Her raison d'être is stellar and is in the Rishi myth, where she is the faint star beside Vasishtha. That explanation is missing from the Sebettu myth. Mesopotamia's Sebettu have no stellar aspect. No reason is given for their companion, and no reason exists apart from the faint star in the constellation; since the constellation is part of the Indian version only, the Indian must be prior. Mesopotamians adopted it in a restricted form and lost sight of the woman's significance through losing sight of the stellar basis.

This heptad is not the whole story. With them too the seven mystique proliferates. The question is how the conception of the Seven Rishis came to Mesopotamia, inspiring a myth that found its way into the *Epic of Gilgamesh*. Not from the Indus Valley and the authors of the *Rig Veda*, if only because the epic was composed before the Indo-Aryans settled there. The only course is to consider those other Indo-Aryans, the ones who branched off at an ill-defined earlier stage and made their presence felt in the Middle East. But first, a different issue must be confronted. It looks as if something else traveled south from Altaic country.

CHAPTER FIVE

The Paradisal Heights

1

Some of the facts that have emerged, and some that will, have been noticed before—by Eliade, for instance. But he and others have resisted the logic, not always totally, but enough to blur. They reject the flow of influence the facts suggest. Ancient civilizations cannot have owed a debt, even a mythic debt, to the barbaric north. It must have been the other way around. A culture with proper credentials, in India or Mesopotamia, must have been the source, and any shamanic parallels are mere decadent borrowings. On this showing, an Altaic seedbed simply is impossible. Shamanism must always have been too primitive, and, in a sense, too trivial, to be an active ingredient in the mystiques and mythologies of more advanced peoples.

Even in itself this is a questionable view. Great oaks, after all, from little acorns grow. In any case, the plain truth is that there is no hard evidence for early transmission of any relevant motifs from India or Mesopotamia to shamanic country. A skeptic might retort that there is no hard evidence for early transmission from shamanic country to India or Mesopotamia, or to anywhere else of interest—movements of Indo-Europeans notwithstanding. But there is. The far-flung maze spiral, with its seven circuits, has already raised that issue. And we can do better, not going back as far as we might wish, but going back a considerable way.

In the fifth century B.C., the Greek historian Herodotus, writing of India (meaning chiefly its nearer portion; his horizon is limited), gives a surprising account of the tribute paid to the king of Persia.

The way in which the Indians get the plentiful supply of gold, which
enables them to furnish year by year so vast an amount of gold-dust
to the king, is the following. Eastward of India lies a tract which is
entirely sand . . .

He may be thinking of somewhere in Afghanistan, but as he goes on, his
readers will perceive difficulties in accepting that this is the story's true
locale. The Indians close to the sandy tract, he says,

. . . are more warlike than any of the other tribes, and from them
the men are sent forth who go to procure the gold. For it is in this
part of India that the sandy desert lies. Here, in this desert, there
live in the sand great ants, in size somewhat less than dogs, but bigger
than foxes. The Persian king has a number of them, which have been
caught by the hunters in the land whereof we are speaking. Those
ants make their dwelling under ground, and like the Greek ants,
which they very much resemble in shape, throw up sand-heaps as
they burrow. Now the sand which they throw up is full of gold. The
Indians, when they go into the desert to collect this sand, take three
camels and harness them together, a female in the middle and a male
on either side, in a leading-rein. The rider sits on the female, and
they are particular to choose for this purpose one that has but just
dropped her young; for their female camels run as fast as horses. . . .
When the Indians therefore have thus equipped themselves they
set off in quest of the gold, calculating the time so that they may be
engaged in seizing it during the most sultry part of the day, when
the ants hide themselves to escape the sun. . . .
When the Indians reach the place where the gold is, they fill their
bags with the sand, and ride away at their best speed: the ants,
however, scenting them, as the Persians say, rush forth in pursuit.
Now these animals are, they declare, so swift, that there is nothing
in the world like them: if it were not, therefore, that the Indians get
a start while the ants are mustering, not a single gold-gatherer could
escape. During the flight the male camels, which are not as fleet as
the females, grow tired, and begin to drag, first one, and then the
other; but the females recollect the young which they have left behind, and never give way or flag. Such, according to the Persians, is
the manner in which the Indians get the greater part of their gold.[1]

Herodotus is reporting what genuinely has reached him from India. His
ants make an independent appearance in the *Mahabharata*. The prince
Duryodhana is enviously describing the glories of his cousin Yudhishthira,
who has a realm of his own and receives tribute from subject rulers.

The kings who live by the river Sailoda between Mount Meru and Mount Mandara . . . brought the gold called Pipilaka, which is granted as a boon by the *pipilaka* ants, and they brought it by bucketsful and piles.

Another translator is more specific: the gold is "raised from underneath the earth by ants."[2]

So this ant story is told in India, Persia, Greece. It is told, however, in China too. It did not originate in any of those countries, but in Mongolia— proof that a long-range dissemination out of the north could, and in this case did, happen.[3]

2

The fabulous ants, in a mysterious gold-rich country, raise a larger issue. In the Indian version they live between Mount Meru and Mount Mandara. What and where are these mountains? The question is best approached indirectly.

In Siberia and Mongolia, as will be recalled, aboriginal peoples have the conception of a sky pillar or world axis connecting earth and heaven while also holding them apart. It is at the center of the universe. Altaic shamans frequently picture it as a mountain, and sometimes it is by this route that they ascend to Bai Ülgän, climbing in spirit through the seven celestial levels. In Mongolian guise the central mountain, with the polestar overhead, is the home of the Seven Old Men, the stars of Ursa Major. The center also may take the form of a tree. Artifacts such as poles can deputize for the center, whether mountain or tree, and represent it. Altaic shamans keep posts, notched to correspond to the heavenly levels.

An Altaic myth, as will further be recalled, says that the god who made the world sat on the mountain in the middle of the sky. When he had an earth to attach it to, he attached it. The mountain is described as golden. There is probably an echo here of the cults of actual mountains, such as "Lord Altai." "Altai" means "golden," and deposits of gold exist thereabouts.[4] The Mongol earth mother Etugen has a personal domain called *Altan Delekei*, the "Golden World."

The gold motif finds its way, in association with the seven mystique, into the Ob Ugrian creation poem previously quoted.[5] The birch tree behind the house of the god and goddess has golden leaves and branches. The seven cuckoos that sit on its boughs, sustaining human life by their power, are golden-winged and golden-tailed. The seven beetles in the next verse are golden-backed.

Again we can trace possible Indo-Aryan borrowing. A world axis or pillar figures in the *Rig Veda*. It is called the *skambha*.[6] In the beginning, earth and heaven were united. After their separation, a god—variously said to have been Varuna, Vishnu, or Indra—fixed them in position and measured out the space in-between. The maintenance of the sky in place sometimes is attributed to a power put forth by the sun. This Vedic imagery is undeveloped, but in mature Hinduism the conception resurfaces in fullness with a great deal more. It may be said to explode.

The Indo-Aryans came to believe most explicitly in a center of the world. Unlike some other peoples, they never located it in their own country at a royal city or holy place, even when they had spread through most of India. *Mahabharata* geography makes it central to a grandiose scheme ranging far beyond. This envisages a more or less round continental landmass, girdled with water.[7] East-west parallel ranges divide it into seven sections. India itself comprises only the southernmost section, or most of it, with a long coastline. Inflated figures are given for the world-island's size, sometimes making it hundreds of thousands of miles across. These reflect a Hindu penchant for numerical hugeness and are contradicted in practice by stories of human journeys and military campaigns extending over large parts of it.

Its center lies far to the north, beyond the Himalayas and other ranges, and is a circular mountain central to earth and heaven, to the whole universe above and below.[8] This is Meru. It may have had two names, Meru and Mandara, but in classical works, such as the epic, it is Meru only, and the name Mandara is given to another one.[9] These are the mountains between which the ants' gold-rich habitat lies. According to one passage, Meru is 84,000 *yojanas* high. The *yojana* is an elastic unit varying from two miles to six. In view of its vagueness, the old word *league*, as in seven-league boots, is a fair translation. Meru's size has no meaning more exact than "incalculably high" or "immensely higher than anything else." In a more temperate but still extravagant passage its height is thirty-three of the same unit.[10]

Meru, like the Altaic central mountain, is made of gold.[11] This is stated repeatedly. As the hub of the universe it "stands carrying the worlds above, below and transversely." In an early cosmic diagram it is at the center of an earth that rises in steps from the perimeter and is laid out on a geometrical plan, as are the orbits of the celestial bodies above. Sometimes Meru is said to have seven faces, each differently colored, or seven levels.[12] Neither feature is attested very early, but there is no doubt about another—Meru's connection with the Seven Rishis, who form Ursa Major, the chief of the constellations wheeling around it. Here, says the *Mahabharata*, "the seven divine seers daily rise and set, led by Vasishtha" (strictly speaking, they don't set, but the meaning, presumably, is "sink").[13] They alight on the mountain on certain special days and are at home on it, like their apparent partial prototypes in the north, the Seven Old Men.

The *Mahabharata* goes into some detail about the behavior of the sun.[14] Its daily circuit is related both to Meru and to Mandara, which lies southwest of the greater mountain. It "circumambulates" Meru at a great distance— walking around being a sign of respect—and, at the close of day, enters a western zone of dusk in the direction of Mandara, which is called the Sunset Peak. From there it continues north and around the far side of Meru, so that our portion of the world is plunged into night. In a passage where a brahmin is speaking of these mountains to the exiled King Yudhishthira, he says:

> "Brightening the north there rises the famous great Mount Meru. . . . The blessed Lord the Sun, who dispels darkness, circumambulates it, pulling all the stars. The shining sun, on reaching Sunset Peak and passing through dusk, then takes the northern course. Having circled the Meru the God Savitar [the sun] reappears in the east, bent upon the well-being of all creatures."

Where is the sun between Meru and its easterly rising for India? One clue lies in the east-west ranges traversing the terrestrial disk; another, possibly, lies in the stepped structure. When the sun emerges from behind Meru, the intervening mountains and the earth's general configuration prevent its rays from striking India immediately. There is a phase of half-light while it is on its way, and when it finally comes into view, it is in the east. At the day's end, in the west, the reverse happens. The sun slips beyond direct vision and dusk prevails. It passes Mandara and vanishes behind Meru again, so that night is total.

The epic tells an amusing tale about another mountain in India, in a mythic antiquity.

> The Sun used to perform at his rising and setting a circumambulation of great Mount Meru, the golden mountain, the king of ranges. Upon seeing that, Mount Vindhya said to the Sun, "Perambulate me in the same fashion, Maker of Light, as you every day circumambulate Meru!" The Sun replied to that lord of mountains, "It is not by my own desire, mountain, that I circumambulate him: that is the path that was assigned to me by Him who created the world."
>
> Upon hearing this the mountain became angry and began to grow suddenly, endeavouring to obstruct the paths of sun and moon.[15]

The gods failed to cope with this crisis, but the hermit Agastya went to Mount Vindhya, told it he was going on a journey to the south, and persuaded it to stop growing till he came back. He walked past and came back by a different route, so that Vindhya never saw him again and the suspension of growth was permanent.

Meru is not vacant. It is paradisal and an abode of gods. In the first of the passages just quoted, the brahmin tells of its divine inhabitants, including Vishnu, here (as generally in the epic) the Supreme Being. The speaker refers to him by an old name, Narayana.

"Behold the pure land, the superb peak of the Meru, where the Grandfather [Brahmā] dwells with the Gods, who are content with their souls. Beyond the seat of Brahmā shines the supreme abode of the lord Narayana, God without beginning and end, whom they call the lasting cause of the causes of all creatures. . . . Ascetics go there to Narayana Hari through their devotion, yoked with the utmost austerity and perfected by their holy deeds. Great-spirited, perfected by yoga, devoid of darkness and delusion, they go there and no more return to this world. . . . This, lordly Yudhishthira, is the lasting, indestructible, and imperishable place of the Lord: always bow to it!"[16]

Elsewhere, when an envoy of the gods is discoursing to a holy man about the divine regions, he mentions Meru, quoting its more moderate but still farfetched altitude:

"It is there that the golden Meru sits, king of the mountains, thirty-three leagues high, where the gardens of the Gods are situated."[17]

Another passage gives further details of these paradisal places, where divine and semidivine beings disport themselves.

That mountain possesses celestial fruits and flowers. . . . Jewels and gems and all precious stones belong to Meru. . . . On the northern side of Meru there is a charming and beautiful forest. . . . It is ever covered with flowers.[18]

In a mythic episode, a bard gives a description of Meru as preface to an account of the way the gods obtained the elixir (amrita, "ambrosia") and became immortal. At that time the sun and moon were not yet in position, but Meru was.

There is an all-surpassing mountain that blazes like a pile of fire. . . . Mount Meru! . . . Awesome beasts range over it, divine herbs illumine it, and the great mountain rises aloft to cover with its heights the vault of heaven. . . . It abounds in rivers and trees and resounds with the most beautiful flocks of many-feathered birds.

It was this mountain's bright and many-jewelled peaks of almost boundless height that all the august Gods together ascended where it thrusts up yonder. The celestials, austere and restrained, foregathered and seated themselves and began deliberating how they might win the Elixir.

Among them God Narayana spoke thus to Brahmā, while the Gods sat around pondering and deliberating: "The bucket of the Ocean must be churned. . . . Thus the Elixir shall spring forth."[19]

The gods went over to Mount Mandara, uprooted it, and, with the aid of a giant serpent, twirled it into the ocean. Amid a cataclysmic upheaval, the sun and the moon, among much else, rose from the depths. Finally a god appeared with a white gourd holding the elixir. After some trouble with the demonic Asuras, whom Narayana outwitted, the gods secured the elixir and restored Mandara to its place.

In this primitive tale, Narayana, who commands the churning, is equated with Vishnu, as he is elsewhere. But here he is the chief god among many, rather than a theological supreme being. In the churning episode, and in other places, we may be glimpsing Narayana in a former independent role.

Meru's life-giving energies radiate into a nation on the far side, the Northern Kurus.[20] These dwell among golden sands (doubtless like the sands where the ants live) and delicious orchards. The men are handsome, the women beautiful. They live together in loving equality, free from sickness and old age, for ten thousand years or more, drinking juice from the fruit of an "eternal tree" that forms a stream flowing to them past Meru. In the same region is a similar country where the people remain forever young by drinking the juice of another tree. On the heights of Meru itself is the source of the Ganges.[21] The sacred river tumbles tumultuously into a lake and flows southward from this, passing Mount Mandara and vanishing for part of its course (underground?), finally emerging in India in queenly glory.

Two religious systems that branched off from Hinduism kept much of this, with variations. One, the Jain sect, built Meru into a colossal cosmology.[22] In a Jain work of about 200 B.C., the earth is a disk with Meru at its center and the polestar vertically above it, and around the disk are seven concentric oceans and ring-shaped continents. Later Jain texts say that Meru has sixteen names, and the universe extends for light-years upward and downward from it, on seven levels. Meru is not septenary but remains paradisal. Its main bulk is composed of truncated cones, one on top of another and of diminishing size, so that it has a series of encircling terraces. Each terrace has parks and groves on it, with houses for the resident deities. On the top is a platform with a sanctuary, where the Tirthankaras, successive Jain teachers, are consecrated at birth. Meru is buttressed by two lower ranges, both also golden. They curve around to enclose the land of the Northern Kurus and a corresponding land on the opposite side, "Kuru of the gods." The long-lived wedded couples have wish-granting trees and are contented, though their passions are a hindrance to spiritual progress.

The Buddhists, who also branched off from Hinduism, retained the mountain likewise.[23] Its Buddhist name is "Sumeru" or "Sineru." This is the Sumeru that some have cited as the inspiration of northern mountain myths but that the Mongols know to be only a late-coming contributory factor. It is still the center of the earth and the axis of the universe. Instead of being round, it has four sides, and there is a quadrangular city of gods on top. Its divine population is thirty-three, a number taken from the *Rig Veda*. One Buddhist cosmology pictures the world in concentric rings, as in the Jain scheme. Sumeru is at the center, and there are seven circles of rock, seven oceans between them, and an outermost rocky rim.

3

Centrality; a cosmic mountain; Ursa Major's Seven Seers inhabiting it; gods and gold. As in the north, so in the south. Or as in the south, so in the north. There are side resemblances. Something like India's churning of the ocean figures in the folklore of the Kalmucks and other Siberians, even with the world-mountain itself in the role of churning stick.[24] In theory such parallels can cut either way. Transmission can be explained by either a north-south drift, with linkage through development, or a south-north drift, with linkage through decadent imitation. Eliade asserts an "influx of Oriental religious ideas" into the northland, while acknowledging that this is not the whole story, and that prior northern beliefs existed.

It is growing clear, though, that a shamanic package carried south is coming into focus as the better hypothesis. It fits into the ancient drift supported by evidence, the Indo-Europeans' spread from the steppes and the Altai toward India. Traces of the drift seem to linger between Mongolia and the Caspian Sea, where folk myths persist about a mountain with gods living on it. The polestar is its peak, or is the tip of the golden spire of a temple crowning it. Claims about influence going the other way cannot be sustained by a mere "must have."

If we appraise the golden mountain itself, comparing the Hindu version with the Altaic, the Hindu is far richer and more imaginative. Yet even this carries a hint of something dropped en route. The Altaic mountain begins as the Creator's throne in the center of the sky, first of all material things, and then descends when the earth is ready. It is easy to see how, once grounded, it could have suggested golden Meru. It is less easy to see how Meru could have suggested the mountain. Meru's summit is central to the sky, but it is always terrestrially rooted. It has no prehistory as the primal building block of creation. The Altaic tale, naive as it is, has a dimension which the myth of Meru has not . . . has lost?

There is another parallel favoring a north-south drift with development, rather than a south-north drift with decadence. The shamanic motif of representing the mountain with a notched post, and correlating its notches with the stages of an ascent heavenward, has a sort of apotheosis in Hindu and Buddhist sacred architecture.

Long ago, Hindu temple builders were representing Meru by sanctuary towers, or *vimanas*.[25] A *vimana* had a roof structure in several tiers. They stood for levels of the mountain itself, or the heavens; the two realms, in any case, were interfused. Contact with gods could be effected up the tower's vertical axis. Sinhalese shrines used to have a square stone in the middle that stood for Meru. The Khmers of southeast Asia built stepped pyramids that likewise stood for Meru, though that meaning may have faded. Farther afield still, in Java, a sacred spring at Jalatunda still gushes out of a hillside with a carved stone above, which is Meru's summit.[26]

In about the eighth century A.D., the Buddhism that was powerful then in Java produced the most spectacular of surviving models, the temple of Borobudur, called by Eliade "a veritable *imago mundi*, built in the form of a mountain."[27] It was made by encasing a natural hill in gray stone. Most of the way up it consists of one great square on top of another, diminishing in size. On each resulting terrace, the wall along the inside is full of sculptured reliefs depicting stories of the Buddha. Theoretically, pilgrims climb a stairway to the lowest terrace and walk all around it, meditating on the reliefs, then go farther up the stairs to the next and walk around that, and so on upward.

These levels symbolize the realm of material existence. The sixth and highest of the square terraces is without images, and transitional. From it the stairs continue up to a seventh level, which is circular. Here the pilgrim is entering the spiritual realm. There are two more circular terraces above, still diminishing in size. They are surrounded by stupas—bell-shaped shrines—and at the very top, crowning the edifice and encircled by the last terrace, is a much larger stupa symbolizing the goal of the human quest, nirvana, liberation.

Buddhist ceremonies are still held at Borobudur. The May full moon is thought an auspicious time. Despite official Islam, related popular beliefs flourish elsewhere in Java. The spirits of the dead are said to plunge into a volcano, Bromo, and to make their way by a subterranean route to a paradise on Sumeru.

Borobudur, the great Buddhist temple in Java.
Mansell Collection

4

To revert to Meru, the question of sources might be settled if a real original could be found. India's world-mountain is a myth, but something factual could have gone into its making; a more accurate word might be "mythification." A real mountain can have world-mountain characteristics, even for people living near it. In the Indonesian island of Bali, which is Hindu in its own style, the "Mother Temple" Besakih is a complex of shrines and terraces up a hill. Beyond rises Mount Agung, the highest in the island, which is itself Bali's world center and abode of gods.[28] Besakih's sacred structures do not symbolize a mythical mountain anywhere else, they are on the spot, more or less. Agung is a volcano. When it erupted in 1963, the gods were assumed to be angry. Crowds prayed in the path of the lava until it stopped advancing.

Could the primary inspiration of Meru have been a primeval Agung in the north, a mountain that was the focus of one of the north's mountain cults? Meru is not completely divorced from geography. The *Mahabharata* sets it in the overall context of the landmass.[29] This, as observed, is said to be divided into seven sections by six ranges that transverse it.

Stretching from east to west, there are six mountains that are all equal
and that extend from the eastern to the western sea.

"Mountain," for Hindus a rather vague term, has an enlarged meaning here
as "range," though its usual sense is the English. "Equal" means equal, or
at any rate comparable, in height. All seven of the earth's sections into
which the ranges divide it are called *varshas* and are inhabited. The most
southerly contains India and is Bharata-varsha.

In this diagrammatic geography, a line drawn northward from central
India crosses the first range, Himavat, then the second, which is Hemakut.
In Hemakut is a god-haunted height known as *Kailasa*, an alternative name
for the second range as a whole. The line goes on across the third range,
which is Nishada. Beyond Nishada, at the center of the great disk, is Meru,
flanked by its subject hills and with the Northern Kurus adjacent. Beyond
again are the other ranges crossing the landmass—Nila, Sweta, and Sringavat. Individual mountains are dotted about here and there; the epic
declares that the earth is covered with them.

The scheme is hardly cartographic, and allusions to the various places,
in relation to one another, cannot be jigsawed together to make a satisfactory
map. Yet the list of transverse ranges is not pure moonshine. The first is
real enough—"Himavat" means the Himalayas. The *varsha* beyond it is,
or includes, Tibet. The second range is Hemakut, and that too can be given
an identity. No range goes right across Asia, but a hint might have been
taken from one that goes a long way, with its ends in obscurity from an
Indian point of view. Kun Lun is a credible candidate. It stretches a full
thousand miles eastward from the Pamirs and has a peak that is more than
twenty-five thousand feet high. If Hemakut is Kun Lun, holy Kailasa is in
the range, and according to Chinese mythology Kun Lun harbors a kind of
paradise.[30]

What about the next *varsha*, the lower land on the far side of Hemakut?
Beyond Kun Lun is the Tarim Basin, partially taken up by the desert of
Takla Makan. The range after Hemakut in the Hindu scheme is Nishada,
and again the real map provides an original. The Tarim Basin is bordered
along the north by the Tien Shan, more or less parallel to Kun Lun and
stretching a thousand miles, with peaks of its own that rival the Himalayas.
On the north side of the Tien Shan is the plateau of Dzungaria. This would
lie in the fourth *varsha*, where Meru is. And a Meru prototype offers itself:
Belukha, the highest peak of the Altai. The Altai would serve as the inspiration of Meru's ancillary ranges.

Arguably, therefore, knowledge underlies the Hindu world diagram as
far as Meru. But after Meru it peters out. There are no ranges farther north
still, no candidates for Nila or Sweta or Sringavat. That absence is interesting. Arguable knowledge stops at the limit of Indo-European expansion

in this direction, the Afanasievo country, where everything beyond actually was terra incognita. The subsequent Indo-European drift south and south-west and contacts with other peoples along the way might have carried traditions of Belukha and the Altai, of the Tien Shan, and of Kun Lun. It hardly could have carried anything about Siberia much beyond the Altai, much beyond the possible Meru prototype; and it is precisely that part of the world diagram that shows no sign of knowledge and is clearly fictitious. The last three ranges are figments only. To judge from some stories, they were formerly located elsewhere and were shifted into a void beyond Meru for the sake of symmetry. The Indo-European ancestors' ignorance would have made this possible.

Near the end of the *Mahabharata* is a confirmation, if an elliptic one. The chief characters traverse a good portion of the disk-earth. King Yu-dhishthira and his wife and brothers quit the world and set off on a final pilgrimage.

> Proceeding to the north, they saw Himavat, that huge mountain [that is, range, as before]. Crossing Himavat, they saw a vast desert of sand. They then saw the powerful mountain Meru, the foremost of all high-peaked mountains.[31]

Their journey is condensed by the author's lack of knowledge or geographic interest. But the sandy desert beyond the Himalayas, which is un-Tibetan, could be Takla Makan. The pilgrims see it, but are not said to cross it, and on a real journey the likely procedure would be to skirt the desert along its eastern side and continue into Dzungaria. In that case we again have an Altaic terminus, and a Meru that may have been suggested, however remotely, by Belukha.

Once again, the name *Altai* means "golden," and Meru is constantly said to be made of gold, not as a mere honorific but as a special and apparently literal attribute. Nicholas Roerich records an aboriginal name for Belukha, "Outch-Sure," said to mean "Orion, Dwelling of Gods."[32] His remark on Orion's linkage with Ursa Major in shamanic worship has been quoted. He even correlates "sacred Belukha" with Sumeru, the Buddhist version of the world-mountain. His biographer states bluntly, "The true natives of the Altai were Turkish tribes who worshipped the mountain Belukha."[33]

We have seen enough about Altaic shamanism and veneration for the Belukha-crowned range to warrant an inference that an embryonic Meru was part of a shamanic package. This also contained Ursa Major, the seven mystique, and notions of paradisal places and dwellings of gods, all closely connected. As Indo-Europeans with ancestors in Altaic country spread far-ther and farther, folk memories of the northern mountain cults could have blended with shamanic lore of the cosmic mountain, to promote Belukha to cosmic status—thus establishing in a remote and mythified Altai a height that Indo-Aryans enlarged into Meru.

This is another case like the bear seers. It carries weight as evidence because it is one-way. It cannot be turned around. Numinous Altai, named "golden" from its real deposits of gold, rising to a worshiped peak, and in a far north beyond three ranges, could have suggested golden Meru or at least been decisive in its making. Influence in the other direction will not work. It is not to be thought of that some Siberian or Mongolian heard of golden Meru in Hindu myth, studied its geography, decided that it would be in the range north of Tien Shan, renamed this "golden" because of Meru (its actual gold playing no part), and persuaded everyone else to call it so.

Granted the Altaic package, other northern details could have contributed. *Tymanitki* ("Toward Morning"), the shamanic name for the upper world, might have supplied a hint for the association of Meru with sunrise.[34] Even the notion of the Ganges rising on Meru has an odd echo of shamanic myth, with its river flowing down from the upper world with seven heavens above and rushing earthward through seven rapids.

It may be objected that belief in a sky center within Asia, and in an Asian world-mountain having the central polestar above it, could not have been based on legends of the Altai, because such a mountain would have had to be far beyond in a more distant north. That, however, is a modern objection based on our knowledge of where the North Pole actually is. Curiously, Marco Polo refutes it. After mentioning the custom of burying noblemen on the Altai, he adds that if you travel forty days' journey north from the range, you cross a low-lying country and reach the ocean, and in doing so, you leave the polestar behind.[35] This is hearsay, but the inhabitants apparently told him that you can get past the celestial pole while still within the Asian mainland. If his informants believed that, then Indians far to the south could have believed it too, and more easily.

With the one-way influences we are slowly piling up evidence that undatable shamanic motifs actually are ancient. If the *Rig Veda*'s dual view of Ursa Major makes sense as an effect of notions identified in the north, those notions were current in the north before the composition of the *Rig Veda*, and probably long before, because of the spatial gap. The same applies to Meru. If the golden central mountain makes sense as an effect of northern mountain cults, northern ideas of centrality, and northern worship of golden Altai, then all of these known phenomena existed before the myth of Meru did.

There is a further point in confirmation, arising from the recurrent American argument. Beliefs about mountains, like beliefs about bears and other matters, occur in native American settings and sometimes sound like echoes. Indians in Arizona say that a peak near Tucson is the center of the universe. Others in California say that Mount Shasta was the first creative work of the Great Spirit, who built the world around it and still lives inside.[36] His daughter mated with a bear and the human race is descended from this couple. Such myths were not brought across the Pacific from India. If imported at all, they came from Siberia. Any myth carried to America by migrant Asians obviously existed back in Asia itself at the time of their departure, and few or none were migrating after about 6000 B.C., when rising water covered the bridge. A naive Asian center of the universe, ancestral to naive centers of the universe in America, might have been Belukha. There is nothing else approaching its height between the Altai range and the Bering Strait. If that is what Belukha was, it had the relevant aura before 6000 B.C. and therefore had it when Indo-Europeans arrived in its neighborhood.

One difficulty remains. The mountain at the world's center appears in Altaic shamanism and it appears in mature Hinduism. It does not appear intermediately in the *Rig Veda*, which never goes beyond the vague image of the *skambha*, the world axis. How did the motif travel from the Altai to India, seeing that the Indo-Aryan document that should reveal it en route fails to do so at all adequately?

The question bring us back again to the other Indo-Aryans, the ones who branched off somewhere in central Asia and expanded through Iran and around Mesopotamia. A Meru-type myth could have been developed more fully in their traditions and could have drifted later to their long-separated Hindu cousins, whom the Vedic *skambha* at least would have kept receptive. Proof that such a myth did reach the Middle East, in an Indo-European context, is supplied by the Iranians. They transferred it, with less definite cosmic bearings, to Mount Elbruz in the Caucasus.[37] They called Elbruz *Harā* and said that stars circled around it, that its summit rose to a realm of light and bliss, and that the Bounteous Immortals, exalted beings in the teachings of Zoroaster, built a dwelling above it for the god Mithra.

The suggested package, reaching Mesopotamia with these Indo-Aryans, could have converted the Seven Rishis into the Seven Sages aforesaid. The Rishis were linked with Meru and, as the stars of Ursa Major, with cosmic centrality. The next logical step is to look more closely at Mesopotamia. Did the seven mystique assume any other forms in that setting, and if so, did it play any significant part in the mythologies of the region, of Sumer and Babylonia? Did those include centrality and a world-mountain too, and if so, was it because a chain of influence continued? Anyone familiar with Indo-Aryan problems already will have seen a large obstacle in the path; but it is not insurmountable.

An Altaic seedbed may look more and more plausible. However, it will raise yet another question: Are we finding support for Gimbutan prehistory, with its primordial Goddess and its tranformations through space and time, or has the prehistory merely put us on the track of a discovery that has little to do with it, the discovery of a source of influence that was not Goddess influence at all? Up to this point, the second alternative may look more likely, but for now, judgment must be suspended. And before any of these topics can be explored, a fundamental matter needs to be clarified.

CHAPTER SIX

Numerology and Psychology

1

With the seven mystique surfacing among shamans and Indo-Aryans and perhaps beginning to show itself beyond, we face a phenomenon that is still part of our world and our thinking, for no obvious reason. It is absurdly easy to dash off a list of sevens—the seven-day week, the seven wonders of the world, the seven seas, the seven deadly sins, the seven sleepers. It even appears in show business—*The Seven Samurai, The Magnificent Seven, Seven Brides for Seven Brothers*. Why seven?

Between the societies thus far considered and the modern West, the gap of time and space is enormous. Surprisingly, perhaps, Eliade may be prepared to help bridge it. He makes a magisterial statement: "It is probable that the shamanic ideology has played a part in the dissemination of the number 7."[1] On Eliade's authority, this is a serious inquiry and not a fantasy. Hampered, however, by his preconceptions as to who influenced whom (or who *could* have influenced whom), he fails to trace the course of the dissemination. Here we have defined a first step, from shamans to Indo-Aryans, and maybe glimpsed a further step in Mesopotamia. But two issues must be tackled.

First, the notion of bridging gaps may simply be misguided. While particular sevens, like Ursa Major, may have passed from culture to culture in particular myths, it may be a mistake to try following the seven mystique further via dissemination—direct or indirect—from a source. A penchant for sets of seven may be just a universal quirk of human psychology.

Second, even if the mystique does exhibit cause and effect, even if it does reveal influence from the northern seedbed, it may not be significant anyhow. From this viewpoint, likewise, it may be no more than a quirk, not a clue that justifies regarding the seedbed as a source for elements of civilization, a home of Ancient Wisdom in however embryonic a form.

At this point it would be premature to try tackling the second issue. Answers can emerge only as exploration proceeds. It seems clear that the seven mystique, in the cases that have come to light so far, is part of a bundle of motifs and not an oddity to be studied in isolation. But the first issue is the immediate one.

A worldwide survey gives the subject an interest that is seldom appreciated. Psychological quirks can, on the face of it, be forgotten. The mystique is not universal. It is culturally formed and, in its early phases, restricted. Even among Indo-Europeans, those who had it—the Indo-Aryans—were an untypical minority. With Indo-Europeans in general the sacred or magical number was three, a fact that the anthropologist Georges Dumézil relates to a tripartite division of society, though there is certainly more to it than that.[2]

Outside the territories considered already, the seven mystique is confined anciently to a single region, a heartland—the Middle East, plus Greece just alongside.* There we first encounter some of the major instances, such as a week of seven days and an astrology reckoning seven "planets"—the sun, the moon, Mercury, Venus, Mars, Jupiter, Saturn. Also a musical scale with seven notes. Normal as it sounds, it has nothing inevitable about it. Admittedly, its length is fixed by a physical fact. If you go up from C, the next C is a note with twice the vibration rate. But the seven steps on the way, C D E F G A B, are products of an aural conditioning that may have begun among the early instrument makers of Mesopotamia. The scale in Indian music, with its Indo-Aryan ancestry, does have seven notes, but the Chinese scale has only five, C D E G A.[3]

The seven mystique's currency across Europe is later and due very largely to Christianity bringing a Bible written in the heartland that teems with consecrated sevens, from the seven days of creation onward. Before the impact of outside influences there are no clear traces of the mystique in China, or Egypt, or the rest of Africa, or Australia, or the Americas. Scattered, undatable heptads occur in magic and ritual, among the Shilluk

---

*"Middle East" means the portion of Asia extending from Turkey and the Mediterranean coastline to Iran, inclusive. Those who use the phrase sometimes add Egypt. I do not. The term *Near East* was coined when the Turkish empire covered much of the region and most of the Balkans. Some authors still use it, now more or less synonymously with "Middle East."

of the Sudan, for instance, and the Navaho.[4] These are never part of a system and have no air of significance.

China is conclusive as to the limitation, because traditional Chinese thinking not only attached no special value to seven, it did attach value to another number. That was five.[5] Besides their five-note scale, the Chinese recognized five planets, namely the true ones visible before telescopes—Mercury, Venus, Mars, Jupiter, Saturn. These were matched with five elements—water, metal, fire, wood, and earth. And there are five directions—north, west, south, east, and center. Chinese astrology assesses a person under five aspects—life, body, power, fortune, intelligence. The five notes of the Chinese scale are paired with planets and elements. The Chinese rainbow has five colors and there are five social duties.

The motif extends to Tibetan Buddhism, which acknowledges five sovereign beings, Dhyani Buddhas, ruling over five epochs.[6] From the Dhyani Buddhas there emanate the five colors, elements, senses, and vowels. Even Hinduism—the mature Hinduism of the subcontinent—has five elements. They are ether, air, fire, water, and earth. These are matched with five senses—hearing, touch, sight, taste, smell.

We can mark off China and eliminate the seven mystique there as being no part of its cultural heritage. Tibet is not quite so clear-cut. In the Indian systems known as Tantric the human organism is said to have seven centers or chakras, one above another from the base of the spine to the crown of the head, and Tibetan Buddhism has Tantric overtones, with techniques for activating one's chakras. It has a few other sevens as well.[7] Lamas regard life as a progression through seven cycles on each of seven planes of experience. In Tibetan verse the most sacred meter has seven-syllable lines (an equivalent in English: "We wandered down the Broad Walk"). A Tibetan legend tells how, when the Buddha was born, he rose at once and took seven paces toward each cardinal compass point. These details never challenge the cosmic ascendancy of five. In its attitude toward numbers, however, Tibet may be a borderland, in the Chinese orbit but affected a little from a region or population with the seven mystique. Mallory may have given the answer here by suggesting that the Buddhists who spoke Tocharian, an Indo-European language of Chinese Turkestan, were descended from the Afanasievo people in the Altai.

In the seven mystique we apparently have something that is formed culturally and is a product of regional influence rather than society in general, or psychology in general. By way of corroboration, a crucial fact is that a special regard for seven does not "come naturally"; it doesn't "just happen." Quite the reverse. One of the oddest features of the mystique is the contrast between seven's persistence where it does occur and its awkwardness. It acts against the grain.

The magic three of the Celts and other peoples has a plain logic, whether or not Dumézil's social reason is valid. It appeals as neat and complete. It conjures up a triangle, the simplest enclosure; it evokes the whole of space (length, breadth, height) and the whole of time (past, present, future); it sums up the entirety of a thing or event (beginning, middle, end). Freud gave it a physical basis in the male genitalia. The basis of the Chinese five certainly is physical—it corresponds to the fingers. But seven cannot be explained thus. Those who argue otherwise have been driven to such expedients as citing seven features of the head—eyes, ears, nostrils, mouth—or seven orifices of the body.[8] They have never explained why people whose counting is based on the obvious finger tally should have built so much on an obscure alternative count. In practice, would anybody think of two nostrils rather than one nose?

A seven mystique is not merely without foundation in the human makeup, it is, as it were, actively alien. Not only is it confined to certain societies, it is such an unlikely thing for any society to adopt that an explanation is needed. Seven does not correlate with visual perception or mental capacity. Two, three, four, five objects can be taken in as a group without counting. Six is marginal. Beyond six, the objects are not perceived at a glance and have to be counted, unless they form a known pattern, like pips on a playing card. Seven is the first number that is *not* plausible as a standard group. It is just too big to be handled or remembered easily. As a frivolous yet telling instance, Walt Disney made *Snow White and the Seven Dwarfs* in 1937, and in spite of the film's success and staying power, few of the public ever found it easy to name all of the dwarfs offhand. Many could get to five or six, but nearly everybody missed at least one.

Numerologists may not be considered very important, but for what it is worth, no reason can be shown why they should have found seven attractive. It does not lend itself to the kind of thinking that regards six as a "perfect" number because its divisors, one, two and three, add up to itself. Seven is a prime number and has no divisors to play with. It is uncooperative. There is no test for divisibility by it. There are tests for the other numbers up to twelve, but the only way to see whether seven will go into a larger number is to try.

One notion is that seven is special because it is three plus four and combines magical qualities that both of the smaller numbers are held to possess.[9] Three, of course, has mythical and folkloric prominence, not only among Celts. There are three Fates, Furies, Graces. Parents in fairy tales have three sons, heroes get three wishes, heroines have three suitors, and so on. A list of triads would extend far backward in time and over an immense territory. In such cases, however, it is doubtful whether three is thought of as a number, exactly, open to arithmetical handling. Rather, as remarked, the feeling is that it stands for a whole. A triad has an air of being complete in itself. It may be a three-in-one, a divine power or entity (Fate, for example) with a triple aspect. Nobody would have made such a triad up to seven by adding four more members; nobody would have endowed Cerberus with four more heads.

Moreover, why *four*? Where would that have come from? In any relevant past, four has no similar magic. It eventually acquired that, in the broader number mysticism that grew up in Greece with genuine mathematics. But that came only with Pythagoras and his disciples in the sixth century B.C., and there were mystical sevens long before Pythagoras.

True, a few heptads of later times are thought of as three and four added together. Medieval schools taught the seven liberal arts. These comprised the *trivium* of grammar, logic, and rhetoric and the *quadrivium* of astronomy, music, geometry, and arithmetic. But the older and more significant sets are not so comprised. The week is not three plus four. The astrological planets are not three plus four. The musical scale is not three plus four. Where the seven mystique can be pinned down earliest, there is little trace of a prior mystique of any smaller numbers; sevens appear without preexisting threes and fours to add together.

Those who accept the theories of C. G. Jung may urge his "archetypes" as an explanation. They are said to be patterns embedded in a collective unconscious that all human beings share. Some are numerical and inspire such groupings as the Three Fates. Jung claims that four is archetypal as well as three, so he may seem to offer ammunition for the seven-equals-three-plus-four theory. Who knows, this piece of mental arithmetic, which is so hard to catch happening in historical daylight, might have been worked out in the collective unconscious. But while three does have an archetypal look, Jung's case for four is much weaker. It depends, to be frank, on the limitations of his own knowledge.

He talks about four directions corresponding to points of the compass, and about four winds, and four seasons, et cetera, as if all peoples had four and there were some deep-rooted necessity in it. The simple truth is that it is not so. His fours are neither worldwide nor very ancient.[10] The Greeks did not define the four cardinal points until about the fifth century B.C., and in other parts of the world, even where these are recognized, it does not follow that there are four directions. In ancient Ireland and India there were five directions, north, south, east, west, and "here." The Chinese usually counted five directions, sometimes six. In some Polynesian islands they reckon seven—north, south, east, west, here, up, and down. Four has no magic in this matter.

The four winds, north, south, east, west, are rationalized survivors of a larger, vaguer, more primitive brood. They do not appear in the Bible till Jer. 49:36 ("And upon Elam will I bring the four winds from the four quarters of heaven. . . ."), and that passage is much later than others that emphasize seven. A Babylonian text, the creation epic *Enuma elish* ("When on high"), mentions four winds as a set but also mentions seven winds as a set. Seven is already there; it is not a sum of three and four.

With the seasons the notion of a four archetype collapses completely. Across the world, the number of seasons ranges from two (tropical South America) to nine (the Shilluk). The Indo-European languages have no common word for autumn. The Greeks, who can be documented, started with three seasons. In the seventh century B.C., their year sometimes was divided into four but sometimes into three. Classical Greek is a three-season language, its word for "autumn" meaning "the after-summer." Theophrastus, a scientific writer, actually divides the year into five.[11]

Seven cannot be made up of an archetypal three and four if the archetypal four is invalid.

2

The heptad, once again, does not just happen as a natural social or psychological product. An impressive proof is still very much with us, affecting everyone's life so constantly and habitually, and to such an extent, that it seldom is reflected upon. We schedule our work and leisure by the seven-day week. It came from the religious commandments of ancient Israel in the septenary heartland. That, however, is not to say why it was commanded or why it was adopted—or above all, why it is still adhered to.

Not because it is sensible or convenient. It isn't. It cannot, for example, be split into equal shorter periods, whereas a six-day week could be halved or divided into three. It doesn't fit into the year an exact number of times: 7 does not go into 365 evenly. Therefore, Christmas and other special occasions never fall on the same day for two years running. A five-day week would fit. The seven-day week itself could be made to fit, since 7 does go into 364, and the only adjustment needed for a regular calendar would be to keep one day a year separate, say, as a holiday. But even that won't do. Every single day has to belong to the clumsy compulsive cycle. French and Russian revolutionaries tried to get rid of it and failed. The feeling that it is right and sacrosanct, part of the natural order, like the year itself, is too strong.

"Right" and "sacrosanct" in this context are near-mystical words, yet they are the proper ones. To observe that the seven-day week is not part of the natural order is to state the issue moderately. There is not even a practical reason overriding its prima facie awkwardness.

Various nations, in various regions of the world, have had calendric units of the same sort. The motive is usually economic.[12] Months can be defined by the moon or otherwise, but a shorter interval is needed to provide for regular market days, days for trade rather than production. A week-type cycle results. It has not resulted everywhere. India had no "week" before it was taken over by conquerors who did have one. Nor was any in general use among the ancient Greeks. But a time division like this is widely on record, and where it has existed, its length has commonly been fixed by the nature of the economy or the distances buyers and sellers have to travel. These are practical reasons, and it might be inferred that the seven-day cycle began in some society where it was practical. Yet this has never been so. The seven-day cycle has always failed to commend itself for marketing or any other basic activity.

Some tribal groups in West Africa have favored a quasi-week of only four days. A five-day week is attested in Scandinavia and Central America. The Assyrians opted for six. Republican Rome had a cycle of nine counted as eight plus one. Ancient Egypt and pre-Columbian Peru made it ten, and so did a minority of Greeks. The Chinese formerly had two concurrent cycles of ten days and twelve, coinciding every sixtieth. With some of these peoples, noneconomic factors entered. The Egyptians treated their ten-day period calendrically, as one-third of a month. The Spartans did likewise, breaking up the month into three "decades."[13] But whatever the operative causes, a strange conclusion stands out. Neither economic practicality nor calendric convenience can be shown to have dictated a seven-day week, ever, anywhere.

It has been claimed that the Babylonians had one, but this is an error.[14] In the time of their great king Hammurabi, in the eighteenth century B.C., they attached taboos to certain days of the month. These were originally the first, the seventh, the fifteenth, and the twenty-eighth. Much later the fifteenth was dropped and the fourteenth and twenty-first put in its place. Yet even then, no septenary cycle carried over from month to month. Each series was self-contained. Nor did the special days have a sabbatical character. To be precise, they were days when the king did not offer sacrifice, or pronounce judgment, or eat roasted meat, or change his clothes. Most activities went on as usual. The same applies to the quasi-weeks elsewhere. None included a periodic cessation from work. When one of the days was a market day it was precisely not a sabbath, but a day for business. The seven-day week with its recurrent rest day is different from the rest in structure as well as length. It cannot have originated in the same way.

Nevertheless, it ousted its more rational rivals worldwide. It triumphed through the ascendancy of Judeo-Christian culture, chiefly in Europe, and of Islamic culture, chiefly in Asia and northern Africa. Behind both was a shared shaping. The seven-day week was part of a religious package they both inherited, originating in ancient Israel; a package that embodied the seven mystique. The week drew strength from another embodiment of it—

the astrological heptad of planets. Astrologers assigned a celestial ruler to each day, in perpetual rotation, and names resulted that were applied to the days of the week and adopted or adapted in most European languages— Sun Day, Moon Day, and so forth. Religious and magical forces active through centuries overcame adverse factors and customs, quelled the opposition, and imposed a rhythm of social behavior as ancestrally right and wise, though neither its rightness nor its wisdom could stand up to scrutiny.

3

Scholars have tended to neglect or evade the seven mystique. The topic looks trivial, or superstitious, or irrelevant to the problems they have chosen to study. Also it eludes their categories. It doesn't seem to be exactly archaeological, or anthropological, or religious, or psychological. Not being the concern of any specialist in particular, it has been the concern of none. Unhappily, too, it has been given an explanation—one of those pseudo-explanations that stifle inquiry, though a proper look at the data will show its inadequacy. The more closely the septenary matter is examined, the more resistant it looks to facile dismissal.

To revert to Jung for a moment, it is interesting to see what he did with it as a fact in the province of psychology. In spite of his archetypes, he did not himself press the three-plus-four notion. As an explorer of myth and religion he often encountered the mystique.[15] Dreams reported by his patients, citizens of a Christian-conditioned Europe, told the same tale. He acknowledged it yet never came entirely to grips with it or accounted for it in terms of his own theories. But he did drop occasional hints at a prototype seven underlying all others. By doing so he lifted the subject out of the domain of the unconscious—or he would have, if he had followed up on the idea. He touches on it in some remarks about the legendary Seven Sleepers of Ephesus, who, he says, "indicate by their sacred number that they are gods"—by which he means "the planetary gods of the ancients."[16] Here and elsewhere he seems to imply that the whole business of the heptad derives from the seven planets of Western astrology.

This is the pseudo-explanation that has inhibited inquiry. It was put forward in 1903 by Franz Cumont, a historian of religion, and it is approved by several besides Jung who have considered the question, although not many have.[17] Cumont was drawn to it by his interest in Mithraism, a Persian-inspired cult that flourished in the Roman Empire, while Jung was drawn by his interest in other cults of that period, such as gnosticism. These esoteric systems laid stress on the planets as a heptad.

Cumont and Jung were well aware that the seven-planet astrology was older than Mithraism or gnosticism. The trouble is that it was not old enough. It could and did reinforce the seven mystique once that was established. It certainly did not supply a prototype that created it. Indo-Aryan sevens, Sumerian sevens (as we shall see), Israel's seven-day week itself— all are prior to seven-planet astrology.

Nevertheless, a glance at this will help to put the problem in true perspective. It began in Babylonia, where ancient astronomy made its first major strides. In the earliest Babylonian texts where planets are listed, they are jumbled with stars and constellations, and the set of seven is undefined.[18] Nothing proves its recognition as such before the late eighth century B.C., and the astrology based on it was not invented till the sixth century B.C. and not perfected till three or four hundred years later still, when Greek astronomers had worked on it.[19]

The Babylonians knew the sun as a divinity, Shamash, and the moon likewise, Sin, and they assigned the true planets to their deities Nebo, Ishtar, Nergal, Marduk, and Ninib.[20] Greeks transposed the system into their own terms during the last pre-Christian centuries. Previously they had not given the sun and moon a high religious ranking; nor had they regarded the true planets as divine (at least in any sense that concerned humanity) or given them names with that implication.[21] For the Greeks, Mercury was the Twinkling Star; Venus was the Herald of Light, the Herald of Dawn, the Evening Star; Mars was the Fiery Star; Jupiter was the Luminous Star; Saturn was the Brilliant Star.[22] They did not much care at first how many of these bodies existed. It was some time before the Herald of Dawn was agreed to be the same as the Evening Star. The fixed list of seven was definitely Babylonian, but with the progress of astronomy it rooted itself among the Greeks, and their slide into astrology began.

When Alexander's conquests spread Hellenistic civilization over a huge area, bringing Greek language and culture, a need arose for a religion that would transcend the old city cults and be big enough for a larger world. In response to that pressure, Hellenistic Greeks followed the Babylonian lead and did better.[23] The mysteriously moving "planets"—the word *planet* means "wanderer"—acquired a new aura of power. The sun and moon were made more conspicuously divine; Apollo's solar aspect, previously little considered, was brought to the fore with that in view, while his sister Artemis took over the moon. The true planets were matched—indeed, almost identified—with Hermes, Aphrodite, Ares, Zeus, and Cronus. The second planet may have become a goddess because the Babylonian Ishtar was; the fourth may have become the chief god because the Babylonian Marduk was. Each, anyhow, was credited with suitable influence.

Horoscopes and predictions were based on their movement through the signs of the zodiac, which had properties of their own. The planets were called interpreters. Thus Hermes and his colleagues acquired a fresh lease on life just when skepticism was threatening to extinguish them, and they made their way into cults, such as Mithraism.[24] Roman astrologers took over the whole heptad. To the true planets they gave equivalent labels, the ones that are still in use—Mercury, Venus, Mars, Jupiter, and Saturn. These, with the sun and moon, had altars in Rome. In an Earth-centered astronomy the moon was reckoned, correctly, to be closest. Beyond the moon came Mercury, then Venus, then the sun, then Mars, Jupiter, and Saturn, in that order. They were not wandering in a void. They were attached to invisible spheres, one outside another, that rotated around Earth. These concentric spheres were the "heavens"; hence expressions like the "third heaven" used by St. Paul (2 Cor. 12:2). Astronomers added a further heaven outside the rest to accommodate the stars, and another outside that, the Primum Mobile, imparting motion to all the rest.[25]

The crucial point is that the whole process started *after* seven was established as sacred and magical—long after. The planetary heptad was not the cause of the number's mystique. Comparison with other astrological schemes makes the relation between them clear. A seven-planet system has no inherent logic or inevitability. Chinese astrology counted the five true pretelescopic planets and left out the sun and moon. The ancient Iranians made the number nine. In India the true planets were known by the fourth century A.D., and Hindu astrologers dubbed them *grahas* and added the sun and moon, as in Babylonia. But they also added two "nodes'" or foci of influence, Rahu and Ketu, making nine grahas. In Hinduism's island outpost of Bali, Rahu and Ketu were the head and tail of the constellation Draco.[26]

It was only in Babylonia that the planets were made out to be seven, and a little searching reveals what happened. Babylonia already had the seven mystique. Among many other proofs, it acknowledged seven cosmic powers long before its astrologers listed the planets. The city of Borsippa had a seven-tiered "Temple of the Seven Rulers of Heaven and Earth" in the twelfth century B.C.[27] Astrologers made the planets seven—no more, no less—because the preexisting mystique demanded that number. They defined their heavens so as to fit. So we may well be back with the Indo-Aryans, and septenary influence penetrating the Middle East with the ones who branched off and through whom, perhaps, the Seven Rishis became the Seven Sages of Mesopotamia. Influence of some kind—regional influence—might seem to be the sole explanation for the seven mystique's presence in the heartland and absence in so many other places. Yet it is still a question whether the Altaic thread does go all the way, or whether the mystique began in the heartland independently from some other cause. In this case we can get beyond inference and speculation. The literature of the region is not silent; the topic actually is examined and treated most seriously.

CHAPTER SEVEN

The Prototype

1

For the moment let us set shamans and Indo-Aryans aside. An antiquity ignorant of them offers a full discussion of the seven mystique, and on the issue of origins, modern theories have hardly added to it. Its author is Philo, called Philo Judaeus, a learned Jew born in Alexandria in about 10 B.C. He studied Greek philosophy and tried to present Judaism as a philosophic system perfecting the wisdom of the Gentiles. To do this he had to reinterpret the Bible—that is, the Jewish Bible, in Christian terms the Old Testament. While not rejecting it as history, he stressed allegorical meanings which he extracted by rules largely of his own devising.

In an essay *On the Creation of the World*, Philo comes down to specifics about the seven days of creation, in the first chapter of Genesis and the opening of the second.[1] He attributes the book to Moses in person, as everyone did then, and treats him as a great philosophical teacher. The creation story, Philo explains, is not chronological. Moses portrays God as making the visible universe in six days, not because it literally took six days, but because of a symbolism in the number. As for the seventh day, when God rested and the week of creation was complete, that is intended to steer the reader's mind, again through the number's symbolism, to a higher spiritual realm that is the source of God's universal design.

To work out this idea, he plunges into strange intricacies, both here and in another essay, *On the Allegories of the Sacred Laws*, where he explores the topic again. His claims are lofty. "I know not if anyone would be able to celebrate the nature of the number seven in adequate terms, since it is superior to every form of expression," he writes. And: "Seven is honoured by those of the highest reputation among both Greeks and barbarians who devote themselves to mathematical sciences. It was also greatly honoured by Moses."[2]

His numerological notions are the least impressive, because of seven's lack of aptitude for this kind of jugglery. He does try, pointing out that in the basic number series from one to ten, seven is neither a product of others nor a producer of others. What he means is that it is a prime itself, and if you multiply it by anything else, you overshoot and are outside the series. So within the basic ten, it is not generated and does not generate. This fact is made out to connect it with Athene, the goddess of wisdom, who sprang from the head of Zeus without ordinary birth and remained a virgin. Philo does better when he turns to actual heptads—the strings of Apollo's lyre, the alleged faculties of the soul and internal organs, and many more. These are all said to be symptoms of the number's supremacy, built into the world and its creatures.

None of this leads him back to origins. In his view, when Moses embeds seven in the creation story, his sacred text is not the reason for the number's significance, it presupposes it. Moses uses the number to guide readers into reflection on the spiritual order behind appearances. In the first of the two essays, Philo never says why. He mentions the three-plus-four equation, but only as a point of interest, and he never picks out anything as a pro- totype, a supreme heptad determining other heptads. In the second essay he draws attention to three that are eternally written in the sky.

> Nature delights in the number seven. For there are seven planets, going in continual opposition to the daily course of the heaven which always proceeds in the same direction. And likewise the constellation of the Bear is made up of seven stars, which constellation is the cause of communication and unity among men, and not merely of traffic. Again, the periodical changes of the moon take place according to the number seven, that star having the greatest sympathy with the things on earth.[3]

Philo's point about Ursa Major is that it is used as a direction finder in navigation. He remarks in another place that it has enabled seafarers to make voyages of discovery, opening up the world.[4]

While the planetary heptad became so important, reinforcing the seven mystique, we have seen that it cannot be the source because it was not observed or defined early enough. Philo himself does not make much of it. One or two modern writers have tried to account for the mystique by invoking his third instance of nature's septenary delight. To quote Richard Cavendish:

> The significance of 7 comes from its connection with the moon. It is a widespread primitive belief that the cycle of life on earth—the birth, growth and decay of plants, animals and men—is connected with the waxing and waning of the moon as it goes through its endless cycle of births and deaths in the sky. . . .
> The moon's cycle is made of four phases, each lasting about seven days. The Sumerians based their calendar on this cycle.[5]

"This cycle" means the lunar cycle as a whole, without regard for subdivisions. Sumer was the territory of the first civilization in Mesopotamia, created by a gifted people who were neither Semitic nor Indo-European.

The lunar theory has something to be said for it. The moon as an object of worship goes back far enough. There was a time in the Middle East when it enjoyed more honor than the sun. It was cool and benign, never fierce. Its cycle governed some of the early calendars, not in Sumer alone. Even the realization that it had no light of its own failed to destroy its spell.

When Philo speaks of its having "the greatest sympathy with the things on earth," he is referring to the belief that Cavendish cites. According to a treatise ascribed to the astronomer Ptolemy, who lived in the second century A.D., the moon

> . . . as the heavenly body nearest the earth, bestows her effluence most abundantly upon mundane things, for most of them, animate or inanimate, are sympathetic to her and change in company with her; the rivers increase and diminish their streams with her light, the seas turn their own tides with her rising and setting, and plants and animals in whole or in some part wax and wane with her.[6]

Besides the approximate correspondence with the monthly cycle in women, the moon still has its role in popular weather lore, and the notion that it affects the brain survives in the word *lunacy*.

Another witness is Apuleius, a younger contemporary of Ptolemy. An initiate of the goddess Isis, one of whose many aspects was lunar, he wrote *The Golden Ass*, a romance of enchantment that is comic for a good part of the way but finally becomes serious. The narrator, who has been asleep on a beach, wakes up in brilliant moonlight.

> It is at this secret hour that the Moon-goddess, sole sovereign of mankind, is possessed of her greatest power and majesty. She is the shining deity by whose divine influence not only all beasts, wild and

tame, but all inanimate things as well, are invigorated; whose ebbs and flows control the rhythm of all bodies whatsoever, whether in the air, on earth, or below the sea. Of this I was well aware, and therefore resolved to address the visible image of the goddess.

Jumping up and shaking off my drowsiness, I went down to the sea to purify myself by bathing in it. Seven times I dipped my head under water—seven, according to the divine philosopher, Pythagoras, is a number that suits all religious occasions.[7]

Though Apuleius does not relate the number to what has gone before, the association seems hopeful.

The moon's septenary quality is supposed to lie in the phases—new to half, half to full, full to half again, half to new, each about seven days in length, together making twenty-eight, roughly a lunar month. Philo adds two numerological touches. If you add together the numbers up to seven, one plus two plus three, and so on, their sum in twenty-eight. Further, twenty-eight is a perfect number, equal to the sum of its divisors: one plus two plus four plus seven plus fourteen equals twenty-eight. Perfect numbers are very scarce. From one to forty million the only ones are 6, 28, 496, 8,128, 130,816, 2,096,128, and 33,550,336. A perfection so rare surely is significant.

In seeking origins we can set such calculations aside. The lunar cycle's real claim to be the prototype is otherwise. It might be strong if it could be shown that the phases ever actually got into the calendar, ever produced a seven-day week, but evidence is lacking. Not only was ancient Israel alone in having such a time division, but the Bible never hints at a lunar reason for it. A further difficulty is like that over the number of planets. Just as these are not "naturally" seven and are reckoned differently in different countries, so the lunar phases are not naturally four or even naturally equal in length. Primitive peoples seldom divide the cycle like this. Some Australian aborigines recognize only two phases, waxing and waning. The Andamanese and others have three unequal phases, waxing, full, and waning. The Karaya in Brazil break up the cycle into five. The Greeks at first had only the Australian two, waxing and waning, and then they had the Andamanese three, waxing, full, and waning, matching them with divine triads, such as the Fates and Graces.[8]

The division into four seven-day phases seems to have been invented in Babylonia, as was the planetary heptad, and for the same reason: that seven was magical already.[9] The process can be seen beginning in the Babylonian story of creation. Here the god Marduk commands the moon to rule the night and mark months. He ordains that the transition from new to half shall take seven days. But this is not followed up. The rest of the cycle is defined differently, and the author tries, rather obscurely, to harmonize it with a thirty-day solar month. It was because of further developments on the same lines that the Babylonians changed their taboo days from the first, seventh, fifteenth, and twenty-eighth of the month to the first, seventh, fourteenth, twenty-first, and twenty-eighth. These days were associated with the moon god Sin.[10] But none of it happened until long after the seven mystique was well established.

As to the relation between the mystique and the moon, Philo has a passage making the same point after his fashion. Seven, he says, "affects even the periodical changes of the moon."[11] In other words, while he accepts the seven-day phases, he says that the moon behaves as it does because of the number's prior power. Seven belongs to the archetypal divine realm, and the moon acts in conformity with it. His metaphysics may be less than persuasive, but in substance he is right. The lunar cycle is not the prototype. Its seven-day phases, as eventually agreed on, did not cause the seven mystique, they are a consequence of it. Even if the lunar cycle were not excluded for that reason, it would suffer from a drawback that would exclude the planets too, if chronology did not. For a phenomenon occurring in early and unsophisticated contexts, a prototype depending on prolonged study, or calculation, or calendric reckoning, is bound to be dubious. What is wanted is something direct and clear-cut, and Philo provides it with his other celestial heptad, the Bear, Ursa Major. By elimination he brings us to a credible answer.

Ursa Major is direct and clear-cut. It is neither inferred nor constructed. It is simply *there*, taken in visually. One of its main stars is fainter than the rest, but they are easily seen as seven on a clear night. Eighteen lesser stars have been included with the Bear in celestial charts, but they are dimmer beyond comparison. The Roman astronomical writer Hyginus admits that they were counted in with it only to make it more bearlike.[12] Throughout most of the northern hemisphere, and specifically in the early homes of the seven mystique, it is visible at all times of the night and all times of the year. Conversely, the Australian aborigines, who do not see it, have an imaginative star-lore but no seven mystique. We already have noted its directly observed quality and the way this is attested in myth and folklore among Egyptians, Mexicans, Lapps, Sioux, Arabs, and the way this is shown in its more familiar guises as a dipper or a plow or a vehicle.[13]

To take the further step of accepting it as the prototype seven, we would need to find a human context or contexts where it had an appropriate aura, a numinosity. But this is exactly what we have done already, by tracing the shamanic myths of the constellation and the adoption of its stars by Indo-Aryans as the Seven Rishis, sources of cosmic harmony and perennial wisdom. The possibility that Ursa accounts for the whole northern seven mystique already has arisen. Philo's argument leads to the same solution by a very different route and is not invalidated by the mystical way he expresses it. The convergence is mutually confirming. There seems to be no alternative, Ursa Major has no competitor. The mystique of seven was caused, in "the dark backward and abysm of time," by reverence for it.

However, this does not show how far it is possible to push the northland's claims as a seedbed, a primordial source of motifs in known civilizations. We need to ask what status Ursa Major had in the Middle East and whether it was conspicuous enough to promote a mystique derived from it. We also need to ask whether the mystique took shape there independently or came as an import, its nearer origin among Indo-Aryans and its remoter origin among shamans. It appears that the Seven Rishis might have entered Mesopotamia as the Seven Sages, but, plausible as this may be, it is not a sufficient ground for general statements.

2

In Mesopotamia, Ursa Major had a place in a sort of preastrology before the listing of the planets.[14] Several constellations were named and linked with the world below by mystical correspondences, though nothing like astrological influence was defined as yet. Pisces was the heavenly analogue of the great rivers, Tigris and Euphrates. Cancer corresponded to the city of Sippar, and Aries and Cetus, combined, to Babylon. Ursa Major itself was Mar-gid-da, the Waggon of the Heavens, and it was matched to another city, Nippur.

That matching conferred distinction. In the third millennium B.C., when Sumer flourished, Nippur's position was unique.[15] Not only was it said to be very old (even prehuman; its first inhabitants were gods), but it was deeply venerated and regarded as Sumer's central point. Never the seat of a royal dynasty, Nippur was the religious capital. Here the chief deity Enlil had a temple, the Ekur, with primacy throughout the land. His blessing was essential to welfare everywhere else. Kings competed in sending gifts to Nippur and went there to be "elected by Enlil" and win suzerainty over other kings.

Nippur's dignity implied a special status for the star group paired with it. The apparent reason for the pairing lay in centrality. To quote Eric Burrows,

> The Great Bear is the most notable constellation near the celestial pole, the centre and axis of the heavens; thus it is analogous to Nippur, the old summit and centre and perhaps navel of Sumer.[16]

It is hard to be sure how early such correspondences are, and it is hard to be sure what these starry affiliations meant. The constellations might have been viewed as dwellings of gods or as diagrams of divine ideas or intentions.[17] Whatever its true age, and whatever its significance, the Bear's linkage with Nippur shows awareness of it and respect for it, long before planetary astrology. But—a caution—it was seen as a whole. The stars were not individualized or counted as seven.

Philo is right to stress Ursa's role in direction finding and therefore in travel, commerce, and human interrelations. The word *arctic* is from the Greek for "north" and means the Bear's place. The part of the sky it dominates is centripetal—as it sweeps round and round, its two pointers guide the eye inward to the polestar. During a period before Christ when no single star was very close to the pole, Ursa Major was even more definitely the north marker. Jung puts this in his own terms: "The 'Chariot' in the sky, Charles' Wain (Ursa Major or Big Dipper) . . . marks the celestial Pole, which was of great significance in the history of symbols. It is a model of the structure of the Self."[18]

Use of it for navigation at sea is of long standing. Homer refers to this in his account of Odysseus's departure from the island of the goddess Calypso:

> It was with a happy heart that the good Odysseus spread his sail to catch the wind and used his seamanship to keep his boat straight with the steering-oar. There he sat and never closed his eyes in sleep, but kept them on the Pleiades, or watched Boötes slowly set, or the Great Bear, nicknamed the Wain, which always wheels round in the same place and looks across at Orion the Hunter with a wary eye. It was this constellation, the only one which never bathes in Ocean's Stream, that the wise goddess Calypso had told him to keep on his left hand as he made across the sea. (*Odyssey* 5:275)

Something is said about this by Aratus, a Greek poet who flourished in the third pre-Christian century.[19] He is the poet whom St. Paul quotes in Acts 17:28, speaking of God in Athens: "For we are also his offspring." Aratus gives Ursa Major the descriptive title *Helice*, meaning "That Which Turns," and confirms its role in Greek seafaring. Some myth-makers took up the Helice point, that the Bear "always wheels round in the same place," and pressed it further. The constellation, according to these, is not merely carried around and not even merely self-propelled. It is the motive power of the whole starry heaven that keeps it rotating in equilibrium.[20]

Such notions take us out of the Middle East and forward in time, but they illustrate attitudes and potentialities that may indeed have existed much earlier. In classical Latin the word for "north" is *septentrio*, which is derived from the constellation as "arctic" is and is a contraction of *Septentriones*, meaning the "Seven Oxen," a team turning a cosmic mill.[21]

Mystical writers of the early Christian era adapt this image, sometimes weirdly. A Greek magical papyrus, perhaps under influence from the Mithraic cult, describes a manifestation of a god "in a white robe and trousers, with a crown of gold on his head, holding in his right hand the golden shoulder of a heifer, that is the Bear that sets in motion and keeps the heavens turning in due seasons." The trousered apparition is heralded by seven virgins called the Seven Fortunes of Heaven, and seven youths with bulls' heads called the Pole-lords of Heaven, the latter being in charge of the rotation.[22]

The motif continued in a more important body of writing, the Hermetic treatises. These were composed in Greek by several anonymous hands during the heyday of the Roman Empire.[23] A medley of Greek and Jewish ideas went into them. They were supposed to contain the teachings of Hermes Trismegistus, "the thrice-great Hermes," a sage identified with the learned Egyptian god Thoth. They showed remarkable staying power and were influential in the Renaissance and even later. Paracelsus, Bruno, and other eminent figures regarded Hermetic lore as Ancient Wisdom. Newton himself believed that he was rediscovering Hermetic truths. Readers of Laurence Sterne will recall that Tristram Shandy received his name because the nursemaid at his christening had trouble with "Trismegistus," which was what his father had intended.

The putative Hermes introduces a discourse on God with a question that is not in the Bible.

The Bear up there that turneth round itself, and carries the whole cosmos with it—Who is the owner of this instrument?[24]

While Hermes does not enumerate the stars in this passage, he does in another, where he speaks of the Bear "composed of seven stars" as occupying the center of the zodiac. This is inaccurate, but he wants to enlarge on its cosmic function, and he goes on thus:

Its energy is as it were an axle's, setting nowhere and nowhere rising, but stopping [ever] in the self-same space, and turning round the same, giving its proper motion to the Life-producing Circle [that is, the zodiac], and handing over this whole universe from night to day, from day to night.[25]

The Hermetic treatises have other septenary touches.[26] Some, as we might expect, are derived from the seven-planet astrology. But not all. As to that, two modern writers, Giorgio de Santillana and Hertha von Dechend, offer a striking suggestion (it may, with due respect, be better to call it an intuition) that is thoroughly in keeping with the idea that has emerged. Ursa Major, they say, has fixed the astrological scheme itself through a direct correlation.

> The Seven Stars of Ursa . . . are normative in all cosmological alignments on the starry sphere. These dominant stars of the Far North are peculiarly but systematically linked with those which are considered the operative powers of the cosmos, that is, the planets as they move in different placements and configurations along the zodiac.

Elsewhere:

> Each planet is represented by a star of the Wain, and vice versa.[27]

The authors do not make it very clear who worked this out, or when, but their discussion shows insight in another respect, as will appear in a moment.

Some of the notions about the Bear are expansions of the plain facts—its visible location and motion, its practical usefulness. While it would be unwise to assume anything like its Hermetic quality three or four thousand years ago, it was important enough to create a favoring milieu for a seven mystique. But to look for the mystique's beginnings in the Middle East, and consider whether it arose independently or as an Indo-Aryan import, we have to delve back into the history of Sumer, where it was already flourishing in about 2500 B.C.

While the Sumerians may have honored the constellation as one of several heavenly patterns, nothing is on record that takes the matter further. Since they were not deep-water sailors and had no need of direction finding at sea, its chief practical value was lost on them. They were aware of it as central, and apparently matched it with their central city; they may have invented a term that was applied to it later: "Bond of Heaven."[28] But however receptive they might have been to a seven mystique derived from it, nothing shows that they themselves did the deriving. In common with nearly all peoples, they seem to have viewed it as a whole, not as made up of seven individual stars. When they looked upward they concerned themselves with the weather rather than with the sky above it, which they believed to be made of tin.[29] It was not they who made the first great strides in astronomy.

If the seven mystique in the Middle East was a product of Ursa Major, the Sumerians were not responsible. Nor were the settled Semitic peoples, the Canaanites, for instance. Though the Canaanites' Phoenician descendants were great seafarers, they steered by Ursa Minor.[30] Yet Semites had the same mystique as the Sumerians. An outside influence is needed, coming from a context in which Ursa Major was numinous and its stars were explicitly seven. That is what we already have, the Indo-Aryan context, with a specific link. Santillana and von Dechend hit on it in the passage quoted, where they say that the cosmic ordering is mythically "dictated by the 'Seven Sages,' as they are often cryptically mentioned in India and elsewhere," who "turn out to be the seven stars of Ursa." They are the Seven Rishis or Seven Seers of the Indo-Aryans, identified with the stars, whom we have glimpsed apparently passing into Mesopotamia as the Seven Sages, the Sebettu, founders of seven cities.

3

Given Ursa Major as the source of the seven mystique, the Goddess issue in the north may eventually turn on the question of whether the constellation was always firmly associated with her, as it is in Roerich's story of Manzalgormo and Gesar.

The mythification of Ursa would have been brought by the western Indo-Aryans, the ones who branched off. We shall have to ask more carefully when and how they reached the Mesopotamian neighborhood. Meanwhile, it is worth recalling the ancient Iranians, who were akin to them. More is known about the Iranians. They were alongside Mesopotamia in the latter half of the second millennium B.C. How long they had already been there is an open question. While they were not the bringers of the seven mystique, they picked it up, as they picked up some version of Mount Meru. They are evidence for its currency thereabouts, an Indo-European currency, though the dating is vague.

Religion played an important part in their development. At first they had a pantheon like that of their Indo-Aryan cousins. Then they produced their great prophet Zoroaster.[31] His teaching came close to monotheism. God was Ahura Mazdah, the Wise Lord, creator of the universe. He had several aspects or emanations, personified as the Bounteous Immortals. One of them, Truth, was opposed by an evil principle called the Lie. Another, the Holy Spirit, was opposed by a twin called Angra Mainyu. Angra Mainyu embraced the Lie and became destructive, an enemy of order. So the world was in a state of conflict. That belief had deep roots in Iranian society, where the peasantry lived in perpetual struggle against marauding highlanders. For reasons that are not clear, Zoroaster turned against the old Vedic gods, the *devas*, and proclaimed that *daevas* were demons and their worshipers were lined up on the evil side. But the conflict would not last forever. Evil finally would succumb. Zoroaster's religion was taken up by the Magi, an order of priest-magicians, and they distorted it, exaggerating the evil spirit till he became an antigod and the system was dualistic—in later terms, Ormuzd versus Ahriman.

Where Iranian ideas belong on the time scale is hard to tell. No one knows Zoroaster's date.[32] Greeks who mention him put him thousands of years back, and modern attempts to transfer him to the sixth century B.C. are unconvincing. But with whatever implications, the seven mystique occurs here. Ahura Mazdah's prime emanations, the Bounteous Immortals, are seven in number (though the Holy Spirit tends to be fused with the Wise Lord himself, so that the set could be reckoned as either seven or six).[33] Some of the old Iranian mythology was preserved by the poet Firdausi, who lived from about A.D. 940 to 1020 and wrote an epic entitled the *Shah-Namah*. Minor sevens in this work often can be discounted as Islamic touches due to Firdausi himself, but a few have genuine interest and can be supplemented from other sources.

The mythical history begins with a "Pishdadian" dynasty of superhuman kings.[34] First is Gayumarth or Gayomart, a mountain dweller who ruled all the world and subjugated demons and beasts. When he died, his blood flowed into the earth and formed the seven metals known to the alchemists—gold, silver, mercury, copper, iron, tin, lead.[35] His successor Hushang found how to work them and also invented agriculture. Next was Tahmurath, who won a victory over Ahriman and forced the demons to teach him the secret of writing.

Fourth and greatest was Jamshid, familiar to readers of the *Rubaiyat* of Omar Khayyam because of a septenary treasure:

> *Iram indeed is gone with all its Rose,*
> *And Jamshyd's Sev'n-ringed Cup where no one knows.*

The cup was of gold and held the Elixir of Life. Its rings had magical properties, but it is not clear whether they resided in the number itself or in something to which the rings corresponded. Genii, under Jamshid's command, buried it on the future site of Persepolis. It was dug up when the city was founded, but its final fate is obscure. Jamshid reigned for seven centuries. He had a flying throne and introduced precious stones and other refinements. When he aspired to be a god, his pride laid him open to a counterattack by Ahriman, who, through an agent named Zahhak, overthrew him.[36]

Historically, the sixth century B.C. brought a martial upsurge creating an immense empire, named after one Iranian element, the Persians, who ruled in concert with the Medes. Its kings adopted Zoroaster's religion. Sensing, perhaps, an affinity between the Wise Lord and the God of Israel, they showed favor to the Jews.[37] Zoroastrianism affected Judaism and, through Judaism, Christianity. One of several results was that the Jewish Satan, previously a minor nuisance tolerated at God's court (Job 1:6–12, 2:1–6), became the Devil and almost an Ahriman.

The biblical book *Esther* is set in the Persian capital Susa during the reign of Ahasuerus, otherwise Xerxes, the would-be conqueror of Greece. Its first chapter tells of a banquet lasting seven days, of seven royal chamberlains, and of seven princes who "saw the king's face and sat first in the kingdom" (1:5, 10, and 14). *Esther* is not history, but some of its local color is plausible. Persian kings had a sort of cabinet of seven wise men. In the more historical *Ezra* (7:14), when Artaxerxes appoints Ezra to reorganize the Jewish community, the commission is given as from the king and "his seven counsellors."[38]

Persia had an aristocratic caste composed of descendants of a group of conspirators who put Darius I on the throne.[39] There were seven of these, Darius himself being one, and "the Seven" is what the group habitually is called, not only in Persian records but in the Greek history of Herodotus (3:70–88). Descent from the Seven conferred status throughout the lifetime of the empire and even afterward. Their families had unique privileges, including, it is said, a monopoly of supplying wives for the kings. Writers in Latin, centuries after the conspiracy, speak of prominent Persians as descended from one or other of the Seven.[40]

Herodotus also tells (1:98) of the Median capital Ecbatana, which had seven walls, one inside another. He says they were all painted different colors—white, black, scarlet, blue, orange, silver, gold. Admittedly this description sounds unlikely. He may have heard some garbled account of the Assyrian city Nineveh, which had a colored septenary crenellation.

Whatever weight may be given to Iranian heptads and Iranian myths about Mount Elbruz, we have reason to think that certain motifs entered the Middle East with Indo-Aryans. These had existed farther back in Asia among their ancestors, some of whom went off in another direction and carried the motifs to the Indus Valley. And the ancestors' ancestors apparently acquired the motifs in the shamanic northland, with its reverence for Ursa Major, its personifications of the seven stars, its bear cults, its other heptads, and its ideas about mountains. The package traveled all the way from the northland and impressed itself on Mesopotamia.

CHAPTER EIGHT

Sumerians and Babylonians

1

What is suggested is that Mesopotamia acquired the seven mystique from the western Indo-Aryans and that a persuasive instance of this is the conversion of the Seven Rishis into the Seven Sages. But the latter heptad was different in kind. It was not a constellation beyond mortal reach; though mythical, it was planted in earthly realities. Whereas the Seven Rishis were wisdom figures in a general sense, the Seven Sages were the founders of seven real cities that formed the basis of civilization.[1] This urban heptad was perhaps rather ill defined and selective. Written sources attest more than a dozen early cities.[2] Among them were Nippur, Uruk (the biblical Erech), Ur (Abraham's birthplace in the Bible), Eridu, Adab, and Lagash. The point, as in other cases, is that for the purposes of the theme, there had to *be* seven.

The cities grew out of tiny settlements where pre-Sumerians lived, known to archaeologists as Ubaidians.[3] These had begun the transformation of barren land by farming. Sumerians carried it further by irrigation. The Tigris and Euphrates supplied abundant water—sometimes they flooded—and the terrain was level. Mainly it was a matter of distribution.

Sumer was Mesopotamia's southern portion, and there, in the words of an eminent scholar's book title, *History Begins*. No one knows where the Sumerians came from. Their language was neither Indo-European nor Semitic. Making their debut during the fourth millennium B.C., they were pioneers not only in the building of cities but in monarchical government,

Sumerian representation of Iru, an aspect of the god Nergal, about 3000 B.C.,
showing an early formative stage of the script that became cuneiform. *Hulton-
Deutsch*

law, cuneiform writing, and myth-making. Their myths developed from
ritual. Sometimes they were politically united, sometimes not. The importance of Nippur as the religious center was permanent.[4]

Their economy was based on agriculture, but the cities were substantial,
with populations in the tens of thousands.[5] Each was dominated by the
temple of its chief god, usually in the form of a ziggurat, a kind of stepped
pyramid. Brick was the commonest building material. Most houses were
single storied with rooms grouped around a small court. The nobles had
extensive estates worked by slave labor, but even the poorest often had
plots of land of their own. Besides farmers and fishermen, Sumer's population included doctors, scribes, merchants (using a rudimentary kind of
money), masons, smiths, potters, jewelers. Sculpture flourished, and so did
poetry and music, played on harps, pipes, drums, and tambourines.

During the third millennium, the people of Akkad (or Agade) grew
powerful, farther up the rivers.[6] They were Mesopotamia's first Semites.
Their difference from the Sumerians was at first linguistic only. Their King
Sargon, the dates of whose reign are given as 2371 to 2316 B.C., conquered
Sumer but treated its religion and culture with respect. A partial Sumerian
recovery was ended by Hammurabi (1792 to 1750), who put together a
major Semitic state centered on the huge city of Babylon. Politically it
fluctuated. The old Babylonian empire did not maintain ascendancy long,
but Babylon continued as the center of civilization.

Within that framework an ethnic and cultural mix had taken shape.
Babylonian priests adopted Sumerian mythology and gave it new literary
forms. Some stories exist to this day in both Sumerian and Akkadian versions. While the latter are apt to be more accomplished, it is misleading
to draw a line between one corpus and the other.

The conception of a network of ancestral cities, founded by the Seven Sages, shows the seven mystique beginning to be functional as an ordering factor, a tool for mentally organizing life and the world at large. In the Indo-Aryan setting it is not. In the rising, creative societies of the Tigris and Euphrates it becomes so, with a climax in the seven-planet astrology. That culmination is a long time coming, and much happens along the way.

Another early septenary step involved a goddess, the mightiest and most beloved of the Sumerian pantheon. This was Inanna (Queen of Heaven).[7] She had a temple in each of seven cities, the set being possibly her own version of the civic heptad: Uruk, Badtibira, Zabalam, Adab, Nippur, Kish, and Akkad. Her temple in Uruk, now Warka, was probably the finest. It was called Eanna, the House of Heaven, and was about thirty by thirty meters in extent. The brick structure rested on a limestone base, which was unusual. Two aisles flanked a nave with a holy of holies at the end enshrining a statue of the goddess. An open court had walls enlivened with red, black, and yellow mosaic.[8]

Inanna, the goddess of love, procreation, and fertility, was spoken of sometimes as a manifest deity, sometimes as a woman, strong willed and passionate. On the whole she was beneficent, and she received popular homage expressed in seven hymns.[9] She was the goddess of the Morning and Evening Star, and in the eventual astrological scheme, where she had her Babylonian name Ishtar, this brightest planet continued to be hers. It is now, naturally, Venus.

Her most important myth is the oldest known version of one made famous by Frazer in *The Golden Bough*, introducing a young god who appears in various guises—for example, as Tammuz (mentioned in the Bible, Ezek. 8:14) and as Adonis.[10] He flourishes for a while, is slain, goes down to the realm of the dead, and returns. This cycle reflects rituals having to do with fertility and the seasons, from spring through summer to autumn and winter and back to spring. A goddess may play a part, as the god's mother or spouse or both, and she is originally the senior figure. In some cases her seniority is obscured, but Inanna takes us back toward beginnings and the primacy of the goddess.

Her consort is Dumuzi, or more fully Dumu-zid-absu, meaning Faithful Son of the Abyss.[11] Tammuz is a later version of him. He was probably a real person, a king of Uruk in about 2700 B.C., shortly before the epic hero Gilgamesh. The Sumerian myth has been pieced together from thirty-odd clay tablets unearthed at Nippur and Ur, dating from about 1750 B.C. The original is doubtless older, but not enormously so, since there has been time for Dumuzi to be mythified—say between 2500 and 2000 B.C. The myth is entitled *The Descent of Inanna*—that is, to the netherworld, pictured by Sumerians as the land of no return, a subterranean space corresponding to the space between earth and sky, though not so large. The dead went down to it through various openings, and eked out a wretched half-existence as shades.

In an exploit previous to her descent, Inanna had gone to Eridu and obtained tablets from the wisdom god Enki bearing the *me*, the divine ordinances governing civilized life.[12] On that occasion, as she journeyed back to Uruk, where her chief temple was, Enki tried to repossess the *me* and sent emissaries to seven places where Inanna paused, but she kept them and used them to benefit Uruk's citizens. Her temple there, with the other six, expressed her majesty on the earth's surface. But in the netherworld her sister Ereshkigal presided, together with seven fate-decreeing gods or judges, the Anunnaki. Inanna began to wonder about it.[13] She "opened her ear to the Great Below" and resolved to go down and visit her sister. Equipped with the seven principal *me* as talismans, she set off, leaving Dumuzi and her temples. A priestess, Ninshubur, had instructions to ask other deities for help if she failed to reappear.

Inanna wore a robe and crown, a gold bangle, and glittering beads. Protected, as she assumed, by the *me*, she descended. She had to pass through seven gates. By Ereshkigal's order, the gatekeeper explained that the rules of the netherworld required her to shed clothing or equipment at each gate. In Ereshkigal's palace she confronted her sister and the seven judges completely naked. Treating her as dead, they refused to let her go.

Ninshubur, back on the surface, persuaded Enki to intervene. Knowing that Ereshkigal was suffering pain, he created two tiny flylike animals, which went down to the netherworld and sympathized with Ereshkigal. Gratefully, she agreed to release her prisoner, but the judges decreed that Inanna must find a substitute.[14] The goddess made her way up again, recovering her garments and other gear but escorted by seven watchful demons. Reunited at Uruk with her consort Dumuzi, she found that he had been

Goddess, probably Inanna, on the right, with sacred tree and serpent; the unidentified figure on the left may be her priestess Ninshubur. *Mansell Collection*

enjoying her absence shamelessly, and she acquiesced in the demons' leading him below as the substitute her sister wanted. They smashed a reed pipe he was playing and upset seven churns of milk he had by him. With some difficulty they dragged him down to the netherworld. . . . For a long time the conclusion was lacking, and it was thought that the mythical cycle was not completed. However, a tablet published in 1963 showed that Dumuzi was allowed to return aboveground for half of the year.[15] When his spouse reappears in her Babylonian guise as Ishtar, a similar tale is told.

In terms of imagery, the main part of the story is not only septenary, it is a shamanic trance-descent to the underworld as performed by Altaic shamans—or shamanesses. Inanna dons a septenary outfit with septenary magical gear. On the way she passes through the ordeal of the seven gates, just as the shaman passes through the seven *pudak*, or obstacles. She faces an underworld deity with seven companions, as the shaman faces Erlik Khan with his seven sons and daughters. But Sumer's myth-makers have used the imagery to give structure and order to something that is not shamanic—the seasonal myth of a long-established agrarian world—and Inanna's ordeal takes an unshamanic form because the myth requires her to be reduced to the nullity of a shade. This adaptation raises the question of motive. The shaman undertakes the descent to intercede for a client in danger of death, or to escort the soul of one who actually is dead. Inanna does neither; the purpose of descent has been dropped. But nothing replaces it. She has no clear motive at all, and she gives the gatekeeper a reason for her visit that is so palpably a pretext that he does not even mention it to Ereshkigal. The story must get her down there somehow, and that's that. This is another case like the vanishing of the reason for Arundhati when the Seven Rishis appear as the Seven Sages. Here too, if there was influence at all, it went one way rather than the other.

Once adapted, of course, a theme can be adapted again. Inanna is a favorite with today's Goddess devotees, and some of them make her descent an equivalent for what Christian mystics call the Dark Night of the Soul.[16]

This myth witnesses to the early presence of the seven mystique in Sumer, and so do other details about Inanna—for example, that she rode in a chariot drawn by seven lions and was patroness of a city called Aratta beyond seven mountains, perhaps in Anshan in southwestern Iran.[17] Further proof comes from the cult of another goddess, Nintu, or Ninhursag. In about 2500 B.C., a king named Lugalannemundu, in Adab, built a temple for her. He called it Enamzu. It had seven gates and seven doors, all with names—the Lofty Gate, the Great Gate, the Gate of the Divine Decrees, the Lofty Door, the Door of Refreshing Shade, and so on. He dedicated the temple with a sacrifice of seven-times-seven oxen and fatted sheep.[18]

2

A serious question, however—some might say a make-or-break question. If the seven mystique came to Sumer with the western Indo-Aryans, and they alone were responsible for it, then they must have been in that part of Asia by 2500. Is there any evidence that they were? Indeed, could they have been? Do the priorities work? Does the chain of influence work? Until recently, conventional scholarship would have rejected all of this. No Indo-Aryans, no Indo-Europeans of any kind, could have been in contact with Sumer early enough. Today the studies by Renfrew and Mallory, in spite of their disagreements, have provided grounds for rethinking. So, perhaps, has a very curious artifact.

An etymological oddity deserves notice at once. Several languages of the Middle East, including Sumerian, have terms for a wheeled vehicle that are akin. The Sumerian is *gigir*, and there was an early Semitic form, *galgal*. A word allied to these is inferred in Proto-Indo-European. In the orthography used for this, it is k^wek^wlo.[19] The parallels reveal more than interchange. The Indo-European word would have been derived from another that denoted twisting or turning, rotary motion, as with a wheel. There is a logic here that is absent in the other languages. They seem to have taken over the "vehicle" word bodily. If so, the Indo-European is the original and the others stem from it. Therefore, Indo-European terminology made its way to the Middle East, including Sumer, extremely early.

This, however, is not much help with the Indo-Aryans. Since the seven mystique is in Sumer around the middle of the third millennium, influence from Indo-Aryans would require them to be in a position to affect Sumerians as far back as that. Sumer already had trading links eastward that might have extended as far as the Indus Valley, a fact, if it is a fact, that may momentarily suggest an alternative source.[20] The trouble is that Indo-Aryans were not there as yet, and according to the orthodoxy favored until lately, they were not anywhere else either. They still had no distinctive existence. Their ancestors were in the neighborhood of the Aral Sea or farther north, as part of an undifferentiated mass that included the Iranians' forebears as well. The arrival of recognizable Indo-Aryans in the Indus Valley was no earlier than 1500, and the *Rig Veda* was composed after that. True, it contained oral tradition of unknown age, preserved in the memories of preliterate priests. Ursa Major as the Seven Rishis, or something of the kind, may be much older. Even so, it could not have inspired the seven mystique in Sumer, because at any relevant date, the spatial gap would have been too wide.

But fresh possibilities are now being aired. Renfrew offers two hypotheses to account for Indo-Europeans in this part of the world.[21] He accepts that the conventional model may be correct but demotes it to hypothesis B. His own suggestion, hypothesis A, is that Indo-Europeans expanded from Asia Minor or thereabouts thousands of years before, advancing slowly eastward and eventually reaching India. Such a process could have provided Sumer with early Indo-European contacts. However, these people would not have been Indo-Aryan and would not have had the northern background. There would be no reason for the Seven Rishis or any other heptad in that setting. If, as Renfrew allows, hypothesis B is true as well, then India received Indo-Europeans in two waves, one from the west and one from the north. On his showing, the second wave would not have come close enough to Sumer, or come early enough.

Mallory's model is closer to orthodoxy, but with a difference.[22] He has Indo-Europeans drifting down from the north and dividing. He makes a crucial addition, or at least takes hold of a factor hitherto on the sidelines and gives it prominence. It is Mallory who has made it clear that the Indo-Aryans who got into India were not the only ones, and he has propelled the westerners onto the stage—the Indo-Aryans who could have planted the seven mystique in Sumer if they got there soon enough.

The septenary argument does not call for Indo-Aryans en masse. A wandering or scattered minority can make itself felt, as the dispersed Jews did in the Roman Empire. The traces of the western stream do suggest a minority, but an outstanding one: Prince Indaruta in Palestine, the gods in the Mitanni-Hittite treaty, the horse-training words among the Hittites, and the horse-color words among the Hurrians. These Indo-Aryans close the spatial gap. Perhaps they can close the temporal gap also.

That possibility is raised by a strange artifact, a metal head acquired in India by Harry H. Hicks and studied in the United States by the Foundation for Cultural Preservation, with the aid of Professor Robert Anderson and other scientists.[23] It was rescued from destruction in 1958 but not subjected to testing until long afterward. Approximately life-size, it is hollow, suggesting a skewed bell with a face, ears, and hair. The metal is a copper-zinc alloy. Its crystallization and other data are said to indicate an age of four or five thousand years, and carbon dating of a particle embedded inside is consistent with that, pointing, if anything, to greater rather than lesser antiquity. The composition of the metal would fit a source in Elamite country just east of Sumer, perhaps a mine at a place called Sialk.

Features of style show that the head represents an Indo-Aryan god, and an inscription on its base, added much later, identifies him as "ancient Narayana." Narayana was a god and ancient indeed. When Vishnu rose to supremacy in Hinduism, Narayana was reduced to an aspect of him, and in the *Mahabharata* "Narayana" is used as a synonym for Vishnu; but passages in the epic—the churning of the ocean, for instance—may give archaic glimpses of independent divinity.

Archaeologically, the metal head stands alone. The group that studied it saw its implication for early Indo-Aryan presence but focused on the better-known Indus Valley context. This is a long way from Elam and they were following a false trail. Their artifact should have led them to the western Indo-Aryans. If valid, it means that they were near Sumer in the third millennium B.C. and could have introduced the seven mystique.

Mallory's scheme of Indo-European movement shows how they might have gotten there on time, bearing the mystique from the shamanic north. He has Indo-Europeans around the Altai by 3000 B.C. or earlier, the Afanasievo culture. From here and from the neighboring steppes expansion goes southward and southwest, creating the Andronovo culture. Within this the Indo-Aryan element takes shape, and some of the Indo-Aryans reach the Indus Valley while others branch off as the western group.

If the metal head is set aside, the objection is as before: we have no evidence for the western ones prior (say) to the sixteenth century B.C. Yet that is an argument from silence only, in a context of scanty records. We find some of their gods in the Mitanni treaty and not before, but there is no firm basis for the inference that no Indo-Aryans were there before. In Mallory's own words, "the symbiosis that produced the Mitanni may have taken place centuries earlier," and "the discovery of a single datable text could advance the Indo-Aryans to greater antiquity in the Near East."[24] Ceramic studies by Roman Ghirshman point to people who may have been "Proto-Indic" southeast of the Caspian Sea in the third millennium.[25] Perhaps it was only among the Mitanni that the western Indo-Aryans grew important enough for their gods to be named in treaties. Such a process could have taken an indefinitely long time, and if it did, it started indefinitely far back.

The possible story is that Indo-Europeans were near the Altai by 3000 or sooner and in contact with shamanism; that descendants drifted south, and some created a partly shamanic Indo-Aryan mythology; and that further drifts took this to the Mesopotamian neighborhood by 2500. The chronology is rather tight, and the views of the Soviet archaeologist V. Dergachev, who puts the Afanasievo culture later, would tighten it further. However, radiocarbon dating does indicate a beginning by 3000. The generations carrying their motifs to Mesopotamia would have had to traverse fifteen hundred miles in five hundred years. That may be on the fast side for folk wanderings, but these particular folk could have been mobile, not tied down by rooted farming commitments. Some theories of Indo-European expansion have assumed a similar pace, and the Russians crossed Siberia much faster in the course of the sixteenth and seventeenth centuries A.D.

A supportive fact is the history of the domesticated horse. Horses were probably brought to the Middle East from Indo-European country. As

Sumerian horse-drawn chariots on battlefield:
mosaic from Ur. *Hulton-Deutsch*

noted, Indo-Aryan terms were employed in equine matters. That was where
the expertise lay, and was known to lie. Previously, wheeled vehicles in
Sumer were drawn by oxen or asses. Cuneiform texts begin to mention
horses in the latter half of the third millennium, after which both the horse
and the horse-drawn chariot enjoy widening popularity.[26] This timing agrees
quite well with the Indo-Aryan advent around 2500, bringing horses. Those
who brought them could have brought mythic and religious motifs as well,
such as their interpretation of Ursa Major.

To indulge a fancy . . . a Sumerian king hears of the wonderful creature
and imports a few dozen with their Indo-Aryan trainers. He happens to
mention the link between holy Nippur, once a city of gods, and the seven-
star constellation seen as vehicular. A trainer replies: "Ah, yes, Sire. We
believe that those seven stars are the Seven Seers, the source of all earthly
wisdom." The process has begun . . .

3

Sumer had many deities.[27] They ranged over the world like Inanna, but,
like her, had cities especially their own. The four principal were An, the
sky god, a very ancient figure; Enlil, Lord Air, king of the gods, bestower
of sovereignty and patron of Nippur; Enki, god of fresh water, the wise

being who befriended Inanna; and Nintu, or Ninhursag, the Lady of the Mountain, who started her career as an earth goddess under the name of Ki. Prominent besides these were Nanna, the moon god of Ur; his son Utu, the sun god; and Inanna herself, who fitted into the pantheon as Utu's sister. The Anunnaki whom Inanna met in the netherworld were sons of An. Babylonians adopted these gods and goddesses with changes of name. An became Anu, Enki became Ea, Nanna became Sin.

While these leading deities were seven, they were far from being the only ones, and they were not treated as a heptad. However, the conception of a principal seven emerged, like the conception of seven cities, and a ziggurat at Borsippa, built in the twelfth century B.C., had seven tiers and was called the Temple of the Seven Rulers of Heaven and Earth. When the planets came to be seen in this light, their definition as a heptad was a logical consequence.

We cannot get behind the pantheon to the hypothetical reign of the Goddess. Not directly, at any rate. Inanna may date from before 3000 B.C., and her style, "Queen of Heaven," implies some kind of supremacy, but in the cuneiform records she is a composite, and divine colleagues generally are present as well.[28] She has been given relationships to them, just as Greek goddesses, such as Aphrodite and Artemis, formerly independent of Zeus, were attached to his family by his myth-makers. As the daughter of Nanna, himself a son of Enlil, she is not even senior. Some would add that the dead-end negativity of the netherworld reflects a god-centered view of human destiny already established; and it is a god, Enki, not a goddess, who saves Inanna from it. There is certainly a case for detecting the masculine gaining ground and inferring an earlier implied Female who is being reduced, dismembered, denigrated. The question is whether the present line of inquiry is any help in suggesting what happened, and in showing to what extent, if any, Indo-European intrusion was to blame.

Here enters Gilgamesh. In early Inanna texts he is her earthly brother, friendly to her. He was apparently a king of Uruk in about 2650 B.C., Dumuzi's successor. As a mythified hero he is the leading character in a long epic.[29] This was popular, and there were several versions, even translations. It has been pieced together from fragments that are not always consistent. The story was taking shape in Sumer during the latter part of the third millennium, and most of it reached its present form in Akkadian during the early centuries of the second. Inanna has become Ishtar, and her role, though brief, is eloquent of a shift in attitudes. The whole story is worth reviewing, partly because of a passage relevant to the Bible and partly to show the persistence of the seven mystique in Babylonia. Sevens are sprinkled through it. Mostly they are not central like Inanna's, and to pick them out of the text is to make them look more important than they are, but they do have a cumulative effect.

The epic tells how Gilgamesh wished to perform a deed that would leave a lasting reputation.[30] He would go to the Land of the Living and bring back some of its wonderful cedars. He set out with some companions, the chief of them being his friend Enkidu, a sort of Tarzan who had distinguished himself by copulating with a harlot for six days and seven nights and rapidly swallowing seven goblets of wine. Leaving Uruk, which had a gate with seven bolts, they crossed seven mountains. Gilgamesh foresaw trouble with the forest's giant guardian, Huwawa, or Humbaba, who was a "sevenfold terror" with seven coats of armor. However, they succeeded in chopping down some cedars. Gilgamesh felled the tree of his choice with a bronze ax weighing seven talents and seven minas, over four hundred pounds.[31] Aided by Enkidu he slew Huwawa, and they returned to Uruk in triumph.

As a result, Ishtar fell in love with him. (Their brother-sister relationship has dropped out; "brother" may always have been employed loosely to mean a cousin.) He repelled her advances, reminding her of the fate of previous male partners of hers—Dumuzi, for instance. He also accused her of cruelty to animals: she had dug seven pits to trap a lion and whipped a stallion to make him run seven leagues. Ishtar, now a woman scorned and a fury, complained to the sky god Anu. Seven years' drought ensued, and the death of Gilgamesh's friend Enkidu. He watched by the corpse for seven days and nights till a worm fell out of its nose and decomposition was palpable. Grief followed grief. His friend's death oppressed him with the horror of mortality. He went to consult the one immortal human couple, Utnapishtim and his wife, who lived far off. Utnapishtim was the chief survivor of the Flood.

His special status needs explaining. Flood myths are numerous, but in Mesopotamia the theme was given unusual weight by folk memories of real inundations.[32] Sir Leonard Woolley, excavating at Ur in low-lying country toward the Persian Gulf, found a deep stratum of silt with traces of human occupation above and below. The silt had been laid down by a deluge of muddy water. Neither Woolley nor anyone else found evidence that this was widespread, but with lesser disasters of the same type it would have played its part in the making of tradition. A Sumerian account of the Flood treats it as a definite break—history is divided into pre-Flood and post-Flood.[33] Sumer's Noah is a king named Ziusudra, who is divinely warned and rides the waves in a boat. The Flood lasts seven days and nights. Afterward the gods make Ziusudra immortal, and he goes away to Dilmun, an earthly paradise in "the place where the Sun rises."

Utnapishtim is Ziusudra's Babylonian equivalent. The epic tells how Gilgamesh reached his distant retreat and heard about the Flood at some length. Utnapishtim explained that it was caused by a cabal of gods, chiefly Enlil, with a view to destroying an unsatisfactory human race. Ea (Enki restyled) had misgivings and warned Utnapishtim, advising him to build a ship, which he did. His ark had seven decks. In seven days' work it was completed, and he loaded his family, craftsmen, and goods aboard, together with animals. The weather grew "frightful to behold" and he shut the door. At dawn a black cloud surged over the horizon, followed by a tempest of lightning, thunder, and rain. Water covered the land.

On the seventh day, the storm died down and the sea quieted. The ark came to rest on Mount Nisir, Pir Omar Gudrun in the Zagros range. After another seven days Utnapishtim sent out a dove, which returned; then a swallow, which also returned; then a raven, which did not, having found dry land. The water was subsiding. He disembarked and offered sacrifice, using "seven and seven cult-vessels." Enlil was angry at his escape, but Ea defended him, and Enlil relented and made Utnapishtim and his wife immortal like gods. They were sent away to live "at the mouth of the rivers," this abode also being a kind of paradise.

Utnapishtim tested the hero's own will for immortality by seeing how long he could stay awake. Gilgamesh, exhausted by travel, fell asleep almost at once and slept for seven days. Utnapishtim's wife baked a loaf of bread every day he slept, and she proved the lapse of time when he woke by showing that each was at a different stage of freshness. Though Gilgamesh had failed the test, Utnapishtim told him of a plant growing beneath the sea that would restore youth. Gilgamesh dived down and plucked it, but on the way home a serpent stole it from him. At last he accepted the evanescence of life and returned to Uruk, reflecting on its enduring walls, the work of the Seven Sages.

In this poem the hero rejects the goddess, and she is vengeful and unlovely. While she is not explicitly blamed for his final loss, the artistic association of serpents with goddess figures, clearly attested in Mesopotamia, should not be forgotten. The change in the Gilgamesh-goddess relationship and the change in her character are symptomatic.

Another Babylonian work projects the shift in attitude into cosmic realms, evoking a primordial female in order to damn her and make her horrible, but nevertheless evoking her, not denying her. This is the epic of creation.[34] It was composed, in substance, about the time of Hammurabi, in the eighteenth century B.C. There may have been an earlier version, and the text as we now have it may include matter that is later. There are gaps and ambiguities. Priests recited it in Babylon on the fourth day of the Spring New Year Festival as a rite of cosmic renewal. The king had a key role in the ceremonies, going through a ritual of abdication and reenthronement and entering into a sacred marriage.[35]

Scholars refer to the epic by its first words, *Enuma elish*, meaning "When on high." It confronts us once again with the seven mystique, because it is divided into seven sections or chapters written on seven tablets, but the mystique is far less marked. Its story is thronged and elaborate.[36] The Creator is Marduk, otherwise Bel, the presiding god of Babylon, but unlike the God of Genesis he is not there "in the beginning." There is no beginning in the biblical sense. Primordial chaos is a preworld of dream or nightmare.[37] The oldest being is Tiamat, a sort of ocean mother. Directly or indirectly she is the source of all other beings. That is admitted. But from the epic's standpoint she is evil. She is the femininity of a repudiated past—the Goddess, advocates of the Goddess might say—converted into a monster, nowhere described in detail, but repulsive; probably a kind of dragon. In the same spirit the Titans of Greek mythology, the gods who reigned before Zeus's Olympians, were made out in retrospect to be violent and barbaric. Greek rewriters of myth could not efface the tradition that their reign was the golden age, so the Titans remained ambiguous. Any such attributes of Tiamat are suppressed. She has no redeeming features.

When the epic opens she has evolved two companions, Apsu and Mummu, personifying fresh water and clouds.[38] Out of the waters' commingling the gods and goddesses emerge. Ea becomes their chief. Apsu complains that they are turbulent and subversive and disturb his peace. Ea forestalls an attempt by the elder beings to wipe them out, paralyzing Mummu by a magical spell and killing Apsu. To effect a *revanche* Tiamat generates a demonic army.

All of the deities are alarmed. By now, Marduk has appeared on the scene. His father is Ea, though in some sense he is the son of the pantheon collectively. He agrees to tackle Tiamat if the others will vest him with sovereign authority and the power to work miracles. At a gathering lubricated by drink, they agree to his terms. Marduk's principal weapons are winds.[39] He stations four of them to prevent any escape and prepares to attack Tiamat with seven more—the Evil Wind, the Whirlwind, the Hurricane, the Fourfold Wind, the Sevenfold Wind, the Cyclone, and the Matchless Wind. As he nears the monster in his chariot, he flings a net over her. She opens her jaws and he drives the winds into her body and inflates it, then shoots an arrow into her heart—an archetypal dragon-slaying. Her cohorts, including their commander, Kingu, are rounded up.

The author has not yet come to creation at all. When he does, it is a byproduct of Marduk's victory, even an afterthought. To do something constructive with Tiamat's corpse, the god splits it into upper and lower halves, forming an internal space, and this is the universe; we are all inside her.[40] Her upper half is the sky. There he makes places for the appropriate gods, including the sun and moon. He creates the stars and Nebiru (Jupiter). *Enuma elish* mentions no other planets, and the astrologers' conceptions are still far off. Having lit up Tiamat's colossal interior, Marduk turns his attention to her lower half, where the earth is. With Ea he makes human beings out of the blood of Kingu.[41] The purpose is strictly utilitarian, to provide creatures who will serve him and his colleagues with worship and sacrifice.

Order has replaced chaos. The assembled divinities build Marduk a temple in Babylon, confirm him in his supremacy, and hail him as "the Son, our avenger." The end of the epic's sixth tablet and the whole of the seventh are taken up with their paean of praise to him under fifty titles. One is Nebiru, showing that Jupiter is already his planet.[42]

The Assyrians, who for a time ruled over Babylonia, adopted this myth. An Assyrian seal depicts Marduk fighting Tiamat, though not with enough detail to be interesting.[43] What is more impressive, indeed startling, is the theme's reappearance later, though its sexual aspect fades out. Ancient Israel's creation story in Genesis also has a watery primeval chaos, but it is depersonalized; God is alone, he has no enemies to overcome before his creative work begins. In Christianity, however, Babylonian motifs creep back. Christians developed a belief that before the foundation of the world many angels rebelled under Satan's leadership and were cast out of heaven, becoming devils. The scriptural basis is Rev. 12:7–9, a text that speaks of war in heaven and gives Satan a dragon form, which commentators have seen as a direct echo of Tiamat.[44] Christians ventured farther along the Babylonian path, maintaining that our world was a consequence of the Evil One's overthrow. God resolved to create it and stock it with humans so that new creatures could fill the gap left by the angels' fall.

These ideas attain their supreme literary handling in *Paradise Lost*, where the story told to Adam by the archangel Raphael, in the fifth, sixth, and seventh books, is a Christian counterpart of *Enuma elish*. Some of the parallels are striking and a few are extraordinary, since Milton could not have known the epic.[45] Whether that is an argument for Jungian archetypes, there is no need to debate. The notable point is the ability of such motifs to persist.

Milton shows that the persistence can be traced forward into other cultures. Can it also be traced backward? Is *Enuma elish* itself a kind of *Paradise Lost*? Did it grow out of imported imagery, as Inanna's descent seemingly did? In this case, there is no record of anything much like it in shamanistic mythology. But in the *Rig Veda* there is. It has several discrepant creation stories, some of them primitive. One of these could have supplied hints for Marduk and Tiamat. The god Indra is hailed as the slayer of a dragon, Vritra, and his victory has cosmic results. The world, or some of it, is formed through the dragon's destruction.

1 Let me now sing the heroic deeds of Indra, the first that the thunderbolt-wielder performed. He killed the

> *dragon and pierced an opening for the waters; he split*
> *open the bellies of the mountains . . .*

> 4 *Indra, when you killed the first-born of dragons and*
> *overcame by your own magic the magic of the magi-*
> *cians, at that very moment you brought forth the sun,*
> *the sky, and dawn. Since then you have found no*
> *enemy to conquer you.*[46]

If these verses embody a myth of Indo-Aryans before the branching off of the western group, that group might have taken it with them—together with the Seven Rishis and other mythical baggage—and passed it on to Mesopotamia, where a blending with indigenous themes could have built up the creation epic. The Mitanni-Hittite treaty shows that Indra was among their gods.

While the seven mystique is not conspicuous in the epic, apart from its overall structure, Mesopotamia provides further instances. The seven-note scale, C D E F G A B or the equivalent, was known in Sumer in the third millennium B.C. A relief portraying a harpist shows a harp with seven strings. Other heptads include the seven heads of a dragonlike monster on a seal dating from 2350 to 2150 B.C. They also include "seven ill winds, the seven whirlwinds which stir up the dust," called the Seven-of-the-Battle. The Sumerians had a set of seven demons personifying bad weather.[47]

A mother of seven is mentioned in a proverbial or colloquial way, as also in the Bible (1 Sam. 2:5—"the barren has borne seven"). The author of a prayer confesses that his transgressions are seven times seven. There are cryptic allusions to "seven lyres standing at the horizon" and to a "house directed by the seven lyre-songs, given over to incantation." The lyre songs might have been sung in a mythical seven-day festival at the foundation of a temple, attended by gods.

Babylonia, with its Semitic Akkadian language, adds two further points peculiar to itself. One is evidence for the promotion of seven to philosophical status. In Akkadian, "seven" comes to stand for wholeness.[48] That may shed further light on the listing of seven celestial bodies as the "whole" planetary system.

The other point concerns Semitic languages generally. If Indo-European languages are compared with them, the overlap is slight. Few words are shared; the two linguistic families are almost distinct. The difference comes out in such basics as the series of numerals up to ten. With these, however, there is a solitary exception. Names for seven do have a likeness. The Proto-Indo-European "seven" is reconstructed as *septm*. In its assumed counterpart, Proto-Semitic, "seven" is *sab'*.[49] According to philologists the two words are more akin than they look, and it does not take a philologist to contrast the total dissimilarity of the rest. Coincidence, surely, not influence. Yet an Indo-European seven could have been more acceptable as strong magic to speakers of Semitic languages if its echoes in those languages carried a hint of preordination.

4

At this point, feminist historical models can be tentatively tested. Here is an ancient civilization with plentiful records. It is fair to ask whether, in Mesopotamia, a Goddess-focused "gylanic" society does appear to have given way to a patriarchal or "androcentric" one, with male gods reflecting and sanctifying male power. It also is fair to ask whether, if such a change happened, Indo-European incursions played any part in it. Some feminists do assert this, though they look to a later wave, not Indo-Aryan, a theory that presents chronological difficulties.

Sumer's laws reveal a society that was male-dominated but not exclusively so.[50] Government and officialdom were male. Women had significant rights—to hold property, for instance, and to engage in business. On the other hand, a husband could divorce his wife on slight grounds, and if she was childless, he could marry another. Some historians have claimed that a comparison of different periods shows a decline in women's status. The present question is whether there were religious changes, or importations from outside, that correlated in any way with society.

Once again, we cannot get behind the known pantheon to a Goddess era. The Goddess, in Gimbutan terms, might have been supreme once, but the only real hint is in the creation epic, and little can be inferred about her nature from the hateful Tiamat. The epic doubtless implies a religious shift, and the reduction of regal Inanna to spiteful Ishtar certainly does. But the beginnings are lost in mist. Golden-age mythology is no help, because Mesopotamians did not look back to such an age in any specific way. They did have its corollary, a notion of degeneration, as in Greece and India. This, however, was expressed in limited and entirely male terms. Ancient kings were said to have lived fabulously long, and Gilgamesh's colossal ax has implications about his size and strength. As the Bible puts it, there were giants in those days. But nothing is said about giantesses.[51]

As for the early Indo-European incursion, now hypothetically Indo-Aryan, if it happened as it seems to have happened, it was an incursion of influence, not a conquest. It came in male-oriented motifs, and that quality carried over. The Seven Rishis, male, became the Seven Sages, also male. The creative monster-slaying of Indra, male, may have suggested the comparable deed of Marduk, also male. But it does not follow that the Rishis or Indra affected the existing bias of religion or myth-making. Sumerians were quite equal to adopting imported themes in goddess contexts without any alteration of gender. In the story of Inanna's descent there may have been masculine encroachment, but it comes in the person of a Sumerian god, Enki. There is no sign that the imposition of all the sevens has anything to do with it.

Inanna's colleague Nintu offers a clue to the course of events. Her temple at Adab, with its seven gates and doors and its dedication with seven-times-seven sacrifices, was the work of a king in about 2500 B.C. Lugalannemundu is alleged to have reigned for ninety years and made Sumer, briefly, a powerful empire.[52] However wildly his career has been exaggerated, the temple had a political point. Rebellious *ensis* (regional rulers) had been brought to heel on all sides. Envoys came to the dedication from several tributary lands, including Elam to the east, which was vital to the Sumerian economy. The record ends with a prayer that Nintu may grant long life to the *ensis* of these lands, on the understanding that they will bring offerings to her Adab temple.

Here Nintu and the seven mystique are associated with a display of majesty. Mesopotamian mythology stresses the institution of kingship, which reputedly had a beginning and descended from heaven.[53] Whether or not it descended from heaven, it did have a beginning. According to one theory it arose from military needs. According to another it arose—in Sumer, as elsewhere—from ritual customs corresponding to the "young god" seasonal myth. Formerly, a priestess-queen, representing the Goddess, was a fixture; her consort, representing the god, was a sacred king who reigned for a set period (originally perhaps only a year) and then was put to death. Then came a time when kings asserted themselves and refused to die, and their rise to dominance began.

It may be so. Kingship at any rate appeared, and Sumer's ministates were drawn together in varying combinations by the varying relative power of their sovereigns. Monarchy brought expanded organization, building, public works such as irrigation, and, of course, warfare. Such things involved coercion and mobility, physical strength and violence, and were inevitably for men more than women. If there was a shift in relations between the sexes, these are enough to account for it. As for Sumer's goddess figures, royal building programs could include temples for them, like Nintu's; they could remain popular and, within limits, powerful; but their accommodation to a god-governed pantheon was a natural process.

All of this could have been internal. Subversion from outside is superfluous. Indo-Aryans may have introduced horses and horse-drawn chariots, useful in war and therefore advantageous to kings, but this was incidental.[54] The Indo-Aryan factors affecting thoughts and attitudes seem to have been subtler.

Within Mesopotamia the seven mystique is unexplained. It is simply there. Its Indo-Aryan importation, if accepted, may be seen as bringing not a change in religion or society, but a new kind of mental ordering—a numerical ordering of life and the world and the forces governing both. While at first it may have been purely mythic or magical, it led to Babylonian astrology and the immense effect astrology had. It also spread into other lands, with even more sweeping consequences.

If it began as part of a shamanic package and was carried by Indo-Europeans, we have a double provisional conclusion—thus far, provisional only—that is curious and ironic. Indo-Europeans did influence Mesopotamia, as some feminists assert, but not at all in the way asserted. And the influence they brought with them was rooted in the far northland, an implied primary Goddess country, but its Goddess content had (on the face of it) been lost on the way.

CHAPTER NINE

The Bonded World

1

The septenary thread was not all. Another was interwoven with it. The numerical ordering factor was accompanied by a spatial one.

In India the Seven Rishis were linked with Mount Meru. To demythologize that statement (partly at least), Ursa Major, circling the celestial pole, was linked with a world center. This was the hub and heart of the universe, golden, god-inhabited, paradisal. Around Meru in one guise or another the whole panoply of earth and heavens was built. Behind the Hindu image we have reason to detect a shamanic package, drifting down from the Altaic region. Meru as a developed myth is absent from the *Rig Veda*, which does not go beyond the ill-defined *skambha*, or world axis. But it could have been known to the western Indo-Aryan branch. The Iranians' reduced version of the mountain as *Harā* (alias Elbruz) shows not only that the motif reached the Middle East but that it was probably Indo-European. Meru could have passed from there to the Hindus at a later stage. Otherwise it is hard to see how it reached India at all, complete with the Altaic goldenness and geography that did not go by way of the *Rig Veda*.

If the western Indo-Aryans brought the Seven Rishis to Sumer, did they also bring the linked motif of Mount Meru? Or, again to demythologize somewhat, if they transmitted the seven mystique, did they also transmit the linked motif of cosmic centrality? Did Mesopotamians impart order to their world by structuring it around a center? And if so, did they work this out for themselves or are there any signs that in this too they were influenced by the Indo-Aryans?

Ideas of centrality in themselves prove nothing. The people of a country often have believed that some particular place was central to it. Druids used to assemble at what they imagined to be the center of Gaul, probably Chartres. Welshmen, to judge from a legend in the *Mabinogion*, indulged the bizarre fancy that Britain's central point was Oxford.[1] As ideas of earth as a whole developed, ideas of a central place for the whole earth sometimes developed with them, on the assumption, of course, that the earth was flat. Peking and Cuzco were both cast in that role. But Mesopotamians, in common with Hindus, as well as with Greeks and Jews, related centrality to an image of the earth's shape that was a beginning of world geography.

As in the Hindu scheme, it was regarded as a disk. Peripheral water surrounded the home of humankind, which was a circular landmass, possibly rising from the rim to the center. In Hebrew this was the *tebel*. When Greeks came to write about it they dubbed it the *oecumene*, or "inhabited world." Romans used the term *orbis terrarum*, "circle of lands," though they realized, as did the Greeks by then, that the outer rim was not smoothly circular.[2] Greeks partitioned the landmass into three divisions, Europe, Asia, and Libya—that is, North Africa. Most of its rivers ran directly or indirectly into the Mediterranean, and the water found its way out via the Straits of Gibraltar. It flowed into the girdling ocean; "ocean" probably means "that which surrounds." Ocean was the greatest river of all, perpetually circling counterclockwise.

Sumerians never got as far as this. Babylonians were not so specific or quasi-geographic, but their conception was akin. They called the peripheral water the Earthly Ocean, to distinguish it from the Heavenly Ocean above the sky, and the Bitter River. A Babylonian map, ascribed to the fifth century B.C. but embodying older ideas, portrays the landmass as a neat circle with the Earthly Ocean surrounding it.[3] The cartographer, as he may politely be called, feels that this diagram is not enough. Spaced out around in the Earthly Ocean like rays of a star are seven triangular islands (seven!). While they cannot be identified with real islands, the captions show traces of hearsay knowledge. In an easterly island "the sun rises," in the northern one the sun is "not seen," and the northwestern island is a place of "semi-obscurity."

In this map, Babylon is at the world's center. Unlike Hindus with their faraway Meru, Mesopotamians recognized an earthly center in their own country, though originally it was not Babylon. Given an increasingly urban society it was natural for a city to have that status. As in one or two other countries, a more precise conception took hold. It has been defined as "hierocentric."[4]

Its older versions date from an era when people were still thinking of the territory they knew rather than of the world as a whole. The central point of the known land was a particular city and, more than that, a particular sacred precinct at its heart, a temple. Centrality was not so much a matter of measurement as of focusing. It was there that lines of force, so to speak, converged; it was a threefold mystical bond—among the districts of the land, between surface and underworld, between earth and heaven. A word sometimes used was *dimgal*, meaning a binding post, and the emphasis in earliest times was on the bond-of-the-land aspect. The temple was a visual bond, a landmark seen from afar over flat country. But the binding post extended down, though invisibly, and libations were poured to the deities of the underworld, apparently through actual pipes.

Several Sumerian temples filled this role, when rulers and worshipers looked no farther than a fairly restricted neighborhood. Then, with widening contacts, Nippur rose to its paramountcy. It became the sacred center of Sumer and, in a vague way, of the world, with Enlil's temple marking the exact spot. Here the god had cleft the earth's crust and ushered the first humans into daylight.[5] Nippur's centrality was confirmed by its pairing with Ursa Major, which was the "bond of heaven," just as the temple was the bond of the world below. A map drawn in about 1500 B.C. shows that Nippur then had seven gates.[6] This applies to a period long after it had lost its importance and long after the advent of the seven mystique. The number may be accidental, since the arrangement of the gates has no symmetry. Still, it is interesting.

Such claims passed to Babylon when Nippur declined and centrality shifted to the younger metropolis. Babylon was more explicitly the world center. Its focus was the temple of its patron Marduk, built for him, according to the creation epic, after his victory over Tiamat. However, the "bond" spread out and embraced the royal palace, because with the growth of imperial power, bonding gained a political aspect.

While there could be echoes here of shamanic notions about a world center and a post representing it, nothing, so far, need imply outside influence. Nothing like Meru has come within sight as yet. Nevertheless, with further elaboration, a kind of Meru becomes involved.

The Sumerians seem not to have had a creation myth like the slaying of Tiamat. Their story was more impersonal.[7] Long ago a vast mountain rose from primordial waters. At first a single mass, it split into earth below and heaven above. The split was not total. Somewhere, a residual Mountain of Heaven and Earth soared skyward. It was frequented by gods. On it the sky god An had created the fate-decreeing seven, the Anunnaki. An, however, had yielded primacy to Enlil, Lord Air, and the mountain was principally his.[8]

It seems to have been revered in the earliest times as a source of strength and fertility.[9] Enlil's winds wafted its energies over Sumer. Sumerians were hazy about its location. Another name for it was the Mountain of the Aromatic Cedar, which could reflect knowledge of the Zagros range to the northeast, or Lebanon.[10] The mountain, however, was never identified with an actual one. Like Meru it caused the alternation of day and night. At nightfall the sun dipped in the west and made a circuit, bringing it around behind the mountain. Dawn's first light began to gleam when it emerged on the other side, so that the mountain contained "the place of sunrise," a phrase that rules out Lebanon.[11]

Sumerians believed in an earthly paradise, Dilmun, where their flood survivor Ziusudra lived. It was said to be in the sunrise place and therefore, we may conclude, on or near the mountain. Dilmun was pure, clean, bright, and peaceful, without sickness or death. Originally it lacked fresh water, so Enki arranged for water to well up from below and make it fertile. Dilmun, however, is puzzling, and it betrays an inconsistency. Despite its sunrise aspect, there are pointers to southwestern Iran and even Bahrain, and also references to a real Dilmun, a source of gold, silver, dates, and ivory goods, that continued to flourish after Sumer's eclipse.[12]

The mountain, and, in some sense, Dilmun, carried over into Akkadian literature and the *Epic of Gilgamesh*. When he goes on his quest for Utnapishtim he arrives at the mountain.[13] It has a name, Mashu. Its twin peaks reach the vault of heaven, its "breasts" reach the netherworld below, and it is guarded by monstrous creatures. They allow the hero to pass. He follows the occult solar path—here it seems to be a twisting tunnel inside—and comes out at the sunrise place, finding a jeweled garden. But this is not Dilmun, because Dilmun is where Utnapishtim lives and Gilgamesh still has a long journey ahead of him.

The data now begin to mesh with India and the northland. Representation of the mountain was an accepted motif, as in places eastward. Mesopotamia had its counterparts of the Hindu *vimanas*, the Khmer pyramids, and Borobudur. This was the primary inspiration of the ziggurat, which began as a sacred mound, an artificial mountain that was a replica or magical model of the great one.[14] The ziggurat concentrated its life-giving energies. Temples grew more architectural, ziggurats developed into stepped pyramids, and the motif persisted. The rapport between temple and mountain—in effect, their mystical identity—was a means of divine communication.

This process enhanced the hierocentric majesty of Nippur. When the holy city was at its height, Enlil's temple was the Ekur, meaning the Mountain House.[15] He sometimes was called the Great Mountain himself. One of his temple's epithets was Duranki, the Bond of Heaven and Earth. As such it was expressly declared to be "in the centre of the four corners of the universe." ("Corners" probably refers to quarters rather than angles; the Sumerian who hit on the above phrase no more implied that the world was square than Shakespeare, who referring to its *three* corners, implied that it was triangular.)

Several hymns underline Enlil's sovereignty and the Ekur's significance. The temple "rose like the sun," built "in accordance with the great *me*," the divine ordinances. One hymn says that the Ekur itself is "a mountain great" and that "in its midst is the Mountain of the Aromatic Cedar." The two are equivalent. Where one is present, so is the other. Enlil's claim, however, was not absolute. Inanna had temples of her own—the Mountain of the Land, the Bond of Heaven and Earth, and the Dilmun House.[16] Still, she acknowledged Enlil's supremacy, and he, for his part, granted her the exclusive right to enter his Ekur without asking permission.

A larger representational building was the giant ziggurat in Babylon called the Etemenanki, Temple Foundation of Heaven and Earth.[17] It was more than two hundred feet high, with external steps and ramps going up through seven stories of lessening size to a holy of holies on the seventh. Herodotus, who describes the Etemenanki, makes it eight. But he is counting the summit structure, which was probably like the big central stupa on the top story of Borobudur.

2

At some stage the mystical correspondence of temple and mountain became involved with cosmology. The temple at the earthly center, at Nippur or Babylon, was a triple "bond," and while two of its bondings were straightforward, the third was not. It easily could be the bond of the land, as a focus of divine forces and human activity and more prosaically as a landmark. It could be the bond of surface and underworld, a point of contact with subterranean powers. But the third bonding, of earth and heaven, grew more complicated.

Ritually it could be symbolized by the priests of a mountain-imitating temple, with their upward track to the summit and the encounter with gods.[18] But ocular observation raised a troublesome issue. If a central temple was a bond uniting the universe, this ought to mean that an invisible shaft or pillar ran up from it to the zenith and the starry dome spun around the top. Yet this was obviously not so. The heavens did not revolve around the zenith at Nippur or Babylon, they revolved around a pole away to the north, at the hub (more or less) of the circle traced by Ursa Major.[19]

Hindus were well aware of that fact, and Meru gave them the answer, presenting no problem because there was no earthly center in India; Meru in the far north could be the center of everything. But Mesopotamians did have an earthly center, whether at Nippur or Babylon. To conserve unity they carried representation further.[20] The earthly center was linked with the celestial pole, and its rapport with the mountain took a more specific form, because it was now the mountain itself that had to be the bond of heaven and earth. It had to become a cosmic peak upholding the sky, with the dome of stars pivoted on it and turning around it. Logically it now should have been given a location in the north. In practice this was not spelled out. Mesopotamian ideas had taken shape within a confined geography and could not expand with any assurance. The mountain remained an undefined mass, stretching across a region that was mostly, by implication, in a higher latitude but was no more precise than that.

Scholars have recognized that Meru and the Mesopotamian mountain were related. Some have argued that Meru was first, some the opposite. But if either inspired the other, Meru had the priority. It is a single universal center; it is unified and coherent; it is paradisal; it has a location; it can be derived credibly from the actual Altai. What Mesopotamia offers has the air of a Meru disintegrated, or a conception partially cobbled together from features of it. The images are scattered, scrappy, incoherent. There are gaps. To take an obvious point, no cuneiform text is explicit about the mountain being northern at all. Its direction can be inferred vaguely from the sun's nocturnal transit behind it, but that is not saying much. It is possible to assemble the pieces and contrive a cosmic mountain something like Meru, but only on the basis of extensive modern research. Myth-makers thousands of years ago could not have done it; no such artificial construct could have traveled to India and become the Meru we know. Also, Meru's apparent traces of a shamanic source, and its apparent echoes of actual geography, have no Mesopotamian equivalents. It was brought there, let us say, by the western Indo-Aryans, and it made an impression on the mythology of the region, but in Sumer and Babylonia it was not fully acclimatized.

Nevertheless we have a second ordering factor linked with the seven mystique—a spatial factor, organizing the universe and preparing the way both for real geography and for potent storytelling, about an earthly paradise, for instance. In Mesopotamia the disk-earth was focused on a central city, a central holy place. At Nippur with its seven gates possibly, at Babylon with its seven-tiered ziggurat certainly, the seven mystique was present at the center. The Indo-Aryans had more spectacular ideas, and to some extent these made their way into the Middle East, though imperfectly.

Working backward from the texts we can infer the concept of a divine mountain away to the north. It rose from the center of the earth to the center of the sky, with a dome of stars rotating around it so that its summit was actually above them, or some of them. Ursa Major was conspicuously connected with it, and the sun, moon, and planets also circled it. The sun vanished behind it at night and came round to a sunrise place where its light reappeared at dawn.

This world-mountain was the special dwelling of a Supreme God. Other exalted beings were there as well, deities or spirits. The Supreme God and the rest could, of course, manifest themselves elsewhere. On the mountain was a paradise, a kind of garden, perhaps. This was on the summit, or at the sunrise place on the mountain's flank; or there might be a paradise at both points, and for that matter, others. The mountain radiated beatitude, well-being, length of life, even immortality. Its energies were expressed in a material fact—it was the source of at least one mighty river, which flowed from it, bringing life-giving fresh water to humanity.

All of this applied to Meru, and Sumerians and Babylonians absorbed most of it in a piecemeal way, but they never properly put it together, because of their incompatible earthly centers. They solved the problem after a fashion by representation. A temple at the earthly center, or an elevation on which it stood, magically or mystically *was* the mountain, a place where it bilocated.

Behind all this, far away and long ago, we can detect the world center of Altaic shamanism and perhaps the hallowed peak of Belukha, the tallest in the golden range. Some scholars have seen even that affinity, yet cannot admit that the priority could be this way around. Santillana and von Dechend supply valuable hints on other points, but when they come to this one they see fit to trace the whole cosmic conception back to "the most ancient Near East, whence India and Iran derived their idea of a 'cosmos.'" The unlikelihood of that last statement is becoming clear. They proceed:

> The shaman climbing the "stairs" or notches of his post or tree, pretending that his soul ascends at the same time to the highest sky, does the very same thing as the Mesopotamian priest did when mounting to the top of his seven-storied pyramid, the ziggurat, representing the planetary spheres.
>
> From the majestic temple at Borobudur in Java to the graceful *stupas* which dot the Indian landscape, stretches a schematized reminder of the seven heavens, the seven notches, the seven levels. Says Uno Holmberg: "This pattern of seven levels can hardly be imagined as the invention of Turko-Tatar populations. To the investigator, the origin of the Gods ruling these various levels is no mystery, for they point clearly to the planetary gods of Babylon, which already in their far-away point of origin, ruled over seven superposed starry circles."[21]

No need to pause over the recurrent delusion that the seven-planet system explains things that are much older—in this case, the "seven-storied pyramid." With the first sentence the irony is that it can be turned around. If the shaman is doing what the priest does, then the priest is doing what the shaman does. If the shaman's ritual could be a barbarous imitation of the priest's, then the priest's ritual could be a sophisticated development of the shaman's.

The authors mention orientalists who have thought (anticipating the present argument) that shamanic beliefs and practices did come first. They ridicule the "grievous blunder" of such scholars, who "lost all contact with astronomical imagination." But it seems that these ignorant characters may well have been right. As for the final quotation, it is pure assumption unsupported by any data, or by a scrap of evidence for a northward drift of population or influence. Evidence of that class, as we have seen, points the other way. The only qualification is that Buddhism did spread to Mongolia, bringing its own cosmic mountain. But that had nothing to do with Babylonia and did not happen until well into the Christian era, while the kindred Mongolian motifs, independent of Buddhism, are amply attested.

3

From Mesopotamia a sweep of country extended northwest and west and finally south, skirting the desert and stretching down through Syria and Palestine—anciently Canaan—toward Egypt. This was the populous "Fertile Crescent." Lines of trade, migration, and communication ran along it. In the second millennium B.C., many of its inhabitants were Semitic, as the Babylonians were, and nomadic Semites of the desert moved in and out. That may be why, long before Mohammed, Arabs swore oaths of friendship on seven stones moistened with their blood.[22] The seven-note musical scale, known to Mesopotamians, was known also to the Canaanites in the Mediterranean coastland.[23] These show other traces of influence from Mesopotamia, proving that the impulses generated there were not confined or exhausted.[24]

To their historical disadvantage, the Canaanites are remembered chiefly for being dispossessed and reviled by invading Israelites. The Bible complains of Israelites flirting with their cults. Thanks to the finding of inscribed tablets at Ras Shamra, site of Ugarit, on the coast, something is known about these cults and Canaanite myth and literature.[25]

Two goddesses, Astarte and Anath, were very prominent and much concerned with sex and fertility. The scriptural pejorative *Baal*, meaning "owner," was a divine title rather than a name. There was a great Baal named Hadd who lived on a mountain, Safon or Zaphon. It lay to the north but was not imagined as far away or as having the cosmic character of a Meru. It was in fact identified with Jebel al-Aqra, which some Canaanites could see from where they lived.[26] Hadd was a Canaanite counterpart of Tammuz and other dying and rising gods. But the Baals who attracted Israelites were local male nature powers, probably thought of as guises or deputies of the great Baal.

Canaanite mythology had its sevens; the mystique took this further step. Spells of drought and famine were supposed to last seven years, because every so often Baal's subterranean sojourn was prolonged for that length of time. Kings may have been liable to replacement after a seven-year reign, or at any rate, their reigns may have passed through seven-year phases.[27]

A sage named Daniel, in a Canaanite tale, offers oblations on seven days and mourns his dead son for seven years.[28] The biblical prophet Ezekiel refers to him (Ezek. 14:14 and 20, and 28:3); at least, the person the prophet has in mind can hardly be the Daniel for whom the book following his own is named. There are Canaanite allusions, as in the Epic of Gilgamesh, to an event or train of events going on till the seventh day. A curious instance is the burning of a fire to melt metal for the construction of Baal's house.[29] Such periods have an air of completion but are not calendric; Canaan had no seven-day week.

While these sevens concern days or years, the number's significance is not restricted to time. Stress is laid on seven speeches repetitiously uttered by El, the chief god.[30] Also there are relevant touches in the Tell el-Amarna letters. These were discovered in 1887.[31] A peasant woman was digging at Tell el-Amarna between Cairo and Luxor, the site of a short-lived capital founded by Akhenaten, the "heretic pharaoh" who tried to convert Egypt to the worship of a single god. She found some clay tablets with cuneiform writing on them and took them to a dealer. At first suspected of being a fraud, the find eventually attracted attention and the site was examined. A total of 377 small but decipherable tablets survive. They are official letters to the pharaohs Amenophis III and Akhenaten himself, written between 1391 and 1335 B.C. Many are from local Canaanite rulers, vassals of Egypt. These give glimpses of a time of trouble, due in part to a turbulent element in Canaan called the Habiru. Their tone is sometimes urgent but always reverential. The Canaanite scribes often preface them with the formula "At the feet of the king, my lord, seven and seven times I fall," or "seven times, seven times."[32]

Canaanite myth has a direct if partial echo of Babylonia, the divine destruction of "the serpent tortuous, Shalyat of the seven heads," also called Lotan.[33] In one text the monster's slayer is Baal, and in another it is Anath. A seal that depicts two deities performing the feat together may resolve the discrepancy. The serpent finds its way into the Egyptian underworld as Apep and may be another guise of the seven-headed creature on an Akkadian seal.[34] It cannot be equated with Tiamat, who, unfortunately for her, had only one head. In the biblical context of Ps. 74:13–14, Lotan turns up as Leviathan and still has several heads, though the psalmist fails to state how many. Shalyat, or Lotan, may be the inspiration of the seven-headed dragon in Rev. 12:3.

While Canaan does not have much to offer in the present respect, it is worth appreciating what it does offer. First, it shows that themes already traced to Mesopotamia spread beyond. Second, it sketches in more of the background of a further spread, which was far more important, not only in ancient times but in all succeeding centuries.

CHAPTER TEN

The Israelites

1

Both the seven mystique and cosmic centrality made their way into the thinking of ancient Israel. In that setting the significance of both expanded again. The Israelite legacy lifts them out of antiquarian study and shows them having enduring effects beyond Israel itself and into the modern world. The threads of apparent influence from the northland now grow longer but, perhaps surprisingly, stronger.

An entity called Israel appears first in an Egyptian inscription dated about 1224 to 1214 B.C., in the reign of the pharaoh Merneptah.[1] This is a paean naming various minor nations as cowed into submission by Egyptian victories. One line says: "Israel is laid waste, his seed is not." The inscription is imprecise as to Israel's whereabouts. Archaeologically, its tribes begin to be identifiable in upland Canaan, away from the seacoast, around 1000 B.C. They are a Semitic people using a primitive form of Hebrew writing. "Hebrew" may be a variant of "Habiru." A mixed swarm of people called Habiru are on record in several countries, including Canaan, where they left their mark on the Amarna correspondence. But the Israelites cannot be equated with them; they began as a small Semitic group within a larger and more miscellaneous Habiru complex and seem to have antecedents among nomads who strayed in and out of Egypt. Egyptians disliked the nomads and called them "sand-ramblers."

The Old Testament books from Genesis to Judges were slowly taking shape from about 1000 B.C. They give the account of Israelite origins that was affirmed by the tribes' religious leaders. Abraham, their common ancestor, is said to have lived in the Mesopotamian city of Ur about a thousand years previously. His original name was Abram, but it was changed. He is further said to have migrated, going first northwest with his father and other relatives and then, divinely guided, southward, taking his wife, nephew, and servants. Settled in Canaan after traversing the whole Fertile Crescent, he received a promise from God that the land would belong to his descendants and that they would be a great, numerous, and favored people—God's Chosen, in fact. "Israel" was a name given by God to Abraham's grandson Jacob. However, several generations of the descendants lived not in Canaan as possessors but in Egypt as slaves, employed on pharaonic building. Despite increasingly harsh treatment, they multiplied. At last, when they numbered many thousands, they found a liberator in Moses.

God revealed himself to Moses under the awe-inspiring style "I am."[2] When God is spoken of in the third person, the usual form of the name is Yahweh, rendered "the Lord" in English. This would mean "He is"; it becomes "I am" when God speaks of himself. Through Moses' agency, God enabled the Israelites to escape, working tremendous miracles, such as dividing the Red Sea to let them pass and then letting it flow back to drown the pursuing Egyptians. That was the Exodus. After long wanderings in the wilderness of Sinai and east of the Jordan, they occupied most of the Promised Land, massacring the Canaanites and other inhabitants. Moses was dead by then. Their conquering chief was Joshua. Twelve tribes, descended from the twelve sons of Jacob, constituted ancient Israel.

Outside the Bible itself, the only evidence for any of this is circumstantial. An Egyptian priest, Manetho, wrote a history alleging that the Israelites were expelled because they were diseased, but his version is so much later, and so obviously a mere retort, that it has no serious value.[3] Still, the Exodus in some sense may be accepted as factual. Its date has been much debated. A theory long favored is that the pharaoh in the story is Rameses II and the Exodus happened in the thirteenth century B.C. Another theory puts it in the fifteenth and associates Israel's conquests with the Habiru upheaval bemoaned in the Amarna letters.[4] On this showing, Joshua was the leader of one Habiru group, that is, the Israelites, some decades after they left Egypt. The Habiru already in Canaan began a long-drawn peasants' revolt against the rulers of city-states under Egyptian suzerainty. It may even be that Joshua took the lead and incited them. At any rate, the Israelites played a part in a general uprising and land seizure, and when Egyptian rule crumbled, they came out on top. This latter theory squares somewhat better with the chronology of the Bible. Its advocates claim that the early dating also agrees better with the archaeological record, which includes some of the scriptural events, notably the collapse of the walls of Jericho.

For two or three centuries the newcomers in the Promised Land had no king. The tribes formed a loose confederacy with governors whom the Bible calls judges. Unity came from the religion of Yahweh and traditions about the mighty deliverance. The Israelites were slow to take over the towns. Their use of Canaanite houses was limited, and their own style of building was a mere heaping of unshaped stones on stones, with pebbles stuffed in the crevices. Yet they were enterprising in their own way, clearing patches of forest, bringing new land under cultivation, and founding villages. A few of the indigenous people survived as serfs.

During the Israelites' wanderings in the desert, the Lord is said to have dictated laws and ritual precepts to Moses, including the Ten Commandments. The Decalogue inscribed on stone tablets may not have been due to Moses himself, but the main text embodying it cannot be later than the ninth century B.C. and may well be earlier. It is there, in Exodus 20:8–11, that we find the most lastingly important of Israelite heptads—the seven-day week, which is still with us, expressed as a cycle of six plus one.

> Remember the sabbath day, to keep it holy.
> Six days you shall labour, and do all your work,
> but the seventh day is a sabbath to the Lord your God; in it you shall
> not do any work . . .
> for in six days the Lord made heaven and earth, the sea and all that
> is in them, and rested the seventh day. Therefore the Lord blessed
> the seventh day and hallowed it.

In the order of narrative, if not in the order of composition, this commandment formalizes a teaching already stated (Exod. 16:22–30).

Modern languages give names to the days of the week, usually derived from the astrological gods or, as with four of the English days, from gods held to be equivalent. But Israel created the week long before astrology, and its days were not named for the planets. Apart from the sabbath, which means "rest," they were not named at all. The reason for the week's existence was not practical. The Israelites' ancestors may actually have had a practical "week." In Gen. 24:55, Rebekah's family want to detain her for "at least ten days." That may be a vestigial instance of the ten-day period used in neighboring Egypt, but if so, it succumbed to the mystical seven. When the week is proclaimed in an Israel under the tutelage of Moses, it is quite different and has no parallel anywhere else.

The decree about it in Exod. 20:8–11 is repeated in 31:12–17, where the sabbath is called a sign of the covenant of the Lord, and breaking it by doing work is made a capital crime. That edict had to be modified (understandably), but in the Jewish religion that evolved from ancient Israel's, the sacred pattern of six plus one was treated with ever-growing reverence.

Any notion that recurrent market days had something to do with it, as in some other calendars, should be dispelled by Neh. 13:15–22, where marketing on the holy day is firmly condemned. Doctors of the law debated in immense detail what *could* be done on the sabbath, with results that still affect orthodox Judaism.

Such questions had more than individual importance. Around the beginning of the Christian era, Jewish armed forces were handicapped by reluctance to fight on the sabbath, since fighting, apart from strict self-defense, counted as work.[5] Rabbis who rejected the hope of a conquering Messiah claimed it was a contradiction in terms, because the Messiah's soldiers would have to suspend operations every sabbath, and his gentile opponents, not being similarly bound, would take advantage of the pause to outmaneuver him. This actually had happened when the Romans under Pompey captured Jerusalem.

Obviously, in ancient Israel the seven mystique acquired a new kind of weight and a new kind of solemnity. Exodus bases the septenary cycle on the acts of God in creation. He made the world in six days and rested the seventh, hallowing that day, the prototype sabbath. What is odd is that the first two chapters of Genesis, which itemize his week of creation, betray the fact that this was not Israel's only version. The seven-day account runs through chapter 1 and the first verses of chapter 2, step by majestic step, and closes in 2:3 with God's blessing on his rest day. But the compiler goes on to a more primitive story, which refers (2:4) to "the day" when the Lord God made the earth and heavens and describes creation more naively and in a different order. The "day" discrepancy is no quibble of modern higher critics. Medieval theologians were conscious of the crux, and St. Thomas Aquinas, the greatest of them, grappled with it ingeniously, if inconclusively.[6]

It seems that Israelite belief first envisaged a one-day creation, with the whole of the world's main structure coming into being together. Living creatures followed in no clear sequence. Then Israel's teachers adopted the seven-day version, which was more detailed and literate. They subordinated the older one without eliminating the difference. Their new version was the basis of the week. The process reveals the seven mystique taking hold, strongly enough to override an existing myth and despite inconsistency.

What is the background of the septenary story? And why did the Israelites preface their history with such a story at all, and take so much trouble over it? The answers shed light on the way in which the seven mystique reached them, together with other things, and on the enormous consequences.

Genesis is more than a prologue, it is an apologia. Israelites realized that the invasion of the Promised Land had been, on their own showing, a ruthless business involving the conquest and slaughter of many of its inhabitants—the Canaanites proper and six other groupings, listed in Deut. 7:1–2 as Hittites, Girgashites, Amorites, Perizzites, Hivites, and Jebusites. These would have been small minorities in a mixed population, some— such as the Hittites—perhaps only traders or mercenary troops, but all came under attack. God had ordered the tribes of Israel, his Chosen, to destroy these peoples utterly, make no covenant with them, show no mercy to them. The justification of such conduct depended on the nature of the God who commanded it. The central purpose of Genesis was to establish that Yahweh, who had chosen the Israelites, given them the Promised Land, and ordained the ruthlessness shown in taking it, was the only Higher Power that mattered and always had been so. He had created the world and acted with magisterial force in its history. Against his decrees there could be no appeal, from outraged victims or anyone else. This is not a modern skeptical explanation. It is the one given by Rashi, doyen of Jewish commentators, whose medieval work is still used in teaching.[7]

For the pre-Abraham part of the apologia, going back beyond ancestral tradition, the Genesis authors had to look for materials outside. The folklore of the Habiru medley of which Israel was a fraction seems not to have provided enough. They could hardly borrow from the Canaanites them- selves. Canaanites with a higher culture survived unconquered in the coast- land, and some of their shrines in the Israelites' own territory remained operative. Many Israelites were attracted to these, but fraternization was condemned. Israelites who flirted with local nature powers, or "Baals," may not have seen this as apostasy. Canaanites, as remarked, probably thought of them as guises or deputies of the great Baal, and some Israelites may have considered them guises or deputies of Yahweh. But such attempts to have it both ways were not approved. Yahweh, the Lord, the Eternal, could not be a dying-and-rising spirit of fertility, and as for Baal's goddess companions, they were totally unacceptable. Therefore the Israelites, confronted with the shrines of the conquered, were to break down their altars and dash in pieces their pillars and burn their graven images (Deut. 7:5).

That applied especially to the goddess shrines. Yahweh was the most patriarchal of deities. But—a warning against cliché inferences—the Old Testament does not depict a society holding women in complete contempt or subjection. It has much misogyny in it, from Eve onward, and it has some extremely ugly stories, but it also has many female characters por- trayed with respect, sympathy, and admiration, and even as national her- oines. Its account of Deborah (Judges, chapters 4 and 5) shows that there was at least a phase when it was perfectly thinkable for a woman to be a prophet speaking for Yahweh and to rise to the highest public office. Moses reputedly owed his very life to his mother and young sister, who saved him from massacre as an infant and arranged an advantageous adoption (Exod.

2:1–10). Miriam, another sister, or maybe the same one, is a leading figure throughout the Exodus; she is capable of standing up to him and protesting at his high-handed behavior.

The Canaanites' culture affected Israel through transvaluation, not imitation. They had a chief god, above Baal and the rest, called El, and Israelites sometimes called Yahweh *El Shaddai*, "God Almighty," and *El Elyon*, "God Most High," but he remained utterly different. They adopted the annual festivals of nature worship, spring and summer and autumn, but turned them into commemorations of events in their own history. The spring festival, for instance, became Passover, recalling the Lord's triumph over Pharaoh.[8]

A direct Canaanite influence was literary.[9] The early Israelites had songs, such as the one sung by Miriam in Exod. 15:20–1, which is a kind of spiritual, celebrating the rout of the Egyptians:

> Sing to the Lord, for he has triumphed gloriously; the horse and his rider he has thrown into the sea.

This may be the oldest thing in the Bible, or nearly so. Its antiquity, and its authenticity as a native product, are not refuted by the lack of evidence for Egyptian cavalry; "rider" can mean "chariot rider." But more complex poems, such as the song enlarging on Miriam's that has been incorporated in the same chapter, are Canaanite-derivative.

Only one myth of the Canaanites has clear biblical echoes, the divine destruction of "the serpent tortuous, Shalyat of the seven heads," otherwise Lotan. A similar deed is attributed to the God of Israel, in passages where the monster is called Leviathan. Addressing Yahweh, the psalmist says,

> Thou didst divide the sea by thy might; thou didst break the heads of the dragons on the waters.
> Thou didst crush the heads of Leviathan, thou didst give him as food for the creatures of the wilderness. (Ps. 74:13–14)

While Job 26:12–13 glances at the same exploit, Job 41 and Ps. 104:25–6 imply that Leviathan is still active, and the prophet Isaiah sees his extinction as yet to come:

> In that day the Lord with his hard and great and strong sword will punish Leviathan the fleeing serpent, Leviathan the twisting serpent; and he will slay the dragon that is in the sea. (Isa. 27:1)

But Canaanite myth was of little use to the authors of Genesis, and even the destruction of Lotan or Shalyat had an antecedent in the slaying of

Tiamat. Tiamat herself could point the authors in a more helpful direction. They needed stories that could put their God in the light they wished for. The Middle East supplied what they wanted if they looked beyond Canaan. It had its versions of three fundamental myths. One was that of the dying-and-rising seasonal god, Tammuz or Adonis or Baal. This could not be fitted to Yahweh as conceived. But another theme was creation, with a god confronting primordial chaos, bringing order out of it, forming the world, and setting the heavenly bodies in their places. Babylon's creation epic was the major treatment of this, and Israel could adapt it. Third was the Flood, in which, through some divine act, most of humanity was destroyed by water, with a remnant spared to make a fresh start. Again Mesopotamia offered a literary version, and again it had possibilities. With the myth of the dying-and-rising god, the meaning lay in a cycle of events endlessly repeated, but creation and the Flood were once-and-for-all happenings. The Lord could not die and return even once, let alone endlessly, but he could make the world and he could flood it. So there was matter here for Genesis, though with profound changes affecting its character.

Forms of the Mesopotamian myths may have traveled west with a nomadic drift in which Abraham's migration from Ur could have been an incident. Or they may have been learned through later contacts along the same route. At any rate, the Genesis seven-day creation and some of the stories following it have an ancestry in the senior culture.[10]

2

As it stands, the opening of Genesis is a fairly late production that biblical compilers naturally placed at the start. Older allusions to the week of creation and other details prove its antiquity in substance. It takes up the Babylonian story and submits it to a kind of rationalization. The swarm of gods and demons has vanished and the God of Israel is alone and absolute, "in the beginning." By implication the author answers the conundrum "What was God doing before he made the world?" Time itself is part of creation and there was no "before"; the question is meaningless.

God is called not Yahweh, but Elohim, an alternative style that runs through one strand of scriptural tradition. The Hebrew word translated as "the deep" is *tehom*, which is cognate with "Tiamat," but Tiamat is depersonalized, reduced to a fluid chaos "without form and void." God's spirit moves across the dark waters. The word translated as "spirit" can mean "breath" or "wind," and there may be a very distant echo of the winds raised by Marduk. As the primordial monster is destroyed, so, here, chaos is canceled, first by the divine spirit and then by the divine command "Let there be light," a touch of sublimity putting the narrative in a class by itself.

Tiamat's splitting apart becomes a separation of waters upward and downward, with a domed firmament keeping them out above, dry land emerging from them below, and an open space enclosed in-between.

Genesis is more thoughtful and dignified than the Babylonian epic. The creation of humanity is a more serious matter and confers a nobler status. The final celebration becomes the grave and holy sabbath. On the other hand, Genesis is less colorful. A war of new gods against old ones is a recurrent, deeply rooted mythical theme, and its biblical banishment, though successful in principle, failed to satisfy. It made a partial return through a loophole left by Genesis. When God says, "Let us make man in our image, after our likeness" (1:26), why is it "us" and "our"? He is not using the royal "we," which the Hebrew language never provided for.[11] It came to be inferred that by the time he said this, he no longer was alone. He had created other spiritual beings, presumably angels. Angels are explicit in Job 38:7, where God recalls his foundation of the earth: "When the morning stars sang together, and all the sons of God shouted for joy." God refers to "us" again—"one of us"—in Gen. 3:22. Given angels, fallen angels became possible, with Satan's revolt and the war in heaven restored, as in traditional Christianity. But when Genesis was composed, that was a long way off.

The biblical creation takes the seven mystique further than the creation epic does, and with much more subtlety. Marduk's seven winds, which blow up Tiamat like a balloon, are a prerequisite of creation, but the epic's seven chapters on seven tablets are more or less arbitrary. The Genesis author converts them into the seven days of his step-by-step scheme. He does more. His work is more deeply septenary than it looks. As a perceptive biblical scholar points out, he rings the changes on seven literary elements: (1) an introductory "God said"; (2) the words God speaks, "Let there be . . ."; (3) a phrase marking fulfillment, such as "and it was so"; (4) a description of the creative act; (5) God's blessing or naming what he has made; (6) the seal of approval, usually "God saw that it was good"; and (7) the conclusion, the "evening and morning" refrain closing a day. These do not all appear every time, but their permutations hint at planning and have a sort of symmetry.[12] There is artistry here, governed by the number, and going far beyond narrative need. Though not part of the scriptural record, a notion that the first man, Adam, had seven sons passed into Middle Eastern lore.

A fundamentalist might protest that to argue like this is to lose sight of reality. Genesis tells us that God created the world in six days and rested the seventh, for the simplest of reasons. He did create it in six days and rest the seventh. That is the literal truth, known to the inspired writer, who was further inspired to emphasize it by building seven into his narrative structure. A broader scriptural survey will dispose of that plea. The week of creation is not a self-contained fact. Sevens are much too common and significant in the rest of the Old Testament. If the number as such is denied any special quality, its occurrences outside the creation story are left hanging. If, in that story, God dictated seven to an inspired writer simply because it was factual, it is hard to see why he should have dictated the same number pointlessly to other writers. A Bible concordance will show that while seven has the ubiquitous three as a competitor in frequency, no other number comes anywhere near, and often the only apparent reason for it is the mystique.

It is also in the Flood story. When the Genesis authors took this up (6:9–9:17), they adapted the Babylonian version in the *Epic of Gilgamesh*, or something like it. Their chief contribution was to fit it into a historical scheme, tracing the acts of God from creation to the calling of Abraham. They linked it backward with the beginning of the world by a genealogy descending from Adam to the Flood survivor Noah and his sons Shem, Ham, and Japheth. They linked it forward with Abraham and the origins of Israel by another genealogy (Gen. 11:10–26).

Their Flood story lacks the literary flair of the epic. In particular, Noah lacks Utnapishtim's personality: he is a mute puppet of the Lord, never saying anything except in an unrelated and nasty episode after it is all over. But again Israelite ideas have made a radical change. The cataclysm is not due to divine pique, nor is there any split among celestial beings. God sends the Flood as an act of judgment on corrupt humankind. It happens at a definite time and is related to previous and subsequent history. Humanity's moral relationship with God is at the heart of the story. Noah and his family are exempted because he is righteous, and the handful of humans in the ark are a faithful remnant who can make a fresh beginning, leading to the formation of Israel as the Lord's people. The mechanics of the Flood are derived from the cosmic scheme of Genesis 1: the waters of the deep burst in from below, and the waters of the sky burst in from above, through the "windows of heaven" (7:11). At the end Noah and his wife are not dismissed into isolation, they remain with their sons and their sons' wives to repeople the world, and God makes a covenant with them.

The seven mystique is less conspicuous here than it is in the Babylonian version, but it is present. God gives Noah seven days to load his ark and tells him to take aboard seven pairs of all "clean" animals and seven pairs of all birds (7:1–4).

Further on in the Old Testament, the sevens continue. Here is a small selection:

Abraham, in token of an oath, gives seven lambs to Abimelech (Gen. 21:28–31).

Jacob serves Laban seven years for his first wife and seven for his second (Gen. 29:16–30).

Pharaoh dreams of seven fat cows devoured by seven thin ones, and of seven good ears of grain swallowed by seven meager ones; Joseph interprets his dreams as foreshadowing seven years of plenty followed by seven of famine (Gen. 41:1–7 and 25–31).

Bezalel makes a lampstand for the tabernacle with seven lamps, the original form of the Menorah, familiar as a Jewish emblem (Exod. 25:31 and 37 and 37:17–24).

The Law of Moses, besides ordaining the seven-day week, enjoins an economic cycle based on seven years and seven times seven, which is an extension of it (Lev. 25:1–24).

Balak sacrifices seven bulls and seven rams on seven altars (Num. 23:1–4, 14, and 29–30).

The Israelites win the Promised Land by conquering seven nations (Deut. 7:1).

King Solomon's festival at the opening of his temple lasts seven days (1 Kings 8:65).

Elijah sends his servant seven times to watch for an approaching rain cloud (1 Kings 18:43–44).

Elisha tells Naaman, suffering from leprosy, to wash in the Jordan seven times (2 Kings 5:10–14).

Zechariah sees visions of a seven-faceted stone and another lampstand with seven lamps, described as "the eyes of the Lord, which range through the whole earth" (Zech. 3:9 and 4:2 and 10).

While some of these sevens, and dozens like them, may be dismissed as accidental, instances such as Balak's altars combine them in ways that clearly are more. The conclusive passage is Josh. 6:1–21, telling how, at the Lord's command, Joshua's army marched around besieged Jericho on seven successive days with seven priests blowing trumpets; and on the seventh day they marched round it seven times, and on the seventh circuit the priests gave a signal, the Israelites shouted, and the walls fell.

Again a fundamentalist might protest. All of these sevens occur because all of the passages simply are telling what happened. But even if that were so, it would imply that God, and writers inspired by him, attached a special importance to seven. Furthermore, we find Israelites using the number colloquially, rather like "half a dozen" in English. Israel's enemies flee in seven directions (Deut. 28:7). Naomi's daughter-in-law Ruth means more to her than seven sons (Ruth 4:15). The Lord's blessing enables a barren woman to bear seven children (1 Sam. 2:5). When males are in short supply, seven women will pursue one man (Isa. 4:1).

None of these passages show why seven is special. The seven-day creation is not the prototype. Nothing makes it a reason for other heptads, apart from the calendric week itself. Also, many of the texts having seven in them may well be older than the creation story. There is no visible alternative to importation of the mystique from outside, to the long chain of transmission from Mesopotamia, and Indo-Aryans farther back, and shamans revering Ursa Major farther back still.

The book of Proverbs gives another linkage between the creation story and the number, which is strange and looks like a direct intrusion. Proverbs is mainly a collection of sayings ascribed to Solomon, Israel's archetypal wise man, with additions from other sages. Traditional matter has gone into it, but as it stands, it is one of the latest-written books of the Old Testament, composed about the third century B.C.[13] By then the semienclosed life of the ancient Israelites no longer was possible. Many of their Jewish descendants were scattered about the world, and the Promised Land itself, though it was home for a Jewish population, was open to foreign influences.

In the eighth and ninth chapters, Wisdom takes the stage as a speaking character. The passage is surprising for two reasons. Despite the masculinity of the Lord and the religion centered on him, Wisdom is female. Moreover, she claims to have been present when he made the world, as a companion and even an assistant, unmentioned in Genesis.

"The Lord created me at the beginning of his work, the first of his acts of old.
Ages ago I was set up, at the first, before the beginning of the earth . . .
When he established the heavens, I was there, when he drew a circle on the face of the deep . . .
When he marked out the foundations of the earth,
then I was beside him, like a master workman;
And I was daily his delight, rejoicing before him always,
rejoicing in his inhabited world and delighting in the sons of men."
(Prov. 8:22–31)

The phrase about God's drawing a circle on the face of the deep reflects the ancient conception of a disk-earth, and the "inhabitable world" is the same as the Greek *oecumene*.

In the next chapter Wisdom enters again and we are told more about her.

Wisdom has built her house, she has set up her seven pillars.
She has slaughtered her beasts, she has mixed her wine, she has also set her table.
She has sent out her maids to call from the highest places of the town . . .
"Come, eat of my bread and drink of the wine I have mixed . . .
Live, and walk in the way of insight." (Prov. 9:1–6)

This Lady Wisdom, who has set up seven unexplained pillars, is no mere personified quality of the wise. She existed before humanity. She reappears in the apocryphal book *Ecclesiasticus* or *Sirach*, chapter 24, with a splendor of imagery making it clearer still that she is not a personification but a person. The author, or a pious interpolator, tries to make out that she is an allegory of the teaching of Moses (presumably in the mind of God from the beginning), and rabbis in later centuries try to accommodate her thus. [14] But this is very farfetched. Another apocryphal book, *The Wisdom of Solomon*, tells of her befriending a series of men—Adam, Noah, Abraham, Lot, Jacob, Joseph—long before Moses lived (10:1–14).

Here the Goddess in some sense has got a footing in scripture after all. Even the religion of Yahweh could not keep her out forever, though it still could refuse to concede equality with him. If we care to look for influences, or to identify Wisdom with a specific goddess figure, there are several possibilities. They cannot be conclusive. In the cosmopolitan world of Proverbs and Ecclesiasticus, the world formed by Alexander's conquests, deities were freely assimilated to one another, and in the case of goddesses not too fancifully, if Gimbutan theologians are right, since all goddesses *were* forms of the Goddess—the primordial *Ewig-Weibliche*. Behind Wisdom's enigmatic mask we may detect the Syrian queen Astarte; or Anath, worshiped by the Phoenicians, who were the Canaanites' heirs and whose literature often dwelt on the "wisdom" theme; or the Greek wisdom goddess Athene; or a blend of all of these. [15] By no means a contrived blend. Whether or not the many goddesses really derived from an original one, there is no doubt about an overlap, a psychological oneness and partial interchangeability. [16] An inscription in Cyprus equates Athene with Anath. [17] The prophet Jeremiah found Jews in Egypt worshiping the Queen of Heaven (Jer. 7:18 and 44:15–19). She might have been Astarte, but an Egyptian stele gives Anath the same title. In the fifth century B.C., a Jewish colony up the Nile near Aswan had a temple dedicated not only to the God of Israel, "Yaho," or Yahweh, but to Anath, his companion. [18] That may be a clue to the Wisdom texts.

Whatever Wisdom's background, she is linked with the work of creation. As to her house and the seven pillars, the Bible takes us no further. A papyrus written by a member of one of the gnostic schools, which had views of their own about Wisdom, says that at creation God laughed seven times and seven gods appeared.[19] There is no visible connection. These gods may be the ruling deities of the planets, but while the author of Proverbs could have known the planets, the pillars do not suggest them and he shows no sign of believing in astrology.

Again that compulsiveness of an awkward seven. It is a curious number of pillars for a building to have. How would they be arranged? If at the front in a colonnade, the middle one would block the center and push the doorway aside. If at the corners, they would make the house heptagonal, a most peculiar shape. If along an aisle, three on the left and four on the right, they would not balance. A hexagon with a central pillar would be symmetrical but foreign to ancient norms of design. The Lady Wisdom has to have seven pillars, her nature is bound up with the number, yet the house does not make sense.

It seems likely that the pillars, so called, are not part of the architecture. A natural guess is that the building is the house of the Lord, his temple in Jerusalem, Wisdom's earthly abode. In *Ecclesiasticus* (24.9–11) she says:

> *From eternity, in the beginning, he created me,*
> *and for eternity I shall not cease to exist.*
> *In the holy tabernacle I ministered before him,*
> *and so I was established in Zion.*
> *In the beloved city likewise he gave me a resting place,*
> *and in Jerusalem was my dominion.*

One of the temple's holiest objects at the time of writing was the Menorah, the seven-branched lampstand, replacing and duplicating one that had been lost when the Babylonians destroyed Solomon's Temple. Its branches, which all rose vertically to hold the lamps, may be the seven pillars.

3

To return to Genesis, it has another passage showing awareness of Mesopotamia—the tale of the Tower of Babel (11:1–9). This purports to explain why the world had different languages quite soon after the Flood, a problem if its whole population descended from the group of eight in Noah's ark. The author says Noah's early descendants did speak a single language, presumably his. They conceived the notion of building a city on a plain in the land of Shinar, and "a tower with its top in the heavens." This was to be a center to keep them together, since they did not wish to be "scattered abroad upon the face of the whole earth."

They made bricks and began work, but the Lord did not intend humanity to cluster in one place, and he condemned the project as a display of impious pride. To put a stop to it he confused the builders' language so that they could not understand one another, and then scattered them, each group going off in a different direction with a differently altered speech. The abortive city with its tower was called Babel. "Babel" may be related to a Hebrew verb meaning "confuse," but in this tale we catch an echo of Israelite scorn for the proud heathen metropolis of Babylon, where a hubbub of languages and dialects still could be heard. Shinar was in that region, and brick was its normal building material. The tower may be a reminiscence of the Etemenanki, Babylon's seven-tiered ziggurat, with its shrine on top making contact with the gods. The builders of Babel undertake the work so that they shall not be scattered. Their tower, like the central temples in Mesopotamia, is to be a bond of earth and heaven, and a bond of the land.[20]

However, Israelite knowledge of the hierocentric idea raises larger issues.

CHAPTER ELEVEN

The Two Dwellings of the Lord

1

It was partly owing to Israel's legacy that the seven mystique spread through Europe and farther, planting the week and other heptads. That could happen because the legacy had an inbuilt dynamism, rooted in Israel's version of the sacred world center.

The first manifestation of this new thing was in Judaism, which was the religion of ancient Israel developed. Its exponents, the Jews, began as a portion of the broader Israelite body. Israel's twelve tribes had held tenaciously to the Promised Land, or as much of it as they occupied, and their religion had grown around the conviction that God had granted it to them by covenant. Through Moses, and prophets and teachers in succession to him, the Lord had published his truths and his laws. Their tenure of the Promised Land depended on their fidelity to these. Most of the tribes were removed from the northern part by Assyrian conquerors—according to the Bible, as a divine judgment on apostasy—but the tribe of Judah carried on in the south, with minorities from some of the others. The people of the rump Judahite state held Jerusalem, maintained their identity through Babylonian conquest and deportation, recovered the holy city and some of the Promised Land, and spread and multiplied outside it. This resilient fraction constituted the basic body of "Jews."

Toward the beginning of the Christian era the Jews were claiming to be custodians of the whole sacred inheritance. The lost northerners still existed somewhere and eventually would reappear, but meanwhile, the Jews were the faithful remnant, the visible Chosen; and through their agency, many now thought, the essential truths and laws of God would spread to the gentiles and destroy pagan idolatry. They had a mission. In theory at least, Judaism was a world-converting faith. Jewish communities, scattered through the Roman domains and beyond, preserved their scriptures and ritual observances, maintained ties with Jerusalem and its rebuilt temple, and awaited a Messiah who would establish their lasting kingdom and God's universal reign. Even after an anti-Roman revolt collapsed in A.D. 70 and the temple was destroyed and the dispersal accelerated, the Chosen kept their identity, if with lessening importance.

Meanwhile, the Christian Church, starting as a sect within the Jewish body but soon expanding outside, had proclaimed that its founder Jesus *was* the Messiah ("Christ" is the same word), though not as expected. The Church put together its own Bible, combining the Jewish scriptures as the Old Testament with added Christian ones as the New, to make up the sacred book of its own more cosmopolitan system. From the fourth century onward Christianity became dominant in the Roman Empire, in its successor states, and gradually in the rest of Europe, bringing its Bible everywhere as authoritative. In the seventh century, Mohammed, professing to restore the religion of Abraham that Jews and Christians had corrupted, drew on Judeo-Christian tradition to create Islam, with its own holy book, the Koran.

The world-converting mission envisaged by Judaism passed, with an immense increase of zeal, to both Christianity and Islam. It had no pre-Jewish precedent. The religions of Babylonia and Canaan remained simply the religions of Babylonia and Canaan, and they expired. The Zoroastrianism of Persia made universal claims, but even in the heyday of Persian power very little was done to press them.[1] Buddhism drifted outward from India, but haphazardly, in a variety of forms, with no strong inbuilt impulsion and no disposition to supplant or suppress rival systems. Judeo-Christian energy and exclusiveness, which propagated the scriptures and—among much else—the seven mystique contained in them, sprang from the monotheism evolved by Israel and from a special feature of this: the association of God with a certain structuring of the world, with the belief that it had a center that was a special dwelling of his, uniquely holy and spiritually powerful. This was Nippur and Babylon over again, but because Yahweh was more than Enlil or Marduk, Israel's center was radically different. From it the new dynamism unfolded, through a spatial ordering linked with the septenary ordering. And to examine it closely, to take note of how it developed and what affiliations it had, is to find more in it than meets the eye.

In Israel's early days it was some time before the Promised Land had a center of any sort. The tribes' most treasured possession, an acacia-wood box called the Ark of the Covenant with Moses' stone tablets inside it, was kept at Shiloh.[2] Shiloh was a shrine for communal worship, but it was little more. Presently Israel became a kingdom. According to the Bible its first great king was David, and Jerusalem was founded by him. He captured the site from the Jebusites and planned a capital and temple. For the temple he picked on the ridge of Ophel. Solomon, who actually built it, was his son. Whatever the truth about these kings, the rising ground where the temple stood became the holy hill of Zion, the heart of the city, sometimes identified with it. Here was Yahweh's house and here was Israel's own sacred center. Biblical writers speak of the mountain of the Lord. While the word sounds like a wild exaggeration, it does often mean this hill . . . though, as we shall see, this is not always the case.

The belief that gentiles will find their way to the God of Israel begins to dawn during the eighth century B.C. In the first part of Isaiah it is grounded on the specific place and the topographical image.

> It shall come to pass in the latter days that the mountain of the house of the Lord shall be established as the highest of mountains, and shall be raised above the hills; and all the nations shall flow to it,
> and many peoples shall come, and say: "Come, let us go up to the mountain of the Lord, to the house of the God of Jacob; that he may teach us his ways and that we may walk in his paths." For out of Zion shall go forth the Law, and the word of the Lord from Jerusalem. (Isa. 2:2–3)

No suggestion yet of missionaries journeying about the world, but the holy hill with the Lord's temple on it is to rise higher in some miraculous manner and become a focus for all nations as it is for his Chosen. Others will come to learn and will take the message home with them.

Isaiah may or may not be hinting already at a world centrality. With the conception of the disk-earth, the idea of centrality grew in Israel as it had in Mesopotamia. In the words of the prophet Ezekiel in the sixth century B.C.:

> Thus says the Lord God: This is Jerusalem; I have set her in the centre of the nations, with countries round about her. (Ezek. 5:5)

Further on (Ezek. 38:12) he speaks of the evil aggressor Gog, who will threaten the Lord's people in their Promised Land, where they dwell "at the center of the earth." The word he uses for "center" means "navel."[3]

Ezekiel wrote in exile in Babylonia, after the Babylonians laid Jerusalem waste, destroyed its temple, and carried off its citizens, together with many more from the southern kingdom of Judah. In 539 Babylon fell in its turn to the conqueror Cyrus, founder of the empire of Persia. He allowed the deportees to go home and rebuild their capital. It is from this point onward that "the Jews" are a distinctive body; the word is simply "Judahite."

The anonymous author of the second part of Isaiah, which begins at chapter 40, salutes the God-given deliverance with rapture. Now the exiles can return, he proclaims. The Lord, seated above "the circle of the earth" (40:22), will be acknowledged as supreme everywhere because of his astounding overthrow of the proud oppressors. For the first time he is seen as the prospective God of a world faith, explictly the only one who is real. Through his rescued people he will summon all nations:

> "Turn to me and be saved, all the ends of the earth! For I am God, and there is no other.
> By myself I have sworn, from my mouth has gone forth in righteousness a word that shall not return: 'To me every knee shall bow, every tongue shall swear.' " (Isa. 45:22–23)

This is bound up with the irreplaceable glory of Zion:

> How beautiful upon the mountains are the feet of him who brings good tidings, Who publishes peace, who brings good tidings of good, who publishes salvation, who says to Zion, "Your God reigns."
> Hark, your watchmen lift up their voice, together they sing for joy; for eye to eye they see the return of the Lord to Zion.
> Break forth into singing, you waste places of Jerusalem; for the Lord has comforted his people, he has redeemed Jerusalem.
> The Lord has bared his holy arm before the eyes of all the nations; and all the ends of the earth shall see the salvation of our God. (Isa. 52:7–10)

The actual restoration was less than spectacular. A replacement temple was duly built and eventually there was a phase of independence, but numerous Jews had remained in Babylonia under Persian rule. Their decision not to go back to Zion was one cause of the Jewish dispersal. But wherever Jews might be living, some accepted the vocation to enlighten the gentiles about the Lord's nature and will, and wean them away from what Jews saw as idolatry. The worldwide conversion might be reserved for the reign of the Messiah, but Judaism did begin to attract non-Jews, and the dispersal itself could be made meaningful in that context. God, some rabbis explained, had scattered his people among the nations so that proselytes should be added to them.[4]

Such were the origins of the idea of an apostolate, and Jews who took it up never lost sight of Jerusalem as the holy city, the world's center, destined capital of the Messianic age. Its aura grew steadily more powerful.

The Lord dwelt in it as he had for so many years, and his presence in the temple was symbolized—since the Ark of the Covenant was long since lost—by his seven-branched lampstand, the Menorah. As at Nippur (perhaps) and Babylon (certainly), the seven mystique was at the world's center. Even after Roman repression effaced Jerusalem's character, even when the second temple was gone, tradition made Zion more and more wonderful. Rabbis related its centrality to the creation story, saying that the first solid ground that God brought into being was the rock where the temple stood, and he then built the Holy Land around it and the rest of the terrestrial land mass around that—"from Zion was the world founded."[5] The temple rock was a kind of stopper, sealing up a place where subterranean waters were near the surface. God had created Adam there and transferred him to the Garden of Eden, the earthly paradise where Eve was made as his companion.[6]

2

Jews who extolled the hill of Zion took note of Isaiah's prophecy that it would rise above all others and become the earth's highest point. Cryptically, however, some rabbis claimed that it already had that distinction.[7] On the face of it the claim was absurd. Zion is no Everest. It has been argued that they pictured the landmass as convex, a dome rather than a disk. They may have pictured it so, but the explanation does not convince. Seen from Jerusalem, the nearby Mount of Olives is visibly higher.

A subtler notion was present here, whether or not the rabbis knew what it was—one of a number of strange things that were nearly edited out of scripture, but not quite. Jerusalem's Zion with the temple on it was the mountain of God, but there was another, vaster mountain of God, and the two were mystically identified, as Enlil's temple in Nippur was identified with his Mountain of Heaven and Earth. Zion, let us say, bilocated. In the Bible, orthodox views have prevailed and the emphasis is nearly always on Jerusalem. But traces of the other mountain remain, in a psalm, in two of the major prophets, and in the tradition of Eden.

Psalm 48 begins:

> Great is the Lord and greatly to be praised is the city of our God!
> His holy mountain, beautiful in elevation, is the joy of all the earth,
> *Mount Zion, in the far north*, the city of the great King.

Confronted with the words *far north*, translators have tried various expedients to explain it away. But this northern Zion cannot be exorcized. It is an archaic fragment stuck in the text.[8] Canaanites had their mountain of gods, Safon or Zaphon, and the name is used once or twice to mean Zion. But Safon was an actual mountain, Jebel al-Aqra, admittedly to the north but not very far north, and in any case, the psalmist never would have referred to the abode of Baal as the abode of Yahweh.[9]

In Isaiah 14:12–15 perplexities deepen. The prophet is taunting a proud king of Babylon who has ceased to be fortunate. At first the language is in a recurrent style of prophetic invective, but then it changes.

> How you are fallen from heaven, O Day Star, son of Dawn! How you are cut down to the ground, you who laid the nations low!
> You said in your heart, "I will ascend to heaven; above the stars of God I will set my throne on high; I will sit on *the mount of assembly in the far north*;
> I will ascend above the heights of the clouds, I will make myself like the Most High."
> But you are brought down to Sheol, to the depths of the Pit.

Extravagant language to address to a mortal. The King James Version of the Bible renders the first sentence, "How art thou fallen from heaven, O Lucifer, son of the morning!" Early commentators think Isaiah is comparing the king of Babylon to the proud archangel who sought equality with God, fell, and became Satan. That is probably why, before his fall, Satan's name is said to have been Lucifer. However, the Old Testament's few allusions to him were written much later, and there is no proof that his story was current as far back as Isaiah.

More significant is the "mount of assembly in the far north." The "far north" phrase is the same as in the psalm, and since Isaiah cannot mean Jerusalem's Zion, his words are conclusive against attempts to maintain that the psalmist does. This northern mountain is gigantic and fabulous, towering not only above the clouds but above the stars and reaching up to heaven. With every allowance for hyperbole, it can scarcely be in any part of the world known to Isaiah's audience.

A natural guess is that the king is meant to be thinking of a northern mountain where the gods of Babylon assemble. This is proposed by two twentieth-century translators. James Moffatt has "I will sit on the hill of the gods in the far, far north." Ronald Knox is hesitant and resorts to a footnote, but he cites a majority view that the king is referring to "those northern hills upon which, according to his own mythology, the gods were supposed to meet." In the context, "hill" is a rather moderate word. The reference would be to Mesopotamia's Mountain of Heaven and Earth.

Yet, as we have seen, no cuneiform text puts this mountain clearly in the "far north."[10] And the difficulty cuts deeper. Old Testament authors have very little to say about gentile myths as such.[11] They name foreign gods and denounce their worship but seldom show any acquaintance with them; they are merely idols with an aura of bad magic. Even in the dramatic conflict of Moses and Pharaoh, when Moses is trying to win his people's liberty, the mighty Egyptian pantheon is absent, apart from a vague reference to the Lord executing judgment on Egypt's gods (Exod. 12:12). The author knows of them, but they never are named or mobilized. Gentile myths are touched on in scripture only when Israel itself has adopted them, as in the case of Leviathan, otherwise Lotan, the twisting serpent of the Canaanites.

Isaiah's allusion to this northern mountain implies that it is part of Israel's own scheme of things, whether or not it is another acclimatized import. Since the impious monarch supposes that by setting his throne on it, he can equal the Most High, in some sense it must be the mountain of God again . . . but, again, not Jerusalem's Zion hill. From a Babylonian vantage point the mountain is explicitly in the north, the far north. This fact introduces another prophetic text. When Ezekiel, in Babylonia, sees a vision of the Lord coming toward him in a chariot, it is from that direction and not from the Lord's home in Jerusalem that the vision approaches.

> As I looked, behold, a stormy wind came out of the north, and a great cloud, with brightness round about it, and fire flashing forth continually, and in the midst of the fire, as it were gleaming bronze. (Ezek. 1:4)

The prophet's description of the vehicle, and the four "living creatures" accompanying an enthroned figure, is a notorious riddle. He is stunned by the apparition, and after hearing a divine pronouncement from the heart of the fire, he goes to some of his fellow exiles and sits overwhelmed among them for seven days (Ezek. 3:15).

In rabbinic tradition the interpretation of this vision is called the Work of the Chariot and is said to be a profound mystery. Only a few initiates have ever known it in full. Its recitation causes supernatural happenings, even a visible appearance of Yahweh himself. When Rabbi Eleazar ben Arak repeated a portion of it to Rabbi Johanan, who had taught it to him, fire encircled the field where they were sitting, angels gathered round, and the trees sang a psalm.[12]

Ezekiel implies that the Lord has a duality of presence. He has his familiar home in Jerusalem, but also, it seems, he has a home in the north. Like the psalmist and Isaiah, Ezekiel associates him not merely with the north but with a northern mountain. The prophet knows a mountain of God that is not in the Holy Land, and he introduces it in a passage recalling Isaiah's. Among his God-dictated messages is an address to the king of Tyre, in the same style as Isaiah's address to the king of Babylon. This too begins as a fairly conventional diatribe, and then it changes, again to a passage about the king's glory and fall, but a lament rather than a taunt, and in amazing terms.

> You were the signet of perfection, full of wisdom and perfect in beauty.
> You were in *Eden, the garden of God*; every precious stone was your covering, carnelian, topaz, and jasper, chrysolite, beryl, and onyx, sapphire, carbuncle, and emerald; and wrought in gold were your settings and your engravings. On the day that you were created they were prepared.
> With an anointed guardian cherub I placed you; you were on *the holy mountain of God*; in the midst of the stones of fire you walked. You were blameless in your ways from the day you were created till iniquity was found in you.
> In the abundance of your trade you were filled with violence, and you sinned; so I cast you out as a profane thing from the mountain of God, and the guardian cherub drove you out from the midst of the stones of fire. (Ezek. 28:12–16)

Again the language is unsuited to a human being. Again it sounds as if the king is being compared to a fallen angel. Some translators, grappling with obscurities, make him the "cherub" himself.[13] Yet beliefs about fallen angels still are difficult to prove in Ezekiel's day, two centuries after Isaiah's.

At all events, God's holy mountain reappears. It has the Garden of Eden on it, the earthly paradise; therefore, it is not Jerusalem's Zion. Collation with Psalm 48 and Isaiah, chapter 14, would suggest that it is in the north, and that is just where the Lord comes from at the outset of Ezekiel's visions. Compass bearings cannot be pressed, but "north" must mean, at the very least, in a higher latitude, and two of the texts say "far." It is quite possible, of course, that Israelites simply took over a northward-pointing myth from elsewhere, without bothering about the geography; but Ezekiel seems to have some slight notion of it.

While Isaiah's "assembly" remains cryptic, the mountain clearly is associated with other beings besides Yahweh—exalted beings, whether resident or rejected. Psalm 82 may preserve a relevant scrap of almost-suppressed belief. It describes God as "taking his place in the divine council," "holding judgment in the midst of the gods," rebuking them for their callous attitude to humanity. He even threatens them:

> I say, "You are gods, sons of the Most High, all of you;
> nevertheless, you shall die like men, and fall like any prince."
> (Ps. 82:6–7)

John 10:34–36 shows that Psalm 82 came to be given a nonpolytheistic gloss—humans to whom the word of God came are referred to as gods—yet there is room to wonder what it meant originally, and whether the "divine council" was the body that "assembled."

Ezekiel's locating the Garden of Eden on the mountain of God does not appear explicitly anywhere else.[14] Yet there can be no doubt as to its mythical importance. Ezekiel 28 seems hard to square with Genesis 2, where Eden is introduced in an immediate sequel to the creation story. But Genesis 2, topographically speaking, is not as straightforward as it looks.

3

Various mythologies tell of a Good Place, sometimes a sort of golden age enclave, like the sunset Elysium of the Greeks, where Cronus still reigns. However "other" it may be, however far beyond reach, it belongs to this world. Paradise as a purely spiritual afterdeath Heaven is a later idea. The actual word *paradise* is Old Persian and means an enclosure, such as a royal park. It reflects Middle Eastern notions of what the Good Place ought to be like—a cultivated space, a garden with abundant water and fruit. Greek translators of the Bible took over the word and used it for the earthly paradise of Genesis, God's Garden of Eden.[15]

Hindu myth, as we have seen, locates its paradisal regions on and near Mount Meru, even employing the word *garden*—"the gardens of the gods." The Mesopotamian paradise Dilmun is sometimes on the world-mountain by implication, though not always. Meru is resplendent with "jewels and gems and all precious stones" and has "many-jewelled peaks"; the garden Gilgamesh finds when he emerges from the mountain at the sunrise place is likewise bejeweled, though it is not Dilmun. Ezekiel's Garden of Eden on the mountain of God is positively ablaze with jewels. There are signs of possible contact in all this.

Genesis's account of Eden looks decidedly different. God creates Adam in another place—rabbinic legend says the future site of Jerusalem, the world center—and puts him there. He creates Eve in the garden itself. The story makes her subordinate and disastrous. She is doubtless a goddess figure demoted by masculine myth-making. As "mother of all living" (3:20) she carries a hint of senior mythology, as do the tree and the serpent, both Mesopotamian motifs.[16] The garden actually has two special trees (2:9), the tree of life and the tree of knowledge of good and evil. God's presumed intention is that humans shall be free to eat the fruit of the former and live forever. He forbids the couple to eat the fruit of the latter. Beguiled by the serpent (in later interpretation, a disguise of Satan), Eve disobeys, and, persuaded by her, so does Adam. They lose their primal innocence and instinctive goodness—the "Fall"—and God expels them from paradise so that they cannot eat the fruit of the tree of life. Death and all the woes of humanity have come into the world.

Death in this context is a doom, with no consolations about an afterlife. To judge from burials with grave goods, the earliest Israelites may have had such a belief, but if so, the religion of Yahweh virtually extinguished it.[17] Throughout the Old Testament, except for a few very late passages, the dead simply go down to Sheol ("the grave"), which is as bloodlessly negative as the netherworld of Sumer. For practical purposes they are finished. This present life is the only one, and Genesis shows the decline from Eden by making it gradually contract. The early patriarchs live for hundreds of years. The true, brief golden age in the garden is over, but a sort of afterglow lingers. Adam, despite his fatal error, reaches the age of 930, and Methuselah reaches 969. As the centuries pass, however, humans last for less and less time, the doom overtakes them sooner and sooner. There is a parallel with the long lives of the first Mesopotamian kings but not their successors, though the biblical ages are less extravagant.

The garden is situated "in Eden, in the east" (Gen. 2:8), which, from an Israelite vantage point, could be almost anywhere in Asia. "Eden" means "delight." A Mesopotamian district had a similar name.[18] While the allusion is to quality rather than location, Adam's descendants seem to be living in more or less that region. Noah's repeopling of the world begins from Mount Ararat in Armenia, where his ark has drifted.

Genesis, in fact, gives the story what looks like a Middle Eastern setting. Yet, simple as that conclusion seems, there has always been dissatisfaction with it. The primary reason lies in the quasi-geography, which is specific yet puzzling and hints at a previous version, transplanted and remolded.

A river flowed out of Eden to water the garden, and there it divided and became four rivers. The name of the first is Pishon; it is the one which flows around the whole land of Havilah, where there is gold; and the gold of that land is good; bdellium and onyx stone are there. The name of the second river is Gihon; it is the one which flows around the whole land of Cush. And the name of the third river is Tigris, which flows east of Assyria. And the fourth river is the Euphrates. (Gen. 2:10–14)

Tigris and Euphrates, the rivers of Mesopotamia, present no problem. A map shows how easy it would be to suppose that they had a common source. But Cush is Ethiopia, so Gihon must be the Nile. Pishon is no identifiable river at all, but a strong tradition makes it the Ganges. On the face of it the headwaters of these four rivers could not be in the same place. The author is drawing not on a geography beyond his ken but on a conception of some other kind.

The passage has been explained as allegory. Eden is made the source of all great rivers, because water, for inhabitants of a dry country, symbolizes fertility and blessedness—a recurrent theme with the biblical prophets.[19] Yet a pure allegory seems too sophisticated for a story so early, so naive. More recondite ideas—for example, that the rivers stand for the four cardinal virtues of Prudence, Justice, Temperance, and Fortitude—can be read back into the text, and fairly, given the assumption that the author was divinely inspired. But he could hardly have had them consciously in mind. Even St. Augustine, who approves of symbolic readings, still insists that they are secondary. The passage is historical and the rivers are rivers.[20]

What seems to have happened is that the Genesis author has got paradise from somewhere else and, in transferring it, has lost sight of an aspect that is in fact vital and indispensable. The imagery that must underlie the four rivers is clear. If they all have a fountainhead in Eden and flow from the garden over distances of thousands of miles, the garden must be very high up. It is no mere riverside park such as a king of Babylon might have founded. The Lord walks in it (Gen. 3:8), and this garden that is his must be on a towering height that is also his—the mountain of God. Ezekiel's Eden on the mountain is no aberration, it restores what was there all the time.

Later authors take the essential point about altitude. The Anglo-Saxon Bede, Europe's leading scholar in the eighth century A.D., asserts that paradise was on a level with the moon.[21] Few have gone as high as that. But Milton, in a better-informed age, understands. In his description of Satan's approach in *Paradise Lost*, he guides the eye of imagination up and up.

> *So on he fares, and to the border comes*
> *Of Eden, where delicious Paradise,*
> *Now nearer, Crowns with her enclosure green,*
> *As with a rural mound the champain head*
> *Of a steep wilderness, whose hairie sides*
> *With thicket overgrown, grottesque and wilde,*
> *Access deni'd; and over head up grew*
> *Insuperable highth of loftiest shade,*
> *Cedar, and Pine, and Firr, and branching Palm*
> *A Silvan Scene, and as the ranks ascend*
> *Shade above Shade, a woodie Theatre*
> *Of stateliest view. Yet higher than thir tops*
> *The verdurous wall of Paradise up sprung:*
> *Which to our general Sire gave prospect large*

Into his neather Empire neighbouring round.
And higher then that wall a circling row
Of goodliest Trees loaden with fairest Fruit,
Blossoms and Fruits at once of golden hue
Appeerd, with gay enameld colours mixt.

(4.131–49)

Milton accepts the Middle Eastern location. He explains the fact that paradise is no longer there by a cataclysm in the course of the Flood (11. 825–31). But while most Jews and Christians have agreed till quite recently that it was historical, many have grasped that the location need not have been. There is a long-standing awareness that literalism may not apply here, that the Genesis text has a background that is not obvious.

An important Jewish work, compiled mainly in the second century B.C., is the *Book of Enoch*. It professes to be a revelation from the patriarch whose name is attached to it, Methuselah's father, mentioned in Gen. 5:21–24; as a Christian epistle shows (Jude 14 and 15), some believed it was. According to Pseudo-Enoch, the true earthly paradise is in the remote northeast beyond seven peaks of the highest range in the world.[22] The objection that great height in a northern latitude would make it too cold and windswept is a modern cavil that never would have occurred to those who first told the story, or to Pseudo-Enoch. They might well have pictured it as warmer than the lands they knew, being nearer the sun.

With the passage of time and the growth of knowledge, the mechanics of Genesis were examined further. Augustine, in the fifth century A.D., dismisses Middle Eastern quasi-geography. But, being committed to the four rivers, he faces the fact—no longer challengeable—that their sources are far apart. Or they appear to be. He offers a solution:[23]

> It is probable that man has no idea where Paradise was, and that the rivers, whose sources are said to be known, flowed for some distance underground, and then sprang up elsewhere.

The subterranean theory came to be widely favored, in the context of an Eden like Pseudo-Enoch's, very far away. In the sixth century a merchant named Cosmas wrote an eccentric *Christian Topography*, in which he tried to extort geographical data from scriptural texts. Cosmas puts paradise right across the eastern ocean in a separate continent. This land was the home of the human race till the time of Noah, who drifted westward in the ark and made his fresh start from Ararat when the water subsided and left a habitable Asia. Cosmas solves the river problem much as Augustine does. He claims that the rivers rise in his transoceanic Eden. They "cleave a passage through the Ocean," pass along Augustinian tunnels, and come up in the world we know. Tigris and Euphrates are still Tigris and Euphrates; Gihon, when it emerges, is the Nile; Pishon is the Ganges or maybe the Indus.[24]

St. Thomas Aquinas, in the thirteenth century, endorses Genesis as historical truth. For him too, however, the geography is indefinite. For him too paradise is not in the Middle East but a long way off. Aware of difficulties, he quotes Augustine on the rivers. He also has to cope with the objection that people have traveled widely ("have explored the entire habitable world," as he optimistically puts it) without bringing back any reports of paradise. He replies with echoes of Pseudo-Enoch and Cosmas:

> The situation of Paradise is shut off from the habitable world by mountains, or seas, or some torrid region, which cannot be crossed; and so people who have written about topography make no mention of it.[25]

In medieval romances of Alexander the Great, Alexander nearly gets there, but not quite. Medieval world maps put paradise about as far east as India. The so-called *Travels of Sir John Mandeville*, a book written toward 1356, has several passages attempting to fit it into the map of Asia.[26] "Mandeville," whoever he is, talks of India and Ceylon (bringing in the ubiquitous gold-digging ants) and a wilderness vaguely beyond—he probably means on a more easterly meridian—with paradise adjacent, so far round the world, which he knows to be spherical, that it has its sunrise at Europe's midnight.

Of paradise he says, "I cannot speak properly, for I have not been there; and this I regret." However, he tells his readers that it is the highest land on earth, reaching up to the sphere of the moon—Bede's opinion. The Flood, which covered everything else, left it unscathed. The four rivers run underground at first. Pishon comes up in India as the Ganges. Gihon has a complicated career, emerging in India and flowing through its deserts, diving underground again and, after further vicissitudes, reappearing at last as the Nile. The Tigris and Euphrates run underground all or part of the way across India and rise, finally, into daylight to the northwest of Meso-potamia. There are wells and springs where water from the rivers reaches the surface and shows their presence. One is the Well of Youth in India, which has curative powers. Another is between Jerusalem and the Mount of Olives.

Eden's location is a topic that has never died. It was one of the scriptural riddles that fascinated General Gordon, the hero of Khartoum.[27] Few of the speculations of the literal-minded have much bearing on real geography. But the long record reveals a stubborn conviction, implied or explicit, that the divine garden was on a height, probably a colossal height. It also reveals a stubborn suspicion, even among the literal-minded, that the Genesis indications of place are not as they seem and that paradise was not only high but remote. Ezekiel and the other biblical texts, plus Pseudo-Enoch, combine to point northward or northeast to a mountain of God mystically at one with Zion, as Sumer's Mountain of Heaven and Earth was mystically at one with the temple in Nippur.

Again a fragmented Meru as in Mesopotamia, but with more of the Hindu prototype rather than less. Parallels exist even in detail—with the Hindu belief, for instance, that the Ganges had its source on the mountain and flowed underground, or at any rate, through some unseen channel, to surface in India. Perhaps we are detecting the western Indo-Aryans here too. However, one feature of Genesis is distinctive. It may open a vista suddenly backward, not merely to Indo-Aryans, but all the way to the Altai.

This is the Fall. Other mythologies had their paradises. Meru had its "gardens of the gods." Sumer and Babylonia had Dilmun, and a garden on their own mountain, if that was conceived as another place. But Genesis has more. Neither Hindus nor Mesopotamians imagine the first humans as actually living in paradise, or as losing it through forfeiture of divine favor, or as thereby condemning their descendants to grief and death. The direct involvement with a golden age and its passing is specially Israelite.[28]

Shamanism, however, has something similar. It tends to go with the myths about a lost harmony with nature. As Eliade puts it, describing what he calls a "paradisal syndrome":

> It was not until after a primordial catastrophe, comparable to the "Fall" of Biblical tradition, that man became what he is today—mortal, sexed, obliged to work to feed himself, and at enmity with animals.[29]

Shamans, in their ecstatic state, can briefly recapture the lost communion between humanity and the rest of life, between earth and heaven.

This parallel draws attention again to the opposed theories—the one that sees influence drifting north from major southern civilizations, from Mesopotamia or India, and impressing the seven mystique and the mountain motif on shamanism; and the one that sees it drifting south from the shamans with Indo-European expansion. If the affinity of Fall and Fall signifies anything, it is a further argument against the south-north theory. If, in this case, transmission happened, it was not from a major civilization. The major civilizations did not have the Fall. Israel, which did, was obscure and at a distance. A purely Israelite motif is most unlikely to have overleapt other cultures, to infiltrate shamanism thousands of miles off.

A shamanic Fall could have figured in a "package" diffused from the Altaic region. Seemingly, though, it did not travel with the Indo-Aryans who made their way to India. Traces of it are wholly absent from the *Rig*

Veda and the Hinduism of the subcontinent. It could have traveled with the western Indo-Aryan branch and reached Israel. But we still have to reckon with its absence from Mesopotamian literature as well as Indian.

Perhaps these Indo-Aryans did carry it, but Sumer and Babylonia, for whatever reason, did not assimilate it, whereas the Israelites did—or rather their ancestors in Syria or Palestine. That may be the most economic explanation. Another exists, apart from coincidence—that the Fall did travel from shamanic country, but by a different route, in an ethnic or cultic stream that passed, say, through the Caucasus or Asia Minor, reaching Israel and blending with the Indo-Aryan stream but not reaching anywhere else. It could have been re-created, sharpened, and brought into focus in terms of Israelite belief, as other themes were. A question to be addressed is whether such a stream left its mark.

CHAPTER TWELVE

A Greek God

1

When we track the seven mystique through the Middle East, the impression is that it halts at the Mediterranean. It is found in Sumer and Babylonia. It is found in Canaan and Israel. It is not found in Egypt to any serious extent, or in Asia Minor. During much of the second millennium B.C., Asia Minor was dominated by Hittites.[1] They were Indo-Europeans, and according to Renfrew, their land had been the home of much earlier Indo-Europeans, the first of all. The immediate point is that the seven mystique seems not to have figured in the Hittite culture. It could have. Kikkuli's horse-training manual is evidence for contact with Indo-Aryans. Myths and themes from the Fertile Crescent could have reached Hittite country, and to a slight extent they did, through a translation of the *Epic of Gilgamesh*, for instance.[2] But these remained exotic. Where the seven mystique is concerned, Asia Minor has the air of a limit, a barrier to its further spread.

Yet it existed on the far side. It existed in a strangely restricted way, confined not merely to a single area but to the cult and mythology of a single god. Greece's version was not an offshoot of anything in the Middle East. It was a separate growth, or so it appears.

Ancient Greece was not homogeneous, and it had more than one phase of creativity. Its first named inhabitants, the Pelasgians, may or may not have been Indo-Europeans.[3] The Hellenes, who were, overran the country in several waves from about 2000 B.C. onward; the name *Hellas* comes from

King or priest in a setting of flowers and butterflies, from Minoan Crete, a civilization with no
early imagery of war. *Hulton-Deutsch*

them, and they evolved the Greek language.[4] Minoan Crete, that artistic
and peaceful island rightly loved by Goddess enthusiasts, flourished during
the same period. Cretans used Greek, at any rate in their later days, and
many had Greek names, but they also had another language now lost, and,
with some awkwardness, they employed its syllabic script to write Greek.

On the mainland, the fine Bronze Age culture of Mycenae arose under
Minoan influence, and a group known as Achaeans, with a warrior aristoc-
racy, became generally dominant by about 1300 B.C. The heroic legends
about the voyage of Argo, the siege of Troy, and so on, relate to this period.
Meanwhile, Crete had gone into decline because of conquest from the
mainland, or eruptions and earthquakes, or both.

About 1100 B.C., the cruder Dorians, who had iron weapons, moved down from the north and plunged Hellas into a dark age. However, traditions from the pre-Dorian time were handed down orally; these formed the Homeric epics, the *Iliad* and *Odyssey*.[5] Homer himself is altogether mysterious, but the epics took their present shape somewhere about 800. Religion and mythology were firmly Olympian now, with a pantheon of six gods and six goddesses, controlled by the former and headed by Father Zeus.[6] He was a blend of an Achaean god and a Cretan. An earlier sky god of the same type was turned into Zeus's brother Poseidon and allotted the sea instead. At some point, an added god, Dionysus, displaced the goddess Hestia, producing a male majority.[7] There were always many lesser deities and subdeities. The opinion, not only of Robert Graves but of others of more academic scholarship, is that many of the Greek myths are male-biased recastings of older ones and fully intelligible only in Goddess terms. Heroic legend certainly is retroactive, pushing back the pre-Olympian Titans into obscurity and making out that Zeus's pantheon was in place, with its revised relationships, before it actually was.

Greece's second creative phase, the time of the glory of Athens and other city-states, extended from the sixth century through the fifth and most of the fourth. This was the age of Aeschylus and Phidias, Herodotus and Thucydides, Pericles and Plato. It was superseded in its turn when the northern kingdom of Macedonia conquered Hellas, and its king Alexander harnessed Greek skill and spirit to overthrow Persia. His victories established the "Hellenistic" civilization throughout the ex-Persian territories in Asia and Egypt.

2

With the Greek form of the seven mystique issues of date arise, and it is vital to discriminate. Some heptads in what purports to be mythology have been read back into it from later times. Thus, Homer's hero Achilles is said to have been the seventh son of his parents.[8] But Homer himself never says so. Hellas's true and primal seven mystique is distinctive, explicit, and related to one sole god—Apollo.

Homer and Hesiod, the other early Greek poet, both give glimpses of it. In the *Odyssey* (9:197 ff.) one of Apollo's priests, Maron, presents Odysseus with seven talents of wrought gold. Hesiod supplies an item of information that leads into a whole network of custom. In his poem *Works and Days*, composed in the eighth century B.C., he discusses the significance of the days of the month and what each of them is auspicious for. Three are holy, and among these the seventh is outstandingly so, because Apollo was born on a seventh day (lines 770–71).

As to this birthday, other mythographers tell us more.[9] Zeus had coupled with Leto, a survivor of the Titan brood, making her pregnant with Apollo and Artemis, the sister whom Romans called Diana. Leto gave birth to Artemis first, and the instantly mature daughter helped her to give birth to Apollo on the little island of Delos. That event took place on the seventh day of the month Thargelion, about May 20.[10] Delos previously had floated and moved about the Aegean. A modern theory is that this legend was inspired by masses of pumice drifting after an eruption.[11] But now the island came to rest. Swans, saluting the divine child, circled around it seven times, singing . . . for swans, an unusual feat.[12] That is why Apollo, when he became the god of music, adopted the seven-stringed lyre as his favored instrument. Delians said he revisited his birthplace each year, on the seventh day of another month in their calendar, Anthesterion.

Elsewhere in Greece the same rule applied to all of Apollo's main festivals, as fixed by the local calendars. These named and defined the months variously, but the septenary rule about Apollo was constant.[13] The Laconians' Karneia fell on the seventh of Karneios (August, more or less), and their Hyakinthia probably fell on the seventh of Hekatombaion (May to June). The Attic Thargelia, marking the god's birthday by a reckoning shared with Delos, came around on the seventh of Thargelion. Another Attic observance, the harvest festival of Pyanopsia, was on the seventh of Pyanopsion. A Pythian summer ceremony was on the seventh of Bukation. Spartan kings made offerings to Apollo on the seventh day of every month. All of these were popular occasions, owing nothing to late fancy or poetic embroidery.

Apparently because of his birthday and the customs branching out from it, one of Apollo's epithets was *Hebdomagetes*, "Commander of Sevens."[14] No other Greek deity had a numerical title related to ritual calendars, and the seventh-day festivals were exceptional themselves—Greeks preferred the full moon. Since she was the first born of Leto's twins, Artemis sometimes had festivals of her own on the sixth day, preceding her brother's.[15]

Soon after his manifestation in Hellas, Apollo, it is said, made his way to Delphi. This place had an oracle where people consulted Ge, Mother Earth. Apollo slew a resident dragon or giant serpent, demoted Ge, and became the oracular god himself.[16] As a matter of history he was probably at Delphi from about 1200 B.C., although he had been worshiped in Greece before. The Delphians held a celebration on the seventh day of the month they called Bysios, in early spring, which they preferred as his birthday.[17] The seventh of Bysios was also the day on which he had taken possession of the oracle, and originally it was the only day of the year when it could be consulted. Even in classical times, when inquirers were admitted in other months, they still had to come on the seventh day of whichever month it was.[18] Apollo presided at Delphi three quarters of the year, spending the rest of his time with the Hyperboreans (of whom more in due course).

Delphi rose steadily in importance. Because of it, Greece became hiero-centric like Sumer, Babylonia, and Israel. Delphi with its temple was the bond of the land, not because it was the capital—ancient Greece never had one—but because it was the sanctuary shared by all Greeks, the one focus of Hellenic union.[19] As such, it helped to sustain morale in times of trouble. The union was cultural as well as religious. Apollo's temple complex housed paintings and sculptures from every quarter, and poets and musicians gathered there to present their works.[20] Over the main door were maxims of the Seven Wise Men of Greece. These were the nearest equivalents of the Seven Rishis and Seven Sages. But they were historical figures, and each was associated with a different city—Solon with Athens, Chilo with Sparta, Thales with Miletus, Bias with Priene, Cleobulus with Lindos, Pittacus with Mitylene, and Periander with Corinth.[21]

All of the city-states used to send envoys to consult Apollo's oracle. His cryptic utterances through an inspired priestess were interpreted by officials called exegetes. Some of them were attached to governments on a permanent basis. The company of exegetes was the nearest thing to a church that Hellas possessed.[22] The Athenians credited Apollo with some of their laws. The Spartans claimed that he had dictated their whole constitution.[23]

Plato, founding an imaginary republic on philosophic reason, still concedes a Delphic exception. This ideal republic must have a religion. Its creation is a matter for "the greatest and finest and most important of legislative acts," and they should be entrusted to Apollo, "for he is the national expositor who explains these things to all men from his seat at the navel of the earth." It may be doubted how far Plato believed in the oracle, but he believed in its value as a moral force, uniting and stabilizing.[24]

His phrase about the "navel" shows a growth of ideas. Delphi came to be viewed as the earth's literal center, like Nippur, Babylon, and Jerusalem. Ezekiel, speaking of Jerusalem, also calls it the navel. By Plato's time, indeed, Greeks had come to realize that the circular *oecumene*, or inhabited landmass, was, to say the least, ragged at the edges. Herodotus (4.36) has an amused comment.

> I cannot but laugh when I see numbers of persons drawing maps of the world without having any reason to guide them; making, as they do, the Ocean-stream to run all round the earth [that is, the landmass], and the earth itself to be an exact circle, as if described by a pair of compasses.

Yet on the testimony of this very sentence the notion of a circle persisted, and a circle, even if improved knowledge made it look irregular, could have a center. A legend told how two eagles or swans, at opposite points on the flat world's edge, flew inward simultaneously and met at Delphi.[25]

The exact central point was marked by a stone called the *omphalos* (Greek for "navel"). Kept in Apollo's temple, it was believed to channel mysterious forces that helped to prepare the priestess for inspiration.[26] Hesiod says it was a stone swallowed by Cronus, the chief Titan, under the delusion that it was his dangerous son Zeus. He disgorged it, and Zeus picked it up and deposited it at Delphi. Others say that although the stone in question was to be seen there, it was not the *omphalos*, which was hidden from public view. The object may actually have been a mound or a phallic symbol. Apollo is portrayed sitting on it.

Inscribed over the temple door, besides the maxims of the Seven Wise Men, was the letter *e*—short *e*, the fifth letter of the Greek alphabet, used in numerical notation for the number five. A philosophical dialogue by Plutarch written in the first century A.D. debates its Delphic meaning and gives sidelights on Apollo's development.[27] Plutarch himself, as a speaker in this fictitious discussion, goes on for a long time about five's significance. Another, Ammonius, retorts that you can squeeze all sorts of meanings out of numbers if you try hard enough. Whatever the meaning of the Delphic *e*, it should not be explained numerically. At Delphi seven has the traditional place of honor, and "the sacred Seven of Apollo will consume the whole day before the narration of all its powers is finished."

3

Apollo commonly is thought of as a sun god, but he was the god of music long before he had anything to do with the sun. A vase painting portrays him on the navel-stone with a lyre in his hand.[28] It has seven strings, like Mesopotamian harps. The basis of such a lyre was the seven-note scale, which was known in Sumer and can be inferred among Canaanites in about 1800 B.C. Instruments attest it also on the Indo-Aryan approaches of India. Evidence for lyres like Apollo's has been found on Minoan and Mycenaean sites.[29]

According to myth the young god Hermes (Mercury in the Roman pantheon) made a lyre out of the shell of a tortoise and some cow gut and played it to please his mother Maia, one of a group of seven goddesses, the Atlantides. He presented it to Apollo, whose career as god of music began from that moment.[30] Some say Hermes gave it fewer strings and Apollo himself made the number up to seven. A Melian vase dated about 700 B.C. depicts him playing his lyre in a chariot, attended by two women; his twin sister Artemis is greeting him.[31]

By the time Plutarch wrote his *e* dialogue, Apollo's aspect as sun god had come to be accepted and he could find a place in the astrological scheme.[32] Later still, in the fifth century A.D., mystics of the Neoplatonic

Vase painting of Apollo before Zeus, holding his seven-stringed lyre; his sister Artemis is behind him. *Mansell Collection*

school dwell further on his septenary quality. In the words of one, Macrobius: "Apollo's lyre of seven strings provides understanding of the motions of all the celestial spheres over which nature has set the Sun as moderator." In the words of another, Proclus: "The number seven they have dedicated to Apollo as to him who embraces all symphonies whatsoever, and therefore they used to call him . . . the Prince of the number Seven."[33]

There are Greek myths and legends with a septenary element in which Apollo seems not to be involved, yet on closer inspection it turns out that he is. Hermes, for instance, made another lyre and presented it to a mortal, Amphion, who built the walls of Thebes by its musical magic.[34] Heptads continued in his city. He had seven daughters and made a gate in the walls for each one. The seer Teiresias, at the court of the later Theban king Oedipus, had his life lengthened through seven generations. After Oedipus's famous and fearful doom—he killed his father and married his mother, not knowing who they were, and blinded himself when he found out—seven champions besieged the city in support of his banished heir, each champion facing one of the gates. Their attempt failed, but their seven sons avenged them by coming back and besieging Thebes again, this time successfully.

It may look as if Apollo had nothing to do with this. But it all begins with the magic of the lyre, which Hermes made because the god's approval encouraged him. Apollo plays a direct part in the fate of Amphion's family. By his wife Niobe the king had seven sons as well as the daughters. Niobe boasted truly but rashly of having a bigger family than Leto's, whereupon Apollo and Artemis, urged on by their affronted mother, appeared with bows and arrows and started shooting. Apollo found the boys out hunting and slew them all, with the possible exception of one, who had propitiated Leto with a well-timed prayer. Artemis found the girls in the palace and did likewise, sparing one, perhaps for the same reason.[35] The survivors may have been brought into the story to avoid a discrepancy with Homer, who says (*Iliad* 24:612 ff.) that Niobe lost six children of either sex.[36] Apollo's Theban involvement does not end there. His Delphic oracle has a decisive role in the Oedipus and post-Oedipus phases, and during the warfare, as "Commander of Sevens," he intervenes in the fighting at the seventh gate.

Apollo is in the background of another piece of myth-making, the listing of the Titans.[37] It came to be more or less agreed that there were seven Titans, and seven Titanesses paired with them. Surely this is an ancient heptad unconnected with Apollo? No, it is not. Hesiod mentions only six Titans, with six female partners (*Theogony*, lines 133–37). The list giving seven each is part of the reputed teaching of Orpheus, the semidivine musician.[38] He is said to have been a priest of Apollo and to have worshiped him as Supreme God, being the first to assert his solar nature. Apollo gave Orpheus a lyre—seven-stringed, of course—on which he played magical music. After his death it floated over the sea to the island of Lesbos, where it was enshrined in Apollo's temple and afterward, by the god's wish, translated to the sky as a constellation.[39] From about the sixth century B.C., a number of Greeks claimed to be custodians of poems and doctrines ascribed to the great musician. They may have pioneered Apollo's elevation as sun god, and it was certainly they who fixed the number of Titans as seven, this being part of their Orphic-Apollonian Ancient Wisdom. The number passed into a myth about the Titans rending the infant god Dionysus into seven pieces and his reconstitution by Apollo.[40]

The labyrinth legend is another such deceptive case. King Minos of Crete demanded a regular tribute of seven Athenian youths and maidens as food for the Minotaur, the monster at the labyrinth's center. As with Niobe and the Titans there is a doubt as to how many—again seven wins out, and again Apollo is involved.[41]

In its origin the labyrinth was probably not a building but a dance, following the course of a backtracking spiral from perimeter to center, with seven circuits clockwise and counterclockwise. This is a major instance of the septenary maze pattern that appears far and wide and may have been disseminated from the Altaic region.[42] Homer speaks of the craftsman Daedalus designing a dancing floor for Minos's daughter Ariadne (*Iliad* 18:590 ff.), and presumably the dance was performed on this. Later its plan was used to represent the real or legendary labyrinth where the Minotaur lived. The septenary double spiral is inscribed on Cretan coins; and these have Apollo's profile on the obverse.[43]

The connection is apparently that the dance was performed on Delos, circling around his altar beside a lake. This altar reputedly was made by the god in person, out of the horns of goats slain by Artemis. It counted, on some lists, as one of the Seven Wonders of the World. The traditional explanation of the Delian ritual was that when Theseus went to Crete to kill the Minotaur he learned the dance from Ariadne, or from Daedalus himself. On the journey home with his rescued Athenians he put in at the island and instituted the dance as a regular ritual.[44]

Daedalus lost Minos's favor and escaped from Crete by making a pair of wings and flying. He landed at Cumae near Naples, built a temple for Apollo, and dedicated his wings to the god. The place became another Apollo oracle. Virgil says that the gate had a representation of the labyrinth on it. This, if it existed, was very likely the same septenary design.[45]

In the sixth century B.C. lived Pythagoras, who was a devotee of Apollo and, according to legend, his son. Pythagoras's epochal work in mathematics went beyond any religious cult, and he taught a number mysticism not focused on any single number. His Apollo affiliation, however, underlines the fact that this god was the only Olympian for whom numbers mattered at all. The Commander of Sevens was the divine patron of mathematics as well as music. Pythagoras, by studying the relation between the length of a vibrating string and the pitch of its note, linked the two.

Pythagoras claimed to be a reincarnation of a Trojan, Euphorbus, and to have initiated, in that life, some of the pursuits that he took further in his Pythagoras phase.[46] A visitor to Miletus found Thales, one of the Seven Wise Men, in a temple of Apollo drawing geometrical figures such as Euphorbus had studied. The Trojan's feats, it appeared, included the construction of a "seven-length circle." This puzzling term has been explained as meaning a diagram of the relative distances of the planets. Pythagoras might have had some inkling of these, but hardly in his previous life as Euphorbus, who fought in the Trojan War.

Last, Apollo took an interest in healing and was the father of Asclepius, the semidivine prototype of doctors and patron of their profession.[47] Chief among them in Greece was Hippocrates, founder of scientific medicine, whose name is immortalized in the Hippocratic Oath. One of his ideas was a division of human life into seven stages.

4

Apollo, then, was a septenary god, explicitly so in his festivals, in his title *Hebdomagetes*, in Plutarch's dialogue. Sevens of various kinds keep appearing in his worship and in mythology related to him. They are extremely rare anywhere else in Greek cult or myth, before the irruption of foreign factors, such as astrology.

Outside Greece a few deities have a similar quality—Inanna, for instance. But the only one whom Apollo really resembles is the God of Israel. The parallel goes beyond the seven mystique. Both had their principal places of worship at world centers, Yahweh at Jerusalem, Apollo at Delphi. At these centers both communicated with mortals. The conviction that "out of Zion shall go forth the Law" was the ultimate source of the missionary energies of Judaism and Christianity, and while Delphic Apollo worship was never a proselyte-seeking, exclusive faith, it was the only Greek cult with even the semblance of a mission. It was cosmopolitan, and it radiated outward. Apollo, through his oracle, advised the founders of Greek colonies in Italy and farther afield. His ministers traveled with the colonists and ensured that he had a temple in every new settlement.[48]

Robert Graves put forward the amazing notion that Apollo and Yahweh are the same—or at least that they overlap.[49] Plutarch, in his discourse on the *e* at Delphi, comes close unconsciously to the same thought. The name of the short *e* in classical Greek was *ei* (not, as later, *epsilon*), and *ei* could mean both "if" and "thou art." One of Plutarch's characters, the same Ammonius who mentions the sacred seven, argues for the second meaning. "Thou art" on Apollo's temple is a salutation the worshiper should utter. It refers to his eternal being.[50] He can be regarded, and at Delphi should be regarded, as the one Supreme God. This is not far from the "I am" of Exodus 3:14 in Yahweh's revelation to Moses. The Greek translation of the Bible calls God *ho Ōn*, the Being, He Who Is.[51] The verb *to be* is the same that becomes *ei*, "thou art," in the alleged Delphic reading.

Plutarch allows Ammonius the last word. No one can tell now whether the Delphic *e*'s inscriber intended this, or could have intended it. If he did he was giving his god an extraordinary distinction. Plutarch is willing to do so. To quote him further:

> The god is not several, made up of an infinite number of things, as we are. He is with reference to no time, but only to the eternal, the immovable and the timeless. There is nothing before, nor after, nor more, nor past, nor older, nor younger; but he being one with the "Now" has filled up the "Ever."[52]

Sophistications like this may or may not have a basis in Apollo's original nature; or rather, the nature of some component of a god who comes through to history as complex and composite—whatever Plutarch may say. Graves's argument is quite different. He cites the vision of the Lord's chariot in the first chapter of Ezekiel, the interpretation of which was a mystery entrusted to very few, the "Work of the Chariot." Graves suggests that it contained a dangerous secret about Yahweh, part of which was his identity or semi-identity with Apollo. The word translated as "gleaming bronze" in the Revised Standard Version ("in the midst of the fire, as it were gleaming bronze") is *hashmal*, which usually is taken to mean "amber." Amber, a northern stone from the Baltic, had connections—according to some—with the Hyperboreans, among whom Apollo lived for part of each year. Thus far Robert Graves.[53]

While Apollo had his principal home at Delphi, the earth's center, he had a northern dwelling as well among these Hyperboreans, whose name means "dwellers beyond the North Wind." Likewise the God of Israel. He had his home in Jerusalem, the earth's center, and he had—as Ezekiel and others show—another dwelling in the far north, the mountain of God. Quite apart from Graves's conjecture, Apollo's northern affiliation needs to be looked at. So does another of his relationships, with Artemis. The two are intertwined. What has emerged is that he embodies the same linked motifs we have found in other settings, the seven mystique and centrality. They appear this time in an Indo-European setting, but they are not due to Indo-Aryans, whether directly or indirectly. Without rushing into fantasies about a Yahweh-Apollo equation, we can reasonably wonder again whether influences akin to those in the Middle East traveled by a different route.

CHAPTER THIRTEEN

A Greek Goddess

1

Once more: despite Plutarch, the Apollo disclosed in myth and worship is a composite figure.[1] He has anomalous attributes, such as a connection with mice. Some of his amours and other exploits, which tend to be cruel, may allegorize events during the Hellenization of Greece. He is apt to be ruthless: he makes his literary debut, in the *Iliad*, inflicting a plague. As god of inspiration he not only speaks through his oracles, at Delphi and elsewhere, he has a responsibility for poetry as well as music and is a sort of choirmaster for the nine Muses. His role as god of mathematics very likely grew from his seven mystique. It developed into a broader patronage of science in general, which may account for his interest in medicine. He becomes, in fact, a divine sponsor of civilization, a deity of order, very Greek yet with un-Greek antecedents that rise to the surface in, for instance, the prophetic ecstasy of his priestesses. His belated worship as the sun, supposedly pioneered by Orpheus, may have an Egyptian background.[2]

The question is whether we can shed light on him, and on his roots and their implications, by pinning down a basic constituent, a nucleus around which attributes gathered. It might be easier to do this if there were any consensus as to the meaning of his name. It has no agreed-upon etymology. It has been explained as "destroyer"; as "god of the town meeting"; and as "apple-god," with a remote echo of a Celtic otherworld sometimes inexactly called Avalon. It also has been equated with Apulunas, the name of a Hittite god of gates. The weakness of these derivations is that they seem unrelated to anything Apollo does.[3]

One thing is sure. He—or let us say his main component, the basic Apollo—reached mainland Hellas from outside.[4] Quintessentially Greek as he became, even Delphi never claimed him as native to itself. He had arrived from elsewhere, and that event was commemorated in a mime of his advent and serpent killing. Official myth said he had come from no farther off than Delos. But his Delian birth as Zeus's son was an afterthought, an invention, intended, like other mythical inventions, to fit an outsider into the Zeus-dominated pantheon. Apart from anything else, it fails to explain why he spent three months of every year outside Greece, among the Hyperboreans . . . whoever they were. (During his absence, Dionysus reigned at Delphi as his deputy but did not speak through the oracle.)[5]

A method of approach that some might call lateral is to consider his sister. Homer says they had a joint temple in Troy, across the Aegean, which they shared with their mother, Leto. He tells how Apollo rescued the wounded Trojan Aeneas during a battle and carried him to the temple. "In the spacious sanctuary, Leto and Artemis the Archeress not only healed him but made him more splendid than ever" (*Iliad* 5.445–48). It is noteworthy that at this date, vaguely around 1200 B.C., Apollo is not a healer himself. Brother and sister aid the Trojans against their Greek besiegers. Inscriptions in Asia Minor confirm the early worship of Apollo and Leto there, and of Artemis herself. There are many signs that she too was a migrant, and from farther off than Troy.

One clue has an immediate interest. If the source of the seven mystique was Ursa Major, Apollo's twinning with Artemis might have had something to do with his acquisition of it. The goddess whom the Greeks made his sister and the Romans called Diana was (among much else) Mistress of Wild Animals, and the Great Bear in the sky was hers—indeed, was her astral form. That is why it is a she bear, *ursa*, not *ursus*. Circling the pole, and linked with Ursa Minor at the hub of the circle, she was present at the sky center just as Apollo was present at the earth center.

Artemis was never septenary in the multiple manner of her brother, but two sky heptads as well as Ursa Major had a connection with her. Of the few star groups recognized by the early Greeks, as Homer names them, three had seven principal members—the Bear itself, the Pleiades, and Orion, in which the bright stars of the image are seven, four at the corners plus the belt.[6] Homer speaks of the Bear as "looking across at Orion the Hunter with a wary eye." The Pleiades, daughters of the Titan Atlas by Pleione, were among Artemis's many maiden companions, and Orion was a giant who pursued them amorously for seven years, much to her annoyance. At last Zeus rescued them by translating them to the heavens. When Artemis learned that Orion was planning a massacre of wildlife she lost patience and slew him, but she also translated him to the heavens. In that milieu he pursues the Pleiades still.[7]

There is a strange point here, which may be a product of folk memory but may give another glimpse of seven showing compulsiveness. The Pleiades mark phases of the year by their rising and setting. This cluster therefore has a worldwide importance, even among primitive peoples.[8] The stars in it that can be seen with the naked eye are hard to count and seldom are reckoned as seven by people who simply look at them, uninfluenced by any mystique of the number. The Blackfoot Indians do, and so do some Australian aborigines, in a very clear atmosphere. But under most conditions six is a more plausible count, and six it is in such civilized contexts as the *Mahabharata*.[9]

Now, the Greeks knew this. But they insisted that the cluster had lost one member. In the words of the poet Aratus in the third century B.C., "Seven are they in the songs of men, albeit only six are visible to the eye."[10] The "songs of men" made out that the Pleiades, in their stellar form, were once visibly seven. Then one of them disappeared. Some say she was Electra, ancestress of the Trojan royal house, and lost her luminosity in grief at Troy's downfall; others say she was Merope and hid in shame at the disgrace of her husband, Sisyphus, condemned in the underworld, for his wickedness, to keep rolling a huge stone uphill, never getting it to the top because it broke loose and rolled down again. Whatever the identity of the lost Pleiad, she is still there, only we can't see her. Thus the Greeks made the number up to seven in defiance of ocular evidence.[11] The only reason for wondering whether the story is founded on fact, on the real extinction of a real once-visible Pleiad, is that the Dyaks of Sarawak also maintain that there are six now but there used to be seven.[12] With the Greeks, the compulsiveness of the heptad seems a likelier explanation.

However that may be, the Bears, great and little, are the star groups calling for scrutiny. When Aratus writes about them he calls them Helice ("That Which Turns") and Cynosura and says they were once she bears living in Crete. They guarded Zeus during his perilous infancy, under threat from his father Cronus, and when he grew up and became sovereign he promoted them to the sky. Aratus does not make them creatures of Artemis or any other Olympian.[13] The trouble is that both constellations, if outlined as animals, have tails—a long one with Ursa Major, a preposterous one with Ursa Minor—and it would be absurd to identify them with the only large quadruped that has virtually none. Fainter stars were added to Ursa Major to make it more bearlike, but the tail difficulty was no nearer resolution.[14] It seems that Aratus picked up the bears from an older myth, one belonging to an age of "aniconic" religious imagery—that is, imagery in which pictorial likeness was not required; a stone, for example, could stand for a god as well as a statue could.

An older myth of the Bears is known indeed, and it involves Artemis. It is time to take stock of this impressive lady. She is one of the goddess figures of whom Farnell wrote, in 1896, that the Greek "female divinities" have so much in common as to suggest that they are all basically the same. In Farnell's work this is a throwaway line. His anticipation of what is now meant by the Goddess is remarkable.

Familiar as a virgin huntress, wearing a knee-length dress and carrying a bow, Artemis is actually much more complex. Her name is un-Greek and she was worshiped in Crete as well as in Asia Minor, before the Greek mainland. In Asia she sometimes was identified with Astarte, Cybele, and

The image of Artemis at Ephesus ("Diana of the Ephesians" in the Bible): her many breasts symbolize the productive and nourishing powers of Earth. *Hulton-Deutsch*

other variants of the Great Mother.[15] Her famous temple at Ephesus, one of the Seven Wonders of the World and a cause of trouble for St. Paul (Acts 19:23–34), was by no means the abode of a virgin. This may sound paradoxical, but the word *parthenos*, rendered "virgin," could mean an unmarried female regardless of her physical state. Artemis's *parthenia* originally implied that while she might have had lovers, she accepted no male as lord.[16] Some of her local rituals were orgiastic and phallic.

Classical myth did eventually make her virginal, yet she was also a patroness of childbirth, having assisted in the delivery of her brother, and she sustained women in labor. She is represented as saying, "Even at the hour when I was born the Fates ordained that I should be their helper"—that is, the helper of women bearing children—"forasmuch as my mother suffered no pain either when she gave me birth or when she carried me in her womb, but without travail put me from her body."[17] Leto's painlessness foreshadows a belief about the Virgin Mary, who was the presiding spirit of Ephesus after its temple was destroyed.

Artemis's local cults are apt to have a primitive air. One or two of them hint that she was once an Earth Goddess or, at any rate, had an Earth Goddess constituent in her nature. Homer calls her "Mistress of Beasts and Lady of the Wilds." At early levels she is associated with water, trees, and woodland life, and untamed animals, such as hares, wolves, deer, boars . . . and yes, bears.[18] She has two earthly ursine aspects, Artemis-Callisto and Artemis-Brauronia. The former explains Ursa Major's connection with her. The latter may point to the ancient homeland from which she came, bringing exotic myths and rituals with her.[19]

Arcadia in southern Greece had a bear cult of an archaic type, in which a deity and an animal were blended. It was here that the goddess was worshiped as Artemis-Callisto, and the Arcadians had a shrine of her under that style.[20] An associated myth gave an account of her constellation. Like a number of myths, it detached an aspect of her and turned this into a separate character. Callisto was made out to have been an attendant nymph, one of her entourage, like the Pleiades. Her story is told in several versions. The discrepancies suggest traditions coming down from a long way back.

Hesiod wrote on the theme in the eighth century B.C. His poem is no longer extant, but in substance the story tells how Callisto yielded to Zeus's lust and bore a son, Arcas.[21] Whatever Artemis's own sexual conduct, she preferred maidenhood in her attendants and turned Callisto into a bear. To save her from hunters, perhaps even from Artemis herself, Zeus translated her skyward and she became Ursa Major. Arcas, human himself though his name means "bear," became the ancestor of the Arcadians. According to another version it was Zeus's jealous wife Hera who turned the nymph into a bear, hoping that Artemis would shoot her in ignorance. The real background of all of this is that Ursa Major was Artemis's manifestation in the heavens. The Arcadians, bear folk, as they interpreted their name, personified her local aspect Callisto and created a myth about it. Artemis took an interest in Ursa Minor, Cynosura, as well, although its mythical status is unclear. It may be Arcas, translated after his earthly life, but if so it ought to be masculine. The god Pan, who lived in Arcadia and sometimes is said to have been Arcas's brother, made Artemis a gift of seven Cynosuran bitches. The word may mean simply "Arcadian," but the number, as ever, is noteworthy and perhaps related to the stars.[22]

As for Artemis-Brauronia, she was the goddess of the town of Brauron, on the coast of Attica east of Athens. It had a temple housing an ancient wooden image of her. In the festival of Brauronian Artemis, held every five years, two girls aged five and ten danced in ceremonies that survived into the classical era. Their dance was called the *arkteia*, or "bear dance." They wore yellow bearskin robes and doubtless corresponded to Ursa Minor and Ursa Major. Callisto had no part in the ritual or the stories relating to it, and her absence confirms that the bears were entirely Artemis's concern, she being the common factor in the two very different settings. There will be more to say about this Brauronian cult.[23]

As a Greek deity and, to a lesser extent, in her Roman guise, Artemis has been called the most feminine of goddesses.[24] That may be so, but not in the conventional sense. She has a tough, aloof femininity favored by liberated women in modern times. One account of the Callisto affair even alleges that Zeus coupled with the nymph by assuming Artemis's shape and effecting a lesbian union. A query may arise as to how pregnancy resulted, but Zeus could have contrived it if he wished. Artemis had a whole train of nymphs, reputedly eighty, whom she recruited when very young.[25] She was apt to be angry if they were heterosexually entangled—hence the Callisto trouble. In some of her folk festivals male dancers took part, but even when they did they were dressed as women.[26]

Her femininity, in the sense defined, and her connection with bears and with the stars of the Bear—do these features lead anywhere? Do they suggest any thoughts about her brother Apollo?

2

Artemis's temple at Ephesus contained an old wooden image of her. Inside its headdress was an object known as the diopet, said to have fallen from the sky—perhaps a Neolithic implement, perhaps a bronze pestle.[27] There is a scriptural reference to it in Acts 19:35, where the phrasing has perplexed translators. The Revised Standard Version hesitantly makes it a "sacred stone." Legend declared that the original shrine and image were set up by Amazons, the matriarchal warrior women of Greek mythology. Before the siege of Troy they made war on Athens. Marching through Asia Minor on their way to Greece, they paused at Ephesus and founded the temple of Artemis as their patroness, dancing to the music of pipes.[28]

For Amazons she was the natural goddess. Greek authors speak of them early and revert to them often but remain uncertain about their homeland. According to the oldest accounts they lived in the Thermodon Valley near the southern coast of the Black Sea. It was reported that men were tolerated among them only for breeding purposes, or even that they had no men at all but made an annual visit to the Caucasus for temporary mates. Girl children that resulted were kept, boys were sent back to their fathers. When Greeks explored the Thermodon Valley and found no Amazons, they inferred that they had been exterminated by enemies or driven out. Herodotus favors the latter version. He says the uprooted Amazons wandered for some time and finally settled in what is now southern Russia.[29]

He may have picked up a morsel of fact. Burials in that region—the Pontic-Caspian—show that women sometimes were interred with weapons and presumably were warriors. It is a fair guess that such women would have had a divine patroness, a prior form, credibly, of the goddess who reached Hellas as Artemis. The Amazons' shifting locations, in the Caucasus and Asia Minor, may even reflect the progress of her cult toward Greece, bringing stories of her Amazon worshipers.

Before any attempt to confirm that guess, a curious fact is worth noting. "Artemisia" is a term applied by modern geographers to an arid area north of the Caspian Sea. The reason is that a plant of that name characterizes the vegetational zone.[30] Why the plant should have been named so is uncertain; possibly it was because of its arrow-shaped barbs. It is intriguing that the plant should have evoked the archeress in just that setting.

The question of an Artemis beyond the Black Sea brings us back to the goddess's image at Brauron, scene of the bear ritual. Like the Ephesian object, it was supposed to have fallen from the sky, but not at Brauron. It stood first in a temple in the Crimea, on a cliff by the sea. Greeks called the people of that country the Taurians, and the temple belonged to a goddess whom they called Tauric Artemis. One of her titles was Artemis Tauropolos, and it was under that name that Amazons reputedly worshiped her.[31]

Legend relates that her image and cult reached Brauron as a consequence of the Trojan War. The fleet of the Troy-bound Greeks was held up by contrary winds at Aulis, between the island of Euboea and the Greek mainland, owing to Artemis's enmity to their leader Agamemnon. He was about to try to appease her by sacrificing his daughter Iphigenia. Artemis, however, wafted her off to the Crimea, where she became a priestess in the Tauric temple and was revered as the goddess in human form. Long afterward Iphigenia's brother Orestes, seeking to expiate his guilt for killing their mother, consulted Apollo's Delphic oracle and was bidden to go to the temple and bring back the celestial image. He went there and was amazed to find his sister alive, having always assumed that she actually had been sacrificed. With her aid he carried out the assignment. They sailed to Brauron together and installed the image in a temple, where Iphigenia continued to serve Artemis as priestess and the girls performed their quinquennial bear dance.

The Tauric cult existed. Herodotus records a report of it as barbaric.[32] Anyone who was wrecked on that coast or even put in because of bad weather was liable to be sacrificed to "the Virgin." The ritual involved beating the victim's head with a club, cutting it off, and nailing it to a cross, while the rest of the corpse was tossed over the cliff or burned. A man of high rank was given special treatment. The priestess killed him herself with a sword and dropped the body into a sacred fire.

It has been argued that the Tauric Virgin was originally someone else, and the Greeks merely equated her with Artemis when they explored that part of the Black Sea littoral, long after Artemis was established at home.[33] But it need not have happened thus. A Proto-Artemis in the Pontic-Caspian region would be an arguable candidate for the original, or at least a basic ingredient.[34] Greeks could have encountered her when they voyaged beyond the Black Sea, but she had been there from time immemorial and they were right to conclude that they were recognizing rather than speculating. It seems hard to understand why Greeks with a fairly civilized Artemis should have identified the barbaric Virgin with her at all, unless they had prior reason to think that the Virgin, despite appearances, *was* Artemis.

We have not one but two stories of Artemis coming to the Grecian world from this northern region. Legend brings her worship through Asia Minor to Ephesus with the Amazons and may not be entirely baseless. Legend brings her celestial image from Taurian country, an image carried across the sea to Brauron by the priestess of an Amazonian cult. Both stories may reflect traditions about her actual advent and the part of the world from which she came. Also we have her ursine aspect. The notion of a bear goddess, or of the Goddess as bear, is foreign to Greece. As in the *Rig Veda*, myth is introducing a creature that was far more familiar and far more numinous in northern lands.

Let us recall what emerged earlier about bear cults and bear myths, from Lapland to the Pacific. They have a unique role in the folklore and ritual of the speakers of Finno-Ugric languages and, more generally, of the Uralic language family that extends into Siberia, to which the Finno-Ugric belong. They occur also among tribes far eastward. The peculiar awe that the bear excites and its air of being semihuman have inspired distinctive beliefs—that bears are ancestors of the human race, a notion very widespread in Siberia; that dead humans can proceed to an ursine rebirth; that occasional men are bear sons, born of a mating between the species. Shamans in ecstasy can "become" bears, and when this happens they do not sink lower than humanity, they are exalted above it—hence, perhaps, the fact that in Indo-Aryan myth the seven stars are both bears and Rishis.

While Artemis's name is not Greek, variants of its first syllable figure in other Indo-European languages, with the meaning "bear." That is true of the Greek *arktos* itself. While "Artemis" could not have been derived from *arktos*, Indo-European forms farther afield hold out possibilities. "Bear" in Welsh is *arth*. Arcas is probably, in his origins, both a bear son and a bear ancestor, hinting at motifs traveling with Artemis from a region where they were normal. A Pontic-Caspian location would plant her in what, by broad consent, is early Indo-European country, where a goddess who acquired ursine associations could have evolved a name with the ursine syllable.

We might even guess at the area where the bear motif was attached to her. The Finno-Ugric people in Lapland and by the Baltic are thought to have migrated from a Uralic homeland between the middle Volga and middle Ob.[35] Any bear cults they brought with them had existed, presumably, in that homeland. For linguistic reasons Mallory and others believe that this was in prolonged contact with Proto-Indo-Europeans. Archaeology points to a specific zone on the middle Volga, the milieu of the "Samara" culture. That is not far from the area where the Amazon legend suggests worship of Artemis . . . or Proto-Artemis.

There is now an evident overlap with the shamanic world. A possibility is dawning that the reverence for Ursa Major in the background of Artemis is the same as the reverence for it in the background of the Seven Rishis— that is, the shamanic reverence. A hope may be taking shape that the Altaic seedbed can be confirmed by a different and convergent route. That will not solidify, however, till it can be seen whether Apollo fits in. Meanwhile, Artemis can be pursued further.

3

Indo-Europeans were spread out across the steppes by 3000 B.C. They had spread as far as the Altai, creating the Afanasievo and related cultures, where contact with shamanism, its seven mystique, and so on might have occurred. An Indo-European continuum stretched from the Pontic-Caspian region to the Altaic. There is reason to believe that shamanism flourished in parallel all the way and had done so from an immemorial past. It has offered an explanation of the Indo-Aryans' seven bear stars. It may offer an explanation of the same stars as the Bear in Artemis's scheme of things.

It is right to recall another topic: shamanism's feminine aspect, and a related theory that may be relevant to Artemis—the theory that women in Siberia were originally the only shamans. Scattered tribes all have the same word for a female shaman, *utygan* and its variants, but not for a male shaman. More can be said, and has been said, about the possibility that male shamans began as smiths who made magical gear for female ones and gradually took over their powers, and also about the curious nostalgia that impels male shamans to dress like women and otherwise become feminized.

Siberian mythology may be expected to include goddesses, and as we saw, it does, with resemblances to Artemis in her oldest-known guises. An Earth Goddess is acknowledged, and so is a Great Mother of the Animals, in whom Eliade detected an "image of the ancient matriarchy." Shamans, Eliade assures us, are on excellent terms with her.

Roerich attests shamanic worship of Ursa Major, and underlying it is a cluster of motifs that may almost settle the Artemisian question. Their discoverers were Dordji Banzaroff and Gregory Potanin. Banzaroff, born in 1822, was a Buryat; he attended a Russian university and held a government post, but he died young. Potanin, a Russian born in 1835, has been mentioned already. His Altaic researches are especially valuable.[36]

Both took an interest in the female shaman word, *utygan*. They judged that it was derived from Etugen, a name for the Earth Goddess.[37] Potanin ventured further. He studied the Earth Goddess's names among Altaic and Finno-Ugric groups and found them to be related to names of constellations, especially the Bears. Connected with all of this is the fact that in one dialect *utygan* means not only a female shaman but a bear.

An Earth Goddess and Mistress of Animals, associated with Ursa Major and terrestrial bears, who could take the form of a bear herself, and manifested through female shamans having an ursine aspect? A reconstruction, but a sustainable one. She might have been the same as the "wise Manzalgormo," creator of Ursa Major in the highly septenary myth recorded by Roerich. Noteworthy also is the fact that even when the constellation is an elk, as in Evenk folklore, it is a she elk.

As always there is the question of how far back the data can take us. But at least it can be said that if such a deity was worshiped early enough she would explain Artemis in some detail. Artemis would have begun on the steppes as a version of the same deity among Indo-Europeans and acquired some of her characteristics through interchange with Uralic and Altaic peoples. She would have been an Earth Goddess and Mistress of Animals, associated personally with bears and having Ursa Major as her sidereal image. These roles could have accompanied her to Greece in one wave or another of Indo-European movement. If the original cult was con-

ducted by female shamans, Artemis's feminine exclusivity and her train of
maidens could be vestiges of that female monopoly.

The Artemis of the Greeks acquired other attributes, but she also may
have retained other vestiges. She figures in Hercules's third labor. He was
commanded to catch the golden-horned Ceryneian hind and bring her back
to Mycenae. The hind was one of five belonging to Artemis, who had
harnessed the other four to her chariot and kept a proprietorial eye on the
fifth. Hercules tracked the hind for a whole year, reaching the Land of the
Hyperboreans. There he met Artemis herself, who, after a parley, allowed
him to take her holy beast away.[38]

The tale's immediate interest lies in the animals and the use she makes
of them. Greece had no species of deer with horned females and no species
that could be harnessed to draw vehicles. The only kind that answers in
both respects is the reindeer, a denizen of the Eurasian northland.[39] (Hence
Santa Claus's well-known team.) Rumors or reports of it could have drifted
into the goddess's saga . . . if, at some stage, she was reasonably close. The
shamanic Mother of Animals has a special fondness for it. In Lapp and
Samoyed paganism the reindeer is sacred like the bear. Far in the east the
Evenk have a myth of their own ancestry that connects the two. A primordial
bear was dismembered. Evenks were created from parts of it and reindeer
from other parts—to be specific, its intestines and feet.[40]

Jung published an astonishing dream recorded by a patient of his.

"We go through a door into a tower-like room, where we climb a
long flight of steps. On one of the topmost steps I read an inscription:
'Vis ut sis.' The steps end in a temple situated on the crest of a
wooded mountain, and there is no other approach. It is the shrine
of *Ursanna*, the bear-goddess and Mother of God in one. The temple
is of red stone. Bloody sacrifices are offered there. Animals are standing about the alter. In order to enter the temple precincts one has
to be transformed into an animal—a beast of the forest. The temple
has the form of a cross with equal arms and a circular space in the
middle, which is not roofed, so that one can look straight up at the
sky and the constellation of the Bear. On the altar in the middle of
the open space there stands the moon-bowl, from which smoke or
vapour continually rises. There is also a huge image of the goddess,
but it cannot be seen clearly. The worshippers, who have been
changed into animals and to whom I belong, have to touch the goddess's foot with their own foot, whereupon the image gives them a
sign or an oracular utterance like 'Vis ut sis.' "[41]

Vis ut sis is Latin and probably should be taken as meaning "You will that
you may be." Jung calls the goddess in the dream "Cybele-Artemis," but

his patient could not have constructed it from any classical legend. The temple is on a mountain and Ursa Major is seen at the zenith; hence the mountain is in a fairly high latitude. The whole atmosphere is foreign to the Artemis of mythical convention but appropriate to what she may have been in her origins. To explain this, whether by folk memory or by some obscure tradition, is an even greater problem than explaining Milton's echoes of the creation epic.

Proto-Artemis would make sense as a goddess of the shamanic world— of parts of Siberia and European Russia. She would be entirely consistent with the hypothetical primary goddess and perhaps, all things considered, more like her than any other recorded deity. But she would be a late derivative form in a Proto-Indo-European milieu. Artemisian inquiry supports the Gimbutan position strongly on its more positive side but puts a query over it in another respect, since it makes the Indo-Europeans more creative and less obsessively masculine.

When the Greeks bring Artemis into focus she has retained a good deal of independence. Her stellar connections imply that Zeus (or Proto-Zeus?) did not have a monopoly, even in the heavens. While he and some of his colleagues may have moved into Hellas from the north, Artemis was not part of that movement. She came through Asia Minor and could challenge Zeus on his own ground, disputing the center of the sky with him. Greeks annexed her to his family as a matter of course and made out that it was really he who had created her constellation. Yet her cults in Asia Minor eluded him, and even in Greece the annexation was far from total.

Because of Ursa Major, Artemis could have invested her brother Apollo with the seven mystique, or at any rate confirmed him in possession of it. The obvious question is how they came to be paired. Does the answer bring us closer to his own origin, or to the Altaic seedbed proposed for those other Indo-Europeans?

CHAPTER FOURTEEN

Beyond the North Wind

1

Apollo and Artemis are twinned as far back as Greek literature takes them, in Homer's lines about their temple in Troy. The mythical reason is that they actually were twins. The real reason for their bonding, and for their joint presence at Delos, never emerges.[1] When the brother-sister relationship appears it is a *fait accompli*, complete with Leto as the mother of both. Only one explanation of it has any substance. It arose from their both being associated with the Hyperboreans, and so with each other. That was the judgment of Farnell nearly a century ago, and it stands, supported by facts unknown to him, although they put it in a different light.[2] It suggests the thought that if we can make out who the Hyperboreans were, they will bring us nearer to a localization—perhaps not for Proto-Artemis, whose antecedents may stretch across the Soviet Union; but perhaps for Proto-Apollo, revealing him somewhere in the Artemisian spread.

The Hyperboreans' name is supposed to mean "Dwellers Beyond the North Wind."[3] This etymology probably is right. It is given in Greece in the sixth century B.C., and it certainly corresponds to the idea the Greeks had of them. Strictly speaking, though, "north wind" is an anachronism. The names of the winds are older than the compass points. The Hyperboreans were dwellers beyond Boreas. Boreas was the strong cold wind that, in Greece, does blow from the north, so he came to be assigned to that quarter when compass bearings were fixed. In Russia, however, the cold wind blows from the east. From a Greek standpoint "dwellers beyond

Classical Apollo: the Apollo Belvedere from the Vatican.
Hulton-Deutsch

Boreas" could have been anywhere from the Balkans to farthest Siberia.
The essential notion was that Boreas had a point of departure and blew
from there, and the Hyperboreans lived on the far side of it, in a country
untroubled by his chilly blast.[4]

Mythology portrays them, or some of them, leading carefree lives in a
sort of Elysium, attaining an age of a thousand years. This idyllic abode
was not at ground level. In the words of the poet Pindar, "Neither by ship
nor on foot couldst thou find the wondrous way to the assembly of the
Hyperboreans." But they also were thought of as a real, earthly people,
whatever paradisal privileges some enjoyed.[5]

For Artemis they were part of her northeasterly landscape, and in classical legend they are a reminder of this. It was in their country that Hercules
met her with her team of reindeer. Plainly she was at home there, though

Classical Artemis: Diana the huntress, from the Louvre.
Hulton-Deutsch

the story suffers from a geographical muddle that makes "there" imprecise.[6]
More interesting are traditions telling of Hyperboreans coming to Delos
itself.

Two Hyperborean maidens, Arge (or Hekaerge) and Opis, were said to
have arrived on the island when Artemis and her brother were young, and
to have died there. Their reputed tomb was behind her temple, and Delians
used to scatter the ashes of sacrifices on it, singing a hymn in the maidens'
honor.[7] The Roman poet Claudian speaks of them as demigoddesses of the
chase known in Scythia, more or less southern Russia. Claudian is a late
authority but probably on the right track. The two were aspects of Artemis
herself, like Callisto, mythicized like her as distinct characters and definitely
northeastern.[8]

Later, legend related, two other maidens named Hyperoche and Laodice brought Hyperborean offerings to the shrine, starting a custom that went on into classical times. Five men accompanied them, so that the party numbered seven. Both died on Delos, like their predecessors. They too had a tomb in Artemis's precinct, and Delian youths and girls laid locks of their hair on it. Since neither the maidens nor their companions ever returned, the Hyperboreans became cautious. When they sent further offerings they employed a relay system, wrapping them in straw for protection and entrusting them to Scythians. The Scythians passed them to neighbors on the west and they progressed from hand to hand in the same way, reaching the Adriatic coast and, eventually, Delos.[9]

When Apollo went to the Hyperboreans for his annual visit, he flew in a chariot drawn by swans along the route that could not be followed either by ship or on foot. Possibly it was the Milky Way. Northern folklore, Lithuanian for instance, makes this a Road of Birds leading to a celestial realm.[10] However, while his swans carried him to the Hyperboreans' exalted "assembly," he did not neglect the more mundane ones below. They honored him with the unusual homage of sacrificed asses, accompanied by music and dancing. In some sense the Hyperboreans were his people, and must have been so before his Hellenic epiphany, whatever the Delos birth story pretended. According to a Delphic legend the oracle itself was set up for him by a group of Hyperboreans. Among them was a certain Olen, who instituted the custom of translating the god's messages into hexameter verse. Olen also is credited with composing hymns sung at Delos, including the one addressed to Arge and Opis. Some say Olen was a native of Lycia in Asia Minor, but he might have joined the Hyperborean party as a guide . . . who knows?[11]

Since Artemis, or Proto-Artemis, was at home in the northeastern spaces, the Hyperboreans deserve to be taken seriously, in a geographic sense. They may supply a context for Proto-Apollo.

Imaginative Greeks wrote of them as highly enlightened and not wholly out of touch with the known world. Apollo's ostensible son Pythagoras was said to have been on friendly terms with a wandering Hyperborean sage, Abaris, who came to him bringing a magical golden arrow. It was a gift from the god and conferred powers of healing and invisibility. Abaris rode through the air on it, or by means of it, going around the world without needing food.[12] Tales like this were combined with romanticization of far-off peoples—distance lending enchantment, as it so often does—to foster the notion of a kind of northern wisdom, Hyperborean wisdom.

But if we ask more precisely where the Greeks located them, the first impression is one of utter confusion drifting farther and farther from credibility. Herodotus allots them a country lying vaguely east of the Urals and extending to "the sea."[13] He has no knowledge of the Arctic Ocean or the Pacific and may simply be following normal belief, picturing the inhabited world as having water all around it. He says nothing that can be positively faulted. But in his own time, the fifth century B.C., an idea had gained currency that Boreas blew from the Rhipaean Mountains, so the Hyperboreans must live there, or just beyond.[14] "Rhipaean" was derived from a word meaning "blast" and was tautological rather than geographic—Boreas's blast issued from the blast place. The Rhipaean Mountains were supposed to be in Scythia, and that carried confusion a step further. The Don and the Dnieper flowed out of Scythia and so, presumably, rose in the Rhipaean Mountains; and unfortunately, the Danube too was regarded as a Scythian river, so the Danube too rose in the Rhipaean Mountains. Therefore Pindar puts the Hyperboreans at "the shady sources of the Danube."[15]

Herodotus knew better about the course of this river, but even when other Greeks caught up with him, it was no help.[16] Since the Danube's source was now fixed in the Rhipaean range, the range itself had to be shifted west. The Rhipaean Mountains became the Alps, even though there was no way Boreas could have blown from that direction. The Hyperboreans, who had been through a Balkan phase, now showed signs of blending with the druids of western Europe. In the fourth century B.C., Hecataeus of Abdera found them in Britain.[17] Other pseudo-clues, however, pointed to the Baltic coast, from which amber came. The foreigners who sent Artemis tribute to Delos may have been equated with her brother's Hyperborean friends because of one of these roving localizations.

It might be inferred that the guesses that moved the Hyperboreans thousands of miles prove them to be creatures of fantasy, with no true anchorage on the map. Not so. Actually they were located before the fatal drift began. Growing geographic awareness was to blame for the later vagaries—a case of a little learning being a dangerous thing. When Greeks knew enough about Russia, and the Danube, and the Alps, and Britain to jump to false conclusions, they duly jumped, losing sight of knowledge that already was available. A viable answer had been given before the obfuscation began. It was due to a pioneer explorer named Aristeas.

2

He was born in Proconnesus, now Marmara, an island in the small sea of the same name between the larger Black and Aegean seas. Early in the seventh pre-Christian century he became a priest of Apollo. Fascinated by the god's annual sojourn among the Hyperboreans, Aristeas set out to look for them. Somewhere around the year 675, he returned. The results of his expedition were embodied in a poem entitled *Arimaspea*, after a nation mentioned in it, and written by himself or by someone who took down his report.[18] Only fragments and partial summaries survive, but they are enough to show that he went a long way. Herodotus used his work, in a skeptical spirit.[19]

His descriptive touches about the nomads of Scythia and the steppes suggest firsthand acquaintance. Continuing eastward he reached the Issedonians and traversed their territory. That was as far as he got. However, they told him of the Arimaspi living beyond and an adjacent country rich in gold guarded by griffins from which the Arimaspi carried it off. Beyond again was a nation of wise and righteous vegetarians, the Hyperboreans.[20]

His journey seems to have taken him as far as Lake Balkhash and the distant approaches of the Altai.[21] As noted before, "Altai" means "golden," and deposits of gold exist thereabouts. Aristeas gives some striking bits of folklore, as when he speaks of the dwelling place of Boreas, from whose blast the Hyperboreans were exempt. He is fairly specific, saying that it is a cave from which the cold wind blows. And here he scores. East of Lake Balkhash is the Dzungarian Gate, where the winds are terrific, and according to Altaic mythology they issue from a cave. That motif is not Greek. Boreas's cave is mentioned by several Greek authors, but all of them are later than Aristeas and they probably picked it up from him. One is the poet Callimachus, in a *Hymn to Delos*. He pictures the cave as closer, in keeping with the kind of remythologizing that moved Artemis closer; but, interestingly, he calls it seven-chambered—another case of a Greek seven with an Apolline connection.[22]

It has been suggested that when Aristeas claimed to have traced the Hyperboreans, he really had heard some rumor of the Chinese.[23] Yet surely they were too far away. His account fixes Hyperborean country in and around the Altai. He speaks of it as extending to the sea, a statement that Herodotus echoes, but the vast Lake Baikal might explain a report to that effect. Tungus shamans actually call it "the sea."[24] So did he hear of actual people who, because of some prior knowledge, are dimly recalled as Hyperboreans in the myths of Apollo? Or did he merely apply the name to some tribe whom the Issedonians told him about and who struck him as fitting the description? Wishful thinking might have impelled him to do the latter. He would have wanted to believe he had attained his goal, even at secondhand. But there are reasons for seeing more in his report than this.

First is the fact, abundantly shown, that Hindu mythology points to much the same area and evokes parallel imagery.[25] It tells of a golden mountain far to the north and of the Northern Kurus in a paradise of golden sands and wonderful orchards, happy and healthy and immensely long-lived. When Alexander's conquests took Greeks to India they heard of the Northern Kurus and took them to be the Hyperboreans, who were described in terms so similar. They may well have been right, in the sense that both Hyperboreans and Northern Kurus reflect legendary stories of

Altai dwellers. This does not prove Aristeas correct, but it does prove that he was not merely fantasizing.

A point in his favor, fabulous as it sounds, is his tale of griffins guarding gold that the Arimaspi purloined, on the Hyperborean approaches.[26] These are the monstrous ants in the *Mahabharata* and in Herodotus, interpreted as griffins by a Greek with a limited repertoire of monsters. The source of the ant legend is Mongolian, and if Aristeas heard it he was surely somewhere in that direction. He was not in India, or China, or any other country where it is known to have spread.

Second, his account looks toward the same area previously focused on. This seeker for Hyperboreans, the people of the god with a seven mystique, found them at or near the homeland of shamans with a seven mystique, its apparent inspiration among Indo-Aryans and the rest. Things are linking up in the same place. Quite apart from Aristeas, several Hyperborean items fit in. For instance, the golden arrow that enables Abaris to fly is a shamanic object. Arrows symbolize the magical flights that shamans claim to perform. In rituals for healing and other purposes, an arrow is pointed at a person for whom prayers are offered, and it may have pieces of gold attached to it.[27] Even the odd detail of Hyperboreans sacrificing asses could be relevant. It could be a garbling of the Siberian horse sacrifices. Siberian horses were small, so they could easily have been confused with their humbler relatives.[28]

3

All of this has a weightier aspect. Apollo is the god of poetic inspiration, and, as Eliade has remarked, shamanic experience very possibly underlies the beginnings of poetry. One may well blend into the other.

> What a magnificent book remains to be written on the ecstatic "sources" of epic and lyric poetry, on the prehistory of dramatic spectacles, and, in general, on the fabulous worlds discovered, explored, and described by the ancient shamans.[29]

Even in the civilized Greek Apollo, scholars have recognized a much more specific shamanic quality, which continues to cling to him. Guthrie, Dodds, and others have argued, with Eliade's approval, that this is the inwardness of his Hyperborean connection.[30] His cult, and the acts ascribed to some of his devotees, suggest that one of the chief factors in his making—even *the* chief factor—was a Proto-Apollo worshiped in the distant northeast, a shamanic deity. This worship would have spread to Asia Minor and eventually to Greece. Other figures would have gone into the final divine composite, but the great god of Delphi retained shamanic features and his annual Hyperborean stay can be seen as a reminder of his antecedents.

Ecstatic prophecy, mantic utterance through communion with the god, occurred not only at Delphi but at some of his Asian shrines—at Claros, Branchidae, Patara.[31] In his oracles he spoke through women—Virgil gives a classic description of the inspired frenzy of his Cumaean Sibyl—and that recalls the fact that women as well as men could be shamans, and once may have been the only ones.

Abaris, with his wonder-working gift from Apollo, is plainly a kind of shaman.[32] He is a Hyperborean, but Greek adherents of the god also have shamanistic tales told of them. Aristeas himself is one such. He is said to have experienced ecstasies when Apollo "seized" him, and to have embarked on his expedition under that influence. Significant legends gathered around him. He could bilocate. He dropped dead in his hometown, Proconnesus, but the body vanished, a traveler reported meeting him in a distant place, and seven years later (seven!) he reappeared in Proconnesus and wrote the *Arimaspea*. Then he vanished a second time, but it still was not final. He was seen by Greek colonists in Italy, whom he told that he now attended Apollo in the shape of a crow. Shamans often turn into birds.[33]

Other persons attached to Apollo appear in similar legends. Hermotimos of Clazomenae had out-of-the-body experiences. He was credited with astral travel over long distances and long periods, after which he foretold future events. Enemies set fire to his body while his soul was absent, and he never returned.[34] Epimenides of Crete is said to have lived 299 years and to have spent fifty-seven of them in a cave, where he received prophetic powers. He went to Athens in about 596 B.C., stopped a plague, and worked with Solon on constitutional reforms. Even in the Bible he is acknowledged as a prophet (Titus 1:12) and quoted as saying "Cretans are always liars, evil beasts, lazy gluttons."[35] A kindred character is Zalmoxis, whose disappearance and reappearance, in Thrace to the north of Greece, led to his being worshiped.[36] He is less clearly shamanic, but legend links him with Pythagoras, an Apollo worshiper of far greater stature, and Pythagoras has shamanic features apart from the Abaris connection. Allegedly he too could heal and prophesy and bilocate. He founded a community of disciples that admitted women to membership.

A late-classical philosopher, Porphyry, makes out that "Zalmoxis" means "Bear-god." Rhys Carpenter, a modern folklorist, accepted this etymology and argued that bears' hibernation affected not only the story of Zalmoxis but the stories of Aristeas and Epimenides too. A philosopher of the same school as Porphyry, Iamblichus, tells an odd tale of Pythagoras himself taming a bear.[37]

The myths of Apollo's follower Orpheus point the same way. He descends into Hades to recover his dead wife, Eurydice. Shamans descend to the underworld for similar purposes. As a diviner, a healer, a companion of animals, Orpheus has traits in common with some of the greater shamans. His severed head, preserved on the island of Lesbos, has oracular life. The skulls of deceased Yukagir shamans used to be enshrined and employed for divination.[38]

There is something beyond this, and more profound. As Greeks were conscious of Apollo's septenary aspect, so they were conscious of the shamanic element in his cult, although they knew nothing of shamanism as such.[39] Aristotle pointed out that Apollo's prophets and prophetesses were not merely passive to the god, not merely possessed. They were not like the crazy hallucinating maenads inspired by Dionysus, who are portrayed in Euripides' drama *The Bacchae*. They made a contribution out of their own inner psyche and never totally lost control.

This is shamanic behavior, and it has deep implications. In Apollo's scheme of things a human being has a soul that can cooperate with the god, opening itself to his inspiration, embracing ecstasy, but still, so to speak, "there." It can detach itself from the body—hence such feats as Hermotimos's astral traveling. Christianity has made the idea of a separable soul familiar, whether valid or not, but in Greece it is not a thought-out conception until Aristeas and the rest. Homer's world recognizes no soul distinct from the body and capable of existence apart from it. All that survives death is an ineffectual shade, or ghost, which is far less than the living personality. The soul that first figures among Apollo's devotees is closer to shamanic beliefs than to native Greek ones—at any rate, during the reign of Zeus.[40]

What is at issue is not whether a migrant Proto-Apollo is credible but whether the data really imply him. Dodds is willing to accept such a god, but not as "Proto."[41] The Greeks, he thinks, heard of a northern Apollo, perhaps a god having a similar name. They equated him with their own and amalgamated the two. This was a fairly late development, after their own Apollo was well established. The shamanic phenomena, it is urged, are not recorded till the Greeks colonized north of the Black Sea around Aristeas's time. They could then have made contact with shamanism in Scythia, to which it extended, and with whatever quasi-Apollo the shamans worshiped. Dodds's argument is along the same lines as the one about Tauric Artemis, making her out to be a separate goddess whom the Greeks discovered when they crossed the Black Sea, and assimilated to the Artemis they already had.

Yet it seems a strange coincidence that both of the deities twinned at Delos should have turned out, centuries later, to have counterparts beyond the Black Sea. The northland data have evoked a Proto-Artemis not merely tacked on to the Greek one but fundamental in her making. With Apollo they may do likewise, in which case his Hyperborean bonding with Artemis was long prior to their advent in Greece.

The Delphic Oracle existed in very early times, and the prophetic ecstasies of Apollo's priestesses cannot have been due to influence from beyond the Black Sea if that reached Hellas only hundreds of years later. Eliade queries whether their inspiration was shamanic in type, but its continuity with Apollo-worship's later developments makes it close enough to be evidence.[42] Then again, there is the ubiquitous seven mystique. That too is attached to Apollo before the Black Sea colonization, being touched on by Homer and Hesiod and apparent in the god's festival dates. The proposed Proto-Apollo could have acquired the mystique from his shamanic connections or from his linkage with Artemis and Ursa Major, or both. Dodds claims that number mysticism, which Apollo exhibited in a restricted form and Pythagoras enlarged on, was not shamanic.[43] But it was, and in the Altaic region seven was the outstanding number. The mystique could have been part of a package having a common source with the one that reached the Indo-Aryans, but not the same, which also included the motif of centrality applied to Delphi and entered Greece with Apollo-worship and Artemis-worship.

If so, we have a second ethnic or cultic stream, flowing from the Altaic source by a different route. There seems to be no way of associating this with a known movement of migration or expansion, as in the Indo-Aryan case. It would have happened in a settled Indo-European continuum. The flow could have passed through the Caucasus and Asia Minor. A long drift of deities like this is perfectly credible. Pre-Columbian America had a whole chain of gods, from Quetzalcoatl in Mexico to Viracocha in Peru, who were variants of one ancestor. To judge from artistic evidence and chronology, this was a god or deified hero of the Olmecs on the south coast of the Gulf of Mexico. They were all, in their shared nature, derived from him.[44]

The "second stream" was a guessed-at reason for the shamanic Fall doctrine reaching Israel but not the senior civilizations east of Israel. Whether Apollo helps is a question. While one absence might be explained, another would take its place. We would have to ask why the Fall—being, presumably, in the second package—is not in the Apollo mythology! Israel's uniqueness on the point still would be a problem. Yet we might, for a wild moment, revert to the Yahweh-Apollo echoes. False clues must be firmly set aside. To detect shamanism in Israel's seers and prophets would be a mistake. Scripture does not portray them as using techniques to achieve visions and revelations; the Lord speaks to them, and through them, otherwise. Still, the Yahweh-Apollo affinities do exist, and when Ezekiel sees the Lord's chariot, strict geography would require it to be approaching from the Caucasus.

4

In the Altaic seedbed that the data converge upon we can find most of the elements that occur outside and *as if* they had been diffused from there—shamanic beliefs and practices; reverence for Ursa Major and mythical personifications of it; the seven mystique; cosmic centrality and symbolic representation of the center; ideas about golden and divine mountains. Proto-Artemis is plausible, if inexactly located. Proto-Apollo, at the source, is a matter of inference rather than evidence. He is bound up with the paradisal theme; and here there seems to be a gap.

At a distance the testimony is multiple. Greeks tell of Apollo's Hyperboreans in their paradise or subparadise, located by Aristeas near golden Altai. Hindus tell of the Northern Kurus in theirs, near golden Meru, and likewise point to the Altai. The two legends were current so far apart that neither could have inspired the other, yet their affinity is so clear that when Greeks could compare them they judged that the Hyperboreans and the Northern Kurus must be the same. Meru itself had its paradisal heights, its "gardens of the gods," apparently hinted at in the cuneiform tablets of Mesopotamia and, more explicitly if also mysteriously, in the sacred texts of Israel.

All of the elements could have been diffused from the Altaic northland they look toward. But whereas, with the seven mystique and so forth, the conclusion that this happened is based on prototypes in the northland itself, the paradise motif is hard to substantiate on the spot. Mountains, real and imagined, are dwellings of gods or ancestral spirits, but neither on the heights nor in the valleys and lowlands is there any word of a paradise or subparadise. Shamans have their golden age, a past paradise that is lost; they re-create it in ecstasy, transcending time; but it was, and is, a state rather than a place, not to be thought of as anywhere in particular or as physically accessible. Nothing shows that beliefs ever were otherwise. They could have been. Celtic folklore, for instance, tells of fairylands in Wales and Ireland, delightful if perilous, that mortals can enter under special circumstances. Altaic counterparts seem to be lacking.

Yet perhaps it was not always so. Evidence for traditions about a paradisal place in that region does exist outside it, but not so far away as to be irrelevant, in Lamaistic Buddhism. It would be rash to claim that the evidence is adequate. In its documented forms it cannot be old enough to carry much weight. It is muddled and elusive and has become entangled with fantasy, Western as well as Eastern. Nevertheless, it deserves a mention.

For some time, no one knows how long, Tibetan and Mongolian lamas have spoken of a place called Shambhala.[45] Its name means "quietude" or "bliss." Pioneer European travelers testified to hearing about it, among them early Jesuit missionaries and a Hungarian explorer, Csoma de Körös, who was in Tibet in 1831.[46] Successors have taken it up, if with unequal credibility. Fancied locations for it are scattered over the map, from the Aral Sea neighborhood to the Gobi Desert and across a good deal of central Asia generally. Its wanderings can be largely discounted, as being caused, like those of the Hyperboreans, by attempts to connect the legend with known places. Such attempts account for a Himalayan theory from which James Hilton probably took a hint for his Shangri-la.

A Tibetan story clarifies the direction at least. When its hero, Padma-Sambhava, has to go into exile, four places are considered, Shambhala, India, China, and Persia—in other words, north, south, east, and west from Tibet.[47] Shambhala's full name is Chang Shambhala, North Shambhala. It is the "northern place of quietude," a curious echo of the meaning of "Hyperborean," with its implied tranquillity at the back of the north wind.

Shambhala is of immemorial age, and it still exists, though perhaps only in the sense that the topography is unchanged. It is, or has been, an abode of Ancient Wisdom, a point of spiritual contact between earth and heaven. Mongols maintain that Buddha went there for initiation, so that Buddhism itself is of Shambhalic provenance.[48] Descriptions evoke it as concealed in a mountain cluster enfolding secret valleys and as barred from easy access by a lake or dried-up lake bed, with entry through a narrow defile, even a cave. Its atmosphere is temperate. Nicholas Roerich quotes a lama as saying to him: "In the midst of high mountains there are unsuspected enclosed valleys. Many hot springs nourish the rich vegetation. . . . Perhaps you have noticed hot geysers in the uplands . . . Who may know the labyrinths of these mountains?"[49]

As the lama implied, Shambhala is sometimes imagined as still active, still functioning. Hidden away in it, according to those who think so, is the residence of its king. Shambhala's kings live longer than ordinary humans. Some or all of them have been incarnations of Manjushri, the god of divine wisdom. W. Y. Evans-Wentz, a scholar whose work interested Jung, regarded Manjushri and Apollo as equivalent.[50] Another distant and tenuous echo like the Hyperborean echo; coincidental all the same.

Shambhalic lore is embodied in a system called Kalachakra, meaning the Wheel or Circle of Time.[51] According to tradition it originated in Shambhala itself. While Buddha did not invent it, he expounded it there before one of the kings who was Manjushri incarnate. The king wrote it down in a Book of Divine Wisdom. A book purporting to give the substance of this was in the possession of the Tashi Lama in the 1920s. Kalachakra lays stress on astronomy and astrology, and cosmic conceptions in general. Reputedly it somehow reached India, not by way of Tibet, and was known there in the seventh century A.D. It was not specifically Buddhist then, but it became so, if rather loosely, in the tenth or eleventh century A.D. A Bengali teacher named Atisha brought it to Tibet in 1038. He too was an incarnation of Manjushri. The same god, in another of his guises, taught the legendary exile Padma-Sambhava, who became the chief astrologer of the school. Manjushri is credited with knowing seven astrological systems, appropriately, if he is the same as Apollo.[52]

No explanation is offered for Kalachakra's roundabout journey from Shambhala to India and thence to Tibet. However, one feature of the mythos may shed a little light. In the eyes of those who believe Shambhala to be still active it has an apocalyptic aspect.[53] A messiah is destined to issue from it. This prophecy has taken different forms. He may be Shambhala's monarch in person. Or he may be Maitreya, the next Buddha. Or he may be a more militant figure, the epic hero Gesar, who had a share in Manzalgormo's creation of Ursa Major. Gesar's return is foretold like Arthur's, and he vanished into Shambhala a long while ago and will emerge from it. Now, Hinduism has its messiah too, namely Kalki, the final incarnation of Vishnu; and the *Mahabharata* says he will manifest himself at the close of the present era, in an Indian village called Sambhala.[54] The lamas' Shambhala is neither a village nor in India, but they could have picked up a hint for the name— not necessarily the idea itself—from Indian beliefs reaching Tibet.

Their own statements about its location are enigmatic.[55] It may be among the mountains of a known region. It may be over a sea. It may be in a north that is inaccessible, sending up the Aurora Borealis as a signal of its presence. Despite written descriptions of the road to it, lamas insist that travelers cannot simply go there. They have to be summoned. One clue is that stories of Shambhala were carried across the Russian empire by migrant Kalmucks and passed into the folklore of the Old Believers, a Russian sect persecuted for refusing to comply with religious reforms. They restyled it Belovodye, White Waters, and cherished daydreams of it as a safe haven out of the reach of earthly powers. Some went in search of it. They went in a more or less Altaic direction, though, predictably, it never was pinned down; it tended to be pushed into an uncertain beyond, not far from the range but definitely on the southern side of it.[56]

Further clues, if bizarre ones, emerge from comparatively modern events.[57] Shambhala was still a popular myth in the early 1920s, so much so that a Mongolian nationalistic ferment fastened on it and on Gesar's promised return as leader. This eliminates some of the wilder guesswork— Mongols would hardly have attached such hopes to a Shambhala near India or the Aral Sea. An anti-Bolshevik Russian, Ungern von Sternberg, tried to exploit the excitement with a view to detaching part of Siberia from Moscow.

Legends and superstitions began to proliferate. Shambhala's image was expanded by adding notions of an underground country, Agharti, supposed to be associated with it.[58] Agharti had tunnels leading hundreds of miles, and the mythical Shambhalic ruler became a "King of the World" with occult powers over the course of history and plans for Asia's future and a new golden age going far beyond Mongol nationalism. The chief Western "authority" on Agharti was Ferdinand Ossendowski, an acquaintance of Ungern von Sternberg. His book *Beasts, Men and Gods*, which came out in 1922, was a best-seller.

Roerich took the Shambhalic apocalypse seriously, though as a religious event rather than a political one.[59] On his Asian expedition he studied the idea among indigenous peoples. His travel diary, published under the title *Altai-Himalaya*, shows that he believed Shambhala to be real and even believed in Shambhalic sages who would declare themselves shortly. In spite of his credulity, he remains one of the few Western observers to have probed the mythos at close quarters and brought Western thinking to bear on it.

While his geographic allusions are cautious, it is fairly clear where he thought the tradition pointed. He speaks of "the general reverence for Altai"; "the coming of the Blessed Ones to Altai"; "the true significance of Altai." He singles out the highest peak of the range, "sacred Belukha," and associates it with the myth of the cosmic mountain. Elsewhere he mentions Meru by name and connects Shambhala with it as an "equally legendary height" in the north.[60] His thoughts, in fact, are not fully worked out, but they do show him to have been on a promising track, as do his items concerning Ursa Major. He mentions the Gesar legends, and geographically these are supportive, since they are popular in the Altai and toward Lake Baikal.[61]

Roerich's Shambhalic foray, which was roundabout, came to a curious end.[62] During July and early August of 1927, his party was encamped in the Shara-gol valley in China's remote northwest. Expectation was at a high pitch. What actually happened was that he and his companions saw a celestial portent, or, at least, a phenomenon in the sky that he took to be one. His description, as a matter of fact, is oddly like the accounts of flying saucers that began to be notorious in the late 1940s. Whatever it was, the lamas told him it was "the sign of Shambhala" and meant that he should move southward. He did, and eventually made his home in the Himalayan foothills, where his views on Shambhala grew more cloudy and noncommittal, though he still held it to have some spiritual meaning.[63] But his opinions when he was close, and less influenced by the lamas' mystification, remain on record in what he wrote at the time.

Shambhala has been dismissed as a Buddhist invention, or even a political one, with no real ancient antecedents. Yet antecedents are possible. Buddhism itself, in its lamaistic form, owes a large debt to Tibet's pre-Buddhist religion, which was called Bön and fades off into indefinite prehistory. It might have been a source for the Kalachakra material and, more to the point, it was shamanic in character and akin to the shamanism of the Altaic region. Enough of it survives in lamaism to make this clear—initiations, dancing, ecstatic astral flying, communication with gods, magical healing. Eliade describes the famous Tibetan Book of the Dead as "shamanic in structure."[64] None of this can be pressed far, but it may be that shamanic cults once were continuous from the Altai through Mongolia into Tibet, and that the idea of Shambhala grew around traditions that looked to the Altai as a paradisal dwelling place of the greatest shamans. Or some part may have been played by the Indo-European Tocharian speakers who shared in the Buddhism of this part of the world and, if Mallory is right, had an Altaic ancestry in the Afanasievo culture.

If so, we come back to the same place again as a paradisal enclave, like the Land of the Hyperboreans. We also may catch a glimpse of a resident god, Manjushri, compared to Apollo by a scholar unconcerned with Hyperborean myth, and possessing at least one septenary attribute. Since Shambhala underwent a transplant into Russian folklore as Belovodye, presumably Shambhala (or, let us say, Proto-Shambhala) could have undergone a transplant into Greek mythology as the Hyperborean land.

The claim that Kalachakra was taught in Shambhala in Buddha's time—that is, in the sixth century B.C.—and then reached India, not by way of Tibet, is very strange indeed. It is all the more so in the light of the drift of Altaic motifs toward India, not by way of Tibet, which surely has come to look plausible. Strange; but at present, little more can be said.

POSTSCRIPT

Jean Sylvain Bailly, a great eighteenth-century French astronomer, studied certain astronomical tables brought from India and found them to be—from the Indian vantage point—erroneous. He worked out that they must have been recorded in "Tartary," about 49° north of the equator, and taken to India from there, unadjusted. This is the latitude of Mount Belukha. Bailly involved his findings with a theory about migrants from a Spitzbergen that used to be warmer, and was the real Atlantis. But his astronomical facts are intriguing if they are right, even only roughly or arguably. The most accessible summary is by James Bramwell in *Lost Atlantis*.

CHAPTER FIFTEEN

Expansion

1

While the lamas offer these flickering sidelights, their septenary contributions are few, and they are confined to oddments along the seven mystique's fringes. What has been argued is that in the "heartland" where it anciently flourished, it injected an ordering factor into human thinking. That made its way via the Apollo cult, especially in the hands of Pythagoras; via the seven-planet astrology, as launched in Babylonia and developed by Greeks; and via the Judeo-Christian religious system. We return at last to the question of whether the mystique, even if it does vindicate the Altaic seedbed, was a mere quirk or actually was a kind of wisdom with an ongoing role in intellectual history . . . whatever the implication for Goddess theories. The first step is to see what happened when the streams flowed together.

In the Hellenistic world created by Alexander, Apollo was still a mighty god and Pythagoras's ideas of number and measurement were advancing the sciences. Astronomy was one of the chief of these, and during the last centuries B.C., Greek astronomers were refining the seven-planet astrology and helping it to take hold. Classical civilization did now produce heptads that were non-Apollonian, and the mystique was extended.

The seven-note musical scale, corresponding to the strings of Apollo's lyre, was well established. But Greeks of esoteric interests went further. They matched the notes to the planets. They also brought in the Greek alphabet. It happened to have seven vowels—*a*, short and long *e*, *i*, short and long *o*, and *u*. These were drawn into the mystical network and paired with planets like the notes of the scale. Vowels and planets were regarded as *stoicheia*, or "cosmic elements," and magical formulae combining vowels were supposed to exert control over planetary influences.[1]

Egypt, thanks to Alexander, was now ruled by a Greek dynasty of which Cleopatra is the most famous member. The city of Alexandria had large Greek and Jewish populations and was a center of intellectual ferment. The seven mystique at last entered Egypt. In the first century B.C., a certain Demetrius writes: "In Egypt the priests sing hymns to the gods by uttering the seven vowels in succession, the sound of which produces as strong a musical effect on the hearer as if flute and lyre were used."[2] Vowels and notes, vowels and planets, notes and planets—a triple linkage of heptads had come into being.

These speculations became involved with the "music of the spheres." Pythagoras, in the course of his explorations, had found that a musical string twice the length of another string gave out a note an octave lower. This he correctly judged to be due to a slower vibration rate. He, and Plato after him, imagined the planets emitting notes as they moved, the differences of speed suggesting differences of pitch.[3] Astrology improved the conception. Allegedly the music was made not by the visible orbs but by the invisible concentric spheres assumed to convey them, or by beings inhabiting these. Outside, the sphere of stars and the Primum Mobile added their voices, and all nine notes, seven plus two, harmonized. Hearing the music of the spheres was normally a privilege of creatures higher than humans.[4]

Milton endorses the old cosmos poetically, even after its discrediting by Copernicus and Galileo. In his dramatic piece "Arcades" he introduces a Genius of the Wood speaking of the hush of night . . .

> *Then listen I*
> *To the celestial* Sirens *harmony,*
> *That sit upon the nine enfolded Sphears,*
> *And sing to those that hold the vital shears,*
> *And turn the Adamantine spindle round,*
> *On which the fate of gods and men is wound.*
> *Such sweet compulsion doth in musick ly,*
> *To lull the daughters of* Necessity,
> *And keep unsteddy Nature to her law,*
> *And the low world in measur'd motion draw*
> *After the heavenly tune, which none can hear*
> *Of human mould with grosse unpurged ear.*

And in a more familiar poem, "On the Morning of Christ's Nativity," with a paradisal echo:

> *Ring out ye Crystall sphears,*
> *Once bless our human ears,*
> *(If ye have power to touch our senses so)*
> *And let your silver chime*
> *Move in melodious time;*
> *And let the Base of Heav'ns deep Organ blow,*
> *And with your ninefold harmony*
> *Make up full consort to th'Angelike symphony.*
>
> *For if such holy Song*
> *Enwrap our fancy long,*
> *Time will run back, and fetch the age of gold . . .*

Greek insistence that the Pleiades were seven created the term *pleiad* meaning a group of seven outstanding persons, stars in some activity. It was applied, in retrospect, to the Seven Wise Men whose maxims were inscribed over Apollo's temple door. They were the Philosophical Pleiad.[5] About 285 B.C. the Alexandrian Greeks had a Poetic Pleiad. Poets of stature not being plentiful among them, mediocre ones, such as Philiscus, were ranked with good ones, such as Theocritus, so that the magic total could be made up.[6]

The Seven Wonders of the World were listed by Greeks in the second century B.C.[7] They were, usually:

> Pyramids of Egypt
> Hanging Gardens of Babylon
> Tomb of Mausolus at Halicarnassus
> Temple of Artemis of Ephesus
> Colossus of Rhodes
> Statue of Zeus by Phidias at Olympia
> Pharos (that is, Lighthouse) of Alexandria

Miscellaneous sevens in the classical world could be piled up further. Seven cities competed as the birthplace of Homer. The belief in a seventh son as exceptional can be traced to a late legend of the Trojan War—Achilles, without whom the Greeks could not win, was the seventh son of his parents.[8] Near Sparta were seven pillars, and according to Pausanias, in the second century A.D., they were arranged in "the ancient pattern." It would be interesting to know what that was. Rome was built on seven hills, as Cicero, Virgil, Ovid, and other Romans assure us. The point is not that the hills existed but that they were counted and became proverbial. The seven hills of the persecuting city are mentioned in Christian scripture (Rev. 17:9).

2

Judaism developed Israel's seven mystique along with other themes, and the missionary impulse, which began with the going forth of the Law from Zion, branched out into Christianity and later Islam. This was a major reason for the mystique's passing to hitherto unseptenary peoples in Europe and Africa.

Jewish scriptural composition came to an end, Judaism's evolution did not. Uncanonical writings like the *Book of Enoch* continued to be written. Judaism became less political, more purely religious, after A.D. 70 saw the Romans' recapture and devastation of rebellious Jerusalem. Among other trophies they carried off was the Menorah, the great seven-branched lampstand. A last revolt in 132–35 ended in the final eclipse of political activism. With the destruction of the temple, the extinction of its priesthood, and the further dispersal of Jews, the rabbis in charge of the local synagogues rose to dominance. For sheer survival they tightened Judaism up. They subjected scripture to minutely detailed interpretation, making a fence around it. The teachings of gnosticism, in part a Jewish invention, built a bridge to the astrology now entrenched everywhere, and the biblical seven mystique was reinforced by the seven planets.[9] But the Judaism of the rabbinic mainstream had no need of them to create heptadic extensions of its own.

An apocryphal book, *Tobit*, already had introduced seven archangels who entered into the Lord's presence (12.15). More was now said about the Menorah, retrospectively, since it no longer was there.[10] Amulets were made with formulae in seven letters or seven verses, arranged in its distinctive shape, and it was expounded as symbolizing the week of creation, with the central light representing the sabbath. The Jewish historian Josephus even gave it a planetary aspect. Its branches also could stand for seven continents in legendary geography, and for the seven heavens, guided by the light of the Lord. Journeys in spirit could be made through them up to the seventh, where his throne was (another shamanic idea, but by this time there could have been other sources).[11]

Rabbis taught that God had seven principal names.[12] The holiest was the one revealed to Moses (Exod. 3:14), "YHWH" or "JHVH," in the vowelless writing of old Hebrew. This, the Tetragrammaton, is the name now usually pronounced "Yahweh," the Christian version, "Jehovah," being out of favor. To Jews it was so sacred that its true pronunciation was kept a secret, and the sages who knew it conveyed it to their disciples by signs, once every seven years.[13] Jewish writers promoted a doctrine of the human constitution being sevenfold, which for them had implications about the nature of God, since human beings were made in his image (Gen. 1:26–27 and 5:1).[14]

Christianity inherited Jewish scripture with all of its heptads, and added more. The Lord's Prayer consists of seven petitions. The Fourth Gospel describes seven miracles of Christ. He speaks seven times on the cross. One of the earliest steps in Church organization is the appointment of seven "men of good repute" to be deacons (Acts 6:2–5). The New Testament's final book, the Revelation, is the most septenary text anywhere, bringing in the number fifty-four times. Its author writes of seven churches, candlesticks, stars, spirits before God's throne, angels, trumpets, vials of wrath, and hills, and of visionary creatures with seven horns, eyes, and heads.

Understandably, in view of all this, Christians came to terms with pagan ideas about planetary heavens and astral influences. Heretical gnostic sects went further, but the orthodox were not rigidly hostile. Occasional authors hit on a linking image. Pope Gregory the Great says that Christ, "coming in the flesh, joined the Pleiades, for he had within himself, at once and for ever, the work of the sevenfold Holy Spirit."[15] With their shared septenary emphasis, Christianity and astrology were like two trees side by side, their branches touching.

They converged in the Christian imposition of the seven-day week. Part of the Hellenistic development was the custom of assigning a day to each planetary power, in a perpetual rota. Romans took it over, using their own names for the deities. The Latin day names were:

> *Solis dies* (Sun's day)
> *Lunae dies* (Moon's day)
> *Martis dies* (Mars's day)
> *Mercurii dies* (Mercury's day)
> *Jovis dies* (Jupiter's day)
> *Veneris dies* (Venus's day)
> *Saturni dies* (Saturn's day)

The modern French day names are derived from these, except for the first, which has become *dimanche, Dominica dies*, the Lord's day. All of the others, *lundi, mardi, mercredi, jeudi, vendredi*, and *samedi*, show their origin. Three of the English day names are Roman still, while the other four, Tuesday, Wednesday, Thursday, and Friday, are taken from Anglo-Saxon deities, chosen as equivalent to the Roman.

By the first century A.D., astrology was popularizing the seven-day cycle through most of the Roman Empire.[16] The actual calendar, however, had not absorbed it. That happened only when it was assimilated to the Jewish week, which non-Jews confused with it, and which was well known not only because of the Jews' ubiquity and unwillingness to work on the sabbath but because of the spread of Christianity and hence of the Bible.

Accidental factors aided the process. In the Jewish week, the day of rest was the seventh. As Romans like Tibullus and Ovid note, the astrological seventh day, Saturn's, was thought inauspicious for work or travel. On the first day of the Jewish cycle, Christians commemorated Christ's resurrection. The astrological cycle made this the sun's day. Church fathers pointed out the coincidence of the Lord's day with the day of light, and the rising of the Sun of Righteousness with the ascendancy of the visible sun.

For reasons such as these, Christians could live with the planetary rota. When the emperor Constantine decided to support the Church he gave legal recognition to the recurrence of the day of the sun and made it a day for both rest and worship, thus drawing together pagan, Jewish, and Christian threads. With the hallowed day coming around officially and regularly, the week as a whole got a footing in the calendar, and there it remains. Christian authorities accepted it because a seven-day cycle was in harmony with scripture. They tried to replace the day names with numbers and had some success in the East, but most Western languages (Portuguese is an exception) retained or adapted them, though with some the sun's day became the Lord's day, as in French. Islam presently took the same path. The two conquering religions carried the seven-day week through the world, supplanting other "weeks."

The Catholic Church spread through Europe and the seven mystique advanced with it, becoming ever more deeply impressed. The Church had a whole septenary scheme of its own. It listed seven sacraments, seven virtues, seven deadly sins, seven gifts of the Holy Spirit, seven works of mercy, seven sorrows and joys of the Virgin Mary, seven penitential psalms. It adopted the seven Jewish archangels and favored a division of history into seven ages. Late medieval symbolism sometimes threatened to stray into sheer numerology. In the words of the medieval historian Huizinga, "A regular cluster was formed of systems of seven."

> With the seven virtues correspond the seven supplications of the Lord's Prayer, the seven gifts of the Holy Spirit, the seven beatitudes, and the seven penitential psalms. All these groups of seven are again connected with the seven moments of the Passion and the seven sacraments. Each of them is opposed to one of the seven deadly sins, which are represented by seven animals and followed by seven diseases.[17]

Actually there are eight beatitudes (Matt. 5:3–11, verses 10 and 11 counting as one). Even the words of Christ had to be forced into the mold.

The cult of Mary associated her with the female Wisdom of Proverbs, perhaps having begun partly because of this. St. Peter Chrysologus, writing in its first phase of major growth during the fifth century, says that Mary is the seven-pillared dwelling built by Wisdom for herself.[18]

Islam split off from the Jewish and Christian systems. Mohammed denounced both as falsifications, but he respected some of their principal figures, including Jesus, and claimed that he was restoring the true faith of Abraham. Hence he drew on the Old Testament and Judeo-Christian tradition, giving them his own gloss. Islam has seven heavens, together with seven hells and, in the teachings of some of its exponents, a purgatory with seven enclosures that souls must climb out of.

The Koran gives direct warrant for various related beliefs.[19] Besides the seven heavens, the prophet rather cryptically declares, there are seven earths. There are also seven seas, gates of hell, and mansions of paradise— on which a commentator, Wahb ibn Munabbih, observes, "Of almost all things there are seven—seven are the heavens, the earths, the mountains, the seas . . . the days of the week, the planets . . . the gates and floors of hell. . . ." Some of these heptads already were familiar when the Koran was written. It may have launched the proverbial Seven Seas on their career, though it is doubtful which seas the prophet had in mind. Islam adds further touches of the same sort. Another of its scholars, Jabal-ul-din, says that Adam was made from earth having seven colors, and that is why some of his descendants are brown, some white, some yellow, and so on.[20] Pilgrims to Mecca walk around the Kaaba seven times. In the same spirit Firdausi's Persian epic the *Shah-Namah* sprinkles heptads through pre-Islamic mythology. The poet has groupings of seven men, seven ordeals undergone by heroes, and so forth.

To revert for a moment to the mountain theme, Judaism and Christianity did not enlarge on it much, apart from the occasional guesswork about the earthly paradise. (There is one towering exception—Dante's *Purgatorio.* More of that hereafter.) Islamic legend does take it up, in a confused way, disintegrating Meru further. Sometimes the mountain continues to be the highest on earth. Sometimes it loses its unique altitude while keeping its paradise. Speculation shifts it about, to Syria, Persia, India. India comes to be a favored location. The name "Adam's Peak" for a mountain in Sri Lanka, with Adam's huge footprint at the top, is a result of these wanderings.[21]

In an Islamic version that did place the mountain in its original north, the prophet Elijah—whom Muslims, like Jews and Christians, believed to be still alive and immortal—was reputed to have his home on it. That was where the fiery chariot had taken him (2 Kings 2:11–12). Another legend, which retained the mountain's centrality, averred that its ascent was purgatorial and that a bridge called Chinvat led from the summit to heaven. Zoroastrian tenets may have left an imprint here.

Though Christians were not greatly concerned with the mountain, they accepted the earthly centrality of Jerusalem, and its unique holiness. The reverence they learned from the Jews was reinforced by the fact that Jerusalem was the birthplace of the Church. They improved the Jewish legends of Adam, saying not only that he was created on Jerusalem's destined site but that he returned there to die and was buried under Golgotha, where the death of Christ, the "second Adam," canceled the doom incurred by the first.[22] Their conviction of the city's importance to Christendom inspired prodigious and tragic efforts in the Crusades. Medieval maps show the land mass as a disk, still, with Jerusalem at the center and the East and the earthly paradise at the top. That spatial ordering, inherited from India and the Middle East, persisted—even in an age when the earth was widely known to be spherical and its size had been quite well estimated.

3

Once astrology and the Church had together planted the seven mystique, it ramified and continued ramifying in various fields.

In thinking about the human constitution. The soul was held to have seven faculties or senses. These were animation, feeling, speech, taste, sight, hearing, smell.[23] Naturally, each had its ruling planet. Some religious teachers—not orthodox Christians—said the soul descended from higher realms, acquiring its faculties on the way down. If it attained salvation it returned them on the way up, shedding the human condition and soaring into an empyrean where all was different.[24] The body was subjected to the same kind of analysis. It was divided into seven main portions, with seven internal organs and seven secretions. Hippocrates's classification of seven stages of life, probably an Apollonian offshoot, was recalled. It may have been the source of Shakespeare's Seven Ages of Man (*As You Like It*, 2.7).

In Christian Europe's first formative system of education. Medieval schools, drawing on the classical heritage, taught the seven liberal arts— grammar, logic, rhetoric, astronomy, music, geometry, and arithmetic. According to legend their elements were inscribed by Adam on seven stone tablets after his banishment from paradise—a notable proof of the belief that he was created with innate knowledge as well as instinctive goodness, that even the short Christian golden age incorporated Ancient Wisdom.[25] He left the tablets in the Vale of Hebron in Palestine, where they survived the Flood. Their discovery and curricular use were due to Hermes Trismegistus, "the thrice-great Hermes," purported author of the Hermetic treatises that inspired so much respect during the Renaissance.[26]

In traditional groupings. The Greeks' application of the Pleiades to earthly sets was repeated in European Christendom. There, as almost everywhere, the star cluster was well known, and because of the influence of classical myth it was reckoned as seven. The Pleiades may be the stars that King Lear's Fool riddles about.

> FOOL. The reason why the seven stars are no more than seven is a pretty reason.
> LEAR. Because they are not eight?
> FOOL. Yes, indeed; thou wouldst make a good fool.

Here the allusion might also be to Ursa Major. But with several historic groups of seven the Greeks' pleiadic motif was revived. Emperor Charlemagne plus his six court scholars, Alcuin being the chief, constituted Charlemagne's pleiad. France had two poetic pleiads, the first in the sixteenth century, the second under Louis XIII. The former, which included Ronsard, made lasting contributions to literature. The latter did not. Both, however, were fitted into the mold by including minor versifiers.[27]

Apart from the pleiads, the heptad defined other groups. A medieval legend of the Seven Sages of Rome was a framework for tales of Sinbad the Sailor and King Arthur.[28] Seven national patron saints were the Seven Champions of Christendom. Apart from their honor in the Church they had little in common. George of England was a fourth-century Levantine martyr. Andrew of Scotland and James of Spain were apostles. Patrick of Ireland was a fifth-century British missionary, David of Wales was a sixth-century monastic founder. Denys of France was a third-century Gallic martyr, Anthony of Italy was a thirteenth-century Franciscan. Yet all became contemporaneous heroes of romantic adventure, as told, for example, by Richard Johnson in *The Famous History of the Seven Champions of Christendom*, published in 1596.

Septenary patterning reaches into the adventures themselves. St. George is imprisoned for seven years by the king of Morocco. St. Denys lives for seven years in the form of a hart. St. Andrew delivers some ladies turned into swans for the same period. St. James loses his eyesight for seven years because of his love for a Jewish woman. St. David sleeps for seven years in a garden, under a malign enchantment, till St. George rescues him. All of the champions are spellbound in a castle where seven lamps burn, and they cannot wake until St. George's sons extinguish them.

This last theme of a prolonged sleep has septenary connections itself. Legend tells of the Seven Sleepers of Ephesus, Christians who hid in a cave in the year 250 to escape persecution and woke and emerged two centuries later.[29] Slumbers of the same type are attributed to various heroes, such as Arthur. Arthur himself, as a sleeper, has no septenary aspect. But Frederick Barbarossa, the hidden German emperor in the Kyffhäuser mountain, turns over every seven years. Ogier the Dane, a companion of Charlemagne, sleeps in a hall in Avalon and beats the floor with a mace at the same interval. Some characters step outside normal time into an otherworld, without actually going to sleep there; the Scottish poet Thomas the rhymer and (in some versions) Tannhäuser, the hero of Wagner's opera, are absent for seven years in this manner.[30]

To return to groups, it is interesting in view of golden-age myth that individuals combined in sevens usually are good. Snow White's seven dwarfs are more attractive than many dwarfs of fairy tale and romance. A Western-influenced Japanese filmmaker invented the Seven Samurai, protectors of a village from bandits, and their American counterparts are the Magnificent Seven. English history supplies a case of the converse. Some ecclesiastics who defied King James II became public heroes and, being therefore "good," were dubbed the Seven Bishops.

A second list of the Seven Wonders of the World never made its mark as the first did, but it has found its way into reference books. As follows:[31]

> Colosseum of Rome
> Catacombs of Alexandria
> Great Wall of China
> Stonehenge
> Leaning Tower of Pisa
> Porcelain Tower of Nanking
> St. Sophia (cathedral, afterward a mosque)

Stonehenge is far too old to belong here, but as in other groups, the tally had to be made up.

In geography. The seven mystique was active in the Age of Discovery. One motive for Columbus's voyage was a current belief in Antilla, the Island of the Seven Cities, founded by seven Portuguese bishops leading parties of refugees from Moorish conquest. Even after Columbus, explorers sailed out from Bristol in search of the island.[32]

As knowledge of the globe increased, "the seven seas" became a cliché. The list in latter-day Europe was artificial. Six would be logical: the Mediterranean, the Atlantic Ocean, the Pacific Ocean, the Indian Ocean, the Arctic Ocean, and the Antarctic Ocean. The seven are contrived by omitting the Mediterranean as not an ocean and splitting the Atlantic and Pacific into northern and southern sections. With the Atlantic the split is defensible, with the Pacific it is absurd. The sole object of this exercise is to have seven somehow.

A similar compulsion affects the writing of early English history. The Heptarchy, a seven-kingdom division of Anglo-Saxon England, is a persistent notion. Yet this too is artificial. Kingdoms of Kent, Sussex, Wessex,

Essex, East Anglia, Mercia, and Northumbria did exist and were the most lasting, but others are named at sundry times and locatable on the map.

And so on and so forth. A seventh son is clairvoyant. The seventh son of a seventh son has the further power of healing by touch. To break a mirror means seven years' bad luck. And whatever storyteller invented seven-league boots, they became a magical method par excellence of rapid travel . . .

CHAPTER SIXTEEN

Starting Points of Science

1

For thousands of years the seven mystique can be seen taking hold. It travels and grows more serious as a method of mental ordering. It appears among shamans and Indo-Aryans and their Iranian cousins; among Meso-potamians; among Canaanites and Israelites; among Apollo's worshipers and myth-makers. Then it spreads through Europe with a power of conditioning that ensures its survival and further spread in the age of European expansion.

But the question still must be pressed: whether the mystique had any real value for intellectual or cultural progress; whether it was simply an oddity, or a phenomenon with a deeper quality, vindicating—at any rate, excusing—advocates of Ancient Wisdom. The answer must determine whether the Altaic seedbed, even if accepted as factual, had any genuine importance.

Let us look at some of the heptad's major embodiments. We noted the musical scale, C D E F G A B, with its equivalents in other keys, as appearing early in the heartland.[1] European and American ears have been attuned to it, for centuries music has been formed by it, and up to now this has been music in its richest development. Traditional Chinese music with its restricted scale has its own qualities but never has made such progress.

Less obvious but also significant is the seven mystique's role in the science of optics.[2] One of its foundations was the study of the visible spectrum, observed as long as rainbows have been. In the West this is analyzed into seven colors—violet, indigo, blue, green, yellow, orange, and red. They seem to be defined not by optical fact but by the determination to have seven. An innocent eye exposed to a rainbow would be unlikely to distinguish that number of colors, and in some parts of the world they are not thus distinguished. Here China may be thought to do better. A Chinese myth tells of a sky-shattering giant who was defeated by the goddess Nyuka. Rising in fiery armor from the eastern ocean, she "forged the five colours of the rainbow in her magic forge and restored the heavens."[3] Nyuka's feat surely is in keeping with what we actually see, as distinct from what septenary conditioning has taught us to see. The conditioning is of long standing but is no part of universal human nature. Nevertheless, the science of optics is an occidental creation, not a Chinese one.

In these cases it may not be very clear that the advantage is due to the number, to the mental ordering. It becomes so in another science, astronomy. Here the starting point is astrology. To make serious claims for astrology is not to defend it as such, and in any case the astrology of today is not the same as that of the Babylonians and Greeks, because its exponents try to include outer planets unknown to them. What matters is that in the basic classical system there was a septenary root for later scientific development. Subsequent strides could happen because of the structuring imposed.

When it held sway in the Hellenistic world, astronomers confronted a problem: how to reconcile their data with the seven-planet scheme, which astrology taught, which their own predecessors had done the most to create, and which, by common consent, was now sacrosanct. The sustained effort to do so drove them to take a step that made astronomy in the modern sense possible.

The main difficulty was that Earth was placed at the center of the universe, motionless, with the planets' seven transparent spheres revolving around it, one outside another.[4] Outside again was the sphere of the stars. Greek astronomers realized that the observed courses of the planets, the "wanderers," could not be explained by simple rotation. They were forced to invent epicyclic movements, with point A going around point B, which itself went around point C. Ptolemy of Alexandria in the second century A.D. made the scheme work after a fashion—the Primum Mobile, outside all of the other spheres, was an addition of his—and it became a durable orthodoxy, which allowed astrology to flourish untroubled. Earth remained at the center, receiving astral influence from the complicated circlings.

But the cumbrousness of Ptolemy's system was bound, sooner or later, to inspire a search for a simpler interpretation. Before him, a Greek named Aristarchus had hazarded the notion that the whole thing could be handled more easily by putting the sun at the center, with the rest, including Earth, going around it.[5] Hardly anyone took up his suggestion, and when Ptolemy had spoken, Ptolemy ruled. Nevertheless, a change crept in. The sun attained a special position. Astrologers referred to it as the "king" planet and got as far as supposing that it had some control over the others' orbits.[6] Meanwhile, religion played a part. Toward the end of the third century A.D., in the last phase of official paganism, emperors seeking stability set up a universal cult of the "Unconquered Sun."[7] Soon afterward Constantine the Great transferred imperial favor to Christianity, but the Emperor Julian, in a short-lived pagan reaction, tried to substitute a solar religion focused on "King Helios." Julian was influenced by the mystical doctrines of the Neoplatonists. One of them, Macrobius, said in words already quoted: "Apollo's lyre of seven strings provides understanding of the motions of all the celestial spheres over which nature has set the Sun as moderator."

Ideas of this kind gradually prepared the way for a rediscovery of Aristarchus's insight. It was a long time before astronomers made any move, but at last, in the fifteenth century, Cardinal Nicolaus of Cusa indicated the same truth. The tangle could be sorted out by posting the sun at the center as ruler of the system. Copernicus affirmed it positively, and Galileo, aided by his telescope, supplied visual evidence. With the planets unscrambled, whirling through unconstricted space, astronomy could reach out.

Astrologers managed to adapt to the new order. The concentric spheres survived for awhile in poetry but faded away. Copernicus and Galileo had changed the universe, and Newton confirmed the change. Yet the ancient astrologers who reckoned the planets as seven—the sun, the moon, Mercury, Venus, Mars, Jupiter, and Saturn—had supplied what was needed for the Copernican leap. That might have been due to chance, or intuition, or some actual undercurrent of Ancient Wisdom, as Newton believed; but they had supplied it.[8] Arguably the leap could have been effected with a different set. The fact remains that it was not. Astrologers in other traditions never enumerated the seven planets, and astronomers in those traditions never made the leap. Even in Greece, where Aristarchus hit on the answer long before, hardly anything came of his purely astronomical argument.

The reason is apparent, and it did depend on the septenary astrological set. The Chinese counted the five true planets visible before telescopes and kept the sun and moon separate. The Hindus called the planets *grahas* and included the sun and moon, but added two further *grahas*, foci of celestial influence known as Rahu and Ketu, making a total of nine.[9] The Babylonians, needing seven, made the system a heptad by defining the "planets" as the true ones plus the sun and the moon, and the Greeks followed them. It was this ordering that formulated the problem so that it led, partly through the theory of the sun guiding the planets, to a heliocentric solution. Chinese astrologers failed to arrive at that formulation because they left out the sun. Hindu astrologers failed because they incorporated *grahas* that were not planets.

Thence to another science. As astronomy evolved from astrology, so did chemistry from alchemy. In its Western form this may have begun among the Egyptians. The word *alchemy* is said to be related to "Cham," an old name for Egypt.[10] At first it was a quest for the Elixir of Life. However, number magic transformed it, and it did so by way of astrology. About 200 B.C., someone realized that just as seven "planets" were known, so seven metals were known. In due course, metals, like days, were matched to planets, each having its celestial ruler.[11] Thus:

Sun	gold
Moon	silver
Mercury	quicksilver
Venus	copper
Mars	iron
Jupiter	tin
Saturn	lead

The allocation of gold and silver explains itself. The third metal is now actually called mercury, and astrology is the reason. Mercury was deemed correct because the metal's liquidity and mobility suggested the gods' flying messenger. Venus acquired copper because it came from Cyprus—in Latin it is *cyprium aes*, "Cyprus metal"—and Cyprus was her special island, where she had her principal temple, at Paphos.[12] Mars as war god became the ruler of iron because of its use in making weapons. Jupiter's connection with tin is less obvious. It may have been due to simple elimination since lead was appropriate to slow-moving Saturn, and with six metals assigned, only tin was left for the sky-ruling monarch of the gods (though it seems that in Sumerian mythology tin was the metal the sky was made of, and its comparative lack of dignity is modern).[13]

For centuries the heptad of metals was as firmly fixed as the heptad of planets, and closely linked with it, so that alchemists sometimes used the names of the planets to designate the metals. The practice still was flourishing when Chaucer listed them in the *Canon's Yeoman's Tale*:

> *The bodyes sevene eek, lo! hem heere anoon:*
> *Sol gold is, and Luna silver we threpe,*
> *Mars iren, Mercurie quyksilver we clepe,*
> *Saturnus leed, and Juppiter is tyn,*
> *And Venus coper, by my fader kyn!*
> (The Canterbury Tales, *VIII, Lines* 825–29)

As late as the Renaissance metals were believed to grow in the earth under their planets' influence, and mines were shut down at intervals so that the planets would have a breathing space to renew the supply.[14]

It was this systematization of metals that shifted alchemists' attention to their nature and properties, to experiments that could be done with them, and to the dream of transmuting base ones into gold.[15] This latter hope could be entertained because they all were thought of as modes of a single basic matter rather than as immutable elements. The elixir of the old quest was not forgotten, but it was equated with the wonder-working Philosophers' Stone that would effect transmutation. Theories correlated physical processes with the spiritual state of the alchemist . . . a field explored long afterward by Jung.[16] This was not yet chemistry, but it led to it, and alchemists made fundamental discoveries. Albertus Magnus, Roger Bacon, Van Helmont, and Glauber are among many transitional figures.[17]

Here too a contrast can be drawn. There was Asian alchemy as there was Asian astrology. Beginning in China in the fourth century B.C. and remaining mainly Chinese though with Indian offshoots, it was a pursuit of Taoism, that odd wayward religion that claimed Lao Tzu as its founder.[18] Chinese alchemists, like their Western counterparts, were concerned at first with the elixir. They believed that immortal sages who knew the secret dwelt on an island called P'eng-lai. Alchemists embarked on the ocean to look for P'eng-lai. One, Li Shao-chün, said he had found it.

In the Taoist quest for eternal life, two key substances were gold and cinnabar, red mercuric sulphide. Li Shao-chün spoke of transmuting one into the other, cinnabar into gold. His emphasis, however, was on immortality rather than transmutation. The chief use of alchemic gold was to make magic tableware that would prolong the lives of people who ate from it and prepare them to encounter the sages and learn the secret. Another alchemist, Wei Po-yang, prescribed eating gold as part of the preparation; he had no ideas about making it. Later, as in Europe, alchemy became involved with spiritual development.

But it petered out. Chinese astrology did not recognize enough planets for pairing off with the metals, and Taoists never systematized the metals in the same way, or vested them with cosmic relationships, or got far in experiments with them. That was not because they were averse to experimental science. On the contrary, they were pioneers, inventing porcelain and the compass, for instance.[19] In such practical matters they were ahead of most of their European contemporaries. But their alchemy was a dead end. Only Europe's septenary kind evolved into a true science, as only Europe's septenary astrology led to a bursting of celestial barriers. We could rephrase the statement and speak of the seven mystique as underlying both astronomy and chemistry. Though the sciences have long since left it behind, nothing can cancel its role in their emergence or the fact that no other number would work . . . that no other number did.

2

The Ancient Wisdom belief, or will to believe, peers back into the past, conjuring up gods, culture heroes, Rishis, or, in more modern versions, Atlantis and druids, masters and sky people. Much of its allure springs from a sort of long-range nostalgia allied to the theme of a golden age or lost paradise. It now appears that in one of its versions, a very recent one, a reality may underlie it. Whether or not we have hit on a substratum of folk memory or, as some may argue, secret tradition, it is a fact that by taking this version seriously we have attained a glimpse of *something* behind the oldest records of India, Mesopotamia, Israel, and Greece.

At issue here is the claim implied by several women prehistorians, and conspicuously by Marija Gimbutas, that Siberia contained a cultural seedbed a very long time ago. This claim is combined with a feminist version of the lost golden age. The Ancient Wisdom of Goddess worshipers, attested by the symbolism of Goddess artifacts, spread into Europe, laying a foundation in depth for matristic or gylanic societies that were peaceable, sexually balanced, creative. These were overthrown by Indo-European conquerors from the steppes, who, presumably, already had supplanted Goddess worship there.

The primary aim of this inquiry has not been to prove or disprove the feminist account in a broad sense but to ask what evidence there is for a cultural seedbed in a region it points to—the Altaic region, more or less, where Goddess artifacts (if that is what they are) are perhaps oldest and certainly senior to most. Is this the locale of a missing piece of prehistory such as Atlantologists and their kind have groped for under oceans and elsewhere?

Evidence certainly has come to light. There probably was such a seedbed. Nothing has emerged thus far to suggest that it was a lost civilization, an Asian Atlantis. It may have been, but it need not. Rather, we have a rough map or pattern showing elements in a range of traditions as all deriving from an Altaic source, vaguely evoked as primary and paradisal, and from a fertilization of Indo-European communities in that part of the world, through contact with its shamanism and related mythology.

Shamanism included, among much else, the motif of a cosmic center associated with mountain cults. It included also a seven mystique, probably reflecting reverence for the sky-center constellation, Ursa Major, with its seven stars. Indo-Europeans who came in contact carried these things in their dispersal, with a dim ancestral awareness of the source and a consequent belief in a remote northern height, the hub of the world, and a northern paradise. From this belief, and from the institution of sacred centers that could be linked with the northern one, came a sense of spatial ordering and of the world having shape and structure.

They also carried the seven mystique, and it promoted a seminal mode of thinking. An idea was planted in some Indo-European minds that grew and grew and passed into non-Indo-European societies. Number was the key to making sense of the universe, above and below. Wisdom came with groups of seven—with seven Rishis, who sang the harmony of creation and reconstituted life after the Flood; with seven sages, whose arts built seven cities; with seven wise men, whose maxims were over the temple door of a septenary god; and with the seven pillars of a mysterious goddess. As heptad bred heptad the application of the seminal thought led to a further mental ordering of the world that went with the spatial.

And the number had to be seven. At least, no smaller one would have served. Indo-Europeans in general had a special regard for three, but it could not play the same role in their thinking. Three was too small to apply to planets and substances, to musical notes and colors and the calendar. Psychologically, moreover, three is a triad rather than a number. Three objects are simply perceived as such, not counted. A mystique of three never could have inspired the counting that wove numerical patterns into nature and supernature. China's five gave more scope, but not enough. The heptad is the first set that is not, as a rule, directly perceived but has to be counted. Seven was the smallest number that, supposedly recurrent through earth and heaven, could produce counting as a habit beyond immediate need, a way of organizing the world. Measurement and weighing could follow and could lead to science advancing without limits.

Indo-European dispersals supplied media for the mystique's transmission to the Indus Valley and, in the Apollo cult, to Greece. They also brought it, directly or indirectly, to Sumerians and Babylonians and Israelites, who made more of it. In Greece, septenary Apollo with his divine lyre became the patron of music as well as of mathematics. His devotee Pythagoras moved toward new conceptions. Meanwhile, seven-planet astrology arose, at first as glorified fortune-telling but with a potentiality for growth into modern astronomy that five-planet and nine-planet astrology never had. The related seven-metal alchemy opened the way for chemistry. The spectrum fell into line as well as the scale, seven colors as well as seven notes.[20] In Israel the seven-day step-by-step creation put the week in the calendar and, far more important, invested the Creator with a quality of order and purposiveness from the foundation of the world . . . in which (if we are to believe Proverbs and *Ecclesiasticus*) the Lady Wisdom, with her seven pillars, had a hand.

CHAPTER SEVENTEEN

Enigmas and Eccentrics

1

While the facts may indicate simply diffusion, spreading themes and ideas in mythic garb, not everyone would be willing to stop there. Enthusiasts for Ancient Wisdom like to talk of secret tradition handed down by initiates. In fairness it must be said that there are a few points in their favor. Or, to put it less provocatively, there are a few "matters arising" that invite examination, a few cases of authors showing apparent knowledge with no adequate clue as to where it came from—knowledge that goes beyond Milton's quasi-Babylonian touches and the ursine temple in the Jungian dream.

Europeans adopted the seven mystique and extended it. They adopted an earth center, Jerusalem, which came with the Judeo-Christian scheme, as did the earthly paradise. But the world-mountain as paradise's location, indeed, in any form, tended to fade out. Islamic legend preserved a fragmented Meru as the world's highest peak, or its center, or a purgatory, or a paradise, the home of Elijah. From its summit, perhaps, a bridge led to heaven. It might be in the north, but then again it might be in India or some other land. Given these disjointed notions, the prototype Meru was virtually out of sight, and Christian imagination hardly parallels even these . . . until the fourteenth century.

Then something extraordinary happens. Meru reappears in the work of Christendom's greatest poet, taking a form that the vagrant Islamic images may underlie but scarcely can explain.[1] The locale of the second part of

Dante's *Divine Comedy*, which concerns Purgatory, is Meru suddenly re-constituted in Christian terms.

For his poetic evocation of Hell and Heaven, in the first and third parts, Dante drew on familiar ideas. Hell had to be below and Heaven above, whatever deeper truths those directions might symbolize. His vision of Purgatory was not predetermined.[2] Souls in that place were neither lost nor ready for Heaven. They were being purified, through accepted suffering, to fit them for a beatitude assured in the end. Dante did not subscribe to a grim view that made Purgatory in effect a department of Hell. To depict those who were on their way, through however arduous a process, his imagery needed to be open and sunlit.

He made it so. His Purgatory is a conical mountain of gigantic height, immensely higher than any known one.[3] It rises through seven levels. Other levels, less definite, surround its base, but the Mount of Purgatory proper has seven, one for each of the sins being purged. The souls inhabit terraces circling it, at the levels allotted to their sins. Flights of steps lead from level to level. Dante's imagined ascents are much swifter than they actually would be; the transitions are dreamlike. The flattened apex of the cone is the earthly paradise (this is where he makes his point about the golden age being a reminiscence of it). From here, in the third part of his poem, Dante ascends among the planets and stars, meeting the Blessed in the successive spheres and finally leaving astronomical space for the true Heaven, where they all have their home.

Several features of the mount have a peculiar interest. One is its location. Without breaking with Christian tradition, Dante gives it the centrality Meru had. He does this most ingeniously, and he is able to do it because of a development that may seem to be fatal—the realization that Earth is a sphere. For Christians who still believed it to be flat, the center was, as always, Jerusalem. For Christians aware that it was spherical, there was an obvious difficulty about giving it a center at all—that is, on its surface.

Dante was one of many Europeans who did know its shape. Another, a few decades after him, was the author of the so-called *Travels of Sir John Mandeville*. "Mandeville" not only knows the world to be round, he offers two figures for its circumference, 20,425 miles and 31,005 miles.[4] The mean of the two is almost correct. He still insists that Jerusalem is central, quoting Ps. 74:12 ("God is my king from of old, working salvation in the midst of the earth"). His explanation is not very lucid; he seems to think that Earth's position in space puts Jerusalem uppermost. Whatever his meaning, he shows that sphericity need not rule out centrality.

Dante knows similar estimates of the globe's size. That is implied in more than one passage, impressively in his story of the last voyage of Ulysses, whose ship crosses uninterrupted ocean for five months (*Inferno* 26.100–142). With Jerusalem he does better. Dividing Earth's surface into a land hemisphere and a water hemisphere he puts Jerusalem at the center of the former, of the inhabited world. The latter, of course, has a center also. It is entirely sea except for a single island at the antipodes of Jerusalem, the corresponding center of the globe's aqueous half. The Mount of Purgatory rises from it.

No precursor had thought of that. Before Dante, some of the Christians who speculated about the earthly paradise had put it on a mountain in the unexplored southern hemisphere.[5] Dante, however, puts it on a mountain that is uniquely high, septenary, and, in spite of the difficulties, central; a mountain that is Purgatory, receiving the holy souls for their pilgrimage; a mountain linking Earth and Heaven.

He cannot admit gods and goddesses, except symbolically. But he can admit their nearest Christian equivalents, as inhabitants of the mount. The souls make their way heavenward under the tutelage of angels, and at the summit, in the earthly paradise, the poet encounters other celestial beings together with his transfigured love, Beatrice. He could not have admitted the Meru-haunting Rishis, the seven stars of Ursa Major, in the Hindu sense. But he glances twice at the constellation, bringing it in rather oddly, as if because of some unspoken association.

On the highest terrace, where the sin of lust is purged, a company of souls sing the praises of two examples of chastity. One is the Virgin Mary. The other is Diana (Dante, of course, calls Artemis by her Roman name). What is odd here is that the praise is not for her own chastity but for her banishment of the lustful nymph who became Ursa Major; and Dante refers to the nymph not by her mythical name, Callisto, but by her astronomical name, Helice (*Purgatorio* 25.131–32).

> "Dian within the forest dwelt, and chased
> Helice forth, who'd drunk of Venus' bane."

In the earthly paradise he sees an allegorical pageant or masque. Seven candlesticks represent the seven gifts of the Holy Spirit, led by Wisdom. Calling them "the First Heaven's Septentrion" guiding the pageant, he cites Ursa Major, the Roman *Septentriones*, as an analogue:

> When the First Heaven's Septentrion stood still,
>> Which rise nor setting never knew, nor aught
>> To cloud its light, save fogs of sinful will;
> Which there to each his proper duty taught,
>> As ours below teaches the mariner
>> To turn the helm and bring his ship to
>> port . . . (29.43–51, 30.1–6)

Somehow Dante reassembles Meru while, on the face of it, knowing its ingredients at best only in Islamic scraps and knowing nothing of Hinduism. This act is one of artistic creation, with no basis in doctrine or popular belief. It is unlikely that his invention is meant to be taken literally. He defies Genesis—his paradise is a source of rivers, but they are not the rivers named in the Bible, and when he thinks he sees two of these, he is corrected (33.112 ff.). He does not explain, either, how Adam and Eve traveled from a faraway island to the future home of their descendants. His poem is in a different class from the guesswork of paradise hunters.

Are we in the presence of archetypes after all? Or does Dante give a glimpse of undocumented tradition? Centuries later the world-mountain appears in another Christian guise, not with his splendor of poetry or fullness of reminiscence but so strangely, in a context so unexpected, that again it raises questions.

Between 1812 and 1824, a German nun, Anne Catherine Emmerich, had a long series of visions related to the events of the gospels.[6] These were written down and edited and have been published in the form of "lives" of Jesus and Mary. Her editor, Clemens Brentano, stressed that the visions made no historical claims. Much of what Emmerich reports is manifestly inspired by apocryphal legend. However, in the course of her "dream-journeyings" she wandered over a vast expanse of the world outside Palestine, and several times she was lifted above the clouds to the top of a mountain in central Asia that towered above all others. Brentano realized that it was analogous to Meru, and he said so in a well-informed note on the text, without commitment as to the source of her knowledge.[7]

Emmerich called it the Mountain of the Prophet, and her description has echoes of the Islamic legends, though it is hard to see where she could have heard them. The prophet she met was not Mohammed. He was a dweller on the heights whom she likened both to Elijah and to St. John the Evangelist. Elijah was a prophet and John was not; probably she thought of him only because he was another reputed immortal (John 21:20–23). She decided on Elijah and saw what she took to be the chariot that bore him aloft, no longer fiery but disused and overgrown with creepers. The prophet welcomed her on a green island in a lake of clear water. The mountain was full of streams and was the source of the Ganges . . . that recurrent motif, going back to Meru itself.

More surprising, coming from a nineteenth-century nun, is an Ancient Wisdom aspect anticipating the claims of Madame Blavatsky and the theosophists. On the island, said Emmerich, were towers of different shapes surrounded by gardens, and she understood them to be libraries housing the wisdom of many peoples. Close to where the prophet's chariot stood he had a tent in which he kept the scriptures of all ages and nations, including some not yet written. Showing them to his visitor he explained that he was comparing them with a large volume lying in front of him, crossing out or burning erroneous passages. His own volume presumably contained the Truth, but humanity, he told her, was not ready for a full revelation. A new teacher must come first.

2

From poetry and vision to scholarship, or purported scholarship—that of Gerald Massey. He was a Victorian versifier, critic, and mythological theorist. His huge work, *A Book of the Beginnings*, its second part retitled *The Natural Genesis*, came out in 1881 and 1883. It is one of those ominous-looking books that profess to account for myths, symbols, and religious beliefs in general, and most of it justifies the reader's forebodings. Its unusual feature is that here and there, startling insights emerge from a farrago of fancy that is at odds with them.

Massey's main thesis is that all of the myths, symbols, and so on began in Africa and were channeled through Egypt, where they were systematized. From Egypt they passed to other countries. He goes to grotesque lengths trying to prove, for example, that many English place names are derived from an Egyptian sacred vocabulary. Yet from time to time it is as if a lighthouse flashed through the murk.

Not only is he aware of the seven mystique, he picks out Ursa Major as the prototype heptad.[8] Moreover, he associates Ursa with a primary mountain of mythology, the "mountain of the seven stars . . . which represented the celestial north as the birthplace of the initial motion and the beginning of time." This was the seven-stepped Meru around which everything revolved, and a great goddess was enthroned on it.[9] The goddess was Artemis, born in the celestial circle that Ursa traced, and the constellation was numinous as her visible symbol. Of the scriptural Wisdom with her seven pillars he says: "Her foundations were laid in the seven stars which made the first circle in heaven."[10] This circle was the true Eden, on top of the mountain in the north.

Massey notes that seven as a magic number is prior to four, so that the explanation of it as three plus four is invalid.[11] Ursa Major, not numerology, is the ultimate source of all of the sevens. Some of these are contrived and imply an existing magic number imposed on the facts. There is nothing inevitable, Massey observes, about seven planets. These, and the Pleiades, were reckoned as seven for the sake of the heptad.[12] He mentions the Seven Rishis and other groupings and enlarges on the septenary character of the God of Israel. He states plainly that artificial sacred mounds were models or deputies of the mountain at the celestial pole.[13] He even touches on the backtracking septenary spiral that is scattered so widely and becomes the

Troy Town of the Welsh. Its circuits, he says, represent "the seven encirclers of the Great Bear."[14]

In the light of the present exploration, all of this is intriguing. When Massey wrote, much of the supportive research had not been done. It is far more remarkable than a summary can convey, because his insights are not put forward coherently in one place, they are strewn piecemeal through an enormous text, of which the main drift is quite different. A reader would be most unlikely to pick them out and bring them together without knowing the key concepts to begin with. Moreover, these ideas—northern, septenary, Artemisian—run counter to Massey's own African thesis. They could not have been deduced from it. Dealing with Eden, he betrays his inconsistency. He places it, as a myth, in the celestial circle above the mountain, but when he tries to localize it below, his arguments force him to place it on the equator.[15] The northern elements are too potent to reject, yet it never is clear where he got them. He makes no systematic use of archaeology or anthropology or comparative religion, and in the 1880s these disciplines had not reached a stage where their findings would have led anyone to such conclusions. He seems to do it by intuition.

Massey has been claimed as a druid—that is, a neodruid. When his work appeared, societies claiming knowledge of druid lore had been in existence for about a hundred years.[16] They stemmed from theories of eighteenth-century antiquaries and, it must be confessed, from fiction and forgery. The druid lore, even if real and authentically handed down, would have been at best a sort of Celtic Ancient Wisdom, and very little Celtic mythology has any relevance for Massey. Historical druidism may have had remote links with shamanism, even Altaic shamanism. But none of Massey's specifics appear in Celtic lands, except the spiral, which he knew, but which would not in itself have told him much. However far below Dante in literary stature, he too can make a reader suspect unrecorded tradition, and he stands alone in his correct singling out of Ursa Major as the source of the seven mystique.

It was to be expected that Massey should attract the interest of a more notorious figure, whose claims to occult knowledge were made openly. This was Helena Petrovna Blavatsky—HPB, as her disciples called her—revivalist of Ancient Wisdom as part of her complicated theosophy.[17] Today, few but theosophists would regard her teachings as valid. Yet she scores one or two hits that are more impressive than even she ever seems to realize.

HPB had a broader impact than she commonly is given credit for, though most of it was not direct but through influence on others, who went on to attain distinction in pursuits of their own. She founded the Theosophical Society in 1875. It was a springboard for Rudolf Steiner, afterward a guru in his own right and an educational pioneer. Annie Besant, who succeeded Blavatsky as theosophy's high priestess, played a major role in the rising nationalism of India, and a number of Indian leaders, including Gandhi and the Nehrus, passed through a phase of theosophical dabbling. Several writers of best-selling fiction owe HPB a debt (Conan Doyle, Edgar Rice Burroughs, Lovecraft); so do several exponents of unorthodox science (Höbiger, Bellamy, Velikovsky) and unorthodox prehistory (Erich von Däniken).

The point of recalling this is not to rehabilitate Madame Blavatsky but to make it clear that she was more than a negligible crank. Her reading was wide, and when she says something, it may be worth asking why she says it and where she got it from.

Her principal books are *Isis Unveiled* and *The Secret Doctrine*. Her Ancient Wisdom is supposedly a vast system of truths about cosmic law, reincarnation, the nature of life, and other topics. Its custodians are the Masters, or Mahatmas, highly evolved beings who live in distant retreats and dole out portions to humanity as they see fit. All religions have been based on fragments of it, Hinduism and Buddhism having the largest share. In the realm of mythology there are occult "keys" that unlock the myths' inner meanings. A few initiates have been taught the keys, or enough of them to keep truth alive. Paracelsus was one such. HPB said she had gone farther than Paracelsus, though not purely by her own talents. Some of the Masters had taught her telepathically and guided her to sacred texts in concealed libraries, texts that nobody else had read. Nobody else in the West, at any rate.

Much of her work can be dismissed on grounds of plagiarism, charlatanry, or sheer incomprehensibility, but not quite all.[18] In her assessment of mythology, for instance, she was ahead of her time, rejecting the then-fashionable theory that practically everything was a sun myth and foreshadowing issues raised by archaeology and the study of sources when brought to bear, say, on the tales of Troy and Crete and the romances of Arthur.[19] It does not follow that her own interpretations are worth much. Yet we may now have cause to wonder about an insight of some kind shaping her panorama of history. She portrays our species as evolving through millions of years and through a series of "root-races," each divided into subraces; and there are seven of the former and, within each, seven of the latter.

Her choice of seven is the interesting thing. The number is made to structure an elaborate scheme giving substance to various peoples from mythology and prehistory and fitting them all together.[20] The members of her first root-race were not material creatures. Second were the Hyperboreans, who were more solid and, we learn with some surprise, lived on a northern continent since broken up, containing Greenland, Spitzbergen, and parts of Asia. Third came the Lemurians, most of whose homeland is now submerged. Some of them were more or less human in the present sense, though much taller, and with extra eyes and arms. Fourth were the accomplished folk of Atlantis, now also submerged; their high civilization declined, but was ancestral to several known to history, notably Egypt.[21] Fifth were the Aryans, very approximately the Indo-Europeans, and humanity is still in its Aryan phase. Many descendants of older races survive; features such as extra arms have apparently been bred out. The sixth root-race is in process of formation, and after that will come the seventh.

To appraise this is to realize what one is apt to realize reading HPB impartially. Her occasional insight is all, its working-out is fantasy. The easy error is to let the fantasy swamp the insight, which in this case is evident. Here and in other contexts, she does lay her finger on the seven mystique. For the initial inspiration there is no need to look far—certainly not to any Masters. Her awareness of the mystique appears chiefly in *The Secret Doctrine*. In the earlier *Isis Unveiled* she has passages showing an interest in seven and quoting instances, but her main purpose is to prove a priority among certain texts, to establish, in fact, who copied whom.[22] Her consciousness of wider bearings is due to her reading of Gerald Massey. *Isis Unveiled* was published in 1877, Massey's opus in 1881 and 1883, and *The Secret Doctrine* in 1888. HPB mentions Massey without fully acknowledging her debt, and she speaks of him condescendingly as a mere rational scholar, "an initiate in the mysteries of the British Museum."[23]

From Massey she takes his explanation of the seven mystique as originating in Ursa Major. It is ironic to find her knowing better in this respect than the reputable scholars who have followed planetary and lunar trails.

> The first form of the mystical SEVEN was seen to be figured in heaven by the Seven large stars of the *great Bear*.[24]

Massey involves the statement with doubtful stuff about Egyptians and druids, and HPB does likewise. Nevertheless, the point is made.

HPB takes the topic much farther, with a whole septenary extravaganza.[25] In *The Secret Doctrine* she calls seven the supreme number of the higher mysteries, the *"Factor* number" of the present life cycle. She lists numerous heptads, such as the week and the planets, albeit some look like inventions of her own. She even invokes the number to answer a natural question: why her all-knowing and benevolent Masters hoard the Wisdom and do not release it to humanity, apart from a favored few.

> Doctrines such as the planetary chain, or the seven races, at once give a clue to the seven-fold nature of man, for each principle is correlated to a plane, a planet, and a race; and the human principles are, on every plane, correlated to seven-fold occult forces—those of the higher planes being of tremendous power. So that any septenary

division at once gives a clue to tremendous occult powers, the abuse of which would cause incalculable evil to humanity. (Vol. 1, p. xxxv).

She believes that she has got hold of something significant—and she has, however weird and pretentious her handling of it. In her stress on seven she is more perceptive than later occultists. Gurjieff, for instance, talks of seven cosmoses and seven human types, but they seem to be personal notions, divorced from the real heptadic themes that HPB is aware of.[26]

Where she fails is in overreaching herself. Her system requires the seven mystique to be universal. Therefore, instead of asking objectively where it occurs and where it does not, and which society transmitted it to which, she cites not only genuine cases but other, scattered ones that prove nothing. It does not work. She finds no convincing traces of the mystique in China, or in Egypt before the Alexandrian Greeks. Farther afield she practically gives up. If there is secret tradition here, it seems not to have included one of the mystique's most eloquent features, its regional limitation.

3

While believers in tradition may still point to all of this as telling in their favor, HPB's actual handling of the seven mystique is a warning against naive acceptance of theosophical versions or any others of the same type. Much the same could be said of Shambhala. She heard of it, and its legends may have contributed to her ideas about Masters. But she started her readers off wrongly by putting it in the Gobi Desert. Nicholas Roerich, though a theosophist himself for some years, was honest enough to amass data impartially and avoid entrapment in the Gobi delusion.[27] Others blundered into a blind alley.

A Western Shambhala mythos was evolved by a breakaway theosophist, Alice Bailey, and expounded during the 1930s by a disciple, Vera Stanley Alder. The latter's book *The Initiation of the World* is an interesting case study. It includes a theory of secret tradition related to a general sketch, quite a competent one, of the notion of Ancient Wisdom.[28] But her treatment of Shambhala underlines the warning implicit in the vagaries of Madame Blavatsky.

Shambhala, spelled "Shamballa," is "the vital centre in the planetary consciousness"—not so much a place as an institution, founded by higher beings from Venus eighteen million years ago, to be the earthly headquarters of the spiritual hierarchy—the Masters who preserve Ancient Wisdom and exert occult influence on the course of history.[29] It has a tangible existence in some sense, but not the ordinary sense, being composed of "etheric physical matter." Even matter that is etheric must, one would think, have a local habitation. On this the author is contradictory. Sometimes Shamballa is said to be in the Himalayas. Sometimes it is vaguely north of them. The nearest thing to a commitment is the Blavatsky-prompted statement that it is on ground that used to be an island in the "Gobi Lake," since desiccated. Between 60,000 and 45,000 B.C., a bridge led from Shamballa to an Atlantean colony on the south shore of the lake called Manova, the City of the Bridge.[30]

Shamballa is concealed in what is now the Gobi Desert, seven-gated and governed by the Lord of the World. To the profane traveler it is invisible and impalpable. The Masters assemble there annually for the Wesak Festival. Buddha takes part, and so does his brother "the Christ." The Christ's Second Coming will take place before the end of the twentieth century, in the shape of the teacher foretold by Buddhists as Maitreya, an event that will usher in a new golden age.[31] All of this is based on alleged revelations and has only tenuous links with what actually is said about Shambhala in Tibet, Mongolia, or anywhere else.

The briefer saga of Shambhala's underground extension, Agharti, does call for comment. It made its Western debut as "Agarttha," said to mean "inaccessible" or "inviolable," in a book called *Mission de l'Inde* by Saint-Yves d'Alveydre, published in 1910.[32] D'Alveydre influenced Steiner. His assertions about his sources are occultish—he received telepathic messages from the Dalai Lama—and largely worthless. The one point of interest is the emphasis on India. He had conversations with a "high official of the Hindu Church" (the high official, however, was an Indian who kept a pet shop in Le Havre).

Ferdinand Ossendowski, as mentioned, collected Aghartic lore on the spot; there apparently was Aghartic lore to collect; and in 1925 René Guénon published *Le Roi du Monde* (*The King of the World*). Guénon was a genuine student of mythology, and while he read d'Alveydre and Ossendowski, he worked in consultation with Hindu scholars, on this book and others. Discussing the elusive place he uses the "Agarttha" spelling and shows commendable caution.[33] It may or may not be wholly subterranean, it may or may not be physically real. If it does exist, it is somewhere in central Asia, enclosed by a mountain. It is a holy land, the prototype of all holy lands, and a place of immortality. The enclosing mountain, actual or mythical, is the original Meru, or world-mountain, and was regarded long ago as the world's center or navel, other centers, such as Delphi, being representations of it. Guénon notes a connection with Ursa Major, the "celestial balance."[34]

This seems to be the closest anyone comes to a direct linkage of Meru and Shambhala—not to mention the earthly paradise, the sacred center, and the seven-star constellation. Guénon is knowledgeable if cryptic, and he even cites Emmerich. He speaks of a revelation prior to all religions and relates the world-mountain and the rest to the Holy Grail. Montsalvat, or the Mountain of Salvation, where in some legends the Grail is kept, is one of the world-mountain's representations.[35]

Guénon raises the same issue as Massey, if in a less elaborately perplexing form. Where did he learn this? He wrote forty years later, when more was known, but that is not a sufficient answer. Although *Le Roi du Monde* echoes Ossendowski in its title, Ossendowski does not account for more than a fraction of it. Guénon has areas of contact with Roerich, who was on his Asian expedition when *Le Roi du Monde* appeared. Roerich was aware of Agharti as well as Shambhala and, in his *Altai-Himalaya*, showed more clearly than his precursors that they were aspects of the same place . . . or myth. He realized that Ossendowski's King of the World was simply the ruler of Shambhala with a more sensational title.[36] His Asian informants, however, were mostly lamas, and they tended to be equivocal and evasive. Guénon's, who were Hindus, may have divulged something more substantial—some philosophical myth redefining Meru that, when brought into contact with a Western mind, produced *Le Roi du Monde*.

CHAPTER EIGHTEEN

Vindication ?

<u>1</u>

We have been assessing Goddess prehistory and the new version of the golden age, with its implications about a cultural source or seedbed in the Altai-Baikal region, which would, in the eyes of the thoroughgoing, have been a sort of paradise of primitive Goddess wisdom. Support has come to light, if perhaps of an unexpected kind. It is time to ask whether the supportive matter can be assembled to give an ordered scenario, fitting everything in.

Gimbutas's oldest exhibit is the panel of mammoth ivory from Mal'ta, which dates from about 24,000 B.C. Goddess figurines are associated with the same place, and the chronological spread points to a long period of cultic and artistic activity. On one side of the panel are spiral designs of dots; on the other are three serpents. The latter may doubtless be accepted as Goddess images. The dot patterns are interpreted in the same way, perhaps rightly, but they suggest a great deal more. There are seven spirals, and the large one in the center makes seven circuits. That fact in itself indicates that the seven mystique of Altaic shamanism has an immensely long past and may descend from a time when, as some anthropologists maintain, women were the principal shamans or even the only ones. Moreover, the wide dispersal of the backtracking labyrinth spiral, which may be derived from the one exemplified on the panel, favors a belief that dissemination from this region did happen. It is found among the Hopi in Arizona, who call it the Mother Earth symbol, and this is evidence both for dissemination before 6000 B.C. and for the original Goddess character of the spiral.

The septenary design draws attention to the seven mystique that presumably underlies it. Shamanic and other clues suggest that this was due to reverence for Ursa Major, the seven-star constellation circling the sky center, the celestial pole. If so, that reverence is as old as the ivory panel. The studies of Banzaroff and Potanin relate the constellation to an Earth Goddess, bears, and female shamans. The later artifacts in the Altaic region, and data such as the American connection, support the view of Piggott and others (including, it is fair to acknowledge, Goddess-worshiping neowitches) that there has been a continuity in the northland over a very long period and that shamanic and kindred mythology, recorded in modern times, can be evidence for remote antiquity. Legends and traditions elsewhere, which point in an Altaic direction, do not demand the assumption that they reach back twenty thousand years or more; they may be derived from the seedbed at a much later stage, with its ancient characteristics still flourishing. Legends and traditions of this kind occur a long way apart, and their apparent convergence on the same northern source is significant.

In the upshot, the evidence for the seedbed is cumulative and its influence can be inferred very widely in linked motifs. The Goddess evidence is good at the source, but in dissemination the Goddess sometimes fades out, even though the disseminated motifs go on strongly, with effects that make the notion of Ancient Wisdom—in the sense of seminal ideas, not developed systems—by no means absurd.

A defensible scenario would be as follows. Tens of thousands of years ago, shamans in Siberia and Mongolia held the seven-star constellation in reverence. It was all the more important because the pole, which it ruled, was not marked then by a separate polestar of conspicuous brightness. They had myths about the two great wild creatures, the bear and the elk. In parts of Siberia the seven-star constellation was a cosmic Elk, while another one was a Bear. The chief deity was a powerful Earth Mother and Mistress of Animals, with whom female shamans were closely associated. Her cult and symbolism, passing from tribe to tribe, played a part in forming the Paleolithic Goddess substratum across Siberia and Europe. Her chief animal form was as a bear. In the Altai-Baikal region, one of her oldest and most active territories, the seven-star constellation belonged to her. Under whatever name, she was the wise Manzalgormo of the myth recorded by Roerich, directly responsible for the constellation; its stars were seven shamans, vested with the power and spirit of the Goddess's bears, so that the constellation was ursine like her. It inspired a mystique of the number seven that was widely spread in her worship but was most prominent in the Altai-Baikal region. Mongols in the course of time adopted the seven shamans as the Seven Old Men, still identified with the stars.

The constellation built up a unique numinosity, partly because of its relation to the pole and hence to shamans' ideas of cosmic centrality, expressed in the image of a central tree or world-mountain, which they climbed in their trances to meet superior spirits. In the Altai area, actual gold that gave the range a name, and an actual mountain cult, helped to evoke the divine world-mountain as golden. Mongols made it the home of the Seven Old Men. Shamans represented the tree or mountain by actual trees or notched posts mystically identified with it, which they climbed during the ecstatic ascent.

Late in the fourth millennium B.C., around the Altai, Indo-European groupings such as the Afanasievo came under shamanic influence and acquired a mythical "package" comprising some of the ancient themes, which in the hands of these new people took on a rekindled life and energy. The package included the golden world-mountain, in some primary form related to the mountain cult and to Belukha as the highest Altaic peak; this eventually evolved into golden Meru, central to the universe, a paradisal abode of gods. It also included the seven stars, both as bear stars and as seers, and something of the connected seven mystique. The mythical package was carried south and southwest in Indo-European expansion. It was developed especially in the Indo-Aryan body. Here the seven stars became the Seven Rishis, semidivine seers said to have assisted at creation and to be the prime fountainheads of wisdom. Among Indo-Aryans the package generated their own mystique of seven, as eventually attested in the *Rig Veda*. Their male pantheon reduced the goddess, but she still was present as Aditi, mother of the seven principal gods. They also had adopted the shamanic ritual of horse sacrifice. The other Indo-Aryan branch that turned west carried the package to Mesopotamia and beyond. Sumerians and Babylonians adapted the Seven Rishis as the Seven Sages, wisdom figures who founded cities. There too the seven mystique developed, passing on into Israel.

Much the same happened, if confusedly, with the world-mountain. For the Indo-Aryans who planted themselves in India and created Hinduism, the center of the earth and the center of the sky coincided. Folk memories handed down from the time of Altaic contact located the universal center in the far north, with vestigial touches of geographic knowledge. It was golden, paradisal Meru, home of gods, source of the holy Ganges, with the primary heptad Ursa Major—the Seven Rishis—circling it and the blessed Northern Kurus nearby among golden sands. Like the shamans, Hindus set up representations of the center. In Sumer the earth's sacred midpoint was an actual city, Nippur. Likewise with Babylon. But in both places there was representation here also. Each city, or rather its principal temple, was identified mystically with the world-mountain. In Israel the emphasis was so strongly on the earthly center, and on the hill of Zion with the Temple of the Lord, that the tradition of the northern mountain was almost effaced. But not quite. "Mount Zion in the far north," the mountain of God, just survived in scripture. The Garden of Eden with its river source was there, or at any rate it might be, to judge from Ezekiel.

Back in the real north, other Indo-Europeans encountered the original Goddess who had been there for so long—the Earth Goddess and Mistress of Animals, with her ursine form, her female shamans, and her constellation. They made her a deity of their own as Proto-Artemis, with women companions, and the bear as her celestial form. Enriched from Finno-Ugrian sources her cult flourished in the Pontic-Caspian country. Altaic contacts also gave Indo-Europeans a shamanic god or spirit of inspiration, Proto-Apollo. The shamans at the Altaic source were remembered in his worship as Hyperboreans, dwellers in a paradise beyond the Boreal wind, the same, ultimately, as Hinduism's Northern Kurus. "Hyperborean" cults of Proto-Apollo and Proto-Artemis linked them together, wandered over the steppes, and drifted through the Caucasus to Asia Minor and Greece. Ethnic movements need not have been involved. By the time it happened, Indo-Europeans were established from end to end of the steppe-land.

Proto-Apollo had a personal seven mystique. It may have been due to his bond with Proto-Artemis and her stars, or it may have been part of his shamanic background, with his sister's possession of Ursa Major simply confirming it and keeping it alive. It makes little difference, since the mystique began with the constellation in any case. He retained it when he reached Hellas in the second millennium B.C. The shamanism of Greek Apollo worshipers may have owed a debt to later Greek acquaintance with shamans in Scythia, but this would have brought elaboration only; the god's Delphic oracle, with its inspired priestesses and their ecstatic techniques, was far older.

The Apollo and Artemis who took shape in Greece, with new myths fitting them into the Zeus-governed pantheon, resulted from various divine fusions and were more complex and civilized. Yet an alien past still clung to them and some of their northern aspects remained. Proto-Apollo, shamanic and septenary, was still a major constituent of the god of Delphi, as is proved by the stories of Aristeas, Abaris, and others and by the annual departure to renew contact with the Hyperboreans. Artemis kept the ursine quality, together with the constellation, the kinship with animals and wild country, a Hyperborean home of her own, and even the shamanesses in the guise of attendant nymphs. She drove a team of reindeer, and Hyperborean women (in their mythical origins, aspects of her "proto" self) brought offerings to her shrine on Delos, starting a custom that continued, wherever the offerings really came from. Greeks were well aware of her ancient cult, lingering on or only lately extinct in the Pontic-Caspian country—as a reality in the Crimea and as a legendary religion of Amazons east of the Don.

2

The case for this scenario rests on two main bodies of data. First, the main themes occur so far apart. In the repeated linkage of seven mystique and centrality and paradise we have what looks like a repeated end product of diffusion from one starting point, far back; and that starting point cannot be in India, or Mesopotamia, or Israel, or Greece. The parallels are both multiple and peculiar. Apollo was septenary like Yahweh. Israel's scriptures had seven running through them like the myths of Inanna and the hymns of the *Rig Veda*. Delphi was the world's center like Zion and Nippur and Babylon. Yet it was not mystically bonded with a world-mountain, Meru, under whatever name, as they were; yet—again—a polar sky center was the domain of Apollo's twin. Associated paradises or subparadises survived as the Land of the Hyperboreans, the Garden of Eden, Dilmun, the land of the Northern Kurus. The Greeks themselves thought that the Northern Kurus and the Hyperboreans might be the same, yet neither could have suggested the other, let alone Eden, directly. And so it goes.

Taken together the data point not only to an external source but to an Altaic source, and a largely shamanic inspiration. Moreover—the other basic fact—Altaic shamanism does provide the ingredients for these phenomena that appear so far afield. Mongolian cults reinforce its claims, and the lamas' lore of Shambhala, however suspect and distorted, offers at least some support for an Asian tradition of Altaic importance, even of a god who might be Proto-Apollo, or rather the deity from whom Indo-Europeans derived him.

The persistence of the world-mountain beyond antiquity is a curious incidental problem. Its disintegration is understandable. Its reconstitution—by an Italian poet, a German visionary, an English eccentric, a French theorist of myth—is more puzzling. It does almost have the air of a Jungian archetype, lodged in a collective unconscious and surfacing at long intervals. Or it is very easily given a Freudian gloss. But psychology is no solution. The world-mountain is not universal, not a projection of the human psyche in general, and its link with the seven mystique gives it an aspect that is quite un-Freudian and nowhere accounted for by Jung. Psychological clichés may show reasons for the image's power, but not for its nature.

What has been defined, anyhow, is a mental ordering of the world with its origin in the Altaic seedbed, the dimly recalled and mythified paradise. If that is accepted it is fair to speak, in a qualified sense, of Ancient Wisdom. Other mythologies have paradises that are not the same. There is no question here of proposing an all-purpose key to paradisal myth, or indeed any other kind. The point is that certain specific myths and themes do support the idea of a north-Asian prototype that had substance, and transmitted impressions that can be plotted and roughly dated. From this, if it existed, through some of the Indo-European dispersals, the mental ordering was implanted in the thinking of ancient civilizations—but not all. It combined a mystique of number with a conception of numinous world centrality. In the two cases with a direct influence on Western society, Israel and Greece, the mental ordering was focused not only on an earth center but on a septenary god whose place it was, with a dynamic quality resulting—on Yahweh at Zion, whose worship led to Judaism, Christianity, Islam; on Apollo at Delphi, who became the divine patron of mathematics and music, science and medicine. The further and radical effects of the seven mystique, in astronomy and other fields, have been sufficiently traced.

Goddess prehistory makes sense, with certain provisos. We can be more specific now about the cultural elements in the Goddess's northern world, about their going outside it and about their importance when they went. In view of the results, her advocates may fairly claim her as the prime source of Ancient Wisdom, at any rate for a large part of the world. Her legacy tended to be absorbed into male-centered systems and lose some of its original character. Implacable anti-Indo-Europeans, if they admit this process, doubtless will condemn it as male theft and falsification. Yet it may also be argued that the Indo-Europeans gave their Goddess inheritance a new precision, a new effectiveness, when it might otherwise have languished indefinitely. Whichever assessment is preferred, the Goddess was not nullified. Something survived in the stream that flowed to Greece that enables us to say more about her. Among the countless female divine figures, Artemis is the one who actually brings us closest to her—not the restrictedly virginal Diana but the Artemis through whom we glimpse the ancient deity she derives from: committed to no male partner, identifiable with earth mothers in Asia, patroness of birth and primordial life and wild nature, preurban, predomestic. Even the huntress is consistent with Paleolithic levels of thinking.

Where this inquiry does challenge Goddess prehistory is in its implications about the early Indo-Europeans, whether they are exonerated or not. They emerge as people of a different kind, for good or ill. The scenario, if accepted, excludes the notion that they were crude seminomads headed by equestrian warriors who worshiped only male deities, had no ideas beyond macho dominance and warfare, and surged out of the steppes and into Old Europe, wrecking Goddess-oriented societies. There may or may not be something in this, but as in Mesopotamia, changes that admittedly happened may be accounted for in other ways. In any case, the contrast is too harsh. It loses credibility if Indo-Europeans were capable of adopting others' religious themes in a creative blending, of arriving at seminal ideas, and of infusing these into established communities, with momentous results. Further, if Proto-Artemis was an Indo-European goddess, with a cult stretching across the steppe-lands themselves, the contrast breaks down theologically. Indo-Europeans did acknowledge female divinity, and not simply as a nuisance they had to come to terms with when they conquered Goddess worshipers.

Their contribution may have been crucial for the perennial themes we started with—the golden age and Ancient Wisdom. It may be true that the dream of a golden age is at bottom psychological, a projection of nostalgia for idealized childhood, even the safety of the womb. It also may be true that the associated sense of loss, of things closing in, is due not only to leaving childhood behind but to seeing death ahead. Such feelings are not confined to any single mythology or family of mythologies. Only in Western society, however, has the golden age been recurrent and protean, turning up again and again in different guises, reinvented, reimagined, reratio-nalized, in a succession of myths and ideologies.[1]

At the earlier stages it may be that an Altai-inspired paradise reinforced mortal yearnings with a sort of pointing-up factor. To believe in Meru, or the Land of the Northern Kurus, or the Land of the Hyperboreans, or Dilmun, or the Garden of Eden, was to believe in an actual Good Place or Good State now out of reach, which made it easier to give shape to the dream and project it onto the past. It even could be urged that if all of these beliefs derived from the actual seedbed, the golden age as a tradition had something in it.

Monica Sjöö goes farther, arguing that golden-age myth reflects a kind of folk nostalgia due to the passing away of the real Goddess era. This view is difficult to sustain from actual mythology. Golden ages do not seem to have an especially Goddess character. The classical one is originally the reign of Cronus or Saturn; Astraea, the goddess of Justice, is put in later but looks like an afterthought. The happy state of Adam and Eve may once have been under the aegis of a goddess, of whom Eve as we know her is a humanized and defamed version, but it cannot be proved because we do not have the prebiblical story.

The argument, of course, cuts deeper. It is bound up with the claim that the Goddess era was socially different and better, being "matristic" or "gylanic," with a balance between the sexes. It was a real golden age, and the feminist version of that conception is not simply one more instance of a syndrome, it is factually grounded.

To examine this belief in detail would be to go beyond present terms of reference. Presumably, when the Goddess in her various forms was powerful, *some* women enjoyed a status that was lost later—shamanesses, priestesses, female custodians of the tribal magic. It can be argued that in a matrilinear, Goddess-worshiping society, women automatically would have had more importance and would have been respected as images of the Great Mother. But it is hard to be sure about such things, and it is extremely hard to know what is implied by archaeology. The art of Minoan Crete (for instance) is reputedly free from images of male domination.[2] That may be true, or at any rate plausible, but the respected women in Cretan pictures are upper class. *Some* women had status, yes. But does it prove much about society in general? One picture is explained as portraying men bearing tribute to the Goddess, or to a priestess representing her. The woman is much more showy than the men, and they look deferential.[3] The interpretation may be correct. But the poses do rather suggest a great lady in Victorian England giving instructions to her household staff. That happened every day, up and down the country. Yet Victorian England was thoroughly patriarchal.

The larger social aspect, in fact, is controversial. It will be wiser here to stop short at noting the sort of issues this discussion has raised and continue on the psychological line.

The case for the loss of the Goddess being significant is more interesting if we look at the motivation of the golden-age theme from the other end. Human history may be seen as a decline because something else is projected besides pseudo-memories of childhood—namely, the individual's awareness of the movement toward decay and death. Myths of the golden age and paradise are more evidential here because they visibly attempt to defy that awareness by making out that somehow, somewhere, sometime, things might be different. Paradises are always associated with long life, even immortality. That is true of the Hyperboreans, of the Northern Kurus, of

Ladies of Minoan Crete. *Mansell Collection*

Dilmun, or of the Garden of Eden with its tree of life and unfallen couple. Hesiod's golden race had no fear of death. In Mesopotamian legend and the Old Testament, closeness to the pristine state is symbolized by life being still very long, and the decline is symbolized by its growing shorter.

Here the Goddess's withdrawal may well be reflected. It does seem to be a fact that faith in a real afterlife dwindled as deity grew more masculine. The change produced the dreary negativity of the Mesopotamian nether-world, the Israelite Sheol, and the Greek realm of shades. Death was now indeed to be dreaded, and the classical postdeath condition became, for some of the dead, not merely nullity but positive suffering. The Roman poet Lucretius actually thought he was cheering his readers up by proving that death was total extinction. Hope of a happy afterlife had evaporated for most people; the Celts, who still had it, were remarked on as exceptional and surprising. A tragic idea of existence as good-followed-inexorably-by-loss-of-good was what came naturally.

In the Christian era the golden age shows a further development, with a further and special pointing up. Dante, after his fashion, may be right. Europe's long Christian conditioning made the lost golden age central to the human state. Paradise and severance from it supplied the groundwork for the fall-and-redemption doctrine at the heart of Christianity. The sense of a glory and its forfeiture, built into the structure of history, lingered after the fading of Christian orthodoxy. It fostered a tendency, often below the conscious threshold, to translate vague nostalgia or discontent into golden age dreams and speculations, with more persistence than anywhere else and with more variety, because the original dogmatic basis was gone. Rousseau's idyllic natural state and the Marxists' primitive communism will be remembered as examples. That can be said without prejudice to any truth that Christian doctrine, or some of the post-Christian theories, may embody.

Paradise Lost in its Christian form is derived from the Bible. But as we have seen, ancestral mythology of the mountain, carried by Indo-Europeans, may have helped to shape the biblical paradise; and the shamanic Fall, carried likewise if mysteriously, may have made its contribution to the biblical Fall.

Ancient Wisdom, like the golden age, is a conception extending beyond any one mythology. Here too, however, Western society has been uniquely inventive, with its Hermetic treatises, its romanticized druids, its theosophical Masters, and all the rest. Again Christian conditioning may have promoted a pointing up and a development. The Bible sanctified the seven mystique, facilitating adoption of the seven-planet astrology as an Ancient Wisdom and as one that smoothed the path for others.

It would be absurd to pretend that suggestions such as these cover everything. The possibility of unknown traditions may be raised by Dante, Emmerich, Massey, Guénon. True, the vagaries of many who assert such traditions are hardly encouraging. Nevertheless, this inquiry has disinterred a missing piece of prehistory, and the sense of a missing piece, a Something Else, does (I have urged) underlie much of the thinking that has evolved Atlantis and kindred phantasms of glory departed.

3

Indo-European importance reopens a question that frames all of this. Who were these people, where did they come from, and what did they do? The emerging possibilities, if accepted, deal a coup de grace to the old theories of Indo-European dispersal, which put the beginning of the process little prior to the last two pre-Christian millennia. If the scenario is anywhere near to being right it needs to have begun long before, so as to bring Indo-Europeans to the Altai by 3000 B.C. and bring them there from an even earlier homeland. Recent studies have acknowledged that it was so. One way or another they provide for Indo-Europeans the whole length of the steppes in the period required. They might have expanded from a Pontic-Caspian starting point, or they might have had an ancestral homeland elsewhere and farther back. For the present purpose it makes no difference. On any modern showing, the homeland phase is so remote that the steppe settlement would have been completed early enough.

Actually, to recall the most recent discussions is to see that to a large extent the scenario falls within a consensus. It envisages Indo-Europeans widely dispersed before 3000 B.C., through what is now the Soviet Union. It concurs with Mallory's ideas about Finno-Ugrian contact and harmonizes with his opinions in general, subject to one or two chronological queries. Favoring a Pontic-Caspian homeland, he envisages a rapid expansion from it and allows an Indo-European character to the Afanasievo and Andronovo cultures far eastward in Asia. Yet the scenario would not make him right and the others wrong. It fits Renfrew's model too. Renfrew launches his Indo-Europeans from Anatolia and has them fanning out through Old Europe and beyond in an agricultural wave of advance, with people of kindred stock branching off into Russia and turning to a more pastoral life-style. But he dates the initial movements so far back that he gives time for Indo-Europeans to occupy the Pontic-Caspian region just as early as they do in Mallory's model. He says it himself:

> My own proposal of an early agricultural dispersal of Proto-Indo-European-speaking farmers from Anatolia would also situate (Proto) Indo-European speakers in the Pontic-Caspian steppe-lands at pre-

cisely the time of the Finno-Ugrian (i.e. Uralic) contact proposed by Mallory.[4]

Their linguistic descendants could have continued eastward from there. The same applies to the theory of a Danube homeland.

Moreover, one argument deployed against Renfrew may now have dissolved. It has been claimed that the goddess worshipers found by Gimbutas in Old Europe cannot have been Indo-Europeans, with ancestry in Anatolia or anywhere else, because Indo-Europeans did not have goddesses. But if, in the steppes, Indo-Europeans had even the one great goddess—Proto-Artemis—at what was certainly an early stage, they could have had any number of goddesses at any stage; they had nothing against female divinity. Old Europe's goddess-worshiping population could have been mainly Indo-European, as Renfrew maintains. Intrusions by "Kurgan" steppe dwellers are possible whoever they were, but surely a transformation by narrowly patriarchal hordes is dubious in the absence of proof that such hordes existed.

No clear reason has emerged for preferring one Indo-European theory to another. But cultural factors may have shifted the bias. If the steppe-roaming Indo-Europeans were something better than a mob of brutish horsemen and trampled women; if they developed the worship of a great goddess; if they were capable of absorbing, processing, and transmitting creative ideas; if descendants of theirs had a share in early stirrings of civilization—then it may be easier to picture them in Renfrew's style, as kinsfolk of the Old Europeans who had pushed peaceably eastward, than it would be to see them in Gimbutas's style, as aliens who pushed destructively westward. As Claiborne remarks, the river names over most of Europe suggest that Indo-Europeans formed the main population and were responsible for most of the map. The steppe dwellers are quite consistent with a belief that they stemmed from such a population. If the communities of Old Europe were indeed Indo-European, settled from about 6500 B.C. onward, they could have acquired some of their goddess worship from the scanty pre-Indo-European element, religious heirs of the Paleolithic substratum, and they could have passed on a goddess receptivity to their steppe-exploring descendants. To say this is only to say "could have," no more. The point is that there is no disproof of Renfrew in feminist theology.

As for the Middle East and the Indus Valley, Renfrew's hypothesis A, bringing Indo-Europeans directly from Anatolia, may be right. However, it seems irrelevant here. The shamanic connection requires a movement down from the northland, roughly as in his hypothesis B. That can be provided for, if not yet fully sustained, and hypothesis A does not add anything. Renfrew allows that both may be true in principle.

But this inquiry has drawn attention to an issue that may turn out to be crucial—the early presence of Indo-Aryans in Iran, the Mitanni kingdom, Canaan. These Indo-Aryans of western Asia, as Mallory calls them, somehow separated far back from the ones who went to India. The history of the seven mystique suggests that Sumer derived it from them around 2500 B.C. The strange metal head exhibited by the Foundation for Cultural Preservation is the only solid evidence for so early a presence. That in itself is too anomalous to build on. But the septenary argument does evoke an Indo-Aryan context for it as early as the date indicated by tests. Some of Ghirshman's ceramic data at least raise encouraging possibilities.

Carbon dating of the Afanasievo culture, up by the Altai, just about provides time for groups to move southwest from the seedbed area, evolving Indo-Aryan language and myth, and for their descendants to reach the confines of Mesopotamia when required. Renfrew's hypothesis A, of course, gets Indo-Europeans of some kind into that area with millennia to spare, but it fails to give them the northern contacts or the Indo-Aryan character. This linguistic branch is an unsolved problem, or rather a subproblem within the main one. It looks as if it may be of major rather than minor importance. Proof of its antiquity could have a radical impact on ideas about Mesopotamia, Israel, and the roots of Judeo-Christian belief.

And the seedbed? If anyone likes to think of it as more advanced than current knowledge suggests, or to imagine a greater Ancient Wisdom—a Goddess Wisdom—of which shamanism as known is a decadent remnant, no disproof can be offered. A sort of Altaic Atlantis may have existed and, thus far, eluded archaeologists. In a region that is sparsely peopled and mainly wild, the possibility of sensational finds is clearly open, but at the same time the prospect of anybody actually making them may appear slim and may be dependent on luck or accident.

Much of the relevant area, from the Altai toward Lake Baikal, lies in the Soviet republic of Tuva, formerly Tannu-Tuva. The part closest to Mount Belukha is Mongun-Taiga. "Taiga," which usually denotes forested country, here has a more general sense of "wilderness." Mongun-Taiga is the "Sacred Wilderness," an intriguing but cryptic name.[5] It is bleak and rugged, with a seminomadic population herding yaks, sheep, goats, and horses. The inhabitants are much more akin to Mongols than to Russians, and ancestrally they are of the Turkic stock that has dominated this region for a very long time.

Shamanism, despite official hostility, lingers on, with some of its ancient concomitants, such as the cult of mountains and their resident spirits. But while cultural continuity may stretch indefinitely far back, the shiftings of particular ethnic groups and the lack of settled centers before Soviet rule deny this land a historical tradition (apart, it seems, from a vague glorification of Genghis Khan). Hence there are few surface clues for the prospective archaeologist here, or indeed anywhere, in Tuva.

Daydreaming may allow such fantasies as a landslide uncovering a lost temple, on this side of the Altai or the other. From the present point of view, the serious long-term hope may be for a gradual unearthing of artifacts in sequence over a large area, revealing more about a seedbed and more about a spread of influence from it—not only Gimbutan Goddess images but cult objects like the Mal'ta panel with the septenary spiral, figurines possibly ancestral to Artemis and Apollo, groupings of seven stars or shamans or shamanesses, tokens of bear worship or mountain worship. Again, evidence for horse sacrifice between Siberia and India would support the belief that Indo-Europeans carried it with them from the north. Such things, of course, are not specific requirements. There would be no sense in being specific where the gaps in knowledge are so vast. To instance them is simply to suggest how the gaps might be partly bridged and the scenario, in some slight degree, confirmed.

Progress might be made by way of a proper scrutiny of the Shambhala legend. Buddhism has written records where shamanism never had. The lamas' Shambhalic texts remain to be adequately studied and assessed in the light of the convergent traditions of Northern Kurus, Hyperboreans, and so forth. Westerners who made the topic known in the 1920s had mystical or occultish interests that told against objectivity, and the lamas themselves, to judge from Roerich, were inclined to mystify rather than enlighten. How far it is still feasible to do the kind of research that is required, no one can tell without trying. But it may be that somewhere the documentation supplies a clue to an identifiable place. If so, that place might be examined. And aerial photography or some other technique might pick out potential archaeological sites.

In any case, fresh perspectives have opened up on the remoter origins of Western society, and at least partial support has come to light for Goddess prehistory. These results surely encourage further work to reveal what happened in those enigmatic northern spaces; how various groups moved and mixed and affected each other; in what ways they are ancestral to ourselves, culturally and ethnically. Facts from other fields of study besides archaeology and philology may be marshaled and interpreted so as to shed new light. This discussion is not a conclusion, it is a challenge.

Notes

CHAPTER 1: DEPARTED GLORIES

1. Hesiod, *Works and Days*, trans. Dorothea Winder (New York: Penguin Books, 1973), lines 109–201; and Robert Graves, *The Greek Myths* vol. 1 (New York: Penguin Books, 1960), sec. 5.
2. Raimundo Panikkar, *The Vedic Experience: Mantramanjari* (London: Darton, Longman and Todd, 1977), 900.
3. Malcolm X, *The Autobiography of Malcolm X* (London: Hutchinson, 1966), 239–43.
4. J. E. McGuire and P. M. Rattansi, "Newton and the 'Pipes of Pan,'" *Notes and Records of the Royal Society* 21 (1966): 110, 115 ff., and 127–28; and Giorgio de Santillana and Hertha von Dechend, *Hamlet's Mill* (New York: Macmillan, 1970), 9.
5. Thomas Aquinas, *Summa Theologica*, vol. 1, Q. 94, arts. 3 and 4. On Dante's ideas about mythological echoes of paradise, cp. B. V. Miller in *The Teaching of the Catholic Church*, vol. 1, ed. George Smith (London: Burns Oates and Washbourne, 1948), 321 (a Catholic traditionalist view).

CHAPTER 2: THE RETURN OF THE GODDESS

1. Marija Gimbutas, papers and other items, listed in Colin Renfrew, *Archaeology and Language* (London: Jonathan Cape, 1987), 316–17; Marija Gimbutas, *The Gods and Goddesses of Old Europe* (New York: Thames and Hudson, 1974), reissued as *The Goddesses and Gods of Old Europe* (Berkeley and Los Angeles: University of Cal-

ifornia Press, 1982); and idem, *The Language of the Goddess* (New York: Thames and Hudson, 1989).

2. Starhawk [Miriam Simos], *The Spiral Dance* (New York: Harper and Row, 1979), 77–78.

3. Charles Seltman, *The Twelve Olympians and Their Guests* (London: Max Parriser, 1956), 52–53. Cp. Graves, *Greek Myths*, vol. 1, 15–20.

4. Geoffrey Ashe, *The Virgin* (1976; reprint, Boston: Routledge and Kegan Paul, 1988), 17–18.

5. Lewis Richard Farnell, *The Cults of the Greek States*, 5 vols. (Oxford: Clarendon, 1896–1909), vol. 2, 425.

6. Starhawk, *Spiral Dance*, 3.

7. Gimbutas, *Language of the Goddess*, pass.

8. Buffie Johnson, *Lady of the Beasts* (New York: Harper and Row, 1988), 19.

9. Gimbutas, *Language of the Goddess*, 4, 89, 111, and 198; and E. O. James, *The Cult of the Mother-Goddess* (New York: Thames and Hudson, 1959), 13–16.

10. A very few artifacts, such as a figurine from Willendorf in Austria, may be somewhat older; but an earlier dating of the odd object thousands of miles away would not invalidate the point being made here. Cp. E. O. James, *Prehistoric Religion* (New York: Harper & Row, 1988), 147.

11. Aratus, *A Literal Translation of the Astronomy and Meteorology of Aratus*, trans. C. Leeson Prince (London: Farncombe, 1895), 20–21, lines 96–136; and Mary Grant, ed. and trans., *The Myths of Hyginus* (Lawrence: University of Kansas, 1960), 215–16 (*Poetic Astronomy* 2:25). A Greek author known to scholarship as Pseudo-Eratosthenes equates Astraea with Isis and Demeter and makes her, in effect, a general goddess figure.

12. Johnson, *Lady of the Beasts*, 19.

13. Joseph Campbell, *The Masks of God*, 3 vols. (London: Secker and Warburg, 1960–65), vol. 1. 329–31; Gimbutas, *Language of the Goddess*, 89; and Jill Purce, *The Mystic Spiral* (New York: Thames and Hudson, 1974), 100–101.

14. Ashe, *Avalonian Quest* (New York: Methuen, 1982), 180–85; and Purce, *Mystic Spiral*, 100–101.

15. W. H. Matthews, *Mazes and Labyrinths* (New York: Dover, 1970), 92–94.

16. Ashe, *Avalonian Quest*, pt. 2; and Philip Rahtz, *Invitation to Archaeology* (Oxford: Basil Blackwell, 1985), 132–33.

17. John Kraft, *The Goddess in the Labyrinth* (Finland: Åbo Akademi, 1985), 24–25. For the Jain instance I am indebted to Martin Godfrey.

18. Purce, *Mystic Spiral*, 111; and Frank Waters, *Book of the Hopi* (New York: Ballantine, 1969), 29–31.

19. For full recent discussions, see Robert Claiborne, "Who Were the Indo-Europeans?" in *Mysteries of the Past*, ed. Joseph J. Thorndike (New York: American Heritage, 1977); J. P. Mallory, *In Search of the Indo-Europeans* (New York: Thames and Hudson, 1989); and Renfrew, *Archaeology and Language*.

20. Claiborne, "Who Were the Indo-Europeans?" 263–67; and Mallory, *In Search of the Indo-Europeans*, chap. 1.

21. Bridget Allchin and Raymond Allchin, *The Rise of Civilization in India and Pakistan* (New York: Cambridge University Press, 1982), 298–300; and Mallory, *In Search of the Indo-Europeans*, 35–56.

22. Renfrew, *Archaeology and Language*, 1–8 and 75–77.

23. Mallory, *In Search of the Indo-Europeans*, 267–69.

24. Gimbutas, *Language of the Goddess*, xx–xxi. Cp. Elinor W. Gadon, *The Once and Future Goddess* (New York: Harper and Row, 1989), 110–11; and Monica Sjöö and Barbara Mor, *The Great Cosmic Mother* (New York: Harper and Row, 1987), 258.

25. Merlin Stone, *The Paradise Papers* (London: Virago, 1976), 120–42. (The U.S. title is *When God Was a Woman*.)

26. Mallory, *In Search of the Indo-Europeans*, 182–85 and 241–42.

27. Claiborne, "Who Were the Indo-Europeans?" 269–72.

28. Renfrew, *Archaeology and Language*, esp. chaps. 6 and 7; and Thomas V. Gamkrelidze and V. V. Ivanov, "The Early History of Indo-European Languages," *Scientific American*, March 1990, 82–89.

29. Marek Zvelebil and Kamil Zvelebil, "Agricultural Transition and Indo-European Dispersals," *Antiquity* 62 (September 1989): 574–83.

30. Mallory, *In Search of the Indo-Europeans*, esp. 262–65.

31. Claiborne, "Who Were the Indo-Europeans?" 267. Cp. Georges Roux, *Ancient Iraq* (London: George Allen and Unwin, 1964), 186–87, as illustrative of views superseded.

32. Mallory, *In Search of the Indo-Europeans*, chap. 5; and Renfrew, *Archaeology and Language*, 259–62.

33. Mallory, *In Search of the Indo-Europeans*, 129. Janet McCrickard, in *Eclipse of the Sun* (Glastonbury, U.K.: Gothic Image, 1990), proves the falsity of the notion that all solar deities are male. She sees this assumption as a grave flaw in Goddess-oriented scholarship. Solar myths, cults, and imagery have no necessary implications about "patriarchy."

CHAPTER 3: BEASTS, MOUNTAINS, STARS

1. M. A. Czaplicka, *Aboriginal Siberia* (Oxford: Clarendon, 1914), 15–17; and Mircea Eliade, *Shamanism* (Boston: Routledge and Kegan Paul, 1964), 3–8.

2. For Roerich, see, besides his own writings, Jacqueline Decter with the Nicholas Roerich Museum, *Nicholas Roerich* (New York: Thames and Hudson, 1989), pass.

3. Eliade, *Shamanism*, 496–98.

4. Alexandra David-Neel, *The Superhuman Life of Gesar of Ling* (London: Rider, 1933), 19–20; idem, *With Mystics and Magicians in Tibet* (London: John Lane, The Bodley Head, 1931), 9; Eliade, *Shamanism*, 431–34; W. Y. Evans-Wentz, *The Tibetan Book of the Great Liberation* (Oxford: Oxford University Press, 1954), 59–60 and 290; and idem, *Tibetan Yoga and Secret Doctrine* (Oxford: Oxford University Press, 1959), 59–60, 290.

5. Eliade, *Shamanism*, 498–504. See also Gimbutas, *Language of the Goddess*, 175–77; Henry N. Michael, ed., *Studies in Siberian Shamanism* (Toronto: University of Toronto Press, 1972), 76; and Stuart Piggott, *The Druids* (New York: Penguin Books, 1974), 160–64. For further suggestions on the remoter background of druidism, see David Keys, "Academics Shed New Light on Druids' Link with Stones," *Independent* (London), June 21, 1988.

6. Starhawk, *Spiral Dance*, 3.

7. N. Kershaw Chadwick, *Poetry and Prophecy* (New York: Cambridge University Press, 1942), 88.

8. Eliade, *Shamanism*, 67, 99, 171, 265, and 486.

9. Ibid., 257–58 and 395; and Czaplicka, *Aboriginal Siberia*, 243 and 249–50; Erich Neumann, *The Great Mother* (Boston: Routledge and Kegan Paul, 1955), 296.

10. Chadwick, *Poetry and Prophecy*, 17–18; Czaplicka, *Aboriginal Siberia*, 171; and Eliade, *Shamanism*, 39, 221, and 256.

11. Chadwick, *Poetry and Prophecy*, 2–3.

12. Michael, *Siberian Shamanism*, 75. Cp. Campbell, *Masks of God*, vol. 1, 315–18.

13. Czaplicka, *Aboriginal Siberia*, 198 and 244. Cp. Eliade, *Shamanism*, 4; and Michael, *Siberian Shamanism*, 174.

14. Campbell, *Masks of God*, vol. 3, 292; Czaplicka, *Aboriginal Siberia*, 199–200 and 211; Eliade, *Shamanism*, 470–74; and de Santillana and von Dechend, *Hamlet's Mill*, 128.

15. Chadwick, *Poetry and Prophecy*, 93; and Eliade, *Shamanism*, 76–81.

16. On the theology in this paragraph, see Czaplicka, *Aboriginal Siberia*, 253; Eliade, *Shamanism*, 198–99 and 275–76; Walther Heissig, *The Religions of Mongolia*, trans. Geoffrey Samuel (Boston: Routledge and Kegan Paul, 1980), 48–49; and Michael, *Siberian Shamanism*, 27, 75–76, 80, 168, and 175.

17. Czaplicka, *Aboriginal Siberia*, 244, n. 2; and Heissig, *Religions of Mongolia*, 102.

18. Eliade, *Shamanism*, 89–90, 96–99, 156–58, and 403.

19. Ibid., 190–200 and 467–70.

20. Michael, *Siberian Shamanism*, 200.

21. On bears, see, in general, Decter, *Nicholas Roerich*, 83; Gimbutas, *Language of the Goddess*, 116–19; Jane Ellen Harrison, *Themis* (New York: Cambridge University Press, 1912), 206, 328–29, and 450; and "Bear," in *Man, Myth and Magic*, 7 vols., ed. Richard Cavendish (London: B. P. C. Publishing, 1970–72).

22. Erich Neumann, *The Origins and History of Consciousness* (Boston: Routledge and Kegan Paul, 1954), 94.

23. Campbell, *Masks of God*, vol. 1, 339–42; and James, *Prehistoric Religion*, 21.

24. Decter, *Nicholas Roerich*, 83; and Michael, *Siberian Shamanism*, 68, n. 41, and 227, n. 157.

25. Harrison, *Themis*, 140–41; and "Lapland," in *Man, Myth and Magic*.

26. Eliade, *Shamanism*, 89–90, 93, 156, and 458–61.

27. Czaplicka, *Aboriginal Siberia*, 45–46, 51, 153, 271, and 295–97.

28. Eliade, *Shamanism*, 297–302.

29. Ibid., 266–69; and J. D. P. Bolton, *Aristeas of Proconnesus* (Oxford: Clarendon, 1962), 97–98.

30. Eliade, *Shamanism*, 269–74; and Michael, *Siberian Shamanism*, 174.

31. Michael, *Siberian Shamanism*, 56–57, 75.

32. Campbell, *Masks of God*, vol. 1, 148; Eliade, *Shamanism*, 266; and Heissig, *Religions of Mongolia*, 82 and 102–10.

33. Marco Polo, *The Travels of Marco Polo*, trans. Ronald Latham (New York: Penguin Books, 1987), 97 and 102–3.

34. Heissig, *Religions of Mongolia*, 106.

35. Ibid., 36, 39, and 45.

36. Michael, *Siberian Shamanism*, 56–57.

37. Eliade, *Shamanism*, 190–200 and 275–76.

38. Ibid., 200–203.

39. Ibid., 261–62, 269, and 275.

40. Ibid., 260–63; and Michael, *Siberian Shamanism*, 50–51.

41. Nicholas Roerich, *Altai-Himalaya* (London: Jarrolds, 1930), 41.

42. Aratus, *Astronomy and Meteorology of Aratus*, 18; and Grant, *Myths of Hyginus*, 137 and 182–83. On Ursa Major in general, see Veronica Ions, *Egyptian Mythology* (London: Paul Hamlyn, 1968), 66; Brinsley Le Poer Trench, *Temple of the Stars* (London: Fontana, 1973), 46–47; Martin P. Nilsson, *Primitive Time Reckoning* (Lund: C. W. K. Gleerup, 1920), 41, 115–16, and 118–19; and de Santillana and von Dechend, *Hamlet's Mill*, 98–99, 101, 383–84, n. 5, and 404–5.

43. Michael, *Siberian Shamanism*, 50–51. With the story of the three hunters (next paragraph), I confess I can't see much difference between the first and third stars. Or is the "small" hunter the fainter one at the corner of the quadrilateral?

44. Ibid., 161–63.

45. Ibid., 227, n. 157.

46. Heissig, *Religions of Mongolia*, 46 and 81–84.

47. N. Roerich, *Altai-Himalaya*, 303–4.

48. Eliade, *Shamanism*, 245.

49. Michael, *Siberian Shamanism*, 27.

50. Eliade, *Shamanism*, 153, 173, and 276.

51. Michael, *Siberian Shamanism*, 56–57.

52. Eliade, *Shamanism*, 263, n. 19, and 276–77.

53. Ibid., 38–43 and 277–78. The quote on page 37 is from page 278.

54. Michael, *Siberian Shamanism*, 24–25.

55. Chadwick, *Poetry and Prophecy*, 2–3.

56. Czaplicka, *Aboriginal Siberia*, 327–28; and Eliade, *Shamanism*, 152–53.

57. Czaplicka, *Aboriginal Siberia*, 221.

58. Waters, *Book of the Hopi*, 3, 29–32, 177, 183, and 193.

CHAPTER 4: THE INDO-ARYANS

1. On the Afanasievo culture, see Mikail P. Gryaznov, *The Ancient Civilization of Southern Siberia*, trans. James Hogarth (New York: Cowles Book Co., 1969), 46–51; and Mallory, *In Search of the Indo-Europeans*, 62 and 223–26. V. Dergachev's somewhat later dating may be reconciled as a *floruit* (V. Dergachev, "Neolithic and Bronze Age Cultural Communities of the Steppe Zone of the USSR," *Antiquity* 63 [December 1989]: 797–98).

2. Mallory, *In Search of the Indo-Europeans*, 62–63 and 263.

3. Ibid., 227–31; and Renfrew, *Archaeology and Language*, 203. A later dating of the Andronovo culture by Dergachev ("Neolithic and Bronze Age Cultural Communities," 799) does not amount to a refutation.

4. Mallory, *In Search of the Indo-Europeans*, 229.

5. Ibid., 47–48 and 230–31.

6. On the *Rig Veda* and the Vedic society and religion, see O'Flaherty's discussions (Wendy Doniger O'Flaherty, ed. and trans., *The Rig Veda* [New York: Penguin

Books, 1981]). See also Mallory, *In Search of the Indo-Europeans*, 37 and 45–46; Stuart Piggott, *Prehistoric India to 1000 B.C.* (London: Cassell, 1950), 255–78; and Renfrew, *Archaeology and Language*, 178–83.

7. O'Flaherty, *Rig Veda*, 1:179 and 10:10.

8. Ibid., 2:12 and 6:75.

9. Ibid., 1:116:15, 4:27:1, 6:75:15, and 10:56:7.

10. Ibid., 1:164:46. See also *The Cultural Heritage of India*, 3 vols. (Calcutta: Sri Rama-krishna Centenary Committee, 1937), vol. 1, 25, Swami Avinashanada, Secretary.

11. O'Flaherty, *Rig Veda*, 139–40 and hymns following.

12. Ibid., 97–98 and hymns following.

13. Ibid., 10:129.

14. Ibid., 245 and 10:72. See also *Cultural Heritage of India*, vol. 1, 7–8, citing *The Rig Veda*, 1:89:10, where Aditi is spoken of as Supreme Being. The Aditi-Daksha relationship is too obscure to be definite about, but a sort of parallel in Egypt is at least more explicit. There, the primordial female, Neith, gives birth to the sun god Ra, yet she is also Ra's daughter. Her myth has a special interest as one of the very few that present the Goddess alone, before any other deities. The theme reappears in Christianity. In the last canto of Dante's *Paradiso*, Mary is addressed as "Virgin mother, daughter of thy Son." However, the doctrine of the Trinity avoids complete paradox: Mary can be regarded as the daughter of the First Person and the mother of the Second. Cp. Ashe, *Virgin*, 13–14 and 60. Also Neumann, *The Great Mother*, 220–21.

15. Piggott, *Prehistoric India*, 255–56.

16. *The Mahabharata*, 3 vols. (incomplete), trans. J. A. B. van Buitinen (Chicago: University of Chicago Press, 1973–78), vol. 1, xxv and 9, n. 12. See also A. Basham, *A Cultural History of India* (Oxford: 1975), 170–71; and Mallory, *In Search of the Indo-Europeans*, 45–46. Indo-Aryan settlement can be correlated with the spread of a "Painted Grey Ware" culture (painted, to be specific, with black or red deco-rations) which flourished from about 1300 to 400 B.C. Places that occur in the epic are datable Grey Ware sites and narrow down the time of the action to somewhere about the middle of this range.

17. A. Basham, *The Wonder that Was India* (New York: Grove Press, 1959), 39; E. J. Rapson, ed., *The Cambridge History of India*, vol. 1 (New York: Cambridge University Press, 1968), 246; *Cultural Heritage of India*, vol. 3, 344; William H. Kenety, ed., *Collector's Choice* (Washington, D.C.: National Association of Private Art Foundations, 1987), 90; and Amaury de Riencourt, *The Soul of India* (London: Jonathan Cape, 1961), 9.

18. O'Flaherty, *Rig Veda*, for example, 1:35:7, 2:28:7, 9:74:7, 10:82:5, including n. 11, and 10:151:3, including n. 1.

19. Mallory, *In Search of the Indo-Europeans*, 42–43; and R. C. Zaehner, *The Twilight of Zoroastrianism* (New York: Weidenfeld and Nicolson, 1961), 39–40.

20. James B. Pritchard, ed., *Ancient Near Eastern Texts Relating to the Old Testament*, 3d ed., with suppl. (Princeton, N.J.: Princeton University Press, 1969), 484, n. 3.

21. Ibid., 206; Mallory, *In Search of the Indo-Europeans*, 37–38 and 131–32; and Piggott, *Prehistoric India*, 252.

22. Mallory, *In Search of the Indo-Europeans*, 37–38; and Piggott, *Prehistoric India*, 253.

23. O'Flaherty, *Rig Veda*, 85 and hymns following. See also Eliade, *Shamanism*, 11, 79–80, 182–83, and 190–97; Mallory, *In Search of the Indo-Europeans*, 135–37; and Piggott, *Prehistoric India*, 249.

24. O'Flaherty, *Rig Veda*, 1:162.

25. Mallory, *In Search of the Indo-Europeans*, 136.

26. Eliade, *Shamanism*, 467–70.

27. Michael, *Siberian Shamanism*, 50–51, 161–63, 200, and 227.

28. De Santillana and von Dechend, *Hamlet's Mill*, 383–84.

29. Alain Daniélou, *Hindu Polytheism* (Boston: Routledge and Kegan Paul, 1964), 316–19; J. E. Macdonell and A. B. Keith, *Vedic Index of Names and Subjects*, vol. 1 (Delhi: Motilal Banarsidass, 1967), 107–8 and 115–18; and Panikkar, *Vedic Experience*, 888–89.

30. O'Flaherty, *Rig Veda*, 10:81:2, 10:82:2, 10:109:4, and 10:130:7, and cp. 4:42:8; and *Mahabharata*, trans. van Buitenen, vol. 2, 584, indexed as 3(37)185 of text.

31. Panikkar, *Vedic Experience*, 889.

32. O'Flaherty, *Rig Veda*, 10:82:2. See also Macdonell and Keith, *Vedic Index*, 117–18.

33. De Santillana and von Dechend, *Hamlet's Mill*, 301, n. 37. For the ingredients of the ensuing story, see *Mahabharata*, trans. van Buitinen, vol. 1, 430, indexed as 1(29)224 of text; vol. 2, 650–51, indexed as 3(37)214–15 of text; and vol. 3, 402, indexed as 5(54)109 of text.

34. O'Flaherty, *Rig Veda*, 1:24:10. See also Panikkar, *Vedic Experience*, 840.

35. Macdonell and Keith, *Vedic Index*, 107 and 117–18.

36. Czaplicka, *Aboriginal Siberia*, 244, n. 2.

37. O'Flaherty, *Rig Veda*, 1:50:8, 2:28:1, 10:72, and 10:101:12 and n. 13. See also Sukumari Bhattacharji, *The Indian Theogony* (London: Cambridge University Press, 1970).

38. F. Max Müller, *Vedic Hymns*, vol. 32 of *Sacred Books of the East* (Oxford: Clarendon, 1891), 251–53.

39. See the indexes of Ralph H. T. Griffith, *The Hymns of the Rigveda*, 2 vols. (Benares, India: E. J. Lazarus, 1896).

40. O'Flaherty, *Rig Veda*, 12, n., and 72 (reference to seven as a favorite number).

41. Müller, *Vedic Hymns*, 251–53, quoting *Rig Veda* 9:114:3.

42. O'Flaherty, *Rig Veda*, 1:164.

43. Bhattacharji, *Indian Theogony*, 233 and 328.

44. "Tantrism," in *Man, Myth and Magic*.

45. De Santillana and von Dechend, *Hamlet's Mill*, 301, n. 37.

CHAPTER 5: THE PARADISAL HEIGHTS

1. Herodotus, *History*, 2 vols., trans. G. Rawlinson (London: Dent, 1910), vol. 1, III:98 and 102–5.

2. *Mahabharata*, trans. van Buitinen, vol. 2, 118, indexed as 2(27)48 of text, and 815, n.; and *The Mahabharata*, 3 vols., trans. M. N. Dutt (Calcutta: H. C. Dass, 1966), vol. 1, II:52:2–4.

3. Bolton, *Aristeas of Proconnesus*, 81–82. Cp. Mandeville, *The Travels of Sir John*

Mandeville, trans. C. W. R. D. Moseley (New York: Penguin Books, 1987), 182–85.

4. Bolton, *Aristeas of Proconnesus*, 100 and 114; Heissig, *Religions of Mongolia*, 102; and Sergei I. Rudenko, *Frozen Tombs of Siberia*, trans. M. W. Thompson (Berkeley and Los Angeles: University of California Press, 1970), xxi and xxiii.

5. Michael, *Siberian Shamanism*, 27.

6. O'Flaherty, *Rig Veda*, 1:154:1 and n. 3, 9:74:2, and 10:121 and nn. 8 and 9. See also Panikkar, *Vedic Experience*, 61–67 and 892.

7. *Mahabharata*, trans. van Buitinen, vol. 1, 324, indexed as 1(11)159 of text; *Mahabharata*, trans. Dutt, vol. 2, VI:5:13; and Collette Caillat and Ravi Kumar, *The Jain Cosmology* (New York: Harmony Books, 1981), 26–28.

8. *Mahabharata*, trans. van Buitinen, vol. 1, 442 and n. on 1(5)15 of text; *Mahabharata*, trans. Dutt, vols. 2 and 3, VI:6:7–10 and XVII:2:1–2; and Caillat and Kumar, *Jain Cosmology*, 27–30.

9. Caillat and Kumar, *Jain Cosmology*, 106.

10. *Mahabharata*, trans. van Buitinen, vol. 2, 703, indexed as 3(41)247 of text; *Mahabharata*, trans. Dutt, vol. 2, VI:6:11; Caillat and Kumar, *Jain Cosmology*, 30 and 48; and "Symbolism," in *Man, Myth and Magic*, 2758.

11. *Mahabharata*, trans. van Buitinen, vol. 2, 422 and 589, indexed as 3(33)102 and 3(37)186 of text; and *Mahabharata*, trans. Dutt, vol. 2, VI:6:10–12.

12. René Guénon, *Le Roi du Monde* (Paris: Les Éditions Traditionelles, 1950), 58–59; "Mountain," in *Man, Myth and Magic*, 1899; and Gerald Massey, *A Book of the Beginnings*, 4 vols. (London: Williams and Norgate, 1881 and 1883), pt. 1, vol. 1, 320.

13. *Mahabharata*, trans. van Buitinen, vol. 2, 533, indexed as 3(35)160 of text; and *Mahabharata*, trans. Dutt, vol. 2, VI:6:21.

14. Ibid.

15. *Mahabharata*, trans. van Buitinen, vol. 2, 422, indexed as 3(33)102 of text.

16. Ibid., vol. 2, 533, indexed as 3(35)160 of text.

17. Ibid., vol. 2, 703, indexed as 3(41)247 of text.

18. *Mahabharata*, trans. Dutt, vol. 2, VI:6:17–24.

19. *Mahabharata*, trans. van Buitinen, vol. 1, 72–73, indexed as 1(5)15 of text.

20. *Mahabharata*, trans. Dutt, vol. 2, VI:7:2–15 and 26–8. The original Kurus were a branch of the royal race in the epic.

21. Ibid., vol. 2, VI:6:28–29; *Mahabharata*, trans. van Buitinen, vol. 2, 308, indexed as 3(32)43 of text; and Caillat and Kumar, *Jain Cosmology*, 29.

22. Caillat and Kumar, *Jain Cosmology*, 20–21, 29–31, 56–57, 156–59, and 168.

23. O'Flaherty, *Rig Veda*, 8:30:2. See also Caillat and Kumar, *Jain Cosmology*, 160; Campbell, *Masks of God*, vol. 1, 148; and Eliade, *Shamanism*, 276–77.

24. Eliade, *Shamanism*, 267.

25. H. G. Quaritch Wales, *The Mountain of God* (London: Bernard Quaritch, 1953), 88–89 and 158–59. Cp. Eliade, *Shamanism*, 267–68.

26. De Santillana and von Dechend, *Hamlet's Mill*, 221; and Wales, *Mountain of God*, 127–28 and 159–70.

27. Ashe, *Avalonian Quest*, 229–32; and Eliade, *Shamanism*, 267.

28. Ashe, *Avalonian Quest*, 232; and Wales, *Mountain of God*, 123.

29. *Mahabharata*, trans. Dutt, vol. 2, VI:6:3–10, 41–42, and VII:2. See also Caillat and Kumar, *Jain Cosmology*, 27–28 and 106–7.

The suggested mythification of real geography is not purely speculative. It can happen. Irish legend shows it on a less grandiose scale in the Voyage of St. Brendan, "Brendan the Navigator." A tenth-century narrative tells of visits he is supposed to have made to a number of Atlantic islands. These include an island of sheep, an island of birds, and an island of giants working at a cyclopean smithy. As described, they are fabulous, like Meru, yet they reflect knowledge of two of the Faeroe Islands and volcanic Iceland, where seafaring Irish monks did settle. See Geoffrey Ashe, *Land to the West* (London: Collins; and New York: Viking, 1962).

30. Francis Hitching, *The World Atlas of Mysteries* (London: Pan Books, 1979), 238–40.

31. *Mahabharata*, trans. Dutt, vol. 3, XVII:2:1–2. See also de Santillana and von Dechend, *Hamlet's Mill*, 76–77.

32. N. Roerich, *Altai-Himalaya*, 112; and idem, *Shambhala* (New York: Nicholas Roerich Museum, 1978), 45 and 140.

33. Decter, *Nicholas Roerich*, 166.

34. Michael, *Siberian Shamanism*, 56–57.

35. Polo, *Travels of Marco Polo*, 102–3.

36. Hubert Howe Bancroft, *The Native Races of the Pacific States*, 5 vols. (London: Longmans Green, 1875–76), vol. 3, 90–93.

37. Eliade, *Shamanism*, 267; R. C. Zaehner, *The Dawn and Twilight of Zoroastrianism* (London: Weidenfeld and Nicolson, 1961), 112–13, 138.

CHAPTER 6: NUMEROLOGY AND PSYCHOLOGY

1. Eliade, *Shamanism*, 177.

2. Mallory, *In Search of the Indo-Europeans*, 130–35.

3. Geoffrey Hindley, ed., *Larousse Encyclopedia of Music* (London and New York: Hamlyn, 1971), 26 and 34; and Piggott, *Prehistoric India*, 272–73.

4. Campbell, *Masks of God*, vol. 1, 165.

5. Ibid., 452–53; and Fosco Maraini, *Secret Tibet*, trans. Eric Mosbacher (London: Hutchinson, 1952).

6. Maraini, *Secret Tibet*, 77.

7. Ibid., 63 and 110–11; Evans-Wentz, *Tibetan Yoga*, 32 and 225, n. 4; and "Tantrism," in *Man, Myth and Magic*.

8. On this kind of approach, see Richard Cavendish, *The Black Arts* (London: Pan Books, 1969), 83–86.

9. "Seven," in *Brewer's Dictionary of Phrase and Fable* (London: Cassell, 1959; reprint, New York: Harper and Row, 1985).

10. See, for example, Bolton, *Aristeas of Proconnesus*, 115–17; Campbell, *Masks of God*, vol. 1, 452; S. N. Kramer, *History Begins at Sumer* (New York: Thames and Hudson, 1958), 310; and Sidney Spencer, *Mysticism in World Religion* (New York: Penguin Books, 1963), 106.

11. Harrison, *Themis*, 184–90; S. N. Kramer, *The Sumerians* (Chicago: University of

Chicago Press, 1963), 91; Nilsson, *Primitive Time Reckoning*, 54–73 and 278. Cp. Graves, *Greek Myths*, vol. 1, intro.

12. *Encyclopaedia Britannica*, 1963 ed., s. v. "calendar" and "week"; and Nilsson, *Primitive Time Reckoning*, 324–36.

13. Herodotus, *History*, vol. 2, VI:57.

14. *Encyclopaedia Britannica*, "calendar"; and Nilsson, *Primitive Time Reckoning*, 329–31.

15. Frieda Fordham, *An Introduction to Jung's Psychology* (New York: Penguin Books, 1959), 66; C. G. Jung—for example, Jung's *Mysterium Coniunctionis*, vol. 14 of *Collected Works* (Boston: Routledge and Kegan Paul, 1963), 11–13, 19, 270, and 403–4; idem, *Psychology and Alchemy*, vol. 12 of *Collected Works* (1953), 54–56; idem, *Symbols of Transformation*, vol. 5 of *Collected Works* (1956), 45, n. 8; and idem, *Two Essays on Analytical Psychology*, vol. 7 of *Collected Works* (1966), 222.

16. C. G. Jung, *The Archetypes and the Collective Unconscious*, vol. 9 of *Collected Works* (1959), pt. 1, 136, n. 7; and cp. Jung, *Mysterium Coniunctionis*, 287.

17. Franz Cumont, *The Mysteries of Mithra*, trans. Thomas J. McCormack (London: Kegan Paul, Trench and Trubner, 1903), 120; and Eliade, *Shamanism*, 274.

18. Pritchard, *Ancient Near Eastern Texts*, 390–91.

19. Franz Cumont, *Astrology and Religion Among the Greeks and Romans* (New York: Putnam, 1912), 10, 14–15, and 26.

20. Ibid., 24 and 59.

21. W. K. C. Guthrie, *The Greeks and Their Gods* (New York: Methuen, 1950), 211–13; and Harrison, *Themis*, 445–46 and 461.

22. Cumont, *Astrology and Religion*, 45.

23. Ibid., 54–56; E. R. Dodds, *The Greeks and the Irrational* (Berkeley: University of California Press, 1951), 245–46; *Encyclopaedia Britannica*, 1963 ed., s. v. "Astrology"; and Gilbert Murray, *Five Stages of Greek Religion* (Oxford: Clarendon, 1935), 143–44.

24. Cumont, *Astrology and Religion*, 89 ff. and 136–37; Cumont, *Mysteries of Mithra*, 119–20; C. H. Dodd, *The Bible and the Greeks* (London: Hodder and Stoughton, 1935), 102 and 138; Murray, *Greek Religion*, 146; and Seltman, *Twelve Olympians and Their Guests*, 29–30.

25. "Primum Mobile" and "Spheres," in *Brewer's Dictionary*; Cumont, *Astrology and Religion*, 119–21; and Murray, *Greek Religion*, 140.

26. *Cultural Heritage of India*, vol. 3, 476; Eliade, *Shamanism*, 274, n. 65; Evans-Wentz, *Tibetan Yoga*, 287; and de Santillana and von Dechend, *Hamlet's Mill*, 123, n. 16.

27. S. H. Hooke, ed., *The Labyrinth* (London: Society for the Promotion of Christian Knowledge, 1935), 60 and 68.

CHAPTER 7: THE PROTOTYPE

1. Philo, *The Works of Philo Judaeus*, 4 vols., trans. C. D. Yonge (London: Bohn, 1854), vol. 1, 26–37 (*On the Creation of the World*, sec. 30–43) and 52–56 (*On the Allegories of the Sacred Laws*, sec. i:2–6). See also Geoffrey Ashe, *The Land and the Book* (London: Collins, 1965), 308–10.

2. Philo, *Works of Philo Judaeus*, 26 and 37 (*On the Creation of the World*, sec. 30 and 43).

3. Ibid., 54–55 (*On the Allegories of the Sacred Laws*, sec. i:4).

4. Ibid., 34–35 (*On the Creation of the World*, sec. 39).

5. Cavendish, *Black Arts*, 84–85.

6. In *Tetrabiblos*, I:2.

7. Apuleius, *The Golden Ass*, trans. Robert Graves (New York: Penguin Books, 1950), 268.

8. Farnell, *Cults of the Greek States*, vol. 2, 552–53; Harrison, *Themis*, 188–90 and 389; and Nilsson, *Primitive Time Reckoning*, 155–56, 168, and 170–72.

9. Nilsson, *Primitive Time Reckoning*, 171–72 and 330; and Pritchard, *Ancient Near Eastern Texts*, 67–68 (tablet 5, lines 12–22).

10. Cavendish, *Black Arts*, 85; and Nilsson, *Primitive Time Reckoning*, 329.

11. Philo, *Works of Philo Judaeus*, vol. 1, 29–30 (*On the Creation of the World*, sec. 34).

12. Grant, *Myths of Hyginus*, 182–83 (*Poetic Astronomy*, II:2).

13. See pages 34–35.

14. Hooke, *Labyrinth*, 60–62; L. W. King, *The Seven Tablets of Creation*, 2 vols. (London: Luzac, 1902), vol. 1, 139, n. 2; and Roux, *Ancient Iraq*, 303–5.

15. Hooke, *Labyrinth*, 50 and 60–64; S. N. Kramer, *Sumerian Mythology* (Philadelphia: American Philosophical Society, 1947), 47; and Roux, *Ancient Iraq*, 84–85 and 119.

16. Hooke, *Labyrinth*, 62.

17. Ibid., 63–64.

18. Jung, *Mysterium Coniunctionis*, 205, n. 492.

19. Aratus, *Astronomy and Meteorology of Aratus*, 18; Grant, *Myths of Hyginus*, 137 and 182–83 (including note).

20. Guénon, *Roi du Monde*, 78.

21. Grant, *Myths of Hyginus*, 182–83 (including note). See also de Santillana and von Dechend, *Hamlet's Mill*, 138. Cp. Robert Graves, *The White Goddess* (London: Faber, 1952), 178.

22. Jung, *Symbols of Transformation*, 102–5; and G. R. S. Mead, *Thrice Greatest Hermes*, 3 vols. (London: Watkins, 1964), vol. 1, 122, n. 1.

23. Dodd, *Bible and the Greeks*, xiv, 100, and 246; and idem, *The Interpretation of the Fourth Gospel* (New York: Cambridge University Press, 1953), 11–12.

24. Dodd, *Interpretation of the Fourth Gospel*, 20; Mead, *Thrice Greatest Hermes*, vol. 2, 66 (in the treatise *Though Unmanifest God Is Most Manifest*, 4).

25. Mead, *Thrice Greatest Hermes*, vol. 3, 31 (in the treatise *On the Decans and the Stars*, 8).

26. See ibid., vol. 1, 293, and various instances under "Seven" in his index.

27. De Santillana and von Dechend, *Hamlet's Mill*, 3 and 236.

28. Hooke, *Labyrinth*, 49–50; Pritchard, *Ancient Near Eastern Texts*, 333 (line 30 of a ritual, admittedly late, that mentions Margidda—Ursa Major—as "the bond of heaven").

29. Kramer, *Sumerians*, 90–91 and 112–13.

30. Aratus, *Astronomy and Meteorology of Aratus*, 18; and Grant, *Myths of Hyginus*, 182–83.

31. Zaehner, *Dawn and Twilight of Zoroastrianism*, 45–47, 60, 63, and 97.

32. Mallory, *In Search of the Indo-Europeans*, 43 and 52.

33. In *Dawn and Twilight of Zoroastrianism*, Zaehner explicitly denies (p. 49) that the planets could have had anything to do with this heptad. Long after Zoroaster, some of his followers superimposed the concept of Infinite Time, Zurvan, as prior to everything else; yet even Infinite Time had seven aspects (pp. 236–37).

34. *Shah-Namah. The Shah-Namah of Firdausi: Described and Introduced by J. V. S. Wilkinson and Laurence Binyon* (Oxford: Oxford University Press, 1931), 13.

35. Dodd, *Bible and the Greeks*, 146; C. G. Jung, *Alchemical Studies*, vol. 13 of *Collected Works* (1968), 337, n. 3; idem, *Mysterium Coniunctionis*, 387, n. 32.

36. "Jamshyd," in *Brewer's Dictionary*; Zaehner, *Dawn and Twilight of Zoroastrianism*, 127. Jamshid is ultimately Yima, an Iranian mythical figure from remote antiquity, who has affinities with a god Yama in the *Rig Veda*.

37. Ashe, *Land and the Book*, 217–21. In the Bible, see Ezra 1:1–4.

38. J. M. Cook, *The Persian Empire* (London: J. M. Dent, 1983), 144–45.

39. Ibid., 18–19.

40. Ibid., 170.

CHAPTER 8: SUMERIANS AND BABYLONIANS

1. Gilgamesh, *The Epic of Gilgamesh*, trans. N. K. Sandars (New York: Penguin Books, 1960), 124; Pritchard, *Ancient Near Eastern Texts*, 73, n. 7; de Santillana and von Dechend, *Hamlet's Mill*, 300–301. In a later revised edition of the Penguin *Epic of Gilgamesh* the pagination frequently differs by two or three.

2. Roux, *Ancient Iraq*, 112.

3. Kramer, in Diana Wolkstein and Samuel Noah Kramer, *Inanna: Queen of Heaven and Earth* (London: Rider, 1984), 115–16.

4. Kramer, *History Begins at Sumer*, 283–84; Roux, *Ancient Iraq*, 76, 80.

5. Leonard Cottrell, *The Anvil of Civilization* (New York: Mentor Books, 1957), chap. 7; and Kramer, in Wolkstein and Kramer, *Inanna*, 119–22.

6. Kramer, in Wolkstein and Kramer, *Inanna*, 117–19; and Roux, *Ancient Iraq*, 127–30, 150–52, 163–72, 198–99, 203, and 206.

7. Gadon, *Once and Future Goddess*, 115–42; Sylvia Brinton Perera, *Descent to the Goddess* (Toronto: Inner City Books, 1981), 16–18; and Wolkstein and Kramer, *Inanna*, xvi.

8. Gadon, *Once and Future Goddess*, 117–18; Roux, *Ancient Iraq*, 68; and Wolkstein and Kramer, *Inanna*, 174–75.

9. Wolkstein and Kramer, *Inanna*, 91–110.

10. Ibid., 124; James, *Prehistoric Religion*, 189–91 and 239, "Dying God," in *Man, Myth and Magic*.

11. Campbell, *Masks of God*, vol. 3, 14; Kramer, *History Begins at Sumer*, 206–25; idem, *Sumerians*, 45; Kramer, in Wolkstein and Kramer, *Inanna*, 124–35; and Pritchard, *Ancient Near Eastern Texts*, 52–57.

12. Kramer, *Sumerian Mythology*, 67–68; and Wolkstein and Kramer, *Inanna*, 11–27.

13. Wolkstein and Kramer, *Inanna*, 11–27.

14. Ibid., 71 and 83; Kramer, *Sumerian Mythology*, 91–92; idem, *Sumerians*, 134, 154,

and 261; "Mesopotamia," in *Man, Myth and Magic*; Perera, *Descent to the Goddess*, 10 and 85–91.

15. Kramer, in Wolkstein and Kramer, *Inanna*, 134.

16. Cp. Perera, *Descent to the Goddess*, 51.

17. Ibid., 17; Kramer, *Sumerian Mythology*, 57; idem, *Sumerians*, 269–70, 273, and 275; and Roux, *Ancient Iraq*, 103.

18. Kramer, *Sumerian Mythology*, 50–52; and Roux, *Ancient Iraq*, 121.

19. Mallory, *In Search of the Indo-Europeans*, 163.

20. Piggott, *Prehistoric India*, 120, 146, 210, and 213.

21. Renfrew, *Archaeology and Language*, 178–210.

22. Mallory, *In Search of the Indo-Europeans*, 36–41.

23. Kenety, *Collector's Choice*, 89–92. References for scientific reports are on page 92.

24. Mallory, *In Search of the Indo-Europeans*, 42. Cp. Seltman, *Twelve Olympians and Their Guests*, 139.

25. Mallory, *In Search of the Indo-Europeans*, 39.

26. Ibid., 41; and Piggott, *Prehistoric India*, 278.

27. Kramer, *History Begins at Sumer*, 130 and 229; idem, *Sumerian Mythology*, 47; idem, *Sumerians*, 118–23; Wolkstein and Kramer, *Inanna*, x–xi and 123; and Roux, *Ancient Iraq*, 83–84.

28. Wolkstein and Kramer, *Inanna*, ix.

29. Gilgamesh, *Epic of Gilgamesh*, 8–9, 12, and 17; Kramer, *Sumerians*, 49–50; Roux, *Ancient Iraq*, 206; and Wolkstein and Kramer, *Inanna*, 7 and 143.

30. Kramer, *Sumerians*, 190–97; Roux, *Ancient Iraq*, 104–8. Cited passages with seven in them occur in Sandars's translation on pp. 63, 65, 69, 75, 80, 84, 85, 93, 111, and 114. In Pritchard, *Ancient Near Eastern Texts*, 75, 77, 80, 82, 84, 90, and 95: tablet I(iv), line 21, tablet II(iii), line 18, tablet III(iv), line 37, tablet IV(v), line 46, tablet VI, lines 52 and 55, tablet X(ii), line 8, and tablet XI, lines 211–18.

31. Kramer, *History Begins at Sumer*, 257; idem, *Sumerian Mythology*, 33–34; idem, *Sumerians*, 202; and Wolkstein and Kramer, *Inanna*, 9.

32. Roux, *Ancient Iraq*, 98–101.

33. Kramer, *History Begins at Sumer*, 203–4; idem, *Sumerian Mythology*, 98; and Pritchard, *Ancient Near Eastern Texts*, 44 and 45, n. 3.

34. Campbell, *Masks of God*, vol. 3, 76–85; L. W. King, *Seven Tablets of Creation*, lxxv–lxxx; "Marduk," in *Man, Myth and Magic*; and Pritchard, *Ancient Near Eastern Texts*, 60–72 and 501.

35. James, *Prehistoric Religion*, 191–92; and Roux, *Ancient Iraq*, 331–35.

36. Roux, *Ancient Iraq*, 85–89.

37. Campbell, *Masks of God*, vol. 1, 107, and vol. 3, 76–85; and Neumann, *The Great Mother*, 213–25.

38. Pritchard, *Ancient Near Eastern Texts*, 60–64 (tablets I, II, and III); and Roux, *Ancient Iraq*, 86.

39. "Marduk," in *Man, Myth, and Magic*; and Pritchard, *Ancient Near Eastern Texts*, 66–67 (tablet III, lines 131–38, and tablet IV).

40. L. W. King, *Seven Tablets of Creation*, vol. 1, 78–79, n. 2; Pritchard, *Ancient Near Eastern Texts*, 67–68 (tablet IV, lines 135–46, and tablet V).

41. James, *Prehistoric Religion*, 213; Pritchard, *Ancient Near Eastern Texts*, 68 (tablet VI, lines 1–34); and Roux, *Ancient Iraq*, 88.

42. L. W. King, *Seven Tablets of Creation*, vol. 1, lxiii; Pritchard, *Ancient Near Eastern Texts*, 68–72 (tablet VI, lines 35 ff., and tablet VII). "The Son, our avenger": tablet VI, line 106. "Nebiru": tablet VII, lines 124–29.

43. Jung, *Symbols of Transformation*, 416.

44. H. B. Swete, *The Apocalypse of St. John* (London: Macmillan, 1907), 149; and Hugh Ross Williamson, *The Arrow and the Sword* (London: Faber, 1947), 30–31.

45. Marduk is the divine Son, as is the Miltonic Messiah. Compare the account of his enthronement, his war chariot with its team of four, and his attack on Tiamat and her host (tablet IV, lines 1–18, 27–41, 49–60, and 101–18) with passages in *Paradise Lost*: book V, lines 600–608 (Hear all ye Angels . . .); book VI, lines 710–18 (Go then thou Mightiest . . .); book VI, lines 749–56 (Forth rush'd with whirl-wind sound . . .); and book VI, lines 824–66 (So spake the Son . . .).

46. O'Flaherty, *Rig Veda*, 1:32.

47. Gilgamesh, *Epic of Gilgamesh*, 89; Kramer, *History Begins at Sumer*, 232 and 271–72; idem, *Sumerian Mythology*, 63; idem, *Sumerians*, 140 and 193; *The Psalms*, trans. Peter Levi (New York: Penguin Books, 1976), cover; Pritchard, *Ancient Near Eastern Texts*, 47 and 87 (tablet VII[iv], line 10), 112, 392, 515, and 650; de Santillana and von Dechend, *Hamlet's Mill*, 450; and Wolkstein and Kramer, *Inanna*, 21 (illustration), 158, and 182.

48. Wolkstein and Kramer, *Inanna*, 158. Cp. Swete, *Apocalypse*, 4, note on Revelation 1:4.

49. Mallory, *In Search of the Indo-Europeans*, 150.

50. Kramer, in Wolkstein and Kramer, *Inanna*, 119–21; and Stone, *Paradise Papers*, 56.

51. Roux, *Ancient Iraq*, 97.

52. Ibid., 121; and Kramer, *Sumerians*, 50–52.

53. Kramer, *History Begins at Sumer*, 201; Graves, *Greek Myths*, vol. 1, intro.; and Stone, *Paradise Papers*, chap. 6.

54. Mallory, *In Search of the Indo-Europeans*, 38–42; Neumann, *History of Consciousness*, 82–83, 120.

CHAPTER 9: THE BONDED WORLD

1. Nikolai Tolstoy, *The Quest for Merlin* (London: Hamish Hamilton, 1985), 108. The notion of Oxford as the center of Britain is in the *Mabinogion* tale of Lludd and Llefelys.

2. Ashe, *Land and the Book*, 81; W. K. C. Guthrie, *Orpheus and Greek Religion* (New York: Methuen, 1935), 138; Harrison, *Themis*, 457, n. 2; Kramer, *History Begins at Sumer*, 128; and idem, *Sumerians*, 112–13.

   While Greek imagination accepted the world-island, it ranged farther. Something lay westward across the ocean—perhaps Cronus's Elysium or the Isles of the Blest. In Plato's Atlantis myth, not only is the ocean the site and grave of a lost kingdom, it has land beyond, a continent enclosing and encircling it. Plutarch takes the same view—the ocean has, so to speak, a rim. But none of this affected the basic idea of the *oecumene*.

3. Neumann, *History of Consciousness*, 10, illustration 3. The map is discussed by

Eckhard Unger, "Ancient Babylonian Maps and Plans," *Antiquity* vol. 9 (September 1935): 311–22.

4. Hooke, *Labyrinth*, 46–50. Cp. "Symbolism," in *Man, Myth and Magic*, 2758.

5. Pritchard, *Ancient Near Eastern Texts*, 583; and Wales, *Mountain of God*, 12–13 and 76.

6. Kramer, *History Begins at Sumer*, 309–13; and Pritchard, *Ancient Near Eastern Texts*, 582, no. 1.

7. Eliade, *Shamanism*, 267; Kramer, *History Begins at Sumer*, 139; and idem, *Sumerian Mythology*, 39–40.

8. Kramer, *Sumerians*, 118–23.

9. Wales, *Mountain of God*, 1, 7, and 12–15.

10. Pritchard, *Ancient Near Eastern Texts*, 582–83.

11. Ibid., 582, n. 4; Kramer, *History Begins at Sumer*, 139; and idem, *Sumerians*, 117.

12. John Armstrong, *The Paradise Myth* (New York: Oxford University Press, 1969), 10; Kramer, *History Begins at Sumer*, 195; idem, *Sumerian Mythology*, 98; idem, *Sumerians*, 147–48 and 281–84; and Pritchard, *Ancient Near Eastern Texts*, 37–38 and 44. Cp. Allchin and Allchin, *Rise of Civilization in India and Pakistan*, 188.

13. Gilgamesh, *Epic of Gilgamesh*, 95–97; see also Pritchard, *Ancient Near Eastern Texts*, 88–89 (tablet IX[ii]).

14. Wales, *Mountain of God*, 7–8.

15. Pritchard, *Ancient Near Eastern Texts*, 574–75, 582–84.

16. Ibid., 578–79.

17. Herodotus, *History*, vol. 1, I:181. See also Roux, *Ancient Iraq*, 329.

18. Eliade, *Shamanism*, 134.

19. Hooke, *Labyrinth*, 47–48.

20. Ibid., 65; Campbell, *Masks of God*, vol. 1, 148; Eliade, *Shamanism*, 264–67; Guénon, *Roi du Monde*, 70; and Wales, *Mountain of God*, 10.

21. De Santillana and von Dechend, *Hamlet's Mill*, 123–24.

22. Herodotus, *History*, vol. 1, III:8.

23. See *Times* (London), March 7, 1974, 8. Cp. Wolkstein and Kramer, *Inanna*, 199.

24. Kramer, *History Begins at Sumer*, 194.

25. On Canaanite religion, see Ashe, *Land and the Book*, 121–23.

26. "Baal," in *Man, Myth and Magic*; and Pritchard, *Ancient Near Eastern Texts*, 133.

27. James, *Prehistoric Religion*, 194–95.

28. Pritchard, *Ancient Near Eastern Texts*, 150 and 155.

29. Ibid., 134, 144, and 145.

30. Ibid., 148.

31. Cottrell, *Anvil of Civilization*, 143; and Ian Wilson, *The Exodus Enigma* (New York: Weidenfeld and Nicolson, 1985), 175–76.

32. Pritchard, *Ancient Near Eastern Texts*, 483–90.

33. Ibid., 137 and 138, n. 10. See also Hooke, *Labyrinth*, 224–25 and fig. 5.

34. Jung, *Mysterium Coniunctionis*, 340; and Wolkstein and Kramer, *Inanna*, 21 and 182.

CHAPTER 10: THE ISRAELITES

1. Wilson, *Exodus Enigma*, 24–25. On ancient Israel generally, see Ashe, *Land and the Book*, chaps. 2–5.
2. Exod. 3:14.
3. Ashe, *Land and the Book*, 38.
4. Wilson, *Exodus Enigma*, 40, 170, and 178.
5. Ashe, *Land and the Book*, 323.
6. Thomas Aquinas, *Summa Theologica*, I, Q. 74, art. 2.
7. Ashe, *Land and the Book*, 72; and Rashi, *Commentary on the Pentateuch*, trans. James H. Lowe (1928), 14–15.
8. Ashe, *Land and the Book*, 102–3, 124.
9. Ibid., 111–12.
10. Roux, *Ancient Iraq*, 196–97. Cp. Wilson, *Exodus Enigma*, 59–60.
11. Bruce Vawter, *A Path Through Genesis* (London: Sheed and Ward, 1957), 43–44.
12. Ibid., 47–48.
13. Ashe, *Land and the Book*, 302–3, and idem, *Virgin*, 26–31.
14. Dodd, *Bible and the Greeks*, 109, n. 2; idem, *Interpretation of the Fourth Gospel*, 85 and 273–75; and W. L. Knox, *St. Paul and the Church of the Gentiles* (New York: Cambridge University Press, 1939), 60 and 70.
15. Knox, *St. Paul and the Church of the Gentiles*, 57 and 60–61; and Williamson, *Arrow and the Sword*, 66–69.
16. Ashe, *Virgin*, 10; and James, *Cult of the Mother-Goddess*, passim. Cp. the salutation to Isis and her reply, in Apuleius, *Golden Ass*, 268–71.
17. U. Cassuto, *The Goddess Anath*, trans. Israel Abrahams (Jerusalem: Magnes Press, Hebrew University, 1972), 64–65; Knox, *St. Paul and the Church of the Gentiles*, 56. Cp. Graves, *White Goddess*, 369, citing E. M. Parr.
18. Ashe, *Land and the Book*, 236–37; idem, *Virgin*, 30–31; James, *Cult of the Mother-Goddess*, 69 and 77–78; and Pritchard, *Ancient Near Eastern Texts*, 491 and n. 10.
19. Jung, *Symbols of Transformation*, 45, n. 8.
20. Hooke, *Labyrinth*, 52–53.

CHAPTER 11: THE TWO DWELLINGS OF THE LORD

1. Zaehner, *Dawn and Twilight of Zoroastrianism*, 23, 40, 102, 281, and 299.
2. Ashe, *Land and the Book*, 60 and 71.
3. Hooke, *Labyrinth*, 54, n. 7, and 56–57.
4. Ashe, *Land and the Book*, 265. In the Bible—or, at least, the Apocrypha—Tobit 13:3–4 expresses the same idea, according to Ronald Knox's interpretation.
5. Hooke, *Labyrinth*, 55.
6. Ibid., 56–57; de Santillana and von Dechend, *Hamlet's Mill*, 219–20, citing L. Ginzberg, *The Legends of the Jews*, vol. 4, 96 and other passages.
7. Hooke, *Labyrinth*, 53–55.
8. Ibid., 65. Cp. "Mountain," in *Man, Myth and Magic*, 1899.
9. Hooke, *Labyrinth*, 66; and Pritchard, *Ancient Near Eastern Texts*, 133, 136, and 147.

10. Hooke, *Labyrinth*, 65.

11. Ashe, *Land and the Book*, 125–26.

12. Graves, *White Goddess*, 412–13; and G. G. Scholem, *Major Trends in Jewish Mysticism* (New York: Schocken Books, 1946), 40–79.

13. Cp. the King James Version of the Bible and W. L. Knox's translation, with his notes, in *St. Paul and the Church of the Gentiles*.

14. Hooke, *Labyrinth*, 66, note 2.

15. Armstrong, *Paradise Myth*, 1; and "Paradise," in *Man, Myth and Magic*.

16. Armstrong, *Paradise Myth*, 10 and 21–22; and Vawter, *Path Through Genesis*, 54 and 64–65.

17. Ashe, *Land and the Book*, 120.

18. "Eden," in *Brewer's Dictionary*; and "First Man," in *Man, Myth and Magic*.

19. Vawter, *Path Through Genesis*, 56.

20. St. Augustine, *City of God*, trans. Henry Bettenson (New York: Penguin Books, 1984), XIII:21.

21. Aquinas, *Summa Theologica*, I, Q. 102, art. 1.

22. R. H. Charles, ed. and trans., *The Book of Enoch* (Oxford: Clarendon, 1912), chap. 32. Enoch (a pseudonym) has other allusions to the seven mountains (18:6–10, 24:2–6, and 77:3–4). One, presumably the most remote of the chain, seems to be identified with the mountain of God in Ezekiel 28:12–16. The passages are doubtfully compatible, perhaps because of differences of source material. However, the earthly Garden of Adam and Eve is definitely northeast.

23. Quoted in Aquinas, *Summa Theologica*, I, Q. 102, art. 1.

24. Ashe, *Land and the Book*, 185–87.

25. Aquinas, *Summa Theologica*, I, Q. 102, art. 1.

26. Mandeville, *Travels of Sir John Mandeville*, 62–63, 86, 111, 113, 123, 167, and 182–85.

27. Lytton Strachey mentions Gordon's biblical speculations in *Eminent Victorians*. Julian Ford (*The Story of Paradise* [Richmond, England: H and B Publications, 1981], passim) detects mythification of the prehistory of East Africa.

28. Armstrong, *Paradise Myth*, 10.

29. Eliade, *Shamanism*, 99, and cp. 171, 431, 486, 492–93, and 508.

CHAPTER 12: A GREEK GOD

1. Mallory, *In Search of the Indo-Europeans*, 24–30; and Pritchard, *Ancient Near Eastern Texts*, 120–38.

2. Gilgamesh, *Epic of Gilgamesh*, 12; and Roux, *Ancient Iraq*, 108.

3. Mallory, *In Search of the Indo-Europeans*, 68–69.

4. Cottrell, *Anvil of Civilization*, chaps. 8 and 14; Graves, *Greek Myths*, vol. 1, 18; Mallory, *In Search of the Indo-Europeans*, 66–71; and Seltman, *Twelve Olympians and Their Guests*, 32.

5. Seltman, *Twelve Olympians and Their Guests*, 109.

6. Ibid., 18 and 37–38; Graves, *Greek Myths*, vol. 1, 19; Guthrie, *Greeks and Their Gods*, 110; and James, *Prehistoric Religion*, 222–23.

7. Seltman, *Twelve Olympians and Their Guests*, 40.

8. Callimachus, *Hymns*, trans. A. W. Mair (London: William Heinemann, 1921; New York: G. P. Putnam's Sons, 1921), 509, giving text of Lycophron's *Alexandra*, lines 177–79. See also Graves, *Greek Myths*, vol. 2, sec. 160h.

9. Graves, *Greek Myths*, vol. 1, sec. 14a.

10. Callimachus, *Hymns*, 62, n. a; and Farnell, *Cults of the Greek States*, vol. 4, 267–68.

11. This suggestion is from J. V. Luce, *The End of Atlantis* (London: Thames and Hudson, 1969), 152.

12. Callimachus, *Hymns*, 48–49, n. c, and 104–5, lines 249–54 of *Hymn to Delos*.

13. Farnell, *Cults of the Greek States*, vol. 4, 259–92; Nilsson, *Primitive Time Reckoning*, 343 and 366–69. Cp. Guthrie, *Greeks and Their Gods*, 86, n.

14. Farnell, *Cults of the Greek States*, vol. 4, 259. The epithet occurs in Aeschylus, *The Seven Against Thebes*, lines 800–801.

15. Nilsson, *Primitive Time Reckoning*, 363.

16. Graves, *Greek Myths*, vol. 1, sec. 21a, b, and c; Guthrie, *Greeks and Their Gods*, 73 and 80; Peter Hoyle, *Delphi* (London: Cassell, 1967), 57 and 185–86. Euripides tells the story poetically in *Iphigenia in Tauris*, lines 1235–84.

17. Callimachus, *Hymns*, 48–49, n. c. See also Farnell, *Cults of the Greek States*, vol. 4, 292; and Hoyle, *Delphi*, 26 and 84.

18. Farnell, *Cults of the Greek States*, vol. 4, 186; and Hoyle, *Delphi*, 26.

19. Dodds, *Greeks and the Irrational*, 75.

20. Hoyle, *Delphi*, 12–13; and Seltman, *Twelve Olympians and Their Guests*, 115.

21. "Wise Men of Greece," in *Brewer's Dictionary*.

22. Dodds, *Greeks and the Irrational*, 75 and n. 73; Guthrie, *Greeks and Their Gods*, 186–87; and Hoyle, *Delphi*, 34–37.

23. Guthrie, *Greeks and Their Gods*, 184–86; and Hoyle, *Delphi*, 134–36.

24. Plato, *Republic*, IV:472H; and cp. *Laws* VI:759c. See also Dodds, *Greeks and the Irrational*, 222–23; and Guthrie, *Greeks and Their Gods*, 186.

25. Plutarch, *The Obsolescence of Oracles*, trans. Frank Cole Babbitt, in *Moralia*, vol. 5, 348–501 (London and Cambridge, Mass.: Loeb Classical Library, Heinemann and Harvard, 1936), 351. See also Hoyle, *Delphi*, 9–10 and 24.

26. Hesiod, *Theogony*, trans. Dorothea Winder (New York: Penguin Books, 1973), line 496. See also Harrison, *Themis*, 385, 396–99, 401, 411, figs. 123, and 424, fig. 127; and Hoyle, *Delphi*, 44–46.

27. Plutarch, *The E at Delphi*, trans. Frank Cole Babbitt, in *Moralia*, vol. 5, 194–253, esp. 225–39.

28. Harrison, *Themis*, 411, fig. 123.

29. Farnell, *Cults of the Greek States*, vol. 4, 325; and Piggott, *Prehistoric India*, 272–73.

30. Grant, *Myths of Hyginus*, 191–92 (*Poetic Astronomy* II:7). See also Graves, *Greek Myths*, vol. 1, sec. 17; and Seltman, *Twelve Olympians and Their Guests*, 71–75.

31. Farnell, *Cults of the Greek States*, vol. 4, 325–26 and plate XXIa.

32. Plutarch, *E at Delphi*, in *Moralia*, vol. 5, 207.

33. McGuire and Rattansi, "Newton and the 'Pipes of Pan,' " 115 ff., citing Macrobius I:19 and Proclus on Timaeus III, 200.

34. Graves, *Greek Myths*, vols. 1 and 2, sect. 76c, 105–107; Hyginus, 67–69.

35. Grant, *Myths of Hyginus*, 31–32. See also Graves, *Greek Myths*, vol. 1, sec. 77.

36. Callimachus, *Hymns*, 92, n. d.

37. Graves, *Greek Myths*, vol. 1, sec. 1d and n. 3. Graves is wrong about seven being the original number, related to the days of the planetary week. The Titans are much older than the week, and, as Hesiod shows in the passage that Graves himself cites (Hesiod, *Theogony*, lines 133 ff.), they were not originally seven.

38. Ibid., vol. 1, sec. 28; Guthrie, *Orpheus and Greek Religion*, 32, 115, and 138; and "Orpheus," in *Man, Myth and Magic*.

39. Grant, *Myths of Hyginus*, 191–92 (*Poetic Astronomy* II:7). See also Graves, *Greek Myths*, vol. 1, sec. 28g.

40. Campbell, *Masks of God*, vol. 1, 101; Graves, *Greek Myths*, vol. 1, sec. 27a; Hoyle, *Delphi*, 73; and "Orpheus," in *Man, Myth and Magic*, 2085.

41. Graves, *Greek Myths*, vol. 1, sec. 98c; and Hooke, *Labyrinth*, 27.

42. Ashe, *Avalonian Quest*, 155–56 and 180–81. Cp. Hooke, *Labyrinth*, 10, figs. 13 and 14.

43. Ashe, *Avalonian Quest*, 191–92; and Matthews, *Mazes and Labyrinths*, fig. 30 (facing p. 45).

44. Farnell, *Cults of the Greek States*, vol. 4, 251–52; Graves, *Greek Myths*, vol. 1, sec. 98t and u and nn. 2 and 3; and Hooke, *Labyrinth*, 27. See also Plutarch's *Life of Theseus*, 21.

45. Ashe, *Avalonian Quest*, 170 and 178; Graves, *Greek Myths*, vol. 1, sec. 92h. Virgil's references to the labyrinth design at Cumae is in *Aeneid* 6:14 ff.

46. Callimachus, *Hymns*, 275–77 and n. a. See also Graves, *Greek Myths*, vol. 2, sec. 163k.

47. Graves, *Greek Myths*, vol. 1, sec. 50.

48. A. B. Cook, *Zeus*, 3 vols. (New York: Cambridge University Press, 1914–40), vol. 2, 455; Guthrie, *Greeks and Their Gods*, 188 and 195; and Hoyle, *Delphi*, 100–101 and 125.

49. Graves, *White Goddess*, 411–13.

50. Plutarch, *E at Delphi*, 194–97 and 237–53.

51. Dodd, *Bible and the Greeks*, 3–4. Cp. Aquinas, *Summa Theologica*, I, Q. 13, art. 11.

52. Quoted in Hoyle, *Delphi*, 66.

53. Graves, *White Goddess*, 412, and cp. 454–56.

CHAPTER 13: A GREEK GODDESS

1. Graves, *Greek Myths*, vol. 1, sec. 14, n. 2, and vol. 2, 158, n. 2; and Hoyle, *Delphi*, 66.

2. Cp. Graves, *Greek Myths*, vol. 1, sec. 21, n. 2.

3. A. B. Cook, *Zeus*, 3 vols. (Cambridge: Cambridge University Press, 1914–40), vol. 2, 487–93; Dodds, *Greeks and the Irrational* 86, n. 32, and 161–62, n. 36; Farnell, *Cults of the Greek States*, vol. 4, 98–99; Graves, *Greek Myths*, vol. 1, sec. 14, n. 2; and Guthrie, *Greeks and Their Gods*, 86.

4. Cook, *Zeus*, vol. 2, 455; Dodds, *Greeks and the Irrational*, 69–70; and Hoyle, *Delphi*, 55 and 88.

5. Guthrie, *Greeks and Their Gods*, 101–2; and Hoyle, *Delphi*, 64.

6. Homer, *The Odyssey*, trans. E. V. Rieu (New York: Penguin Books, 1959), 5:275 ff. A parallel passage in *The Iliad* (trans. E. V. Rieu [New York: Penguin Books, 1959], 18:486 ff.) mentions the Hyades. These stars are generally reckoned as five, but sometimes as seven also. See H. B. Walters's *Classical Dictionary* (New York: Cambridge University Press, 1916). Cp. Grant, *Myths of Hyginus*, 13 and 148–49.

7. Grant, *Myths of Hyginus*, 137, 151, 210–11 (*Poetic Astronomy* II:21), and 237. See also Graves, *Greek Myths*, vol. 1, sec. 41e and n. 6; and Seltman, *Twelve Olympians and Their Guests*, 136.

8. Graves, *Greek Myths*, vol. 1, sec. 45, n. 4; idem, *White Goddess*, 186; and Nilsson, *Primitive Time Reckoning*, 93, 129–30, 136–45, and 274–75.

9. *Mahabharata*, trans. Dutt, vol. 2, IX:44:10. See also Nilsson, *Primitive Time Reckoning*, 122 and 133; and de Santillana and von Dechend, *Hamlet's Mill*, 157.

10. Callimachus, *Hymns*, 401, giving text of Aratus, *Phaenomena*, lines 257–58; and Grant, *Myths of Hyginus*, 210–11 (*Poetic Astronomy* II:21).

11. Callimachus, *Hymns*, 401, n. f; Grant, *Myths of Hyginus*, 148–49 and 210–11 (*Poetic Astronomy* II:21); "Pleiades," in *Brewer's Dictionary*; and Graves, *Greek Myths*, vol. 1, sec. 41e and n. 6.

12. Nilsson, *Primitive Time Reckoning*, 137–38.

13. Aratus, *Astronomy and Meteorology of Aratus*, 18. Cp. "Nymphs," in *Man, Myth and Magic*.

14. Grant, *Myths of Hyginus*, 182–83.

15. Farnell, *Cults of the Greek States*, vol. 2, 480–86; Graves, *Greek Myths*, vol. 1, sec. 22; Guthrie, *Greeks and Their Gods*, 99–106; and Harrison, *Themis*, 504–5.

16. Guthrie, *Greeks and Their Gods*, 103; Seltman, *Twelve Olympians and Their Guests*, 127; Neumann, *History of Consciousness*, 52.

17. Callimachus, *Hymns*, 63, lines 22–25 of *Hymn to Artemis*.

18. Homer, *Iliad*, 470ff. See also Farnell, *Cults of the Greek States*, vol. 2, 427–31, 456, and 472; and Seltman, *Twelve Olympians and Their Guests*, plate facing p. 32.

19. Gimbutas, *Language of the Goddess*, 116.

20. Farnell, *Cults of the Greek States*, vol. 2, 435–37; Guthrie, *Greeks and Their Gods*, 104; and "Nymphs," in *Man, Myth and Magic*.

21. Grant, *Myths of Hyginus*, 181–82 (*Poetic Astronomy* II:1).

22. Callimachus, *Hymns*, 69, lines 93–97 of *Hymn to Artemis*. See also "Diana," in *Man, Myth and Magic*. Regarding Arcas's final destiny, cp. "Calisto and Arcas," in *Brewer's Dictionary*. His skyward translation, with his mother, is affirmed by the Roman poet Ovid in his *Metamorphoses*, 2:505–7.

23. Farnell, *Cults of the Greek States*, vol. 2, 435–37; Graves, *Greek Myths*, vol. 1, sec. 22, n. 4; and Guthrie, *Greeks and Their Gods*, 104. Graves, in *The White Goddess* (286, n. 2), claims that a picture of the two girls in bear costume "rushing savagely at the boys who attended the festival" inspired an alarming story of the prophet Elisha in 2 Kings 2:23–24.

24. "Diana," in *Man, Myth and Magic*.

25. Graves, *Greek Myths*, vol. 1, sec. 22b and d.

26. "Diana," in *Man, Myth and Magic*, 632.

27. Graves, *Greek Myths*, vol. 2, sec. 116, n. 5; and "Diana," in *Man, Myth and Magic*, 632.

28. Graves, *Greek Myths*, vols. 1, 2, sec. 100g and 131d.

29. Herodotus, *History*, vol. 1, IV:110–17. See also Graves, *Greek Myths*, vol. 2, sec. 131b and c; and "Amazons," in *Man, Myth and Magic*.

30. Dergachev, "Neolithic and Bronze Age Cultural Communities," 780. Personal information from Timothy Taylor.

31. Farnell, *Cults of the Greek States*, vol. 2, 440 and 452–54; Graves, *Greek Myths*, vol. 2, sec. 116, 131c, and 161d. See also Euripides, *Iphigenia in Tauris*.

32. Herodotus, *History*, vol. 1, IV:103.

33. Farnell, *Cults of the Greek States*, vol. 2, 452–53.

34. "Nymphs," in *Man, Myth and Magic*.

35. Mallory, *In Search of the Indo-Europeans*, 148–49 and 206–7.

36. Czaplicka, *Aboriginal Siberia*, 326–28.

37. Ibid., 244, n. 2; and Heissig, *Religions of Mongolia*, 102.

38. Pindar, *3rd Olympian Ode*, in *The Works of Pindar*, 3 vols. (London: Macmillan, 1930–32), lines 14–33; and Farnell's note in vol. 2 of *The Works of Pindar*. Cp. Harrison, *Themis*, 236, n. 3. Regarding Pindar's peculiar geography, see page 173.

39. Cook, *Zeus*, vol. 2, 465; and Graves, *Greek Myths*, vol. 2, sec. 125, n. 2.

40. Eliade, *Shamanism*, 41; and Michael, *Siberian Shamanism*, 68 and 71, n.

41. Jung, *Archetypes and the Collective Unconscious*, pt. 1, 195–96.

CHAPTER 14: BEYOND THE NORTH WIND

1. Cook, *Zeus*, vol. 2, 453.

2. Farnell, *Cults of the Greek States*, vol. 2, 465.

3. Bolton, *Aristeas of Proconnesus*, 101 and 115–16. But see also Farnell, *Cults of the Greek States*, vol. 4, 100–103.

4. Callimachus, *Hymns*, 88–89, line 65 of *Hymn to Delos* and note e; also 106 note c, giving various references. Pindar, *3rd Olympian Ode*, line 33.

5. Pindar, *10th Pythian Ode*, in *The Works of Pindar*, lines 29–43. See also A. B. Cook, *Zeus*, vol. 2, 459–65; and Guthrie, *Greeks and Their Gods*, 74–75.

6. Cook, *Zeus*, vol. 2, 465.

7. Herodotus, *History*, vol. 1, IV:33–34. See also Farnell, *Cults of the Greek States*, vol. 2, 465 and 487–88, and vol. 4, 100–105.

8. Claudian: in a poem on Stilicho's consulate, 3:253.

9. Herodotus, *History*, vol. 1, IV:33 and 35.

10. A. B. Cook, *Zeus*, vol. 2, 459–62.

11. Herodotus, *History*, vol. 1, IV:35. See also Hoyle, *Delphi*, 63, citing Pausanias.

12. Dodds, *Greeks and the Irrational*, 140–41; Guthrie, *Greeks and Their Gods*, 78 and 195; and Piggott, *Druids*, 79–82.

13. Herodotus, *History*, vol. 1, IV:13 and 32.

14. Ashe, *Avalonian Quest*, 202–11; Cook, *Zeus*, vol. 2, 498–99; Guthrie, *Greeks and Their Gods*, 79; and Piggott, *Druids*, 80.

15. Pindar, *3rd Olympian Ode*, lines 14–33.

16. Herodotus, *History*, vol. 1, IV:49.

17. Ashe, *Avalonian Quest*, 172–73, 202, and 207–8; and Cook, *Zeus*, vol. 2, 498–99.

18. Bolton, *Aristeas of Proconnesus*, 2–8 and 141.
19. Herodotus, *History*, vol. 1, III:116, IV:13, and IV:16.
20. Bolton, *Aristeas of Proconnesus*, 74–76.
21. Ibid., 74, 93–96, 100, 114, and 118; and Rudenko, *Frozen Tombs of Siberia*, xxi–xxiii.
22. Callimachus, *Hymns*, 88–89, line 65 of *Hymn to Delos*, and n. e. See also Bolton, *Aristeas of Proconnesus*, 93–96. Robert Graves (*Greek Myths*, vol. 1, sec. 48) gives references for this cave motif that are later than Aristeas—none that are earlier.
23. Bolton, *Aristeas of Proconnesus*, 100–101; and Piggott, *Druids*, 79.
24. Eliade, *Shamanism*, 238. Jules Verne, in his novel *Michael Strogoff*, mentions a folk belief that if you call Baikal a sea, it remains calm, but if you call it a lake, it grows rough and angry.
25. *Mahabharata*, trans. Dutt, vol. 2, VI:7:2–14. See also Bolton, *Aristeas of Proconnesus*, 98–99; and Caillat and Kumar, *Jain Cosmology*, 29.
26. Bolton, *Aristeas of Proconnesus*, 81–82 and 92; and Rudenko, *Frozen Tombs of Siberia*, 142 and 257.
27. Dodds, *Greeks and the Irrational*, 140–41; Eliade, *Shamanism*, 152, n. 31, 175, n. 140, 217, 388; Guthrie, *Greeks and Their Gods*, 78; Heissig, *Religions of Mongolia*, 47.
28. Callimachus, *Hymns*, 321, fragment 51; and Pindar, *10th Pythian Ode*, lines 34–35. See also Bolton, *Aristeas of Proconnesus*, 69; and Hoyle, *Delphi*, 63–64.
29. Eliade, *Shamanism*, 511.
30. Ibid., 387–91; and Guthrie, *Greeks and Their Gods*, 204.
31. Dodds, *Greeks and the Irrational*, 69–70. Cp. Herodotus, *History*, vol. 1, I:182.
32. Dodds, *Greeks and the Irrational*, 140–41; Eliade, *Shamanism*, 388; Guthrie, *Greeks and Their Gods*, 195; and Piggott, *Druids*, 82.
33. Herodotus, *History*, vol. 1, IV:13–15. See also Bolton, *Aristeas of Proconnesus*, 120–26; Eliade, *Shamanism*, 388–89, 395, and 403; and Guthrie, *Greeks and Their Gods*, 193–94.
34. Guthrie, *Greeks and Their Gods*, 195–96; and Eliade, *Shamanism*, 389.
35. "Epimenides," in *Chambers Biographical Dictionary*, 2 vols. (Edinburgh: Chambers, 1975); and Dodds, *Greeks and the Irrational*, 143.
36. Herodotus, *History*, vol. 1, IV:94–96. See also Dodds, *Greeks and the Irrational*, 143–45 and n. 60; Eliade, *Shamanism*, 389–90; Guthrie, *Greeks and Their Gods*, 195 and 197–98.
37. Dodds, *Greeks and the Irrational*, 144 and n. 61, and 147 and n. 75; Eliade, *Shamanism*, 390 and n. 55.
38. Eliade, *Shamanism*, 245 and 391; Guthrie, *Orpheus and Greek Religion*, 216–20.
39. Dodds, *Greeks and the Irrational*, 71 and n. 43, 135, and 139–40.
40. Eliade, *Shamanism*, index, p. 603 (numerous "soul" references).
41. Dodds, *Greeks and the Irrational*, 140–42 and nn. 32 and 36.
42. Eliade, *Shamanism*, 387, n. 42.
43. Dodds, *Greeks and the Irrational*, 144 and n. 63.
44. Cp. Ashe, *Land to the West*, chaps. 8 and 9.
45. David-Neel, *Life of Gesar of Ling*, 46–47.
46. Hitching, *World Atlas of Mysteries*, 240; N. Roerich, *Altai-Himalaya*, 49; and idem, *Himalayas, Abode of Light* (London: David Marlowe, 1947), 28.

47. Evans-Wentz, *Tibetan Book of the Great Liberation*, 117.

48. Cp. Alexandra David-Neel, *With Mystics and Magicians in Tibet* (London: John Lane, The Bodley Head, 1931), 244.

49. Hitching, *World Atlas of Mysteries*, 238; and N. Roerich, *Shambhala*, 13.

50. Evans-Wentz, *Tibetan Book of the Great Liberation*, xvii–xxi.

51. Ibid., 59–60 and 122; and "Adibuddha," in *Encyclopedia of Religion and Ethics*, 12 vols. (New York: Scribner, 1908–21), vol. 1, 95.

52. Evans-Wentz, *Tibetan Book of the Great Liberation*, xx, 59–60, 122, and 135–36; idem, *Tibetan Yoga*, 155–56; George Roerich, *Trails to Inmost Asia* (New Haven, Conn.: Yale University Press, 1931), 156–58; and N. Roerich, *Himalayas*, 104.

53. David-Neel, *Life of Gesar of Ling*, 14–15 and 45–48; N. Roerich, *Altai-Himalaya*, 111; and idem, *Himalayas*, 65.

54. *Mahabharata*, trans. van Buitinen, vol. 2, 597, indexed as 3(37)188 of text; *Mahabharata*, trans. Dutt, vol. 1, III:190:93–95.

55. Evans-Wentz, *Tibetan Book of the Great Liberation*, 60; N. Roerich, *Altai-Himalaya*, 110–11 and 372; idem, *Himalayas*, 73, 78–79, and 86–87; and idem, *Shambhala*, 2 and 12.

56. Decter, *Nicholas Roerich*, 166; N. Roerich, *Altai-Himalaya*, 337–38 and 406; and idem, *Himalayas*, 108–10.

57. David-Neel, *Life of Gesar of Ling*, 33–35 and 43–44; Decter, *Nicholas Roerich*, 166–67; and Ferdinand Ossendowski, *Beasts, Men and Gods* (London: Edward Arnold, 1922), 238–41, 247–49, 269–70, and 294.

58. Ossendowski, *Beasts, Men and Gods*, 118, 177–79, and 299–314; and N. Roerich, *Altai-Himalaya*, 37–38, 62, 354, and 396.

59. Decter, *Nicholas Roerich*, 140–41; and N. Roerich, *Altai-Himalaya*, xiii, 143, 149, 353–54, and 391. Cp. G. Roerich, *Inmost Asia*, 156–58.

60. N. Roerich, *Altai-Himalaya*, 35, 112, 289, 306, 314, and 349; and idem, *Shambhala*, 45. Cp. Decter, *Nicholas Roerich*, 166.

61. David-Neel, *Life of Gesar of Ling*, 7.

62. G. Roerich, *Inmost Asia*, 243–45; N. Roerich, *Altai-Himalaya*, 359–62; and idem, *Himalayas*, 50–51 and 81–82.

63. N. Roerich, *Himalayas*, 13 and 21.

64. Chadwick, *Poetry and Prophecy*, 19; David-Neel, *Life of Gesar Ling*, 19–20 and 47; idem, *Mystics and Magicians in Tibet*, 9; Eliade, *Shamanism*, 430–41; Evans-Wentz, *Tibetan Book of the Great Liberation*, 59–60; and idem, *Tibetan Yoga*, 290.

CHAPTER 15: EXPANSION

1. Grant, *Myths of Hyginus*, 179; Philo, *Works of Philo Judaeus*, vol. 1, 36–37 (*On the Creation of the World*, 41). See also Dodds, *Greeks and the Irrational*, 292; and Murray, *Greek Religion*, 142.

2. Graves, *Greek Myths*, vol. 1, sec. 21, n. 10, and sec. 52, n. 8; and idem, *White Goddess*, 285.

3. Callimachus, *Hymns*, 275–77 and n. a. See also "Spheres, the music, or harmony, of . . . ," in *Brewer's Dictionary*.

4. McGuire and Rattansi, "Newton and the 'Pipes of Pan,'" 115 ff.

5. Grant, *Myths of Hyginus*, 158–59 (*Fabulae*, lines 221–23). See also "Pleiad," in *Brewer's Dictionary*.

6. Callimachus, *Hymns*, 480, intro. to Lycophron. See also "The Pleiad of Alexandria," in *Brewer's Dictionary*.

7. "Wonder," in *Brewer's Dictionary*.

8. Callimachus, *Hymns*, 509, giving text of Lycophron, lines 177–79, and n. q. See also Graves, *Greek Myths*, vols. 1, sec. 1, n. 4, and 2, sec. 160h.

9. Dodd, *Bible and the Greeks*, 139–41.

10. "Menorah," in *Jewish Encyclopaedia* (New York and London: Funk and Wagnalls, 1901–6).

11. Spencer, *Mysticism in World Religion*, 178–79.

12. "Seven Names of God," in *Brewer's Dictionary*.

13. Campbell, *Masks of God*, vol. 1, 85, citing the Talmud, *Kiddushin*, 71a.

14. Dodd, *Bible and the Greeks*, 156.

15. Quoted in Jung, *Mysterium Coniunctionis*, 403–4.

16. On the astrological week in the Roman world, see Dio Cassius, *Roman History*, 9 vols., trans. E. Cary (London and Cambridge, Mass.: Loeb Classical Library, 1940), vol. 3, XXXVII:17–18. His ascription of it to Egyptians is a reference to Alexandria, not ancient Egypt. On its development, and calendric adoption by Christians, see Henry Chadwick, *The Early Church* (New York: Penguin Books, 1986), 128–29.

17. J. Huizinga, *The Waning of the Middle Ages*, trans. F. Hopman (New York: Penguin Books, 1985), 199.

18. Ashe, *Virgin*, 146–47; Graves, *White Goddess*, 254; and Williamson, *Arrow and the Sword*, 69.

19. Miguel Asin, *Islam and the Divine Comedy*, trans. Harold Sutherland (London: John Murray, 1926), 88, citing the Koran, 65:12. This verse mentions the seven heavens and earths; other instances are scattered. Regarding the septenary purgatory, see p. 116 in Asin.

20. "Adam," in *Brewer's Dictionary*; and Jung, *Mysterium Coniunctionis*, 386.

21. Asin, *Islam and the Divine Comedy*, 114–16 and 123–24.

22. Eliade, *Shamanism*, 268; Mandeville, *Travels of Sir John Mandeville*, 79 and 129; and de Santillana and von Dechend, *Hamlet's Mill*, 304, n. 45.

23. "Sense," in *Brewer's Dictionary*. Cp. Cavendish, *Black Arts*, 83–86.

24. Cumont, *Astrology and Religion*, 197–98; Hooke, *Labyrinth*, 68; and Williamson, *Arrow and the Sword*, 43–44.

25. Jung, *Mysterium Coniunctionis*, 398–99.

26. Cp. Dodd, *Interpretation of the Fourth Gospel*, 11; and McGuire and Rattansi, "Newton and the 'Pipes of Pan,'" 110.

27. "Pleiad," in *Brewer's Dictionary*.

28. Joseph Palermo, "*Sept Sages de Rome*," in *The Arthurian Encyclopedia*, ed. Norris J. Lacy (New York: Garland, 1986).

29. Alban Butler, *The Lives of the Saints*, 12 vols., ed. and rev. H. Thurston and D. Attwater (London: Burns Oates and Washbourne, 1926–38), vol. 7, 375–80 (July 27).

30. "Seven Sleepers," in *Brewer's Dictionary*.

31. "Wonder," in *Brewer's Dictionary*.

32. Ashe, *Land to the West*, 296.

CHAPTER 16: STARTING POINTS OF SCIENCE

1. Hindley, *Larousse Encyclopedia of Music*, 541 ("octave") and 544 ("scale").

2. Cp. Jung, *Mysterium Coniunctionis*, 287.

3. N. Roerich, *Altai-Himalaya*, 191–92.

4. "Primum Mobile" and "Spheres," in *Brewer's Dictionary*; Franz Cumont, *Astrology and Religion Among the Greeks and Romans* (New York: Putnam, 1912), 119–21; Gilbert Murray, *Five Stages of Greek Religion* (Oxford: Clarendon, 1935), 140.

5. Bertrand Russell, *A History of Western Philosophy* (London: George Allen and Unwin, 1946), 237–38.

6. Cumont, *Astrology and Religion*, 127–28 and 132; Jung, *Mysterium Coniunctionis*, 357–60; and McGuire and Rattansi, "Newton and the 'Pipes of Pan,' " 115 ff., citing Macrobius I:19.

7. Geoffrey Ashe, *Kings and Queens of Early Britain* (London: Methuen, 1982), 44 and 53–54.

8. McGuire and Rattansi, "Newton and the 'Pipes of Pan,' " 110, 115 ff., 127–28, and 134.

9. *Cultural Heritage of India*, 3 vols. (Calcutta: Sri Ramakrishna Centenary Committee, 1937), vol. 3, 347 and 476; Eliade, *Shamanism*, 274, n. 65; Evans-Wentz, *Tibetan Yoga*, 287; and de Santillana and von Dechend, *Hamlet's Mill*, 123, n. 16.

10. C. J. S. Thompson, *Lure and Romance of Alchemy* (London: Harrap, 1932), 10–12.

11. Ibid., 12–24; Cumont, *Mysteries of Mithra*, 120; Dodds, *Greeks and the Irrational*, 246–47 and 293; and Jung, *Mysterium Coniunctionis*, 224.

12. Jung, *Mysterium Coniunctionis*, 93; and Seltman, *Twelve Olympians and Their Guests*, 81–82.

13. Kramer, *History Begins at Sumer*, 128; and idem, *Sumerians*, 112–13.

14. Thompson, *Lure and Romance of Alchemy*, 16–17.

15. Cp. Jung, *Mysterium Coniunctionis*, 19.

16. Jung, *Alchemical Studies*, 349; idem, *Psychology and Alchemy*, 227–28; and Thompson, *Lure and Romance of Alchemy*, 77 and 206.

17. Thompson, *Lure and Romance of Alchemy*, 24 and 240–44.

18. On Asian alchemy, chiefly Taoist, see Spencer, *Mysticism in World Religion*, 109–10; Thompson, *Lure and Romance of Alchemy*, 49–58; and, especially, Holmes Welch, *The Parting of the Way* (London: Methuen, 1958), 90–102, 105, 126–27, and 131–33.

19. Welch, *Parting of the Way*, 134–35.

20. Cp. Jung, *Mysterium Coniunctionis*, 287.

CHAPTER 17: ENIGMAS AND ECCENTRICS

1. Hooke, *Labyrinth*, 70.

2. Asin, *Islam and the Divine Comedy*, 111–17.

3. Dante, *The Divine Comedy*, 3 vols., trans. Dorothy L. Sayers (New York: Penguin Books, 1949–62), vol. 2, Sayers's discussion, 62 and 69–71.

4. Mandeville, *Travels of Sir John Mandeville*, 127–31 (chap. 20).

5. Asin, *Islam and the Divine Comedy*, 122.

6. Anne Catherine Emmerich, *The Life of the Blessed Virgin Mary*, trans. Sir Michael Palairet (Rockford, Ill.: Tan Books, 1970), v–xii.

7. Ibid., 63–65 and n. 1. Cp. Guénon, *Roi du Monde*, 66–67.

8. Massey, *Book of the Beginnings*, pt. 1, vol. 2, 75, 129, and 520; and pt. 2, vol. 1, 219.

9. Ibid., pt. 1, vol. 1, 314–20; and pt. 2, vol. 2, 5 and 15.

10. Ibid., pt. 1, vol. 2, 134; and pt. 2, vol. 2, 25–29, 82.

11. Ibid., pt. 2, vol. 2, 166–67.

12. Ibid., pt. 1, vol. 1, 358–59; pt. 1, vol. 2, 137–38 and 149; pt. 2, vol. 1, 286–91 and 316; and pt. 2, vol. 2, 2 and 221–22.

13. Ibid., pt. 2, vol. 1, 358–59; and pt. 2, vol. 2, 52.

14. Ibid., pt. 1, vol. 1, 312.

15. Ibid., pt. 2, vol. 2, 162.

16. Geoffrey Ashe, *Mythology of the British Isles* (North Pomfret, Vermont: Trafalgar Square, 1990), 124–26; and Piggott, *Druids*, 142–57.

17. On Madame Blavatsky, see (besides her own books) L. Sprague de Camp and Catherine C. de Camp, *Citadels of Mystery* (London: Fontana/Collins, 1972), 228–32; and Francis King, *Satan and Swastika* (London: Mayflower, 1976), 46–59. Both of these accounts are hostile but, in essentials, defensible.

18. De Camp and de Camp, *Citadels of Mystery*, 231; and F. King, *Satan and Swastika*, 50.

19. H. P. Blavatsky, *The Secret Doctrine*, 2 vols. (Pasadena, Calif.: Theosophical University Press, 1970), vol. 1, 303.

20. De Camp and de Camp, *Citadels of Mystery*, 230–31; and F. King, *Satan and Swastika*, 53–57.

21. F. King, *Satan and Swastika*, 56.

22. H. P. Blavatsky, *Isis Unveiled*, 2 vols. (Pasadena, Calif.: Theosophical University Press, 1972), vol. 2, 407–8 and 417–20.

23. Blavatsky, *Secret Doctrine*, vol. 2, 353.

24. Ibid., vol. 2, 631 (quote); Le Poer Trench, *Temple of the Stars*, 50; and Massey, *Book of the Beginnings*, pt. 2, vol. 1, 219.

25. Blavatsky, *Secret Doctrine*, vol. 2, 590–641.

26. P. D. Ouspensky, *In Search of the Miraculous* (Boston: Routledge and Kegan Paul, 1950), 71–72 and 205.

27. Blavatsky, *Secret Doctrine*, vol. 2, 319. On Roerich's theosophy, see Decter, *Nicholas Roerich*, 107; and cp. Claude Bragdon's introduction to N. Roerich, *Altai-Himalaya*, xiii. A book of essays on his work, entitled *The Messenger*, by Frances Adney and others, was published under theosophical auspices in 1925.

28. Vera Stanley Alder, *The Initiation of the World* (London: Rider, 1969), 119 and 143–54.
29. Ibid., 58–59.
30. Ibid., 114.
31. Ibid., 92–95.
32. Guénon, *Roi du Monde*, 3; and F. King, *Satan and Swastika*, 44.
33. Guénon, *Roi du Monde*, 63, 71, and 89–90.
34. Ibid., 58–59, 65, 70–74, and 78.
35. Ibid., 66–67; and Robert Baudry, "Guénon, René," in *Arthurian Encyclopedia*.
36. N. Roerich, *Altai-Himalaya*, 37–38, 337, 354, 396, and 398.

CHAPTER 18: VINDICATION?

1. Geoffrey Ashe, *Camelot and the Vision of Albion* (London: Heinemann, 1971; and New York: St. Martin's Press, 1972), esp. chap. 8.
2. Gimbutas, *Language of the Goddess*, xx. Cp. Neumann, *The Great Mother*, 91.
3. Gadon, *Once and Future Goddess*, 88, fig. 63.
4. Colin Renfrew, "They Ride Horses, Don't They?" *Antiquity* 63 (December 1989): 844.
5. Mongun-Taiga was featured in a television documentary series, "Disappearing World," made by the British company Granada. The programs were published in booklet form in 1989, this one being the work of Dr. Caroline Humphrey. In an early sequence of "The Herders of Mongun-Taiga," a storyteller began a folk tale about *seven* men. This, alas, was not included in the booklet.

Bibliography

Alder, Vera Stanley. *The Initiation of the World*. London: Rider, 1969.

Allchin, Bridget, and Raymond Allchin. *The Rise of Civilization in India and Pakistan*. New York: Cambridge University Press, 1982.

Apuleius. *The Golden Ass*. Translated by Robert Graves. New York: Penguin Books, 1950.

Aratus. *A Literal Translation of the Astronomy and Meteorology of Aratus*. Translated by C. Leeson Prince. London: Farncombe, 1895.

Armstrong, John. *The Paradise Myth*. New York: Oxford University Press, 1969.

Ashe, Geoffrey. *Avalonian Quest*. London: Methuen, 1982.

———. *Camelot and the Vision of Albion*. London: Heinemann, 1971; and New York: St. Martin's Press, 1972.

———. *Kings and Queens of Early Britain*. London: Methuen, 1982.

———. *The Land and the Book*. London: Collins, 1965.

———. *Land to the West*. London: Collins, 1962; and New York: Viking, 1962.

———. *Mythology of the British Isles*. North Pomfret, Vermont: Trafalgar Square, 1990.

———. *The Virgin*, 1976; reprint, Boston: Routledge and Kegan Paul, 1988.

Asin, Miguel. *Islam and the Divine Comedy*. Translated by Harold Sutherland. London: John Murray, 1926.

St. Augustine. *City of God*. Translated by Henry Bettenson. New York: Penguin Books, 1984.

Bancroft, Hubert Howe. *The Native Races of the Pacific States*. London: Longmans Green, 1875–76.

Basham, A. *The Wonder that Was India*. New York: Grove Press, 1959.

———, ed., *A Cultural History of India*. New York: Oxford University Press, 1975.

Bhattacharji, Sukumari. *The Indian Theogony*. London: Cambridge University Press, 1970.

Blavatsky, H. P. *Isis Unveiled*. 2 vols. Pasadena, Calif.: Theosophical University Press, 1972.

———. *The Secret Doctrine*. 2 vols. Pasadena, Calif.: Theosophical University Press, 1970.

Bolton, J. D. P. *Aristeas of Proconnesus*. Oxford: Clarendon, 1962.

Brewer's Dictionary of Phrase and Fable. London: Cassell, 1959; reprint, New York: Harper and Row, 1985.

Butler, Alban. *The Lives of the Saints*. 12 vols. Edited and revised by H. Thurston and D. Attwater. London: Burns Oates and Washbourne, 1926–38.

Caillat, Collette, and Ravi Kumar. *The Jain Cosmology*. New York: Harmony Books, 1981.

Callimachus. *Hymns*. Translated by A. W. Mair. London: William Heinemann, 1921; and New York: G. P. Putnam's Sons, 1921.

The Cambridge History of India. Vol. 1. Edited by E. J. Rapson. New York: Cambridge University Press, 1968.

Campbell, Joseph. *The Masks of God*. 3 vols. London: Secker and Warburg, 1960–65.

Cassuto, U. *The Goddess Anath*. Translated by Israel Abrahams. Jerusalem: Hebrew University, Magnes Press, 1972.

Cavendish, Richard. *The Black Arts*. London: Pan Books, 1969.

———, ed. *Man, Myth and Magic*. 7 vols. London: B. C. P. Publishing, 1970–72.

Chadwick, Henry. *The Early Church*. New York: Penguin Books, 1986.

Chadwick, N. Kershaw. *Poetry and Prophecy*. New York: Cambridge University Press, 1942.

Chambers Biographical Dictionary. 2 vols. Edinburgh: Chambers, 1975.

Charles, R. H., ed. and trans. *The Book of Enoch*. Oxford: Clarendon, 1912.

Claiborne, Robert. "Who Were the Indo-Europeans?" In *Mysteries of the Past*, edited by Joseph J. Thorndike. New York: American Heritage, 1977.

Cook, A. B. *Zeus*. 3 vols. Cambridge, England: Cambridge University Press, 1914–40.

Cook, J. M. *The Persian Empire*. London: J. M. Dent, 1983.

Cottrell, Leonard. *The Anvil of Civilization*. New York: Mentor Books, 1957.

The Cultural Heritage of India. 3 vols. Calcutta: Sri Ramakrishna Centenary Committee, 1937.

Cumont, Franz. *Astrology and Religion Among the Greeks and Romans*. New York: Putnam, 1912.

———. *The Mysteries of Mithra*. Translated by Thomas J. McCormack. London: Kegan Paul, Trench and Trubner, 1903.

Czaplicka, M. A. *Aboriginal Siberia*. Oxford: Clarendon, 1914.

Daniélou, Alain. *Hindu Polytheism*. Boston: Routledge and Kegan Paul, 1964.

Dante. *The Divine Comedy*. 3 vols. Translated by Dorothy L. Sayers. New York: Penguin Books, 1949–62.

David-Neel, Alexandra. *The Superhuman Life of Gesar of Ling*. London: Rider, 1933.

———. *With Mystics and Magicians in Tibet*. London: John Lane, The Bodley Head, 1931.

de Camp, L. Sprague, and Catherine C. de Camp. *Citadels of Mystery*. London: Fontana/Collins, 1972.

Decter, Jacqueline, with the Nicholas Roerich Museum. *Nicholas Roerich.* New York: Thames and Hudson, 1989.

Dergachev, V. "Neolithic and Bronze Age Cultural Communities of the Steppe Zone of the USSR." *Antiquity* 63 (December 1989): 793–802.

de Riencourt, Amaury. *The Soul of India.* London: Jonathan Cape, 1961.

de Santillana, Giorgio, and von Dechend, Hertha. *Hamlet's Mill.* New York: Macmillan, 1970.

Dio Cassius. *Roman History.* 9 vols. Translated by E. Cary. London and Cambridge, Mass.: Loeb Classical Library, 1940.

Dodd, C. H. *The Bible and the Greeks.* London: Hodder and Stoughton, 1935.

———. *The Interpretation of the Fourth Gospel.* New York: Cambridge University Press, 1953.

Dodds, E. R. *The Greeks and the Irrational.* Berkeley: University of California Press, 1951.

Eliade, Mircea. *Shamanism.* Boston: Routledge and Kegan Paul, 1964.

Emmerich, Anne Catherine. *The Life of the Blessed Virgin Mary.* Translated by Sir Michael Palairet. Rockford, Ill.: Tan Books, 1970.

Encyclopaedia Britannica. 1963 ed.

Encyclopaedia of Religion and Ethics. 12 vols. New York: Scribner, 1908–21.

Evans-Wentz, W. Y. *The Tibetan Book of the Great Liberation.* Oxford: Oxford University Press, 1954.

———. *Tibetan Yoga and Secret Doctrine.* Oxford: Oxford University Press, 1958.

Farnell, Lewis Richard. *The Cults of the Greek States.* 5 vols. Oxford: Clarendon, 1896–1909.

———, ed. and trans. *The Works of Pindar.* 3 vols. London: Macmillan, 1930–32.

Ford, Julian. *The Story of Paradise.* Richmond, England: H and B Publications, 1981.

Fordham, Frieda. *An Introduction to Jung's Psychology.* New York: Penguin Books, 1959.

Gadon, Elinor W. *The Once and Future Goddess.* Harper and Row, 1989.

Gamkrelidze, Thomas V., and V. V. Ivanov. "The Early History of Indo-European Languages." *Scientific American*, March 1990, 82–89.

Gilgamesh. *The Epic of Gilgamesh.* Translated by N. K. Sandars. New York: Penguin Books, 1960.

Gimbutas, Marija. *The Gods and Goddesses of Old Europe.* New York: Thames and Hudson, 1974. (Reissued as *The Goddesses and Gods of Old Europe.* Berkeley and Los Angeles: University of California Press, 1982.)

———. *The Language of the Goddess.* New York: Thames and Hudson, 1989.

Grant, Mary, ed. and trans. *The Myths of Hyginus.* Lawrence: University of Kansas, 1960.

Graves, Robert. *The Greek Myths.* 2 vols. New York: Penguin Books, 1960.

———. *The White Goddess.* London: Faber, 1952.

Griffith, Ralph H. T. *The Hymns of the Rigveda.* 2 vols. Benares, India: E. J. Lazarus, 1896.

Gryaznov, Mikail P. *The Ancient Civilization of Southern Siberia.* Translated by James Hogarth. New York: Cowles Book Co., 1969.

Guénon, René. *Le Roi du Monde.* Paris: Les Éditions Traditionelles, 1950.

Guthrie, W. K. C. *The Greeks and Their Gods.* New York: Methuen, 1950.

———. *Orpheus and Greek Religion.* New York: Methuen, 1935.

Harrison, Jane Ellen. *Themis.* New York: Cambridge University Press, 1912.

Heissig, Walther. *The Religions of Mongolia.* Translated by Geoffrey Samuel. Boston: Routledge and Kegan Paul, 1980.

Herodotus. *History.* 2 vols. Translated by G. Rawlinson. London: Dent, 1910.

Hesiod. *Theogony* and *Works and Days.* Translated by Dorothea Winder. New York: Penguin Books, 1973.

Hindley, Geoffrey, ed. *Larousse Encyclopedia of Music.* London and New York: Hamlyn, 1971.

Hitching, Francis. *The World Atlas of Mysteries.* London: Pan Books, 1979.

Homer. *The Iliad.* Translated by E. V. Rieu. New York: Penguin Books, 1959.

———. *The Odyssey.* Translated by E. V. Rieu. New York: Penguin Books, 1959.

Hooke, S. H., ed. *The Labyrinth.* London: Society for the Promotion of Christian Knowledge, 1935.

Hoyle, Peter. *Delphi.* London: Cassell, 1967.

Huizinga, J. *The Waning of the Middle Ages.* Translated by F. Hopman. New York: Penguin Books, 1985.

Ions, Veronica. *Egyptian Mythology.* London: Paul Hamlyn, 1968.

James, E. O. *The Cult of the Mother-Goddess.* New York: Thames and Hudson, 1959.

———. *Prehistoric Religion.* New York: Harper and Row, 1988.

Jewish Encyclopaedia. New York and London: Funk and Wagnalls, 1901–6.

Johnson, Buffie. *Lady of the Beasts.* New York: Harper and Row, 1988.

Jung, C. G. *Alchemical Studies.* Vol. 13 of *Collected Works.* Boston: Routledge and Kegan Paul, 1968.

———. *The Archetypes and the Collective Unconscious.* Part 1. Vol. 9 of *Collected Works.* Boston: Routledge and Kegan Paul, 1959.

———. *Mysterium Coniunctionis.* Vol. 14 of *Collected Works.* Boston: Routledge and Kegan Paul, 1963.

———. *Psychology and Alchemy.* Vol. 12 of *Collected Works.* Boston: Routledge and Kegan Paul, 1953.

———. *Symbols of Transformation.* Vol. 5 of *Collected Works.* Boston: Routledge and Kegan Paul, 1956.

———. *Two Essays on Analytical Psychology.* Vol. 7 of *Collected Works.* Boston: Routledge and Kegan Paul, 1966.

Kenety, William H., ed. *Collector's Choice.* Washington, D.C.: National Association of Private Art Foundations, 1987.

Keys, David. "Academics Shed New Light on Druids' Link with Stones." *Independent* (London), June 21, 1988.

King, Francis. *Satan and Swastika.* London: Mayflower, 1976.

King, L. W. *The Seven Tablets of Creation.* Vol. 1. London: Luzac, 1902.

Knox, W. L. *St. Paul and the Church of the Gentiles.* New York: Cambridge University Press, 1939.

Kraft, John. *The Goddess in the Labyrinth.* Finland: Åbo Akademi, 1985.

Kramer, S. N. *History Begins at Sumer.* New York: Thames and Hudson, 1958.

———. *Sumerian Mythology.* Philadelphia: American Philosophical Society, 1947.

————. *The Sumerians.* Chicago: University of Chicago Press, 1963.

Lacy, Norris J., ed. *The Arthurian Encyclopedia.* New York: Garland, 1986.

Le Poer Trench, Brinsley. *Temple of the Stars.* London: Fontana, 1973.

Luce, J. V. *The End of Atlantis.* London: Thames and Hudson, 1969.

McCrickard, Janet. *Eclipse of the Sun.* Glastonbury, U.K.: Gothic Image, 1990.

Macdonell, J. E., and A. B. Keith. *Vedic Index of Names and Subjects.* Vol. 1. Delhi: Motilal Banarsidass, 1967.

McGuire, J. E., and P. M. Rattansi. "Newton and the 'Pipes of Pan.'" *Notes and Records of the Royal Society* 21 (1966): 108–43.

The Mahabharata. 3 vols. (incomplete). Translated by J. A. B. van Buitinen. Chicago: University of Chicago Press, 1973–78.

The Mahabharata. 3 vols. Translated by M. N. Dutt. Calcutta: H. C. Dass, 1895–1901.

Malcolm X. *The Autobiography of Malcolm X.* London: Hutchinson, 1966.

Mallory, J. P. *In Search of the Indo-Europeans.* New York: Thames and Hudson, 1989.

Mandeville. *The Travels of Sir John Mandeville.* Translated by C. W. R. D. Moseley. New York: Penguin Books, 1987.

Man, Myth and Magic. 7 vols. Edited by Richard Cavendish. London: B. P. C. Publishing, 1970–72.

Maraini, Fosco. *Secret Tibet.* Translated by Eric Mosbacher. London: Hutchinson, 1952.

Massey, Gerald. *A Book of the Beginnings.* 4 vols. London: Williams and Norgate, 1881 and 1883.

Matthews, W. H. *Mazes and Labyrinths.* New York: Dover, 1970.

Mead, G. R. S. *Thrice Greatest Hermes.* 3 vols. London: Watkins, 1964.

Michael, Henry N., ed. *Studies in Siberian Shamanism.* Toronto: University of Toronto Press, 1972.

Müller, F. Max. *Vedic Hymns.* Vol. 32 of *In Sacred Books of the East.* Oxford: Clarendon, 1981.

Murray, Gilbert. *Five Stages of Greek Religion.* Oxford: Clarendon, 1935.

Neumann, Erich. *The Great Mother.* Boston: Routledge and Kegan Paul, 1955.

————. *The Origins and History of Consciousness.* Boston: Routledge and Kegan Paul, 1954.

Nilsson, Martin P. *Primitive Time Reckoning.* Lund: C. W. K. Gleerup, 1920.

O'Flaherty, Wendy Doniger, comp. and trans. *The Rig Veda.* New York: Penguin Books, 1981.

Ossendowski, Ferdinand. *Beasts, Men and Gods.* London: Edward Arnold, 1922.

Ouspensky, P. D. *In Search of the Miraculous.* Boston: Routledge and Kegan Paul, 1950.

Panikkar, Raimundo. *The Vedic Experience: Mantramanjari.* London: Darton, Longman and Todd, 1977.

Pegis, Anton C., ed. *Basic Writings of Saint Thomas Aquinas.* 2 vols. New York: Random House, 1945.

Perera, Sylvia Brinton. *Descent to the Goddess.* Toronto: Inner City Books, 1981.

Philo. *The Works of Philo Judaeus.* 4 vols. Trans. C. D. Yonge. London: Bohn, 1854.

Piggott, Stuart. *The Druids.* New York: Penguin Books, 1974.

————. *Prehistoric India to 1000 B.C.* London: Cassell, 1950.

Plutarch. *The E. at Delphi.* Translated by Frank Cole Babbitt. In *Moralia*, vol. 5, pp.

194–253. London and Cambridge, Mass.: Loeb Classical Library. Heinemann and Harvard, 1936.

——. *The Obsolescence of Oracles.* Translated by Frank Cole Babbitt. In *Moralia,* vol. 5, 348–501. London and Cambridge, Mass.: Loeb Classical Library. Heinemann and Harvard, 1936.

Polo, Marco. *The Travels of Marco Polo.* Translated by Ronald Latham. New York: Penguin Books, 1987.

Pritchard, James B., ed. *Ancient Near Eastern Texts Relating to the Old Testament.* 3d edition, with suppl. Princeton, N.J.: Princeton University Press, 1969.

The Psalms. Translated by Peter Levi. New York: Penguin Books, 1976.

Purce, Jill. *The Mystic Spiral.* New York: Thames and Hudson, 1974.

Rahtz, Philip. *Invitation to Archaeology.* Oxford: Basil Blackwell, 1985.

Rashi. *Commentary on the Pentateuch.* Translated by James H. Lowe. 1928.

Renfrew, Colin. *Archaeology and Language.* London: Jonathan Cape, 1987.

——. "They Ride Horses, Don't They?" *Antiquity* 63 (December 1989): 843–46.

Roerich, George. *Trails to Inmost Asia.* New Haven, Conn.: Yale University Press, 1931.

Roerich, Nicholas. *Altai-Himalaya.* London: Jarrolds, 1930.

——. *Himalayas, Abode of Light.* London: David Marlowe, 1947.

——. *Shambhala.* New York: Nicholas Roerich Museum, 1978.

Roux, Georges. *Ancient Iraq.* London: George Allen and Unwin, 1964.

Rudenko, Sergei I. *Frozen Tombs of Siberia.* Translated by M. W. Thompson. Berkeley and Los Angeles: University of California Press, 1970.

Russell, Bertrand. *A History of Western Philosophy.* London: George Allen and Unwin, 1946.

Scholem, G. G. *Major Trends in Jewish Mysticism.* New York: Schocken Books, 1946.

Seltman, Charles. *The Twelve Olympians and Their Guests.* London: Max Parriser, 1956.

Shah-Namah. The Shah-Namah of Firdausi. Described and Introduced by J. V. S. Wilkinson and Laurence Binyon. Oxford: Oxford University Press, 1931.

Sjöö, Monica, and Barbara Mor. *The Great Cosmic Mother.* New York: Harper and Row, 1987.

Smith, George, ed. *The Teaching of the Catholic Church.* 2 vols. London: Burns Oates and Washbourne, 1948.

Spencer, Sidney. *Mysticism in World Religion.* New York: Penguin Books, 1963.

Starhawk [Miriam Simos]. *The Spiral Dance.* New York: Harper and Row, 1979.

Stone, Merlin. *The Paradise Papers.* London: Virago, 1976 (U.S. title: *When God Was a Woman.*)

Swete, H. B. *The Apocalypse of St. John.* London: Macmillan, 1907.

Thompson, C. J. S. *The Lure and Romance of Alchemy.* London: Harrap, 1932.

Tolstoy, Nikolai. *The Quest for Merlin.* London: Hamish Hamilton, 1985.

Vawter, Bruce. *A Path Through Genesis.* London: Sheed and Ward, 1957.

Wales, H. G. Quaritch. *The Mountain of God.* London: Bernard Quaritch, 1953.

Waters, Frank. *Book of the Hopi.* New York: Ballantine, 1969.

Welch, Holmes. *The Parting of the Way.* London: Methuen, 1958.

Williamson, Hugh Ross. *The Arrow and the Sword.* London: Faber, 1947.

Wilson, Ian. *The Exodus Enigma.* New York: Weidenfeld and Nicolson, 1985.

Wolkstein, Diana, and Samuel Noah Kramer. *Inanna: Queen of Heaven and Earth.* London: Rider, 1984.

Zaehner, R. C. *The Dawn and Twilight of Zoroastrianism.* London: Weidenfeld and Nicolson, 1961.

Zvelebil, Marek, and Kamil V. "Agricultural Transition and Indo-European Dispersals." *Antiquity* 62 (September 1989): 574–83.

Index

Abaris, 172, 176, 216

Aboriginal Siberia (Czaplicka), 25

Abraham, 89, 118, 123, 125, 132, 190

Achilles, 148, 186

Adam, 124, 125, 135, 139–40, 190, 191, 205, 219

Aditi, 43, 49, 215

Adonis, 91, 123

Aeneas, 158

Aeneid (Virgil), 16

Aeschylus, 148

Afanasievo, 40–41, 45, 63, 69, 96, 165, 215, 224

Agamemnon, 163

Age of Discovery, 193

Agharti, 181–82, 211

Agni, 42

Ahasuerus, 88

Ahriman, 86, 87

Ahura Mazdah, 86, 87

Ainu, 31

Akhenaten, 115

Akkadians, 90, 110

Alchemy, 198–99, 201

Alcuin, 192

Alder, Vera Stanley, 210–11

Alexander the Great, 75, 128, 143, 148, 174, 184–86

Altaic culture, 13–17, 22–23, 51, 59, 69, 96, 154, 168, 184, 195, 200, 219, 222, 224

  central mountain in, 59–60, 63–65

  Hyperboreans and, 174

  shamanism in, 24–39, 45, 49, 54, 55, 63, 65, 93, 113, 144, 165–66, 178, 179, 213–17

  Shambhala and, 182

Altai-Himalaya (Roerich), 25, 34, 182, 212

Altai Khan, 33

Altamira cave paintings, 15

Amarna letters, 118

Amazons, 162–64, 216

Amenophis III, 115

Ammonius, 151, 155

Amorites, 121

Amphion, 153

An, 97–98, 109

Anath, 114, 115, 128

Anatolia, 10, 12, 21

Ancient Wisdom, 2, 4–8, 180, 195, 200, 202, 205, 207, 208, 214, 217–19, 221

Ancient Wisdom (*cont.*)
  astrology and, 197
  Christianity and, 191
  numerology and, 68
  in theosophy, 207, 209–10
Anderson, Robert, 95
Andrew, St., 192
Androcentric society, 104
Andronovo culture, 41, 96
Anglo-Saxons, 20
Angra Mainyu, 86
Animals, shamanic role of, 30–32, 45–
  46. *See also* Bears; Elk; Horses
Anthony, St., 192
Anu, 98, 99
Anunnaki, 98
Apache, 32
Aphrodite, 75, 98
Apollo, 75, 78, 148–58, 162, 164, 165,
  169, 170, 172, 173, 175–81, 183,
  184, 186, 195, 197, 201, 216–18
Apsu, 101
Apuleius, 79–80
Apulunas, 157–58
Aquinas, St. Thomas, 120, 143
Arabs, 34, 81, 114
Aratus, 83, 159
"Arcades" (Milton), 185
Arcadians, 161
Arcas, 161, 162, 165
Archetypes, Jungian, 71–72, 74
Ares, 75
Ariadne, 154
Arimaspea, 173, 176
Aristarchus, 196–97
Aristeas, 173–75, 176, 177, 216
Aristotle, 177
Ark of the Covenant, 132, 135
Artemis, 15, 75, 98, 149, 153, 154, 156,
  158–59, 160–74, 177–79, 204, 216,
  218, 223
Arthur, King, 6, 35, 43–44, 181, 192, 208
Arundhati, 47–48, 51
Aryans, 209. *See also* Indo-Aryans
Asclepius, 154
Assyrians, 73, 88, 102, 131
Astarte, 114, 128, 160

Astrea, 2, 3, 14, 219
Astrology, 68, 69, 71, 74–76, 91, 155,
  181, 184
  Christianity and, 188–89, 191
  music and, 184–85
  seven mystique in, 196–99, 201, 221
Astronomy, 75, 181, 183. *See also* Con-
  stellations
  Earth-centered, 76
  seven mystique in, 196–98, 201
As You Like It (Shakespeare), 191
Athene, 78, 128
Athenians, 150, 153
Atisha, 180–81
Atlantides, 151
Atlantis, 15, 183, 200, 222
  modern myth of, 7
  in theosophy, 208, 211
Atlantis: The Antediluvian World (Don-
  nelly), 7
Atlas, 158
Atri, 47
Augustine, St., 141, 142
Australian aborigines, 15, 80, 81, 158
Avebury, 15

Baal, 114, 115, 121–123, 136
Babylonians, 73, 90, 93, 98, 114, 129,
  132–34, 136, 137, 145
  astrology of, 75, 76, 184, 196, 197
  centrality of, 108, 111–13
  creation epic of, 100–102
  Flood myth of, 99–100, 125
  golden age of, 5
  paradise of, 144
  seven mystique of, 65, 72, 76, 80, 98–
    100, 146, 184, 197, 201, 215
Bacchae (Euripides), 177
Bacon, Roger, 199
Baikal, Lake, 13, 174, 224
Bailey, Alice, 210
Bailly, Jean Sylvain, 183
Bai Ülgän, 29, 33, 37, 54
Balak, 126
Banzaroff, Dordji, 166, 214
Barbarossa, Frederick, 192
Basques, 20

Bears, 30–32, 46, 48–49, 161–62, 164–67, 176, 214
Beasts, Men and Gods (Ossendowsi), 182
Bede, 141, 143
Bel, 101
Bellamy, Edward, 208
Belukha, Mount, 62, 63–65, 113, 182, 183, 224
Ben Arak, Rabbi Eleazar, 137
Besakih, 61
Besant, Annie, 207–8
Bezalel, 126
Bhagavad Gita, 5
Bharadvaja, 47
Bharata-varsha, 62
Bias, 150
Bible, 5, 35, 68, 71, 79, 80, 88, 91, 103, 104, 114, 117–20, 122, 125–29, 132–43, 155, 221
  Acts, 161, 162, 188
  Deuteronomy, 121, 126
  Esther, 88
  Exodus, 118, 119, 120, 121–22, 128, 137, 187
  Ezekiel, 133, 137–39, 141, 144, 150, 156
  Ezra, 88
  Genesis, 117, 119, 120–21, 123–27, 129–30, 139–44, 188
  Isaiah, 122, 127, 133, 134, 136
  Jeremiah, 71–72, 128
  John, 205
  Judges, 117, 121
  King James Version, 136
  1 Kings, 126
  2 Kings, 126, 190
  Leviticus, 126
  Matthew, 189
  Nehemiah, 120
  Numbers, 126
  Proverbs, 127, 201
  Psalms, 122, 135, 138–39, 203
  Revelations, 188
  Revised Standard Version, 162
  Ruth, 127
  1 Samuel, 127
  Titus, 176

Wisdom of Solomon, 128
Zechariah, 126
Blackfoot Indians, 159
Black Muslims, 4
Blavatsky, Helena Petrovna, 5, 7, 205, 207–11
Bolsheviks, 25
Bön, 26, 33, 182–83
Book of the Beginnings, A (Massey), 206
Book of Enoch, 142, 187
Boötes, 46
Borobudur, 60, 61
Bounteous Immortals, 65, 86, 87
Brahma, 57, 58
Bramwell, James, 183
Brentano, Clemens, 205
Bronze Age, 3, 147
Bruno, 84
Buddhism, 26, 32, 33, 41, 59, 63, 114, 132, 208, 211, 225
  Lamaistic, 69, 179–84
Burroughs, Edgar Rice, 208
Burrows, Eric, 82
Buryat, 24, 33

Callimachus, 174
Callisto, 161, 162, 171, 204
Calypso, 83
Canaanites, 85, 114–16, 121, 122, 128, 132, 135–36, 146, 151, 195
Cancer, 82
Canon's Yeoman's Tale (Chaucer), 198
Carnac, 15
Carpenter, Rhys, 176
Catholic Church, 189
Cavendish, Richard, 79
Cave paintings, 15, 26
Celts, 20, 70, 157, 179, 207, 221
Centrality, cosmic, 32–33, 54–65, 107–13, 132–38, 200–201
  seven mystique and, 107, 135, 150–51
Cerberus, 71
Chadwick, Nora, 27–28
Chakras, 50–51
Charlemagne, 35, 192, 193
Chaucer, Geoffrey, 198
Chemistry, 198, 199

Chilo, 150
Chinese, 54, 68, 69, 71, 73, 174, 195–99, 201
  golden age of, 5
  numerology of, 68, 69, 76
Chinghiz Khan, 33
Chippewa, 32
Christ, 35, 188, 211
Christianity, 132, 142, 155, 177, 197
  fallen angels in, 102, 124
  fundamentalist, 5
  golden age of, 3, 5, 191, 221
  mountains in, 202–5
  persecution of women in, 10
  seven mystique in, 68, 84, 187–92, 218
  Zoroastrianism and, 87
Christian mystics, 93
Christian Topography (Cosmas), 142–43
Chukchi, 24
Cicero, 186
Circle of Time, 180
Claiborne, Robert, 20, 223
Claudian, 171
Cleobulus, 150
Cleopatra, 185
Cles-Reden, Sibylle von, 11
Columbus, Christopher, 193
Conan Doyle, Sir Arthur, 208
Confucius, 5
Constantine, 189, 197
Constellations, 34–35, 46–49, 51, 206–7, 214–15
  Christians and, 192
  Greeks and, 158–62, 166, 168
  mountains and, 55
Copernicus, 185, 197
Cosmas, 142–43
Creation myths, 29, 32, 38, 54, 65, 100–102, 120, 123–24, 127, 168
Creation Science, 5
Crete. *See* Minoan Crete
Cronus, 2, 3, 75, 151, 158
Crusades, 191
Cult of the Mother-Goddess, The (James), 11
Cults of the Greek States, The (Farnell), 11

Cumont, Franz, 74
Cybele, 160
Cynosura, 162
Cyrus, 133
Czaplicka, Maria, 25

Daedalus, 154
Daksha, 43
Dante, 6–7, 14, 190, 202–5, 207, 222
Darius I, 88
Dark Ages, 44
Dark Night of the Soul, 93
David, 35, 133
David, St., 192
Death
  attitudes to, 11, 220–21
  the Fall and, 140
  Greek beliefs about, 177
Deborah, 121
Dechend, Hertha von, 84–85, 86, 113
Delos, 16, 154, 172–73, 177–78, 216
Delphic Oracle, 149–51, 157, 164, 172, 176, 178
Demetrius, 185
Denys, St., 192
Dergachev, V., 96
Descent of Inanna, The, 91–93
Dhyani Buddhas, 69
Diaghilev, Sergei, 25
Diana, 15, 149, 158, 204, 218
Diogenes, 15
Dionysus, 148, 153, 158, 177
Disney, Walt, 70
Divine Comedy (Dante), 6, 190, 202–3
Dodds, E. R., 175, 177
Donnelly, Ignatius, 7
Dorians, 147–48
Druids, 5, 26, 108, 173, 200, 207, 209
Dumézil, Georges, 68, 70
Dumuzi, 91–93, 98, 99
Dyaks of Sarawak, 159
Dyaus, 22

Ea, 98, 99–100, 101–2
Easter Island, 7
Ecclesiasticus, 128, 129, 201

Eden, Garden of, 6, 7, 138–44, 207, 220–21

Edward III, King of England, 43

Egyptians, 34, 73, 114, 157, 206, 209
  alchemy of, 198
  Canaanites and, 115
  constellations of, 34, 81
  Israelites and, 117, 118, 122, 137
  seven mystique and, 68, 185

Eisler, Riane, 9

El, 122

Electra, 159

Eliade, Mircea, 25–26, 29, 37, 45, 52, 59, 60, 67, 144, 166, 175, 178, 183

Elijah, 35, 126, 190, 202

Elisha, 126

Elk, 30, 35, 46, 214

Elohim, 123

Emmerich, Anne Catherine, 205–6, 211, 222

Enki, 92, 97, 98, 105

Enlil, 82, 97, 99, 100, 109–111, 132, 135

Enuma elish, 72, 100–102

Epic of Gilgamesh, 51, 110, 115, 125, 146

Epimenides of Crete, 176

Ereshkigal, 92, 93

Erlik Khan, 29, 33, 37, 39, 93

Eskimo, 32, 34

Etruscans, 16

Etugen, 30, 54, 166

Euphorbus, 154

Euripides, 177

Eurydice, 177

Evans-Wentz, W. Y., 180

Eve, 121, 135, 139–40, 205, 219

Evenk, 33, 35, 166, 167

Ezekiel, 115, 133, 137–39, 141, 144, 150, 156, 178, 216

Fall, the, 140, 144–45, 178

Famous History of the Seven Champions of Christendom, The (Johnson), 192

Farnell, Lewis Richard, 11, 160, 169

Faust (Goethe), 11

Feminist ideology, 9, 10, 104, 106, 200, 223

"Fertile Crescent," 114, 118, 146

Firdausi, 87, 190

Flood
  Babylonian version of, 99–100
  Hindu version of, 47
  Israelite version of, 125, 142, 191
  Sumerian version of, 99

Foundation for Cultural Preservation, 95, 224

Frazer, James, 91

French Revolution, 4, 72

Fundamentalism, 5

Gadon, Elinor, 10

Galileo, 185, 197

Gamkrelidze, Tomas, 21

Gandhi, Mohandas K., 4, 208

Gayumarth, 87

Genghis Khan, 224

Geography, 108, 193–94

George, St., 192

Gesar Khan, 35–36, 181, 182

Ghirshman, Roman, 96, 224

Gilgamesh, 91, 98–100, 104, 110

Gilyak, 31

Gimbutas, Marija, 9–10, 12–13, 14, 15, 16, 17–18, 19–23, 30, 200, 213, 223

Girgashites, 121

Glastonbury Tor, 17

Glauber, 199

Gnosticism, 74, 128

Goddess worship, 9–23, 66, 200, 213–14, 216, 218–21, 223, 225
  of Canaanites, 114
  of Greeks, 157–68
  Israelites and, 127–29
  in Mesopotamia, 98, 100–101, 104–5
  in *Rig Veda*, 43
  seven mystique and, 91–93, 184
  shamanism and, 27, 29–30, 38

Goethe, Johann Wolfgang von, 11

Golden age, 2–8, 139, 179, 200, 213, 219–21
  Christian, 191
  in feminist ideology, 9
  Goddess worship and, 14, 18, 21, 22
  Mesopotamians and, 104
  seven mystique and, 193

Golden age (*cont.*)
    shamanism and, 28
Golden Ass, The (Apuleius), 79–80
Golden Bough, The (Frazer), 91
Gordon, General, 143
Gotama, 47
Graves, Robert, 11, 148, 155, 156
Great Mother, 11, 161
Greeks, 8, 73, 77, 80, 87, 221
    astrology of, 75, 196
    constellations of, 38, 48, 83, 191, 192
    geography of, 108
    Goddess worship by, 11, 15, 98, 157–
        68
    gods of, 22
    golden age of, 2–5, 101, 104
    Hyperboreans and, 169–76, 183, 216
    Indians and, 52–54
    labyrinth imagery of, 16
    mathematics of, 71
    Persians and, 88
    seasons of, 72
    seven mystique of, 68, 146–55, 158,
        159, 162, 168, 178, 184–86, 201, 217
    shamanism and, 175–79
Gregory the Great, Pope, 188
Griffith, Ralph, 49–50
Grizzly Bear Dance, 30
Guénon, René, 211–12, 222
Gurjieff, 210
Guthrie, W. K. C., 175
Gylanic societies, 9, 19, 20, 104, 200

Habiru, 117, 118
Hadd, 114–15
Hammurabi, 73, 90
Hecataeus of Abdera, 173
Hellenes, 146–47
Hellenistic Greeks, 75, 148
Helmont, Van, 199
Henry V, King of England, 43
Heptads. *See* Seven mystique
Hera, 161
Hercules, 167, 170
Hermes, 75–76, 151, 152
Hermes Trismegistus, 84, 191
Hermetic treatises, 5, 84–85

Hermotimos of Clazomenae, 176, 177
Herodotus, 52–53, 88, 111, 148, 150,
    151, 164, 172–73, 174
Hesiod, 2–3, 148, 151, 153, 161, 178, 221
Hestia, 148
Hicks, Harry H., 95
Hilton, James, 180
Hinduism, 42, 76, 145, 205, 208, 215,
    216
    astrology in, 198
    basic scripture of, 47
    cosmic centrality in, 55–65, 107, 108,
        111, 179
    goddesses in, 17
    golden age of, 3
    mature, 43, 50, 55, 65, 69
    messiah in, 181
    mythology of, 43, 44
    Northern Kurus myth in, 174, 179
    sacred architecture of, 60, 110
Hippocrates, 154, 191
Hittites, 45, 95, 121, 146, 156
Hivites, 121
Höbiger, 208
Holy Grail, 211
Holy Spirit, 189
Homer, 34, 83, 148, 153, 154, 158, 161,
    169, 177, 178, 187
Hopi, 17, 27, 38, 213–14
Horses, 30, 45–46, 96–97, 105, 175
Huizinga, Johan, 189
Hurrians, 95
Hushang, 87
Hyginus, 34, 81
Hymn to Delos (Callimachus), 174
Hyperboreans, 3, 149, 156, 158, 167,
    169–76, 178–80, 208, 211, 216, 217,
    219, 220–21, 225

Iamblichus, 176
Iliad (Homer), 34, 148, 153, 154, 157,
    158
Inanna, 91–93, 97–98, 104, 105, 155,
    217
Indaruta, Prince, 44–45, 95
India, 55, 59, 62, 64, 71, 107. *See also*
    Hinduism

golden age in, 4, 5, 104
Greeks and, 52–54
Indo-Europeans in, 21
nationalism in, 208
Well of Youth in, 143
Indo-Aryans, 19, 41–43, 44–46, 49, 51, 103, 104, 151, 223–24
    cosmic centrality, 54–55, 64, 65, 107–8, 112, 144
    gods of, 22
    horses and, 96–97, 146
    seven mystique and, 67, 68, 75, 81–82, 85, 86, 88, 89, 91, 94–96, 107, 127, 165, 175, 178, 195, 215, 224
Indo-Europeans, 18–23, 40–41, 72, 94–96, 146, 165, 178, 200, 217, 221, 222–23, 225. *See also* Indo-Aryans
    Buddhist, 183
    Goddess worship and, 104, 218–19, 223
    seven mystique and, 68, 201, 215
    shamanism and, 106
    theosophy and, 209
Indra, 42, 45, 55, 102–104
Initiation of the World, The (Alder), 210
In Search of the Indo-Europeans (Mallory), 20
Iphigenia, 163
Iranians, 41, 65, 86–88, 195
Iron age, 3
Iroquois, 32
Isaiah, 135–38
Ishtar, 75, 91, 93, 99, 104
Isis, 79
Isis Unveiled (Blavatsky), 208, 209
Islam, 60, 73, 132, 187, 189, 190, 202, 205, 218
Israelites. *See* Jews
Issedonians, 174

Jabal-ul-din, 190
Jacob, 118, 126
Jain, 58, 59
Jamadagni, 47
James, E. O., 11
James, St., 192
James II, King of England, 193

Jamshid, 87
Jebusites, 121, 133
Jehovah, 187
Jeremiah, 128
Jesuits, 180
Jesus, 190, 205
Jews, 8, 95, 117–46, 155, 179, 221
    in Alexandria, 77, 185
    Canaanites and, 114, 115
    centrality and, 108, 117, 132–38
    creation myth of, 5, 102, 123–24, 127
    Fall doctrine of, 140, 145, 178
    Goddess worship and, 11, 127–29
    seven mystique of, 73, 75, 80, 85–86, 117, 119–20, 124–31, 187–91, 195, 201, 217, 218
    Zoroastrians and, 87–88
Johanan, Rabbi, 137
John the Evangelist, St., 205
Johnson, Richard, 192
Joseph, 126
Josephus, 187
Joshua, 118, 126
Judaeo-Christian tradition, 73, 132, 184, 190, 202, 224
Judaism. *See* Jews
Julian, Emperor, 197
Jung, C. G., 71, 74, 83, 167–68, 180, 199, 217

Kalachakra, 180–81, 183
Kalevala, 31
Kalki, 181
Kalmucks, 59, 181
Karaya, 80
Kasyapa, 47
Khayyam, Omar, 87
Khmers, 60, 110
Ki, 98
Kikkuli, 45, 146
King Lear (Shakespeare), 192
Kingship, institution of, 105
Kingu, 101–2
Knox, Ronald, 136
Koran, 132, 190
Körös, Csoma de, 180
Krishna, 5

Kurgan people, 19–22
Kuryak, 31

Labyrinths, 16, 153–54, 213
Laconians, 149
Lao Tzu, 199
Lapps, 31, 32, 34, 37, 81, 167
Lascaux cave paintings, 15
Lemurians, 208
Leto, 149, 153, 158, 161, 169
Li Shao-chün, 199
Lord's Prayer, 188
Lost Atlantis (Bramwell), 183
Louis XIII, 192
Lovecraft, H. P., 208
Lucretius, 221
Lugalannemundu, 93, 105
Lunar cycle, 79–80

Mabinogion, 108
Macedonia, 148
Macrobius, 152, 197
Magi, 86–87
Magnus, Albertus, 199
Mahabharata, 43, 44, 46, 47, 53, 55, 56,
    61–62, 63, 95, 159, 175, 181
Maia, 151
Maitreya, 181
Malcolm X, 4
Mallory, J. P., 10, 20, 21, 41, 69, 94–96,
    183, 222–23, 224
Malory, Sir Thomas, 43–44
Mal'ta, 13, 15–16, 17, 27, 38–39, 213–14
Manetho, 118
Manjushri, 180, 181, 183
Manu, 47
Manzalgormo, 46, 166, 181
Marduk, 75, 80, 101, 102, 104, 109, 123,
    124, 132
Mar-gid-da, 82
Marx, Karl, 4
Marxists, 4, 221
Massey, Gerald, 206–7, 209, 212, 222
Matriarchy, 9
    shamanism and, 29
Matristic societies, 9, 10, 19, 200

Merneptah, Pharaoh, 117
Merope, 159
Meru, 55–65, 107–13, 144, 179, 190,
    200–205, 211, 215, 217
Mesopotamia, 51, 52, 114, 116, 140, 144,
    145, 221
    centrality in, 107–8, 111, 112, 133
    constellations of, 82, 86
    creation epic of, 103
    Flood myth of, 99–100, 123
    Goddess worship in, 104, 106, 218
    Indo-Aryan expansion into, 65, 86, 88,
        96, 103, 224
    Israelites in, 118
    paradise of, 136, 139, 179
    seven mystique in, 67, 68, 76, 89, 105–
        6, 127, 195, 215
    tower of Babel and, 129, 130
Methuselah, 140
Mexicans, 34, 81
Middle Ages, 43
Milton, John, 102, 141, 142, 168, 185,
    202
Minoan Crete, 10, 13, 16, 146–47, 151,
    153, 154, 160, 176, 220
Minos, King, 153, 154
Miriam, 122
Mission de l'Inde (Saint-Yves d'Al-
    veydre), 211
Mitanni, 45, 95, 96
Mithra, 65
Mithraism, 74, 75–76, 84
Mitra, 45
Moffatt, James, 136
Mohammed, 132, 190, 205
Mongols, 24, 32, 33–34, 38, 54, 59, 175,
    181, 182, 214–15, 217
Moses, 5, 77, 78, 118, 119, 121, 126, 128,
    131, 133, 137, 187
Mother Earth, 17, 38, 213
Mountains
    as cosmic center, 32–33, 54–65, 107–8,
        135–38, 179, 190, 200–205, 215, 217
    temples as representatives of, 109–13
Müller, Max, 49, 50
Mummu, 101

Murray, Margaret, 10
Music of the spheres, 184–86
Mycenaeans, 147, 151

Nanna, 98
Narayana, 57, 58, 95
Narundi, 51
Nasatyas, 45
Native Americans
    cosmic mountains of, 64–65
    shamanism of, 27, 30–32, 34
Natural Genesis, The (Massey), 206
Navaho, 69
Neanderthals, 30
Nebo, 75
Neo-goddess religion, 10, 22
Neoplatonic school, 151–52, 197
Nergal, 75
Newton, Isaac, 5, 197
Nicolaus of Cusa, 197
Ninib, 75
Ninshubur, 92
Nintu, 93, 98, 105
Niobe, 153
Nippur, 82–83, 89–90, 91, 97, 109, 110–
    12, 132, 135, 144, 150, 215
Noah, 125, 142
Northern Kurus, 58, 59, 62, 174, 215–
    17, 219, 220–21, 225
Numerology. See Seven mystique
Nyuka, 196

Odin, 35
Odyssey (Homer), 83, 148
Oedipus, 152, 153
O'Flaherty, Wendy Doniger, 50
Ogier the Dane, 192–93
Old Believers, 181
Old Europe, 9–10, 12, 19
Olen, 172
Olmecs, 178
On the Allegories of the Sacred Laws
    (Philo), 77–78
On the Creation of the World (Philo), 77
"On the Morning of Christ's Nativity"
    (Milton), 186

Optics, 195–96, 201
Orestes, 163
Orion, 34, 63, 158
Ormuzd, 86
Orpheus, 153, 157, 176–77
Ossendowski, Ferdinand, 182, 211, 212
Ostyak, 37
Ovid, 186, 189

Padma-Sambhava, 180, 181
Pan, 162
Paracelsus, 84, 208
Paradise, 139–44. See also Eden, Garden of
Paradise Lost (Milton), 102, 141–42
Passover, 122
Patriarchal society, 10, 22, 104
Patrick, St., 192
Paul, St., 76, 83, 161
Pausanias, 186
Pelasgians, 146
Periander, 150
Pericles, 148
Perizzites, 121
Persians, 54, 87–88, 132–34
Peter Chrysologus, St., 190
Phidias, 148
Philiscus, 186
Philo, 77–79, 80, 81–82, 83
Philosopher's Stone, 199
Phoenicians, 85, 128
Piggott, Stuart, 26–27, 45, 214
Pindar, 170, 172
Pisces, 82
Pittacus, 150
Plato, 7, 148, 150, 185
Pleiades, 38, 158–59, 161, 186, 191–92
Pleione, 158
Plutarch, 151, 155–56, 157
Polo, Marco, 32–33, 64
Polynesians, 71
Pompey, 120
Porphyry, 176
Poseidon, 148
Potanin, Gregory, 38, 166, 214
Primum Mobile, 76, 196
Proclus, 152

Prometheus, 5
Proto-Indo-Europeans, 18–19, 21, 22
Pseudo-Enoch, 142, 143, 144
Psychology
 myth-making and, 6
 numerology and, 67–69, 72
Ptolemy, 79, 196, 197
Pueblo, 32
Pyramids, 110
Pythagoras, 71, 80, 154, 172, 176, 178,
 184, 185, 201

Quetzalcoatl, 178

Ramayana, 17
Ramses II, Pharaoh, 118
Rashi, 121
Realm of the Great Goddess, The (von
 Cles-Reden), 11
Reindeer, 167
Renaissance, European, 5, 84, 199
Renfrew, Colin, 21, 94–95, 146, 222–24
Rig Veda, 41–42, 43, 44, 45, 46–51, 54–
 55, 59, 65, 94, 102, 107, 144–45,
 164, 215, 217
Rishis, the Seven, 46–51, 55, 65, 76, 81–
 82, 86, 89, 93, 103, 105, 107–8, 165,
 201, 204, 206, 215
Rite of Spring (Stravinsky), 25, 31
Robespierre, Maximilien de, 4
Roerich, Nicholas, 25, 31, 34, 35–36, 38,
 46, 63, 86, 166, 180, 182, 210, 212,
 214, 225
Roi du Monde, Le (Guénon), 211, 212
Romans, 73, 120, 187, 221
 astrology of, 76, 188, 189
 Christianity and, 132, 189, 197
 constellations of, 48
 geography of, 108
 gods and goddesses of, 149, 151, 158,
 162, 204
 golden age of, 2
 Mithraism and, 74
Ronsard, Pierre de, 192
Rousseau, Jean-Jacques, 3–4, 221
Rubaiyat (Omar Khayyam), 87

Russian Revolution, 72
Ruth, 127

Sabbath, 120, 124, 189
"Samara" culture, 165
Samoyeds, 24, 31, 37, 167
Santillana, Giorgio de, 84–85, 86, 113
Sargon, King, 90
Satan, 124, 136, 139, 141
Scandinavians, 73
Science, seven mystique in, 195–201
Scythians, 172, 173, 174
Secret Doctrine, The (Blavatsky), 208,
 209–10
Semites, 85–86, 90, 114. *See also specific*
 peoples
 language of, 103–4
Seven mystique, 37–38, 67–76, 77–88,
 89, 179, 201, 202, 206–7, 213–18
 Canaanite, 85–86, 115–16
 in Christianity, 188–92
 cosmic centrality and, 107, 113
 in geography, 193–94
 of Greeks, 146, 148–55, 158, 159, 162,
 168, 175, 178, 184–86
 of Jews, 72, 73, 75, 80, 86, 119–20,
 124–31, 187–91
 in medieval education, 191
 in Mesopotamia, 89–106
 prototypes for, 77–88
 in *Rig Veda*, 46, 49–51
 science and, 195–201
 soul and, 191
 in theosophy, 208–10
 in traditional groupings, 191–93
Shah-Namah (Firdausi), 87, 190
Shakespeare, William, 7, 191
Shamanism, 24–39, 96, 165–68, 213–17,
 224–25
 animals in, 30–32, 45–46, 165–67
 constellations in, 34–35, 46
 cosmic centrality in, 32–33, 54, 55,
 63–65, 109, 113–14, 200, 215
 the Fall in, 144–45
 Greeks and, 175–79
 seven mystique in, 37–38, 49, 67, 93,
 106, 175, 178, 195, 213–14

in Tibet, 183
Shamash, 75
Shambhala, 179–83, 210–12, 225
Shilluk, 68, 72
Siberians, aboriginal, 24, 54, 59. *See also* Altaic culture
Sin, 75, 81, 98
Sinbad the Sailor, 192
Sioux, 32, 81
Sisyphus, 159
Sjöö, Monica, 10, 14, 219
Smiths, 29, 36, 166
Snow White and the Seven Dwarfs, 70
Solar deities, 22
Solomon, King, 126, 127, 129, 133
Solon, 150, 176
Spartans, 73, 149
Starhawk, 11, 12, 14, 27, 29
Steiner, Rudolf, 207
Sternberg, Ungern von, 181, 182
Sterne, Laurence, 84
Stone, Merlin, 10, 20
Stonehenge, 7, 193
Stravinsky, Igor, 25
Sumerians, 21, 65, 89–90, 97–98, 110, 112, 145, 198
 centrality of, 82, 107–10, 113, 144
 constellations of, 85
 Goddess worship of, 91, 104–5
 seven mystique of, 75, 85–86, 93, 94–95, 103, 107, 146, 151, 201, 215, 224
Sumeru, 59

Tahmurath, 87
Tammuz, 91, 123
Tantric cults, 51, 69
Tatars, 24, 28, 33, 37, 48
Taurians, 163, 164
Tazabagyab, 41
Teiresias, 152
Temples, mountain-imitating, 109–13
Ten Commandments, 119
Tengere Kaira Khan, 29
Tezacatlipoca, 34
Thales, 150, 154
Theocritus, 186
Theogeny (Hesiod), 153

Theophrastus, 72
Theosophy, 5, 7, 205, 207, 210
Theseus, 154
Thomas the rhymer, 193
Thomas, Robert P., 16
Thor, 35
Thoth, 84
Thucydides, 148
Tiamat, 101, 102, 104, 109, 115–16, 122–23, 124
Tibetan Book of the Dead, 183
Tibullus, 189
Tirthankaras, 58
Titans, 2–5, 101, 148, 151, 153
Tobit, 187
Tocharin language, 41, 69, 183
Tower of Babel, 129–30
Travels of Sir John Mandeville, 143, 203
Trojans, 3, 154, 158, 159, 163, 169, 180, 186
Troshchanski, 29
Tungus, 24, 28, 29, 33

Ubaidians, 89
Ugrians, 29, 36, 37, 54
Uralic tribes, 24
Ursa Major, 34–35, 38, 67, 81–86, 167–68, 179, 192, 204, 206, 207, 209, 211
 Ancient Wisdom and, 47, 97
 cosmic centrality and, 55, 59, 64, 65, 107, 109, 111, 112, 214
 Greeks and, 78, 81–83, 158, 159, 161–62, 165, 168, 178, 216
 Mesopotamia and, 82, 88
 shamanism and, 35, 46, 54, 127, 214
 Shambhala and, 181, 182
 Sumerians and, 85–86, 94, 97
Ursa Minor, 46, 159, 162
Utnapishtim, 99–100, 110, 125
Utu, 98

Varuna, 42, 45, 48, 55
Vasishtha, 47–48, 51
Vasyuga-Ostyak, 37
Velikovksy, 208
Viracocha, 178
Virgil, 16, 154, 176, 186

Virgin Mary, 161, 189–90, 204
Vishnu, 42, 57, 58, 95, 181
Visvamitra, 47
Vogul, 37
Von Däniken, Erich, 5, 208

Wahb ibn Munabbih, 190
Wei Po-yang, 199
Welsh, 17, 108, 165
Wheeler, Mortimer, 15
Wheel of Time, 180
When God Was a Woman (Stone), 20
White Goddess, The (Graves), 11
Wicca. *See* Witchcraft
Wisdom (biblical personification), 127–
    29, 189–90, 201
Witchcraft, 10–12, 14, 27
Woolley, Sir Leonard, 99
Work of the Chariot, 137
Works and Days (Hesiod), 148

Xerxes, 88

Yahweh, 118, 119, 121, 122, 128, 132,
    133, 136, 138, 140, 155, 156, 178,
    187–88, 217, 218
Yakut, 24, 29, 31, 37
Yudhishthira, King, 56, 57, 63
Yukagir, 36, 177
Yurak-Samoyed, 37

Zalmoxis, 176
Zechariah, 126
Zeus, 3, 11, 22, 75, 78, 98, 101, 148–49,
    151, 158, 159, 161, 162, 168, 177
Ziggurats, 11–12
Ziusudra, 99, 110
Zoroaster, 65, 86–87
Zoroastrians, 44, 87–88, 132, 190
Zvelebil, Marek, 21